PART 2

THE KASHMIR STORY

through the ages

Arjan Nath Chaku
Inder K Chaku

Vitasta
Let Knowledge Spread

Published by
Renu Kaul Verma
Vitasta Publishing Pvt Ltd
2/15 Ansari Road, Daryaganj
New Delhi - 110 002
info@vitastapublishing.com

ISBN 978-93-82711-75-9

First Edition 2016

2nd Reprint 2019

MRP: ₹ 595

Cover and Layout: Vitasta Publishing Pvt Ltd
Printed at Vikas Computer and Printers, New Delhi

The book is dedicated to the cherished memories of

Sumit Chaku

who departed so young, leaving us shattered.

He will always remain in our hearts.

CONTENTS

ACKNOWLEDGEMENTS

The making of the book *The Kashmir Story* started as a joint initiative of its writers Arjan Nath Chaku and Inder K Chaku and soon transformed into a dedicated project for our family. Every single member of the family has been emotionally involved in the progress of this work. Invaluable contributions came from everyone in the shape of interactions, discussions, critical analysis, furnishing of software material and more.

Dr Shiban Chaku's continued support and insightful, perceptive and frank commentary helped immensely in giving a direction and flow to the book.

Opender Chaku, who worked tirelessly towards collecting informative material and his expert inputs in printing, truly gave shape to the book.

Bimal Chaku, who inspired and prompted the authors to pen the History of Kashmir.

Shanta Mirza's concern for the progress of the book became a source of inspiration.

S Sachin Chaku, Natasha Chaku/Kaul, Shivani Chaku/Garyali and Neha Chaku/Tankha also contributed in their own way.

Ms Sushma Zutshi, Guddi as we affectionately call her, for her enormous support in providing the reference material and valuable suggestions from time to time.

I acknowledge my editor Veena Batra with a deep sense of gratitude. Her enthusiasm coupled with meticulous scrutiny, scientific, rational and strictly professional approach is truly laudable.

I am also grateful to:

Ms Indira Laisram, who initially corrected about 18 chapters.

Dr P L Kaul for his passionate interest in the development of the book that really motivated us. His discussions regarding the Flora, Fauna and other subjects enriched the book.

Shri Bansi Kaul, whose discussions helped bring refinement in our thought process.

Shri B K Gaind for his help in shaping the chapters related to Crafts and Art of Kashmir.

Dr Animesh Arya, famous chest and allergy specialist of India, who kept the ailing author Arjan Nath Chaku alive till the last chapter of the book was completed.

One
Sikh Rule In Kashmir

The most remarkable thing about the Sikh community is the way they organised themselves and became the rulers of Punjab. "The Sikh is a fighting man, and his fine qualities are best shown in the army, which is his natural profession," says Sir Lapel Henry Griffin.[1]

By 1767 AD, the Sikhs had organised themselves into more than sixty bands. In course of time, these bands were combined into a number of bigger units which came to be called Misls. According to Joseph Davey Cunningham,[2] "The confederacies into which the Sikhs resolved themselves have been usually recorded as twelve in number, and the term used to denote such a union was the Arabic word 'Misl' (equal)." The Sikh community was divided into twelve Misls. When Maharaja Ranjit Singh took over the reins of the government in 1797 AD, he unified the Sikhs and gave proper shape to the community. In order to extend his territory he made many invasions, initially against the Sikh Misls and then against the adjoining territories and made Punjab as it is known today. Ranjit Singh believed that his kingdom was incomplete without annexing Kashmir with it; so he decided to invade it.

Maharaja Ranjit Singh's Sikh army was successful in defeating Pathan rulers in Kashmir and the valley came under the Sikh supremacy in 1819

AD. It was the end of Pathan rule and the start of Sikh domination. People heaved a sigh of relief when the Sikh army took over the valley. They rejoiced and felt that the rule of tyranny, brutality and cruelty was over. However, even during Sikh rule the conditions for the people of Kashmir did not improve. There was some relief for Hindus in the valley, though the Muslims were harassed during that period. According to Zahid G Muhammad[3] "In 1819, the Sikhs entered Kashmir in great triumph and jubilation. The troops not unexpectedly, indulged freely in loot."

Maharaja Ranjit Singh, 1792-1839 AD

Maharaja Ranjit Singh was born in November 1780, in Gujranwala, North India, which is now located in Pakistan, in Sandhawalia family. His father Sardar Maha Singh was the commander of the Shukerchakia Misl and controlled the territory in west Punjab based around his headquarters at Gujranwala. Ranjit Singh succeeded his father at a young age of 18. After several campaigns, his rivals accepted him as their leader, and he united the Sikh factions into one . He took the title of Maharaja on April 13, 1801, to coincide with Baisakhi day. His mother, Raj Kaur, was the daughter of the chief of Jind.

Maharaja Ranjit Singh spent his time in hunting and indulging in every kind of pleasure activity . He was betrothed at the age of six to Mahtab Kaur, daughter of Jai Singh of Kanhaiya Misl. In his childhood, Ranjit Singh had an attack of small pox, as a result of which he had pocks marks on his face and had lost one eye. At the age of twelve he started accompanying his father to the battlefields and learnt the art of warfare. With the death of his father, he became the ruler of his Misl. Initially, his mother, Raj Kaur and Dewan Lajpat Rai and later his mother-in-law helped him in the administration of the territory. Soon, in 1797 AD, he took the power in his own hands. According to Sir Lapel Henry Griffin,[4] "Maharaja Ranjit Singh was so completely a product of the Sikh theocracy, and embodied the spirit of the Khalsa, that no account of his character and career would be complete without a description of the religious system." The Sikhs organised themselves under the leadership of Sardar Jassa Singh Ahluwalia and Nawab Kapur Singh. They called themselves Dal Khalsa.

The Afghan rule in Kashmir had earned hatred, abhorrence and revulsion from Kashmiris for their acts of brutality from the very start of their rule.. Maharaja Ranjit Singh had made many attempts to capture Kashmir. He tried to invade Kashmir in 1812 and 1814 AD, but failed. The Afghan governor, Azim Khan, who earned victory over Sikh soldiers on the battleground in 1814 AD, became very arrogant. He was ruthless, particularly towards Hindus. The desperate and distressed Hindu nobles of Kashmir turned to Birbal Dhar (a minister during Azim Khans's period)and his son, Raja Kak Dhar, to seek help in overthrowing the Afghan despotic rule. Birbal Dhar and his son went to Maharaja Ranjit Singh and requested him to invade Kashmir. The defeat at the hands of Azim Khan in Kashmir in 1814 AD was fresh in the minds of Sikhs. In the meantime, the political conditions in Afghanistan became horrific on account of the succession war among the Afghan throne claimants. Azim Khan was summoned back to Afghanistan, and in his place, Jabbar Khan was made the governor. He was the last ruler of the Afghans in Kashmir. When Ranjit Singh came to know that Azim Khan had proceeded to Afghanistan with his best troops and that the valley was totally unprotected, he decided to attack Kashmir. In 1819 AD, he deputed his army to proceed to Kashmir. This time it was an easy win for Ranjit Singh's forces who succeeded in driving out the Afghans from Kashmir.

Maharaja Ranjit Singh had two paralytic attacks, the second one in 1838 AD. Doctors had advised him to stop excessive use of intoxicants. However, according to Kartar Singh Duggal,[5] "The Maharaja had ridden the whole day on horseback and had greatly exhausted and overheated himself with his usual carelessness with regard to food. He took nothing that day but watermelons, of which he partook very freely. A heavy storm fell in the afternoon, the rain poured down in torrents, and the piercing winds from mountains of Kashmir suddenly lowered the temperature to a degree inconveniently cold."

Maharaja Ranjit Singh, the Lion of Punjab, died on June 27, 1839 AD, and with him died the Sikh rule. Kartar Singh Duggal writes,[6] "As (prince) Kharak Singh set the pyre alight, there was loud chanting of hymns of all religions. Soon thereafter, there was a gentle shower. Then a pair of pigeons appeared as if from nowhere in the sky. They dipped low and fell into the flames."

Governors appointed during his regime

Dewan Chand, 1819 AD

Dewan Chand was the first governor deputed by Maharaja Ranjit Singh in Kashmir. He remained as governor for a brief period. During this time, the only thing to his credit is that he established law and order in the hilly tracts of the valley. Jia Lal Kilam says,[7] "Dewan Chand had all the qualifications of a great General but he lacked those qualities which could make him a successful administrator." Dewan Chand was summoned back. He reached Lahore, presented a sum of rupees twenty-five Lakh to Maharaja Ranjit Singh, and thus secured his immunity. Dewan Moti Ram succeeded him.

Dewan Moti Ram, 1819-1820 AD

Dewan Moti Ram, son of Dewan Mohkam Chand, was the first regular governor of the Sikh rule in Kashmir. He remained as governor for fourteen months. Although the majority community of Kashmir was Muslims, he had realised that Muslims as well as Hindus were subjected to Afghan tyranny. They had not showed any special favour to Muslims. Nonetheless, this governor knew that Muslims in Punjab were more violent and uncompromising. However Dewan Moti Ram was a peace loving man. Pandit Jia Lal Kilam says,[8] "Dewan Moti Ram was a man of genial temperament and a peace-loving disposition."

Pandit Birbal Dhar was put in charge of the revenue administration. Birbal conducted himself with great ability and tact with the result that Maharaja Ranjit Singh was highly pleased with him. On the occasion of the Dushera festivities, the Maharaja sent him a costly present of a *Chauga*, (Royal gown), *Kalgi* (feather), a pearl necklace and a gold bracelet, etc.

Suddenly the Muslims of the valley became restive. Seeing the way Hindus were being treated more leniently than them, they began making inflammatory speeches in the mosques against the Sikh rule in Kashmir. Agitated by the situation, Dewan Moti Ram closed the Jama Masjid for Muslims to pray inside and decided to demolish Khanqah-i-Maula. He had actually placed guns on the opposite side of Vitasta. There was an uproar amongst the people of the valley. Not only Muslims, even Hindus vigorously opposed this. Pandit Birbal Dhar personally approached the governor and got the destruction of the mosque stopped. Birbal Dhar, who had suffered at the hands of Muslim rulers under the Afghans so greatly that his wife had to commit suicide and his daughter-in-law was taken prisoner, saved the destruction of Khanqah Mosque, and with that, he saved the composite culture of Kashmir and demonstrated his belief in the co-existence of all religions.

Destiny played a strange game with Dewan Moti Ram. His son was killed in Hazara. Dewan was upset, depressed and dejected. He, therefore, decided to relinquish the governorship and start renunciation. According to Lepel Griffin,[9] "When his eldest son was killed in Hazara in 1820, he resigned the appointment and wished to retire to Banaras..." He left Kashmir, and in his place Hari Singh Nalwa was placed as governor of Kashmir.

Hari Singh Nalwa, 1820-1821 AD

Sardar Hari Singh Nalwa was appointed as governor of Kashmir on August 24, 1820. Born in Gujranwala town, now in West Pakistan, in the year 1791 AD, in the house of Sardar Gurdial Singh and Dharam Kaur, Hari Singh was the only son of his parents. His grandfather Sardar Hardas Singh was engaged in the service of Shukerchakia Misl.

Sardar Hari Singh Nalwa, the great Sikh warrior, was the Commander-in-chief of Maharaja Ranjit Singh. His father was also a warrior in Ranjit Singh's army. He earned the name Nalwa after he killed a tiger. His name brought terror into the hearts of the Afghans and the Afghan mothers used to silence their crying babies by saying, "*Khamosh bash—Haria raghle.*" (Quiet Dear Child; Haria is Coming)

During Dewan Moti Ram's tenure, people had stopped paying taxes to the government. However, Hari Singh Nalwa, after taking over, immediately issued a stern warning and started collecting the taxes from the people. He was cruel but a great organiser and military commander. His method of administration was of primitive type and the people of Kashmir were very distressed. He also struck a coin in his own name. The coin came to be known as Hari Singh rupee. Pandit Birbal Dhar continued to be the revenue collector during his tenure. This Sikh Governor also tried to extract the last penny from the hapless Kashmiris. Thus, the change of masters from Afghan to Sikhs proved no better. The Sikhs were no less cruel, rapacious and intolerant. According to Walter Lawrence,[10] "Sikhs seemed to look upon Kashmirian as little better than cattle. The murder of a native by a Sikh was punished with a fine to the government from sixteen to twenty rupees, of which four were paid to the family of the deceased if a Hindu, two rupees if he was a Mohamadian." On account of some misunderstanding, Birbal Dhar was dismissed from service and Ganesh Pandit Dhar was appointed in his place. However, when the charges against Birbal Dhar were cleared, he was re-instated.

It is interesting to note that William Moorcroft, an officer of the East India Company was deputed by the Company to Ladakh to find a good breed of horses. When he visited Ladakh, he started interfering in the relations between Maharaja Ranjit Singh and the Raja of Ladakh. A commercial treaty was concluded with the government of Ladakh by which the whole of Central Asia was virtually opened to British trade in exchange for British protection. This treaty would have required breaking relations with Maharaja Ranjit Singh. The Maharaja made a complaint to the then British Government and in return Moorcroft was censured for this act. Information was sent to Ranjit Singh informing him that Moorcroft was no longer representing the East India Company.

Dewan Moti Ram, 1821-1826 AD

Maharaja Ranjit Singh came to know about the repressive measures adopted by Hari Singh Nalwa. He therefore re-appointed Dewan Moti Ram as the governor of Kashmir. During this period, relations between Dewan Moti Ram and Pandit Birbal got strained. The latter was arrested and put behind bars where he died. Pandit Jai Lal Kilam says,[11] "Birbal died in custody—a strange irony of fate that the person who made it possible for the Sikh rulers to occupy the country and who greatly contributed to the strengthening of the administration should have died as a prisoner!"

Dewan Moti Ram was in charge till 1926 AD. Lepel Griffin writes,[12] "When the family fell into disgrace owing to the sinister influence of Raja Dhiyan Singh, Dewan Chunni Lall, a man of no account, took his place for a year and a half."

Chroniclers say that Dewan Moti Ram was a kind man with humane feelings. However, he was essentially concerned more with revenue collection than looking after the welfare of the people of the valley. The revenue collection was meant to be sent to Lahore to Maharaja Ranjit

Singh and not utilized for the upliftment of the people. Yet, the Sikh rulers in comparison to Afghans were less brutal, says Younghusband,[13] "The Sikhs who succeeded the Afghans were not so barbarically cruel, but they were hard and rough masters."

Dewan Chunni Lall, 1826 -1827 AD

The Government recalled Dewan Moti Ram and in his place Dewan Chunni Lall was made the governor of Kashmir. Chunni Lall proved no better. During his governorship, the collection of revenue fell very short due to abject economic conditions of the people. He remained for a very brief period and Dewan Kirpa Ram succeeded him.

Dewan Kirpa Ram, 1827-1831 AD

Dewan Kirpa Ram, son of Dewan Moti Ram, became the governor of Kashmir and replaced Dewan Chunni Lall. He was a man of magnificent tastes. He loved Kashmir's panoramic scenery and he loved the Kashmiri women. Tradition says that he used to roam on the Dal Lake in a big boat which was rowed by one hundred women nude up to their chest. The dancing girls used to dance in the boat. However, he beautified Srinagar by constructing fine-looking buildings.

Kirpa Ram's magnificent life was disturbed by a severe earthquake which destroyed many buildings and killed many people. The intermittent tremors remained for many months. This natural catastrophe was followed by severe cholera. Both these natural calamities caused heavy loss of life. It is said that many dead bodies could not be provided with shrouds for want of cloth. Meanwhile, Zabardast Khan raised a revolt against Sikh supremacy. Dewan Kirpa Ram had to lead an expedition against this Raja of Muzaffarabad. Initially, Zabardast Khan had succeeded in inflicting heavy losses on the Sikh army but, later on, through the planning of Ganesh Dhar, Zabardast Khan was defeated.

Dewan Kirpa Ram was not a cruel governor; he was to a great extent a benevolent ruler. Yet, during his period the economic condition of the people did not improve much though it was a bit better than his predecessors. According to Godfrey Thomas Vigne[14], "Kupar Ram, (Kirpa Ram) who was governor for four years was the kindest and the best of all. He attended to the wishes and rapacity of Ranjit, and was luxurious without being tyrannical. The dancing girls were his constant companions, and his state barge was always paddled by women, who were not, it may be supposed, selected for their want of beauty." His rule was mild and people made some economic progress. It is said that he used to send 42 Lakh rupees to Maharaja Ranjit Singh annually and at the same time, people were reasonably happy. According to Sir Lepel Griffin,[15] "Dewan Moti Ram and his youngest son Kirpa Ram were on the whole, the best governors that the valley had."

Bhima Singh Ardali,1831-1832 AD

Kirpa Ram was recalled to Punjab and Maharaja Ranjit Singh appointed Bhima Singh Ardali as the governor of Kashmir. During his governorship, terrible Shia/ Sunni riots broke out in Kashmir. The Sunni frenzy burnt Hassanabad and Zadibal, the Shia localities. When Bhima Singh could not control the riots he was recalled. Prince Sher Singh was sent in his place.

Prince Sher Singh, 1832-1834 AD

Prince Sher Singh was the son of Maharaja Ranjit Singh.The Maharaja had decided to visit the valley during Prince Sher Singh's governorship, but later on he abandoned the visit and went back from Poonch. Sher Singh remained in Kashmir for two years. He indulged in enjoyment of all sorts, leaving the country's administration in the hands of his deputy, Basakha Singh. As a result of this arrangement the people suffered. In the meantime, a terrible famine broke out which reduced the population of the valley to one-fourth. As a ruler, Sher Singh proved ineffective. He did not do anything to bring food grains for the starving people. The people complained against him to Maharaja Ranjit Singh who called him back.

During Sher Singh's tenure, a missionary visited the valley. As stated by Joseph Wolff and Alfred Gatty,[16] "He then entered with his companions, the beautiful valley called Shoopeyan, which is covered with lilies and roses; and dancing girls were sent to amuse him." The statement clearly indicates that the Sikh Government in Punjab and the British were very close to each other during the period in question. Prince Sher Singh was recalled and Colonel Mian Singh took charge of Kashmir as governor.

Colonel Mian Singh, 1834-1841 AD

Mian Singh was considered a brave, courageous and fearless soldier. He bore twenty-seven wounds on his body. He had participated in many wars and had earned the reputation of being an able commander. Like a military commander, he first tried to observe the economic as well as social condition of the people. Being a keen observer, he found that people were really in distress. Famine conditions had made people terribly miserable. The first thing he did was to import foodstuffs like rice, pulses, and eggs. He gave interest free loan to villagers for development of agriculture. These measures brought self-confidence among people and agriculture began to show signs of prosperity. Mian Singh initiated many measures such as introducing proper weights and punishment for those who did frauds with the villagers. He decided cases justly without resorting to religious partisanship and bias. His rule is considered as the best period of Sikh rule in Kashmir.

It was during Governor Mian Singh's tenure that an Austrian army officer known as Baron Charles Hugel visited Kashmir and wrote his memoirs. In addition, another traveller known as Thomas Vigne visited Kashmir. Both these travellers penned down their travel memoirs—*Travels in Kashmir and The Punjab* by Hugel and *Travel in Kashmir, Ladakh, Iskardo, the Country Adjoining the Mountains* by Godfry Thomas Vigne.

On his arrival, he tried to present himself to the governor of Kashmir. Writes Baron Charles Hugel,[17] "Mr Vigne and Dr Henderson wished to accompany me, but by the time the breakfast was over, and we were ready to start, it was noon, and Kazi told me it was too late. I was vexed that he had not reminded me of the hour and declared my intention of not going at all. The Kazi was horrified. He whispered in his(Interpreter's) ear, that the governor, desiring that I should see him in all his glory, had held a grand levee, of durbar, at ten o'clock, and that the company, after waiting two hours, had been dismissed—the governor being accustomed daily at that hour to drink two bottles of Kashmir spirits. When Mohan (my interpreter) reported this to me, I most readily deferred presenting myself, not wishing to visit a viceroy and find him in a state of drunken insensibility."

Col Mian Singh remained busy in ameliorating the hardships caused to the people of Kashmir. Meanwhile, the Sikh government in Punjab had to face an assault by Amir Dost Mohammad who ruled over part of Afghanistan in 1835 AD. He launched an attack against the Sikh army to wrest Peshawar from them, which was part of the Maharaja's territory. The Sikh army defeated the Afghan forces and retained Peshawar. It was during Col Mian Singh's tenure that the Lion of Punjab, Maharaja Ranjit Singh, died in 1839 AD.

Maharaja Kharak Singh, 1839 AD

After the death of Maharaja Ranjit Singh, a fight broke out between his sons for the throne. However, Prince Kharak Singh, the eldest son of the Maharaja from Maharani Datar Kaur was made the king of Punjab on September 1, 1839. He was born on 9 February 1801. He was married to Maharani Chand Kaur, daughter of Jaimal Singh Kanhaiya when he was only eleven years old. He remained as king from September to October 8, 1839 AD. He died on November 5, 1840 AD.

Kharak Singh had to encounter a lot of envy from his ambitious ministers. Even the Dogra minister Dhiyan Singh started opposing him and instigated Maharaja Kharak Singh's son, Naunihal Singh, against his father. However, the Maharaja was always advised by his tutor, Chet Singh Bajwa. The conspirators assassinated Chet Singh and arrested Maharaja Kharak Singh and put him in prison with strict vigil. Prince Naunihal Singh took over the reins of the country. Tradition says that he perished because doses of slow poison were given to him.

Maharaja Naunihal Singh, 1839-1840 AD

Naunihal Singh, the grandson of Maharaja Ranjit Singh and son of Maharaja Kharak Singh was coronated as the king of Punjab. Born to Maharani Chand Kaur on March 9,1821, he was very popular among his subjects as well as the army. But his rule lasted only for one year. It is said that he also proved quite useless. He imprisoned his father and went to see him only once. Destiny played a strange trick on him. When he was coming back from consigning his father's body into flames, a wall came down upon him and crushed his head. He died on November 6, 1840. It is not known whether the building's collapse was accidental or deliberate. Some Historians believe that the Dogra rajas, Gulab Singh and Dhiyan Singh, killed Naunihal Singh, as after the accident he was able to walk but he was whisked away from there by them. He was then confined to a room in the fort. After two days it was announced that the Maharaja was dead. Historian Latif does not agree with the view that the Dogra Rajas killed him. He says that it was an accident that he got killed. Cunningham also says that it is not decidedly known that the Rajas of Jammu killed him but they were capable of committing this crime.

The fact remains that he had secured the throne with the help of Dogras but soon there arose mistrust between him and the Dogra chief Raja Dhiyan Singh. Also, Maharaja Gulab Singh was declared an independent ruler of Jammu by Maharaja Ranjit Singh, but Naunihal Singh forced Maharaja Gulab Singh to pay taxes to his administration. According to Cunningham,[18] "Nau Nihal's great aim was to destroy or to reduce to insignificance, the potent Raja of Jummoo who wished to engross the whole power of the state, and jointly held Ladakh and the hill principalities between Ravee and Jhelum in fief besides numerous estates in various parts of Punjab"

Col Mian Singh, 1834-1841 AD

Colonel Mian Singh continued as the governor of Kashmir. Conditions all over had deteriorated and there was turbulence everywhere. In Punjab, with the death of Naunihal Singh there was again the problem of who was to take over the throne. On the other hand, the British forces were becoming active with each passing day. The English army, who were interested in conquering Afghanistan and northern India, did not like the Sikh army's victory against Dost Mohammad. The 'Perpetual friendship Treaty of Amritsar', of 1809, between Maharaja Ranjit Singh and East India Company was severely dented when the Sikhs were not allowed to annex any other territory beyond what they had on the western side of northern India. With this scenario in the background, Maharani Chand Kaur, the mother of Naunihal Singh herself took over as the Regent Queen of Punjab.

Maharani Chand Kaur, 1840-1841 AD

After the death of her son Naunihal Singh, Maharani Chand Kaur took over the reins of Punjab on December 2, 1840, and was titled as Malika Muqaddasa (Empress Immaculate). She was the daughter of Sardar Jaimal Singh of the Kanhaiya Misl. She married Prince Kharak Singh in February 1812 AD when she only ten years old.

With the help of Attar Singh, Ajit Singh, and Lehna Singh Majithia, the powerful ministers of Ranjit Singh, Maharani Chand Kaur became the queen. After taking over the reins she removed the Dogra Ministers from their important posts and appointed Sikhs in their places. Attar Singh became her prime minister. The replacement was undertaken as Raja Dhiyan Singh, prime minister and brother of Raja Gulab Singh was insisting she adopt his son so that he could be the heir apparent to the Kingdom. But she refused and this angered Dhiyan Singh and there arose a rift between the Dogra ministers and Rani Chand Kaur.

Raja Dhiyan Singh connived with Prince Sher Singh, son of Ranjit Singh and launched an attack on her forces and defeated her. The Maharani had issued orders to the forces not to help the Prince. But the regiments stationed outside the city walls joined the Prince. He, therefore, raised an army of 26,000 infantry, 8000 horses and 45 guns, whereas the Maharani was left with only 5000 men and a few guns. The Maharani was trounced and Sher Singh became the King of Punjab.

Maharaja Sher Singh, 1841-1843 AD

Maharaja Sher Singh ascended the throne of Punjab on January 20, 1841, after defeating Rani Chand Kaur. He had the full support of disgruntled and discontented soldiers and European officers. Initially, he put Dogras on important positions but soon he too was fed-up and tried to change them by appointing Sikhs in their place. That aroused rivalry between Sikhs and Dogras. The suspicion and mistrust between Maharaja Sher Singh and Dogra prime minister Dhiyan Singh culminated into a bloody situation.

The Maharaja did not prove an efficient ruler. He was always engrossed in vices. He was married to the daughter of the ruler of Suket. This very beautiful woman was known as Rani Dukno. Soon Ajit Singh Sandhawalia and Sardar Lehna Singh hatched a conspiracy to kill the King and capture the throne. They killed him and also Raja Dhiyan Singh, the prime minister.

John Martin Honigberger, who brought Homeopathy to India and was personal physician to Maharaja Ranjit Singh wrote,[19] "Sirdar Ajeet Sing and his uncle Lena Sing (descended from the family of the Scindawalla, and related to Runjeet Sing) belonged to the party of the ranee, who had fought against Sheer Sing and Dhiyan Sing; but they knew how to insinuate themselves into the confidence of both to such a degree that, without the knowledge of either, they destroyed both the Maharaja and his wuzeer. They conspired with Sheer Sing to murder Dhiyan Sing, but at the same time, they also intrigued with Dhiyan Singh to murder Sheer Sing." He further says that, "Sheer Sing was even repeatedly cautioned by his friends to be on his guard, to which advice, however, he paid no attention and in an immovable manner allowed them to concoct their schemes. Each one believed that the stroke was appointed for his adversary, and, finally, it fell upon both. True is the proverb: 'He, who digs a pit for another, falls in himself;' for Ajeet Singh as well as Lena Sing had laboured for their ruin."

In September 1943, Maharaja Sher Singh was inspecting Ajit Singh's troops for the Guard of Honour. After the first ceremony, Ajit Singh requested him to inspect his carbine. The Maharaja, who was great lover of weapons, put forth his hands to hold the rifle. Ajit Singh pressed the trigger and emptied the loaded barrel into the chest of Maharaja Sher Singh. Instantly he brought out a sword and cut off his head too.

A notable event during Maharaja Sher Singh's reign was the conquest of Ladakh Valley. The expedition under the Dogra General Zorawar Singh conquered Ladakh.

Col Mian Singh, 1834-1841 AD

Colonel Mian Singh continued to be the governor of Kashmir. Meanwhile, his Sikh soldiers raised a revolt against him and before he could pacify them the soldiers conspired against him and he was assassinated on 17 April 1841. Maharaja Sher Singh sent Raja Gulab Singh with a strong force to punish the mutinous army. Writes GT Vigne,[20] "Letters which I received by the July mail, 1841, informed me that Mahan Singh (Colonel Mian Singh) had been murdered in his durbar by the mutinous Sikh Sipahi (Soldiers), who demanded an increase of pay, which he would not grant without a reference to Lahore."

With the death of Mian Singh, two governors, one after the other, Sheikh Gulam Mohi-ud-Din and then his son were assigned the governorship of Kashmir.

Sheikh Gulam Mohi-ud-Din, 1841 AD

After the assassination of Col Mian Singh, the governor of Kashmir, a Muslim, Sheikh Gulam Mohi-ud-Din, was sent as governor in 1841 AD. This Muslim governor had a very tough time though he was a very efficient and enlightened man. He was there for a short period but he left a reputation of a secular and a progressive governor. Sheikh Gulam Mohi-ud-Din earned a lot of goodwill of the people of Kashmir. In the first instance, he opened the Jama Masjid at Srinagar which Dewan Moti Ram had ordered to be closed in 1819. Similarly, he also got the

Shankaracharya temple repaired. Writes PNK Bamzai,[21] "Simultaneously he repaired the temple on the Shankaracharya hill in Srinagar and installed a new Lingam therein."

Maharaja Duleep Singh, 1843-1849 AD

It seems that destiny had played mischief with the children and grandchildren of Maharaja Ranjit Singh, as they were not destined to enjoy the luxury of ruling over the kingdom carved by the Maharaja. After his death, his son Kharak Singh occupied the throne but for a few months. Then came Naunihal Singh, son of Kharak Singh, who died when he was accidently buried under a wall. Maharani Chand Kaur took over the reins of Punjab, turned profligate and was dethroned. Maharaja Sher Singh was killed by Ajit Singh. Finally, it was the turn of Maharaja Duleep Singh to be the king of Punjab.

Maharaja Duleep Singh, the youngest son of Maharaja Ranjit Singh, was only five years old when he was anointed as the ruler of Punjab in the year 1843. His mother, Rani Jind/Jindan Kaur became his regent. In fact, all the power was in her hands. Punjab was passing through very anarchic conditions. The administration was there only in name. Frequent removal of rulers, who were either killed or died, had sent an ominous signal in the kingdom. Law and order had collapsed; the soldiers were in a state of turbulence due to non-payment of salaries.

On the other hand, the English had already captured Delhi and placed Lord Dalhousie as the Governor General of India (1848 to 1856 AD). He is named as the author of the Doctrine of Lapse since annexation was his policy. The English agent who was placed in Punjab was there to make political mischief so that Punjab could be annexed with the English territory. Seeing the chaotic and muddled conditions in Punjab, the English army arrived near Sutlej, ready to fight the Sikh army. Lord Harding defeated the Sikh army in 1846 AD in the First Sikh War. On March 9, 1846, the Treaty of Lahore was signed. In this treaty the Sikhs were made to surrender the important region between Beas and Sutlej rivers. The salient feature of the treaty was that the Lahore Durbar was to pay a war indemnity of one and a half crore of Rupees. The treaty also resulted in the famous Koh-i-Noor diamond falling into British hands. The Sikh treasury in Punjab had only 50 Lakh rupees. They gave the sovereignty of the state of Jammu and Kashmir to Maharaja Gulab Singh for which he paid seventy-five Lakh Rupees.

The first Anglo-Sikh war had not completely cowed down the Sikh army. They wanted to regain their valour by defeating the English. An excuse came when the governor of Multan, Kahan Singh became hostile to Punjab rulers. He murdered the two English agents from Maharaja's government. The English declared war against the Sikhs. The Sikhs lost the war and Punjab was annexed to the British dominion in 1849. The prominent features of the second Sikh war were that Maharaja Duleep was given a pension of 50 thousand pounds per annum and deported to England.

Maharaja Duleep Singh was the youngest son of the legendary Lion of Punjab, Maharaja Ranjit Singh and Maharani Jind/Jindan Kaur. He was born on September 6, 1838. He succeeded his half-brother Maharaja Sher Singh in 1843 AD. He handed over the Koh-i-Noor diamond to the British in controversial circumstances. It ultimately reached Queen Victoria as part of the terms of the conclusion of the war on the 250th anniversary of the East India Company on July 3, 1850.

Maharaja Duleep Singh became a great favourite of Queen Victoria. He was received into the Church of England in 1853 AD and was baptised to the Christian faith. He attempted to return to Punjab in 1886, but was stopped at Aden and turned back. Meanwhile, he escaped to France and persuaded the French authorities to assist him in regaining his throne in India. Suddenly the urge to reconvert to his original religion overpowered him and he converted back to Sikhism in 1888. Failing to excite official interest in France due to British objections, he journeyed to Russia, where he offered his services to the Tsar in lieu of his help. This was the end of Sikh Rule in Punjab and in Kashmir also.

Maharani Jind Kaur

On the death of Maharaja Sher Singh in September 1845, Maharani Jind Kaur, who was popularly known as Rani Jindan, the youngest wife of Maharaja Ranjit Singh, became Regent for her young son Maharaja Duleep Singh. She decided on a policy of aggression towards the British army. The Sikh forces fought valiantly and gallantly with the British army but unfortunately her own men, whom she trusted the most, deceived her. The Sikh forces lost and they had to sign the treaty of Bharowal in

1846. Rani Jindan was deposed as Regent and banished to Sheikhpura near Lahore. Henry Lawrence, British Resident at Lahore imprisoned her. After thirteen years, her son Duleep Singh was allowed to see his mother and he took her along with him to England. She remained in Kensington, London till she died on August 1, 1861.

Sheikh Gulam Mohi-ud-Din, 1843-1845 AD

On the Kashmir front, Sheikh Gulam Mohi-Ud-Din continued to be the governor of Kashmir. Meanwhile, Raja Gulab Singh had sent a military contingent under the leadership of Sardar Zorawar Singh to conquer Ladakh. Raja Gulab Singh sought Sheikh Gulam's help in Kashmir. He helped Raja Gulab Singh by supplying aid to his army in the form of rations and board and lodging for his military contingents. He also provided labourers who carried their luggage to Ladakh to quell the rebellion there. Gulam Mohi-ud-Din was engaged in the activities of Raja Gulab Singh till he died in 1845. After his death, his son Sheikh Imam-ud-Din was appointed as governor of Kashmir.

Sheikh Imam-ud-Din, 1845-1846 AD

Maharani Jind/Jindan Kaur appointed Sheikh Imam-ud-Din, son of Sheikh Gulam Mohi-ud-Din, as governor of Kashmir in 1845 AD. Though highly cultured and well educated, he could not do much in view of the very fluid political conditions in Punjab, the English interference and the restlessness of Sikh soldiers in Punjab and Kashmir. In the year 1846 AD, the Sikh rule in Kashmir ended as Kashmir was taken over by Raja Gulab Singh.Thus, started a new chapter of Dogra rule in the history of Kashmir.

Two
British Occupation of India

The commercial relations between Europe and India have existed since very early times. Alexander the great, the King of Macedonia, invaded and conquered Punjab in 323 BC. This gave impetus to the land route trade with other countries. In fact, the Portugal navigator Vasco-de-Gamma discovered the sea route to India. He came to India in 1497 AD reaching Calicut (in Kerala) on April 22, 1498. The other Portuguese governors strengthened the Portuguese position in India. But on account of their defective system of governance and religious intolerance, they could not hold India for a long time.The Dutch, who were primarily engrossed in European affairs, also tried to occupy India and the first Dutch expedition was sent under De Houtma in 1595 AD. It anchored at Java. By 1619 AD, the Dutch also established a few settlements in India.

By the end of 16th century, the English also decided to establish trade with India. It was in 1599 AD that a resolution was passed by a group of English merchants under the Chairmanship of the Lord Mayor of London to form an association to trade directly with India. Thus, there appeared on the scene a British Company known as the East India Company. The English East India Company was ultimately established in 1603 AD to do business with India. It was the third expedition of the Company under Capt William Hawkins which reached the Indian shores and got permission in 1612 to build a factory at Surat. Curiously enough, the English settlement grew rapidly after getting permission. Sir Thomas Roe secured permission from Emperor Jahangir. The historic meeting between Emperor Jahangir and Sir Thomas Roe of the British East India Company took place in Akbar's Palace in Ajmer. Jahangir permitted them to set up factories at Ahmadabad, Baroch and Agra. The East India Company grew by leaps and bounds and was able to carve out an empire for England.

By 1822 AD, the East India Company, benefitting from the imperial patronage, expanded its commercial trading operations and also increased its military strength gradually. Soon, they conquered Bengal, Bihar, East and West Ghats and then reached Delhi. During early nineteenth century, Napoleon was at the height of his power in Europe. It was feared by the English that he might invade India. In this connection, John Elphinstone was sent to Kabul to meet the King. Shah Shuja, the ruler of Afghanistan, assured him that he would not allow any European army to pass through his country to invade India. In the meantime Shah Shuja was dethroned.

Maharaja Ranjit Singh was the first Sikh ruler who established diplomatic relations with the English. He had realised the strength of British power and therefore wanted to be at peace with them. The first contact was established in 1800 AD. There was a rumour that Zaman Shah of Kabul was preparing to attack India. The English began to feel worried about the safety of their possessions in India. They sent Yusuf Ali with many gifts to the court of Maharaja Ranjit Singh, with the request that he should not side with Zaman Shah. But Zaman Shah got involved in the domestic mess in Afghanistan and the possibility of his invasion of India vanished. With that, the English came close to Maharaja Ranjit Singh. The alert military leader, Sir Charles Metcalf, was sent to the court of the Maharaja. He made the treaty of Amritsar with the Sikh Ruler of Punjab in 1809. By this treaty, the English and the Maharaja declared perpetual friendship with each other.

However, the English began interfering in the internal politics of India with the aim to conquer the country and establish a British Raj in India. By this time, they had conquered Bombay, Bengal and Bihar.

Even Awadh had become subordinate to British rule. It was during the reign of Emperor Farrukh Siyar, the Mughal King, that the East India Company had sent two envoys with thirty thousand pounds worth of presents for Emperor Farrukh Siyar (son of Aurangzeb) who eventually gave them important trade and valuable concessions and exemptions from customs duty. The Company's success was partly due to the fact that an English surgeon named William Hamilton cured the Emperor of a malignant distemper, and the emperor was moved to grant trading rights to the company in 1717 AD.

The war of succession among later Mughal Princes also helped the English to plan intrigues and win power from them. When the Mughal Emperor Alamgir II was murdered in Delhi, his son and legitimate successor to the throne was in Bihar. His name was Ali Gauhar. For twelve years he did not move to Delhi as he was afraid of the wazir Imad-ud-Mulk. He remained under the protection of the East India Company. However, he came to Delhi with the help of the Marathas. He assumed the title of Shah Alam II and sided with Shuja-ud-Daula , Nawab of Awadh and Mir Qasim, Nawab of Bengal against the forces of East India Company. They fought against the English at the battleground of Buxar but were defeated. Emperor Shah Alam was taken prisoner. Meanwhile, in May 1765 AD, Robert Clive was appointed as Governor of Bengal for the second time.

The English forces occupied Ferozepur, which was only forty miles from Lahore. Only one river, Sutlej, had to be crossed to reach Lahore. Maharaja Ranjit Singh also had claimed this place. Seeing the English constructing a fort, the Maharaja thought that the British were encircling his kingdom. The Sikhs had occupied Shikarpur to which the English objected and the Sikhs were forced to withdraw. They began to believe that the next move of the English was to encircle and invade Punjab. As a result of this suspicion, the Sikhs and the English fought many battles in which the English army was victorious . According to Sir Lapel Henry Griffin,[1] "the rising power of English, which, through the eighteenth and nineteenth centuries, ever increased in intensity. The victories of the British Government were won by gallantry or diplomacy, by force or by fraud, but its advance, though sometimes checked, was never long delayed."

In Kashmir, the Sikh governors, Sheikh Gulam Mohi-ud-Din and then his son Sheikh Imam-ud-Din proved ineffective due to the fact that after the death of Maharaja Ranjit Singh his successors proved hopelessly weak and unable to cope with administering the country. The several wars fought between the Sikh army and the British made the Sikh army weak and that hastened the downfall of the Sikh rule in Punjab and in Kashmir.

The British had anticipated that the Durbar would be unable to give the war indemnity. The British officers headed by Lord Henry Hardinge and Henry Lawrence, therefore, decided to give the state of Kashmir to Raja Gulab Singh in lieu of money. They made separate arrangements with the Raja. This infuriated the Sikhs especially Maharani Jind. According to Sukhdev Singh Charak.[2] "The Sikhs reacted venomously and expressed their bitter resentment over this arrangement and once more unsuccessful attempts were made on the Raja's (Gulab Singh's) life. In an angry letter to Henry Lawrence, she warned that if Kashmir was given to Gulab Singh she would appeal directly to Queen Victoria." However, the British continued with the arrangement of transfer of Kashmir to Raja Gulab Singh.

Meanwhile, there arose some differences between the Sikhs and the English. The latter annexed Sind to their territory. The Sikhs objected. Then the English told the Sikh rulers that the areas around Sutlej were being annexed with the British territory. That was the cause of the First Anglo-Sikh war that took place in 1845 AD.

On February 10, 1846, the Battle of Sobraon, between the Sikh army and the British forces took place, which concluded in defeat of the Sikh army. The remarkable thing about this war is that though the Sikhs had huge manpower there was no good leader. In the words of Cunningham, "the Sikh army was lacking in leadership." Although many advised the British rulers to annex Punjab, they did not occupy it. The war ended with the Treaty of Lahore.

This transfer of Kashmir to Raja Gulab Singh was made through a separate treaty, known in history as the Treaty of Amritsar, which concluded on March 16, 1846. According to this treaty, Gulab Singh was recognised as Maharaja Gulab Singh. The British did not feel the necessity of consulting the people of Kashmir while doing this. The Sikh rule in Kashmir ended and Dogra rule started.

Transfer of Kashmir to Gulab Singh

Perhaps Jammu and its Dogra rulers were not alien for Kashmiris as were Mughals and Afghans; even Sikhs were foreigners. Dogras were next-door neighbours.

The foreign rulers such as Afghans and Sikhs who ruled over Kashmir never took the people seriously. In 1379 AD when Sayyid Mir Hamadani (popularly known in Kashmir as Shah Hamdan) came to Kashmir accompanied by hundreds of Sayyid missionaries to preach Islam, Kashmiris were never consulted. When Hassan Shah from Shah Mir's lineage was the king of Kashmir, he had married a Sayyid girl and the Sayyids got royal patronage. The Kashmiris hated them for their rule over Kashmir was hard, cold, ruthless and ugly. Their cruelty and repression and fanaticism had crushed the Kashmiri spirit. In the words of Prem Nath Bazaz.[3] "They (the rulers) had become zulum parast (worshipers of tyranny)." According to William Moorcroft.[4] "The Sikhs looked upon Kashmiris as little better than cattle."

When Maharaja Gulab Singh became the ruler of the valley, the people there were ignorant of the social, political and economical revolution that was taking place in India. M A Stein observed in the introduction of *Rajatarangini*[5]. "In my account of topography of Kashmir, I have endeavoured to show to what extent the great mountain barriers around the valley have, until quite modern times, isolated its population from the rest of India. This isolation has all times exercised a decisive influence on the history of Kashmir."

The nineteenth century was indeed a transitional period between mediaeval times and the dawn of modernism. The British conquest of the whole of India seems to have been a blessing in disguise. In the words of Lord Dalhousie, "The three great engineers of social improvement which science had already given to the west— the railways, the post and telegraph system and modern banking, are adjuncts of modern civilization about which the people of the valley were ignorant."

With the dawn of western influence over India, some social customs like sati, female infanticide and early marriage were considered obsolete, reprehensible and revolting. Great social reformers like Raja Ram Mohan Roy, Swami Vivekananda, and Swami Dayanand helped to remove these social evils. As the ruler of Jammu and Kashmir, Maharaja Gulab Singh had an onerous task to give peace and tranquillity to the state so that people could attend to their economic activities. By the time the Sikh rulers vacated the country, the political, economical and social conditions were in chaos. Initially, Gulab Singh ruled very strictly and bought peace in the valley. There were criminal nomadic tribes like the Bombas, Khakas, and Gulwams who used to visit the valley and indulge in loot, death and destruction. Gulab Singh succeeded in liquidating them.

Earlier foreign rulers had introduced a peculiar system of forced labour, known in Kashmir as 'Begar'. These rulers used to commandeer the services of peasants for the purpose of taking loads from one place to another during invasions by the army. In return, they would get nothing except food. As a result of this pernicious system, agriculture suffered enormously. The system was akin to slavery. Gulab Singh wanted to abolish this evil system, but discretion prompted him to use it selectively. He made selection of peasants and registered their names. When necessary, the government would call them for jobs, and in return, he used to pay them in kind.

Kashmir is perhaps the only place where the Government took the job of rice distribution seriously. The Maharaja introduced rationing of foodstuffs. He constructed storehouses for the storage of rice. It is true that Maharaja Gulab Singh wanted to ameliorate the economic as well as political conditions of the people through various practical steps that he took. But since he had paid seventy-five Lakhs to the British, he also wanted to recover this amount from Kashmiris. He was shocked to learn that the major portion of cultivable land had been taken away from the Kashmiris and distributed to his own men as jageers. The rest was mountainous land from which he could not earn anything. He, therefore, resorted to heavy taxation. Nevertheless, with the return of peace and tranquillity, the economic activity gained extraordinary momentum—the shawl industry thrived. In the words of a British army officer, Lieutenant Colonel Torrens,"Gulab Singh went beyond his predecessors in the acts of undue taxation and extortion. They had taxed heavily, it is true, but he sucked the very lifeblood of the people. They had laid violent hands on a large portion of the fruits of the earth, the profits of the loom and work of men's hands, but he skinned the very flints to fill his coffers."

On the Punjab front the Sikhs were defeated by the British army. They were not only defeated but the British also humiliated them. The treatment meted out to Maharani Jindan by the British added fuel to fire. Lord Dalhousie annexed Punjab on March 9, 1849. All this had made Maharaja Gulab Singh very apprehensive about the British intentions. It is true that the British were interested in annexing Kashmir to their territory. But the Treaty of Amritsar was a handicap for them.

Three
The Dogra Rule in Kashmir

Maharaja Gulab Singh, 1846-1856 AD

The history of Jammu, Kashmir and even of Punjab seems incomplete without the name of Maharaja Gulab Singh. Destiny took such a turn in his life that from a soldier he rose to become a Maharaja. Gulab Singh was the son of Mian Kishore Singh belonging to the Rajput clan. He was born on October 21, 1792 AD. Mian Kishore Singh was the jageerdar of Samba in the Jammu district. His mother's name was Mahadevi. He got his education under the guidance of his grandfather Mian Jawahar Singh. Shiv Nimohi, in his book *Duggar Ka Itihas*[1] has mentioned that his grandfather gave him training in the art of warfare, use of sword and martial art.

At the age of sixteen, in the year 1808 AD, Maharaja Ranjit Singh's army, headed by Bhai Hukma Singh Chimni, attacked Jammu. Raja Jeet Singh, the then Raja of Jammu, deputed his army chief Miyan Mota to fight the enemy. Assisting Miyan Mota in this fight, Miyan Dodi and Gulab Singh also fought gallantly against the Sikhs. The Sikhs were defeated. In spite of the success, Raja Jeet Singh accepted Maharaja Ranjit Singh's sovereignty.

In 1809 AD, Gulab Singh left for Lahore and got an appointment in the army of Maharaja Ranjit Singh. As per Joseph Davey Cunningham,[2] "Gulab Singh took service as horseman in the band commanded by Jamadar Khooshhal Singh. He sent for his second brother, Dhiyan Singh, and then again like the reigning favourite, they both became running footmen under Runjeet Singh's eye." His allegiance towards Maharaja Ranjit Singh earned him recognition, and he was later on appointed as a commander of a small contingent in his army. Gulab Singh fought valiantly for the Sikh army from the year 1815 to 1820 AD. In 1819, he, as one of the commanders with the Sikh army, invaded Kashmir but did not succeed in ousting the Afghan Rule from there. It was the time when Azim Khan was the governor of Kashmir.

The Background

According to Sukhdev Singh Charak,[3] Raja Jeet Singh proved an incompetent man. He was the son of Raja Diler Singh and grandson of Raja Ranjeet Dev. Since he was so useless, his queen Brandrali Rani, an ambitious woman, took over the affairs of the administration. But, among her appointed advisers, Mian Mota refused to work under her. In the year 1816 AD, Maharaja Ranjit Singh ousted Raja Jeet Singh and annexed the Jammu state with his kingdom. The freedom loving Jammu people resorted to guerrilla warfare, which annoyed the Maharaja. He ultimately gave the administration of Jammu region in the hands of Miyan Kishore Singh in the year 1817 AD. Miyan Kishore Singh, during his lifetime, crowned his son Gulab Singh as the legal heir to the throne. Maharaja Ranjit Singh also had made Gulab Singh the owner of Riasi. In fact, Gulab Singh, as a commander of the Sikh army had acquired the town of Riasi from its erstwhile king known as Raja Dewan Singh.

In the year 1819 AD, Gulab Singh joined the forces of Maharaja Ranjit Singh and invaded Kashmir once again. He fought the Afghan forces and defeated them. In fact, Pandit Birbal Dhar had approached Maharaja Ranjit Singh to wage a war against the Afghans in Kashmir. Shiv Nimohi says that when Birbal Dhar got the audience with Maharaja Ranjit Singh, he presented the Maharaja with baskets of fruits as presents.[4] The victory over Pathan rulers in Kashmir enhanced the honour of Gulab Singh in the eyes of Maharaja Ranjit Singh. According to D N Kundra,[5]

Ranjit Singh waged three wars against Kashmir—the first war took place in 1813, the second in 1814 and the third in 1819 AD. The Sikh army came out victorious in 1819 AD. Keeping in view the outstanding contribution of Gulab Singh in strengthening the Sikh rule, Maharaja Ranjit Singh crowned him as the Raja of Jammu on June 16, 1822. As per Shiv Nimohi, the coronation took place on the banks of Chandrabhaga river (now Chenab river) in Akhnoor. According to Victor Jacquemont in his book, *Letters from India: Describing a Journey in the British Dominions of India*,[6] "I spent the evening with my friend the Rose-water Lion (for such is the signification of Gul-ab-Singh: Gul, rose; ab, water; Singh, lion). He is a soldier of fortune, a sort of usurper."

Raja Gulab Singh was a great strategist and possessed wisdom and diplomatic acumen. Even after getting Jammu and its adjoining principalities under his territory, he did not give up serving the rulers of Lahore. When Sher Singh, son of Kharak Singh and Dain Singh, a courtier of Sher Singh, wanted to capture the Lahore throne and oust Rani Chand Kaur, it was because of Gulab Singh's loyalty towards her that he acted swiftly and defeated Sher Singh. Writing about his valour, resilience and undaunted spirit, "In the face of this thundering ocean of arms and artillery (of Sher Singh), Gulab Singh's undaunted spirit of resistance was unwavering," Alexander Gardner says in his memoirs.[7]

According to the memoirs of Alexander Gardner, who was commander of the garrison and attached to Gulab Singh:

> "The Dogras on the walls began to look over and were jeered at by Sher Singh's troops; the little fort was surrounded by a sea of human heads. Gulab Singh made contemptuous replies, and roared out to Sher Singh, demanding that he should surrender. With a wild yell, some 300 Akalis swept up the Hazuri Bagh and crowded into the gate. Just at that moment, when the crowd was rushing in on us, their swords high in the air, I managed to fire the ten guns, and literally blew them into the air. Then Sher Singh fled and grievous carnage ensued. The Dogras, always excellent marksmen, seemed that day not to miss a man from the walls... we counted the bodies of no less than 2800 soldiers, 200 artillerymen, and 180 horses."

After taking over as the Raja of Jammu, Gulab Singh gradually annexed many small principalities to his Kingdom. He then entrusted the governorship of Kishtwar to a brave soldier of the Sikh army, Sardar Zorawar Singh Kahluria, in 1823 AD.[8]

Maharaja Gulab Singh had realised the British army's potential for they had already conquered almost the whole of India except Punjab. He knew that the British would be the future masters with whom they would have to deal. Since he had already risen to the status of an important minister of Punjab even during the lifetime of Maharaja Ranjit Singh, he had maintained friendly terms with the British.

After getting the jageer of Jammu, he spent more time in the development of Jammu province. He took keen interest in the collection of revenue. He subdued Kishtwar, an adjoining territory. This gave a tremendous boost to his army. He decided to send the troops to Ladakh. The army marched from Punjab to invade Ladakh. They had to pass through Kashmir. Once they reached the valley they rested at Nasim Bagh near the Dal Lake.

Col Mian Singh was the governor of Kashmir and he rendered full cooperation to Gulab Singh's Ladakh adventure led by Zorawar Singh. His successor, Sheikh Gulam Mohi-ud-Din too helped them. Finally, Zorawar Singh succeeded in annexing Ladakh under Dogra rule in September 1842 AD, but when Gulab Singh became an independent Maharaja, the monarchy of Ladakh was abolished.

Gulab Singh could not remain long without British interference. British rulers wanted to keep their Resident in the valley so as to keep a watch over the activities of the Maharaja. Initially, he tried to avoid it, but the Second Sikh War between the Sikhs and the British (1848 to 1849 AD), in which the Sikh Army got defeated, resulted in Punjab being annexed with the British ruled India. The Dogras could not but succumb to the pressures put on them by the British masters who were working assiduously to further the imperial interests in Kashmir. Kashmir had acquired a position of importance in their total game plan. The Dogra period of Kashmir history was marked by the British advent into Kashmir.

To keep the British in good humour, Maharaja Gulab Singh had passed orders that any Britisher visiting Kashmir should be given VVIP treatment. In order to give effect to their 'divide and rule' policy, they sent General Reynell Taylor to make enquiries whether the Muslim population of the Kashmir valley was satisfied with the Maharaja's rule. Taylor had to return disappointed as the majority of the people said that they were quite happy with the Maharaja's rule. The British were not to give in easily. They began interfering in the internal affairs of the state on one pretext or the other. At one time they would criticise the high price of rationed rice, at another they would object to the style of the Maharaja's working. Very tactfully they cloaked their interference as their constructive guidance for the ruler of Jammu and Kashmir.

Commander Zorawar Singh conquered Ladakh and then advanced towards Tibet. The English rulers did not favour Sikhs or Dogras invading Tibet. The English authorities, in fact, wanted to have some sort of watchtower somewhere on the northern side of Kashmir to monitor the activities of European and the Russian governments. Now that the British had conquered Delhi and had also annexed Punjab with their territory, they were afraid lest Napoleon Bonaparte of France or the Russians should invade India. However, they saw a change in European politics favourable to the British—an ostensible change as Napoleon got involved in the Peninsular war and the fear of France or Russia invading India receded. Russia was making rapid advance in central Asia and the British began to grow anxious about their hold on India.

The English interference continued from the rule of Maharaja Gulab Singh to the reign of Maharaja Hari Singh. It ceased only when Maharaja Hari Singh gave the Gilgit principality to the English on a 60-year lease on March 29, 1935. Earlier, the Indian British Government (Lord Lytton, Viceroy of India) had already requested Maharaja Gulab Singh and appointed Capt Biddulph as Political Officer in Gilgit in 1877 AD. "Having attained their objective, the British at once relaxed their pressure on Maharaja," writes P N K Bamzai.[9]

Says Sukhdev Singh Charak,[10] "Gulab Singh, a scion of the junior branch of the Jamwal ruling family, took his cue from Ranjeet Dev and aspired to revive the greatness of Jammu Raj with the aid of the sources of Lahore kingdom and his own diplomatic skill." He further states, "Gulab Singh's forward policy in Tibet, however, aroused the bitterest opposition from the British who henceforth viewed his designs with suspicion and objected to any further addition to his powers and possessions. The

British, in league with anti-Dogra element of Lahore Court, intrigued to dislodge the Dogras from their position. This led to the assassination of Dhiyan Singh (Raja Dhiyan Singh, minister of Maharaja Ranjit Singh) at the hands of pro-British Sandhawalia chiefs and afterwards caused the loss of lives of Raja Hira Singh, Mian Sohan Singh, Pandit Jalla and several other Dogras. But Gulab Singh extricated the Dogra Raj from these perils by his shrewd diplomacy and political manoeuvrability. His estates were vast and spread from the borders of Tibet and Karakorum Pass in the north and northeast to Sialkot and the Jhelum in the South and West. He had encircled Kashmir, which he wanted to possess."

During his rule a lady known as Mrs Hervey visited Kashmir in August 1850, and then wrote her travel details as *Adventures of a Lady in Tartary, Tibet, China and Kashmir*. She wrote,[11] "Since Gulab Singh's accession to kingdom of Kashmir, the population is yearly diminishing, through the poverty and disease brought on by his cruel and oppressive rule."

Maharaja Gulab Singh was suffering from dropsy disease. His health started showing signs of deterioration. When the disease became very bad he decided to hand over the administration to his son Ranbir Singh. In February 1856, Ranbir Singh became the Maharaja of Jammu and Kashmir. With the outbreak of the Mutiny in 1857, the British interference in the internal affairs of Maharaja Gulab Singh became less. The Maharaja was a very clever and seasoned man. In spite of his being on the death bed he showed the British authorities that he was a reliable and good ally and offered them financial and military help which was accepted by them. He died in June 1856.

Zorawar Singh's adventure, 1786-1841 AD

General Zorawar Singh was born in 1786 AD in Hamirpur in a Kahluria family. He was a Dogra warrior who joined the army of Maharaja Ranjit Singh and then Maharaja Gulab Singh as a sepoy. Gradually he rose to high positions. On account of his soldierly qualities and military insight he became the governor of Kishtwar in 1823 AD, and earned the title of Wazir. Maharaja Gulab Singh always realised the value of annexing Ladakh with his territory. Ladakh is a territory of Buddhist Lamas. Its adjoining areas are Dardistan and Baltistan. Physically, Ladakh is a territory adjoining the Kashmir valley but it was considered a separate principality since ancient times. It was culturally similar to Tibetan traditions and religion. Ladakh looked a subordinate of the Tibetan temporal authority but practically it was a separate political entity. Ladakh, Baltistan, Dardistan, Kargil etc. were a mountainous region almost inaccessible to the world.

When Maharaja Gulab Singh wanted to subjugate Ladakh and the adjoining territories and get them under his domination, Tsepal Namgyal was ruling over Ladakh from 1790 to 1834 AD. He came to know that there were dissensions among the ruling family of Ladakh. Says Sukhdev Singh Charak,[12] "Raja Giapo-Cho of Timbus wanted to drive out the Raja of Saut from his territories and, therefore, he sent a complaint in this connection to their overlord Tsepal Namgyal, the Gyalpo of Ladakh. The Gyalpo, however, took no immediate action in the matter. Therefore, the Raja of Timbus secretly sought the help of Wazir Zorawar Singh, the Hakim of Kishtwar."

After taking into confidence Maharaja Ranjit Singh and the British, in 1834 Raja Gulab Singh deputed a large army of about 5,000 men under the command of Zorawar Singh to conquer the hilly region of Ladakh. He set out for Ladakh via Bhot Khol Pass and entered Purig. He annexed Ladakh for the first time in the history of Jammu and Kashmir in 1834. Tsepal Namgyal was the last king of Ladakh.

"After subduing the chief of Sod and the reduction of Suru in September 1835 AD, the Wazir marched to Zanskar whose chief together with all the Zamindars waited upon him and agreed to pay tax of three rupees and half for every house," says Sukhdev Singh Charak.[13] Ladakh had fallen and an annual tribute of 20,000 rupees was fixed. Munshi Daya Ram was stationed in Leh as a representative of Maharaja Gulab Singh. In October 1835 AD, Zorawar Singh returned to Jammu to apprise Maharaja Gulab Singh of the situation. Once Zorawar Singh was out of Ladakh, the King of Ladakh revolted. Zorawar Singh had to rush back to Ladakh and he conquered it again. This time the Prince of Ladakh fled to Nubra. After Ladakh, he campaigned in Baltistan among the three states of Skardu, Gilgit and Hunza.

Zorawar Singh decided to attack Tibet. His attack on Tibet and victory over it was shortlived. On December 12, 1841, Tibetan forces were reinforced by the Lhasa forces, which were well trained. Facing defeat, he tried to launch an offensive attack on the enemy. The Tibetan forces overwhelmed the Dogra forces. Zorawar Singh was shot in his shoulder. Unfortunately, this brave wazir fell down from the horse and the Tibetan forces rushed and surrounded him and killed him. They slit his throat and carried away his head. According to Sir Alexander Cunningham,[14] "The Indian soldiers of Zorawar Singh fought under very great disadvantages. The battlefield was upwards of 15,000 feet above the sea, and the time mid-winter, when even the day temperature never rises above the freezing point." For his military skills, inspiring leadership and administrative acumen, Zorawar Singh has been named "Little Napoleon of India" by some historians. The techniques of mountain warfare employed by him are considered textbook examples of military science even today.

Maharaja Ranbir Singh, 1856-1885 AD

Maharaja Ranbir Singh was enthroned as Maharaja of Jammu and Kashmir on 20 February 1856.

He was born in August 1830 AD and his childhood name was Fena Singh. The youngest brother of Maharaja Gulab Singh was Raja Suchet Singh of Ram Nagar who married seven times. However, none of his wives gave birth to any child. He, therefore, adopted the youngest son of Maharaja Gulab Singh known as Ranbir Singh.[15] Ranbir was looked after with great affection and love by all the seven queens of Raja Suchet Singh. Since Suchet Singh was an important and very busy figure in the Khalsa army, he could not look after the education of Ranbir Singh. However, Ranbir Singh learnt the art of warfare. He also learnt Dogri language. When he was fourteen years old, he was married to the daughter of Raja Bijay Singh of Seeba.

Maharaja Gulab Singh had three sons—Prince Randhir Singh, Prince Sohan Singh and Prince Ranbir Singh. Randhir met with an accident and died. Sohan Singh had died young and Ranbir Singh was the sole survivor. Maharaja Gulab Singh anointed his only surviving son Ranbir Singh as Maharaja of Jammu and Kashmir, on February 20, 1856 during his lifetime.

Maharaja Ranbir Singh married five times. His first marriage took place when he had not attained adolescence. Unlike the Mughal and Sikh princes who turned profligate and pleasure loving, he took keen interest in the affairs of his country. During his rule there was, to a great extent, economic prosperity in the state. He also ensured that there was no uprising against his rule from other places. He kept a constant watch over the developments of the country. According to Jaffrey Richard Timm,[16] "Maharaja Ranbir Singh not only took deep interest in the physical well being of the people in general but also was personally concerned with the revival of religious awareness and education throughout his kingdom."

He always enjoyed the work of the state. He personally attended to and heard the grievances of the people. Unfortunately, the officialdom, whether placed at Jammu or at Srinagar still believed in the medieval method of giving harsh treatment to the subjects. His officials tried to extract every penny from the poor people; only some of it they put in the state treasury and the remaining in their own pockets.

Though Maharaja Ranbir Singh had no formal education, he was trained in martial art as well as how to command the army. He was also given lessons in political diplomacy and on how to deal with his subjects. He had complete faith in the religion he practised. He was also aware of the great traditions of Jammu and Kashmir. He appointed scholars to survey the places of pilgrimage. Aurel Stein writes,[17] "Pandit Sahib Ram, who was undoubtedly the foremost among Kashmirian Sanskrit scholars of the last few generations had been commissioned by Maharaja Ranbir Singh to prepare a descriptive survey of all ancient Tirtha of Kashmir. For this purpose a staff of Pandits was placed at his disposal whose business it was to collect the necessary material in various parts of the country." Maharaja Ranbir Singh had a secular outlook and respected all religions.

According to Shiv Nimohi,[18] the name of Ranbir Singh is written in golden letters in the history of Jammu and Kashmir. Even foreign historians have praised the developments undertaken by him. Sir Francis Younghusband has also stated,[19] "Maharaja Ranbir Singh himself was extremely popular, both with his people and with Europeans—being a marked contrast to his father."

The Maharaja also stressed the spread of education in the state. Health was another area which was important for him. He utilised the services of English experts in the field of agriculture, medicine, and education. He allowed English missionaries to open schools and hospitals in the valley. For instance, it was Tev Doxey and Rev J H Knowles, two British missionaries, who established the missionary schools and introduced modern education. Similarly, the Medical missionaries of Christian theology opened modern hospitals where allopathic medicine and treatment was given to the patients. Walter Lawrence writes,[20] "He (Maharaja Ranbir Singh) was extremely hospitable to the Europeans, and his efforts to introduce dispensaries and schools in the state showed that he was an admirer of institutions of the British Government." This way these missionaries served the poor people of the state. Narendra Sahagala has written,[21] "He opened many centres for the teaching and study of Sanskrit, built libraries and made efforts for re-establishing the values of Hindu life."

To streamline the administration of the State, he divided the administration into three departments—Dafter-e-Nizamat (civil administration), Dafter-e-Dewani (finance), and Dafter-e-Jangi (defence). He also appointed two governors—one in Jammu and another in Kashmir. He distributed the state into Districts, Tehseels and Parganas. In Jammu there were seven districts—Jammu, Jasrota, Rampur, Udhampur, Riasi, Nowshera and Manawar. In Kashmir there was six districts—Srinagar, Anantnag, Shupiyan, Pattan, Kamaraj and Muzaffarabad. Similarly, Ladakh, Baltistan, and Gilgit also were distributed into districts, Tehseels and Parganas. An officer general of Police headed Jammu and Kashmir State. Each district had a police inspector and a deputy inspector of police at district headquarter level and each Thana (Police Station) had a Thanedar (Station House Officer) and four policemen. The Maharaja constructed two jails, one in Srinagar and another in Jammu. In the jails, the prisoners were imparted vocational training, so that on their release they could earn their livelihood.

The Maharaja also looked after healthcare. He got as many as 27 hospitals constructed in Jammu and Kashmir. Eulogising his rule and his development schemes, Jia Lal Kilam writes,[22] "Maharaja Ranbir Singh was indeed a very wise ruler. The development schemes which he inaugurated are even now yielding fruit."

The Maharaja announced many gazetted holidays including Id-ul-Fitar, Id-ul-Zuha, Shab-e-Barat, Shab-e-Kadar, Baisakhi, Ekadashi, Lohri, Shivratri, Deepawali, Raksha Bandhan, Ramnavmi, Basant Panchami, Janmashtami and Holi etc. As per Walter Lawrence,[23] "Ranbir Singh was a model Hindu prince devoted to his religion and to Sanskrit learning, but kind and tolerant to the Musalman to whom he allowed the free exercise of their religion."

According to Narendra Sahagala,[24] "Muslims from Poonch and Rajouri and some from the Kashmir valley assembled and appealed to Maharaja Ranbir Singh praying that they be accepted in their basic Hindu religion. It can be treated a misfortune for the country that some contractors of religion always tried to create hurdles. When the Maharaja asked the Pandits about this re-conversion, the Pandits clearly refused to accept them back in Hindu religion. These very Pandits had not allowed Rinchan to adopt Hindu religion, which led to the trampling of Kashmir under the feet of Muslim rulers for 500 years."

Maharaja Ranbir Singh also introduced many changes in sericulture. He got mulberry saplings from China and Japan for cultivation. Says Walter Lawrence,[25] "Maharaja Ranbir Singh made great efforts to introduce new staples into Kashmir, and money was freely spent on sericulture, vines and wine making."

He also introduced the telegraph system in the valley, from Srinagar to Gilgit, and soon it was introduced in the whole of Jammu and Kashmir. Another important thing that took place during his rule was that the Survey of India Department undertook a survey of Jammu and Kashmir State through the services of Major Montgomery.

Unlike those Muslim monarchs who followed a policy of religious intolerance to force the people for conversion to Islam, Maharaja Ranbir Singh allowed Muslims their religious freedom. No mosque was dismantled and no conversion made. Meanwhile, a terrible famine spread in the country in 1878 AD. It was a result of heavy snow and rainfall for many months. Standing crops were destroyed and no new cultivation could take place. This famine was so devastating that sixty per cent of the population of the valley perished. The rains continued even during springtime, and, as a result, even apple trees and other fruit trees were affected and people were left even without this alternative food.

According to Walter Lawrence,[26] "when the hungry people had devoured the blossoms of the apple and pears, and the unripe fruit of the mulberries, they turned to the grasses and roots of the swamps and forests.

The bark of the elm and the yew was ground into flour. Those near the forests lived on herbs while the skim milk lasted, but herbs without milk soon proved fatal and by the summer of 1878 famine was raging. Then that awful sign of demoralisation and helplessness manifested by the non-burial of corpses appeared; wells and holes were choked with bodies and prowling dogs began to pray on human carcasses." He further says, "Many attempted to escape to the Punjab, but at the barrier troops were stationed to prevent the migration of the people, and harrowing tales are told of the fathers of families getting past the barrier by bribing the guardians of the passes, while the wives and children were left to die in Kashmir."

The Maharaja spared no effect to ameliorate the hardships of the people but unfortunately the administration officials—corrupt, greedy and devoid of human values, looked the other way. Another devastating economic condition that prevailed in Kashmir during 1870 AD was almost the end of the shawl industry in Kashmir. According to Walter Lawrence,[27] "The shawl industry is now unfortunately a tradition—a memory of the past. The trade received its death blow when war broke out between Germany and France in 1870, and I have been told by an eyewitness, of the intense excitement and interest with which the Kashmiri shawl-weavers watched the fate of France in that great struggle—bursting into tears and loud lamentation when the news of Germany's victories reached them. If there had been any hope that the industry would revive, and that shawls would again became fashionable, this hope was dashed when the famine of 1877-79 visited the valley."

One important thing that haunted all the Dogra Maharajas was the British interference in the administration of their Kingdom. In order to keep a watch over Central Asia's political developments, they wanted to place their resident in Kashmir who would keep the British officers informed. Maharaja Ranbir Singh diplomatically pointed out to the British government that there was no provision in the treaty wherein they could appoint a Resident. The British government kept the proposal in abeyance.

The Maharaja had learnt from his father the art of diplomacy. His father had ably handled the situation when the British government had sent an officer named Lt Reynell Taylor to Srinagar to enquire if Muslims of the valley were satisfied with the Maharaja's rule. Instead of taking offence, Maharaja Gulab Singh took it as friendly advice from the English and assured them that he would try to improve the condition of the state.

Maharaja Ranbir Singh, like his father, had sent his trusted people to the frontiers to assess the scope for the expansion of his kingdom. This irked the British. "Mahtab Singh", says PNK Bamzai,[28] "an officer of great dash and pluck, travelled deep in Central Asia in 1866-1867, and on his return submitted an interesting and illuminating diary of his travels." Not all the activities of the Maharaja were to the British liking.

The news of the famine and its heavy human toll had reached the British governor at Punjab. "Famine stricken people were being carried across the Wular Lake to go to some adjoining villages. These boats got capsized in the middle of the lake and many people were drowned," says Jia Lal Kilam.[29]

The British government found a valid excuse to interfere in the Maharaja's administration. They used an important Kashmiri Pandit Hargopal Kaul, author of *Gulistan-i-Kashmir*, who had made the complaint about the drowning of people in Wular Lake to the British at Delhi. As a result of this, writes Jia Lal Kilam,[30] "He (Maharaja) had withstood all the overtures of the British Indian Government, for affording them a foothold in the country."

Meanwhile, it was during this period that the Indian uprising of 1857 against the East India Company's control in India took place. These uprisings were mainly concentrated in North and Central India, with some outbreaks elsewhere too. The first signs of brewing discontent appeared in cantonment areas in January 1857. The controversy was that to load the new rifle, the sepoys had to bite the cartridge open. It was believed that the cartridges were greased with lard (pork fat) regarded as unclean by Muslims, or tallow (beef fat), regarded as sacrilege by Hindus.

All these events were, however, limited to a relatively small area—within a town or at the most a few districts. What was unprecedented was the escalation from purely localised conflicts to a large-scale rebellion, which broke out in May 1857. Maharaja Ranbir Singh remained away from this rebellion and kept his kingdom unaffected by this movement.

In the year 1881, the Maharaja fell seriously ill. He was ailing from some dangerous disease and in 1885 AD, he breathed his last in Jammu.

Maharaja Pratap Singh, 1885-1925 AD

After the death of Maharaja Ranbir Singh his eldest son Maharaja Pratap Singh was crowned as Maharaja of Jammu and Kashmir on September 15,1885.

Maharaja Pratap Singh, the eldest son of Ranbir Singh was born on July 18, 1850 AD. He was born from Queen Sibi, the first queen of Ranbir Singh, at Riasi Palace. His younger brother Prince Ram Singh was born in 1861 and third brother Amar Singh was born in 1864. He had two sisters. When Prince Pratap Singh attained the age of 14 he was married to Princess of Chamba on February 10, 1862. Maharaja Pratap Singh married thrice. His second queen was from Katoch tribe and third queen belonged to Pathania tribe.

"Born at Riasi in 1850," writes P N K Bamzai,[31] "Pratap Singh received education in Dogri, Sanskrit, Persian and English. In his youth he was entrusted by his father with the duties of hearing petitions from people and passing suitable orders in consultation with some of his experienced officials." His father Maharaja Ranbir Singh took special care to train his son in administrative affairs. In 1881 AD when the Viceroy of India visited Kashmir Prince Pratap Singh was deputed to receive the Viceroy at the border of the State.

Maharaja Pratap Singh inherited a spoilt and degraded paradise on earth states Walter Lawrence in the introduction of his book *The Valley of Kashmir*[32] "Much has been written of the abuses which have prevailed in the administration of Kashmir. They were numerous and deplorable, and when I first came to Kashmir in 1889, I found the people sullen, desperate and suspicious. Soldiers forced them to plough and sow, and the same soldiers attended at harvest time. People were dragged from their houses to carry loads to Gilgit, and every official had right to their labour and their property." Further, he writes, "The peasants were overworked, half-starved, treated with hard words and hard blows, subjected to unceasing exactions and every species of petty tyranny."

When Maharaja Pratap Singh ascended the throne, there came great natural calamities. A severe cholera epidemic took a very heavy toll during 1885, 1892, 1900, 1902, 1906, 1907 and 1910 AD. As if this epidemic was not sufficient to decrease the human population there came an epidemic of plague in 1903-1904 AD. This was followed by a sever intensity earthquake and then terrible floods. And all the savagery of nature decimated huge portions of human population. The flood destroyed agricultural produce and earthquakes destroyed thousands of houses.

It is rightly said, "Uneasy lies the head that wears the crown." This saying applies to Maharaja Pratap Singh. With his accession to the throne, he had to face the British interfering in his administration. The British government succeeded in getting the consent of the Maharaja for the appointment of a British Resident in Kashmir. Sir Oliver St John was the first to be deputed in Kashmir in the year 1883 as Officer on Special Duty but was elevated as Resident in 1884 AD. According to Jia Lal Kilam,[33] "the British Indian Government changed its former policy of non-interference and deputed for the first time in the history of the state a Resident in Kashmir. Some veiled charges like that of treason having been brought against the Maharaja, he was virtually deposed by the government instead a council was constituted to carry on the government of the country."

When Maharaja Pratap Singh was installed as the ruler of Kashmir, by that time the British had conquered almost whole of India. The Indian states, big or small, had accepted the supremacy of British rulers. In every state, they had appointed their own Resident who not only kept a watch on the British interest but also interfered in the internal matters of those states. As regards Kashmir, till the death of Maharaja Ranbir Singh, the British rulers could not succeed in getting the state's consent in appointing a British Resident. However, Maharaja Pratap Singh was forced to accept the installation of a British Resident in Kashmir.

According to Mridu Rai,[34] "At the same time, the (British) Government of India made it clear that the Resident would have virtual *carte blanche* in Kashmir and impressed on the Maharaja the necessity for consulting him at all times, and following his advice. That the British were successful in forcing these terms on the new ruler was due, in large part, to Ranbir Singh's reluctance to name Pratap Singh, his eldest son, as his successor ; he was leaning instead towards the younger, Raja Amar Singh."

The British authorities in India as well as in Britain were not happy with the terms of the Treaty of Amritsar, particularly wherein Maharaja

Gulab Singh was given a free hand to rule and to work for the expansion of his kingdom. The British interference was not only for placing their Resident in the state—their ulterior motive was to annex the state with the British Indian territory. They began political manoeuvring against the Maharaja.

Viceroy, Earl of Dufferin, on September14, 1885, wrote to Maharaja Pratap Singh confirming his succession to the throne. He also wrote that he was deputing his agent Sir Oliver St John to look after the working of the State. Though the Maharaja objected, yet the British Resident was thrust on him.

In fact, when Maharaja Pratap Singh took over as ruler of Kashmir, the British Viceroy wrote to him that immediate reforms in the administration are needed for the benefit of the people of Kashmir. The British Resident had to keep watch over these reforms to see if the people actually benefited. It seems that the British Resident was not happy with the reforms of the Maharaja. He, therefore, sent a report of the Maharaja to the Viceroy.

Extract of the Report on the affairs of the State of Jammu & Kashmir by the Resident of Kashmir, March 5, 1888:

> "I would assign him a liberal income, to be placed at his absolute disposal, and treat him with full honour as titular Chief, but I would exclude him from all real power. He may reign, but not govern. A great danger with the Maharaja is that his notorious weakness of character and purpose render him an easy tool in the hands of an unscrupulous adviser, and therefore, it is essential that he should be controlled by some agency upon which the Government of India can place confidence. I consider that a reduction of the Maharaja's authority on these lines is an essential condition precedent to all other necessary measures."

According to Narendra Sahagala,[35] "a British Parliamentarian, William Digwe, has given an account of the political powers of these agents. He has written that the powers of the Resident were supreme and one could not do anything without written orders from him. His wish was law. He allowed himself to be surrounded by sycophants and friends and ousted old and loyal servants of the Government. No one in that country could open his mouth and in case any weakling raised a voice of protest, he was warned of dire consequences."

With the opening of a British Residency in Kashmir many Christian missionaries poured into the valley for spreading Christianity. Unlike Muslim rulers, these did not indulge in killing or in violence if the people refused conversion to Christianity They laid the foundation of modern education. They also started hospitals where allopathic treatment was given to the patients.

During these extraordinary times, the British Government in India did not allow the Dogra rulers to misrule the State. It is true that they had no feelings for the miserable condition of the people of Kashmir. They were only in search of some pretext to interfere and to annex Kashmir with the rest of India. They had realised the strategic importance of Kashmir. According to E F Knight,[36] "During the reign of the present ruler, Pertab Singh, the Indian Government has lent to the Kashmir State several selected officers, both civil and military to superintend the much-needed reforms in the administration of the country. Without this interference on our part, Kashmir would have been unable to carry out her treaty obligations. She was threatened by bankruptcy and general disorganisation, while her unpaid and discontented army was in no condition to protect the frontier."

After Sir Oliver St John went back, T C Plowden succeeded him in 1888. Taking charge of the Residency in Kashmir, he started planning the deposition of Maharaja Pratap Singh in connivance with his brother Amar Singh. He wrote to the Viceroy on February 17, 1889, "And I should expect that, after a short time, all the influence which the Maharaja possesses, especially Zenana influence would be brought to bear against Amar Singh. Another probable result of his elevation would be a feud between him and his brother Ram Singh, thereby raising against him another hostile party."

The Indian British Government appointed Colonel Parry S Nesbit as the Resident of Kashmir.[37] Colonel Parry was a personal friend of Raja Amar Singh. The Maharaja was forced to sign a draft *Irshad* by which he relinquished all powers of his government for a period of five years.

On March 8, 1889, he was made to write letters to the members of the council informing them that they were dismissed. The members were then selected by the British themselves and they also selected Amar Singh to head the council. The council was composed of Raja Amar Singh, Raja Ram Singh, Rai Bahadur Pandit Suraj Kaul, and Rai Bahadur Pandit Bhag Ram. In addition, the British government of India kept the provision to add more members to the committee, from time to time. One English member, especially selected on a salary of Rupees 3,000 per month was also deputed. This council had full and sole powers in all the public departments of the state for a period of five years except any interference in the private affairs of the Maharaja.

The British Resident also wrote to Maharaja Pratap Singh and all the members of council that though the members of the council were given full powers of administration, they were expected to exercise those powers under the guidance of the British Resident. This exercise was done to secretly conspire to overthrow the Maharaja.

Luckily for Maharaja Pratap Singh the news of British manoeuvring leaked and there was a noisy clamour and great hue and cry in India particularly when a Bengali newspaper *Amrit Bazaar Patrika* and *Akhbar-e-Aam* of Lahore, published this secret letter and showed how the British Government conspired to depose the actual rulers and tried to install their puppets. Sensing damage to the reputation of the British Indian government, the toppling of Maharaja Pratap Singh from the throne of Kashmir was given up.

Meanwhile, Maharaja Pratap Singh's grant of a go-ahead for establishing a British political agency in Gilgit and other neighbouring places made the British begin treating him leniently and his deposing was permanently abandoned. Colonel A G Durand was installed as the first British political agent in Gilgit. During his time, the chieftains of Hunza and Naagar were ruling near the border of Russia held territories. With the Russian activities near the border, these Rajas began showing signs of independence. However, Colonel Durand had raised an army of well-trained soldiers consisting of Dogras and Gurkhas who lost no time in subduing these two tribal leaders. He then occupied Misghar, a place at the extreme end of the Northern part of the state. But Gilgit was to work under the guidance of the Council of Regency.

As per Victoria Schofield,[38] "British Imperial policy towards the State of Jammu and Kashmir in the late 19th century was guided primarily by fear of a Russian advance towards India through the Pamir Mountains (border with Tajikistan), as well as by events in the expanse of land north of the Hindu Kush and Himalayas known as Turkestan, the eastern part of which was under nominal rule of China."

With such developments in the North-Western areas and the cooperation of the Maharaja with the British Government, the British authorities deemed it fit and proper to restore all powers to the Maharaja by abolishing the council chaired by his brother Raja Amar Singh. However, in order to democratise the functioning of the administration, the Maharaja appointed a chief minister who was assisted by revenue, home, and judicial ministers. They assisted him in providing efficient administration to the people. Unfortunately, these measures did not serve the purpose the British had envisaged. The Maharaja appointed his relatives and offered them high posts. It is true that some uneducated people from Punjab and other states were appointed on important positions but they exploited their authority and amassed wealth and then left the state. On the other hand, the Maharaja's relatives appointed as ministers had no awareness of new and modern ideas, so much so that one of the ministers used his thumb impression instead of signing an order.In the meantime, Raja Amar Singh, Maharaja Pratap Singh's brother died. The elder brother Raja Ram Singh had already died in 1899. Though the death of his brother plunged him into grief, nonetheless, the Maharaja was greatly relieved of anxiety as there would be no meddling from his own relatives.

In 1920 AD, Maharaja Pratap Singh wrote to Lord Chelmsford for restoring full powers. In 1921, Lord Chelmsford restored to him the powers and abolished the council of Regency. It seems that the British Resident was trying to introduce a British type of democracy in the State, and he made the Maharaja a constitutional monarch. According to Shiv Nimohi,[39] the Governor felt that the Maharaja was unnecessarily being harassed, so he dissolved the council of Regency and gave full command of the government to him. Nevertheless, the cabinet Ministers continued to administer the state with the Maharaja himself assuming powers to exercise veto.

In India and Jammu and Kashmir, various reforms were introduced by the British, which enabled India to come up on the map of modernism. For instance, administrative reforms introduced the Civil Services, which subsequently ensured efficient administration to the people. Similarly, they laid the rules for legislative powers granted to the local self-government bodies. Financial reforms established the rate of Income Tax to be levied uniformly. The most important policies made were educational reforms, agricultural reforms and the introduction of railways, post and telegraph and development of roads—considered revolutionary steps towards modernism.

In Kashmir, Urdu was recognised as the State's official language only in 1889 AD. According to Nishat Ansari,[40] "Maharaja Ranbir Singh or Pratap Singh might have made Dogri (their own mother tongue) the State and official language, but for the fact that the Jammu and Kashmir State is physically divided into three heterogeneous units, having different cultures, customs, traditions, modes of living, clothing and mother tongues." He further says, "To string these diverse units, Urdu was accorded the status of link as well as the official language. One more reason was that people in Kashmir, Jammu, and Ladakh had been conversant with Urdu and felt closer to it."

Universities, colleges and schools were established on the pattern of such institutions already established in London. Post and Telegraphs and modern banking were introduced. Surprisingly, though India was humming with such modern activities, Kashmir was still living in the middle age. The Maharaja began to introduce these modern facilities in the State. Modern hospitals for both males and females were established in Srinagar and Jammu. Schools for boys and girls were set up. One degree college each, at Jammu and at Srinagar were established. Technical schools and colleges were introduced. He also introduced reforms in agriculture, sericulture and horticulture. The best quality of cocoons were imported from Italy and France.

Swami Vivekananda, the famous Hindu religious philosopher, visited Kashmir during the reign of Maharaja Pratap Singh. According to Swami

Bodhasarananda, manager of Advaita Ashram, "His first visit to the valley was on 10th September 1897." Geophone Mac Lead, Ole Bull and Sister Nivedita accompanied the Swami. He visited many places of pilgrimage such as Kashir Bhawani (Kheer Bhawani) at Tula Mula, Martanda (the Sun Temple) etc. Says Swami Bodhasarananda,[41] "Throughout the rest of the journey Swami Vivekananda would bathe in the holy water, offer flowers, fruits and sweets to the objects of worship before breaking his fast, make obeisance by prostrating himself on the ground, tell his beads, make ritual circumambulation, and the rest."

Charles E Bates and Deny F Ward visited Kashmir during the reign of Maharaja Pratap Singh. They have mentioned an account of their fascinating journey in their book *Our Summer in the Valley of Kashmir.* Edward Frederic Knight, a Victorian barrister and journalist also visited the valley. He has given an important and absorbing account of Kashmir in his book *Where Three Empires Meet.*

First World War

Meanwhile, the First World War had broken out in 1914 and Dogra forces joined the British army to fight the war. Looking at the contribution of Maharaja Pratap Singh in the war, the British were happy. In 1921, Lord Chelmsford returned total powers to the Maharaja who took all steps to improve the condition of his country. Kashmir experienced the dawn of modernism.

The minority community consisting of Kashmiri Pandits learnt the meaning and the gains of modernism. They took advantage of the presence of modern schools and colleges in Srinagar, which were started in 1905. By 1925 AD, hundreds of Kashmiri Pandits got educated as graduates. Surprisingly, two hundred students were in the first batch but not a single Muslim student had joined the school. Since these schools and colleges were affiliated with the University of Punjab, many Kashmiri Pandit boys went to Punjab, where they got trained as engineers, doctors and lawyers.

Curiously enough, the administration did not take notice of these young, talented and educated Pandit boys who were prepared to help in the smooth functioning of the administration. Unfortunately, the authorities in places of power were Dogras or people hired from Punjab, who were not educated, some of them were even illiterate. Therefore,

Kashmiri Pandits took upon themselves the task of fighting for their due share in the administration. They raised the slogan of "Kashmir for Kashmiris." This slogan subsequently resulted in the "Hereditary State Subject" law. According to Jia Lal Kilam,[42] in the early twenties the resentment took the form of an agitation. Jia Lal Kilam, Pandit Shankar Lal Kaul, Jia Lal Kaul and Jia Lal Jalali—all of them fresh from college started an agitation through the outside press for securing the rights of the state subjects. According to this law, all those persons who had been living in the state before the valley came under Maharaja Gulab Singh's rule and who were born thereafter are known as State Subjects. These persons could purchase immoveable property, and be considered for appointment in the Government services.

The Muslim community largely remained backward because of their prejudice towards modernity. In India, too, owing to the abject poverty of Muslim masses, and due to the injured pride of Muslims, on account of the loss of their rule in India, a sort of helplessness had crept into Muslim psyche. After the Mutiny, Muslims steadily lost ground in education. The English administration's sporadic efforts to educate them did not prove fruitful. Strenuous efforts were putin to set up the Aligarh Muslim University. The opening of Mohammedan Anglo-Oriental College forms a landmark in the history of Indian Muslim Education. In support of this movement, those wealthy and influential Kashmiri Muslims who had left their land of birth during the Sikh rule set up an organisation in Punjab. They sponsored intelligent Muslim students from the valley to whom they gave scholarships for further studies. A small Muslim minority took steps towards educating their children but still the majority of the Muslims remained uneducated.

On account of failing health, Maharaja Pratap Singh breathed his last on September 25, 1925 AD.

Maharaja Hari Singh, 1925-1947 AD

Maharaja Pratap Singh expired without leaving any male child who could be crowned as the Maharaja of Jammu & Kashmir. To hold the crown of the kingdom was the prerogative of a male descendent only and it was found that Prince Hari Singh, nephew of Maharaja Pratap Singh, was the only legal heir to the throne. Thus, Hari Singh assumed charge of Jammu and Kashmir in 1925 AD.

Maharaja Hari Singh's tenure was the beginning of the end of Dogra rule in the state. Born on 30 April 1895, he was the last Dogra ruler of Jammu and Kashmir. At the age of 13, his father Raja Amar Singh sent him to Mayo College, Ajmer, for his academic studies. The college was for princes only. A year later, when his father died, the British took a personal interest in his education and appointed Major H K Brar as his guardian. As per Shiv Nimohi,[43] when he (Prince Hari Singh) finished his studies in Mayo College, he was sent to Imperial Cadet Corps at Dehradun for military training. As soon as he attained the age of 20 he was appointed Commander-In-Chief of Jammu and Kashmir State Forces. On this occasion, Maharaja Pratap Singh had addressed the audience who had graced the occasion. Says F Ward Deny,[44] "On this occasion the Maharaja himself read a somewhat extensive speech in English, beginning with: 'I feel highly honoured by your cordial acceptance of my invitation to grace this festive occasion,' and ending with these words: 'I therefore ask you, ladies and gentlemen, to be good enough to drink to the health of my dear nephew, Hari Singh. May he live long and be happy and prosperous.'

Maharaja Hari Singh married four times. The first three queens died young. He married Maharani Tara Devi last. She gave birth to a son, Prince Karan Singh. Maharaja Hari Singh, son of Raja Amar Singh was thirty years old at the time of his coronation. He was fair, smart, charming and had a dashing and debonair personality. He was the first Dogra ruler who had travelled abroad.

As a Prince, he was a frequent visitor to Europe. A gang once blackmailed him as he became close to an English woman, Mrs Robinson. In that blackmail, his own ADC, Captain Arthur was involved. The British Government was very upset by this episode. According to Ian Copland,[45] "The elderly and ailing Sir John Wood was forced out after he unwittingly placed the heir apparent to the throne of Kashmir, Hari Singh, in the clutches of a nest of pimps and blackmailers."

The Maharaja's modern upbringing

It was not smooth sailing for the Maharaja to run the administration when he took over as the ruler of the country. According to Barbara

N Ramusack,[46] "Jammu and Kashmir were the only remnants of once powerful states in the Himalayas to survive the British onslaught, but to the present day they remain a tragically contested site." Maharaja Hari Singh was not a mediaeval monarch to be guided by whims and fancies like feudal lords; he was man of modern age. His upbringing too was modern. He had remained under the guardianship of English gentlemen. During the First World War, he was deputed to train units of the State army. Those state units earned praise for the art of fighting in many countries where they were sent. Lord Wavell, Viceroy of India, also recognized him as having 'Liberal Ideas.'

Monarchical Prime Ministers

Initially, Maharaja Hari Singh retained the prime ministership for himself until 1927 AD. Then he appointed Sir Albion Bannerji who was Prime Minister from 1927 to 1929. Later on, in 1929, he appointed George Edward Campbell Wakefield as his Prime Minister who remained on the seat from 1929 to 1931. After this, Sir Hari Kishen Kaul became the Prime Minister for two years and then Elliot James Dowell Colvin took over from 1933 to 1936. Sir Barjor J Dalal became Prime Minister in 1936 and after him, the Maharaja appointed Sir N Gopalaswami Ayyengar as his Prime Minister. Sir Ayyengar remained on the seat from 1936 to 1943. Kailash Narain Haksar, who took over the Prime Ministership for one year, from 1943 to 1944, was followed by Sir Bengal Narsing Rao who remained the Prime Minister of Kashmir from 1944 to 1945. In June 1945, Ram Chandra Kak became the next Prime Minister and remained upto August 1947. Janaka Singh was Prime Minister of Jammu and Kashmir for two months only, from August to October 1947. Finally, Mehr Chand Mahajan took over on October 15, 1947, and remained till March 5, 1948. After this Sheikh Mohammad Abdullah became the Prime Minister of Jammu and Kashmir.

Maharaja Hari Singh planned to make Kashmir a true paradise. He started the construction of a boulevard around the lakes with a total mileage of more than 100 miles. To make it beautiful, lampposts were placed at every 20 yards. On the other side of the boulevard, he wanted to make small gardens where flowers would grow. On one side of this boulevard is Shankaracharya Mountain. There are huge boulders at the foot of this mountain. This boulevard was to be constructed only up to Nishat Garden.

The people knew about the modern upbringing of Maharaja Hari Singh. They reposed faith in his ability to introduce measures that could bring prosperity to his subjects. His steps to help the agriculturists and relieve them from the clutches of moneylenders by introducing Debt Reconciliation were very much appreciated by the people.

Maharaja Hari Singh introduced compulsory primary education. In local lingo, these schools were nicknamed as 'Jabbri Schools', (Jabbr is force). In fact, with the introduction of this compulsory education, Muslim students who were admitted in Madrasas had to join these schools.

Another important step taken by the Maharaja was the 'Prevention of Infant Marriage Act', which made liable the parents who performed it. The government made another important declaration that only State Subjects were empowered to purchase immovable property and seek employment in the State. A person would become a State Subject if his parents had lived in the State earlier or from Maharaja Ranbir Singh's time.

The peace and tranquillity of the State got disturbed by constant agitation resorted to by the Muslim Conference. Thus, the road map for making the state a paradise was damaged. The influx of tourists did not increase and the houseboat owners suffered heavy losses. The communal tensions in the state continued for many months. Writes Ian Copland,[47] "To make matters worse, the sittings of the JSC coincided with a period of unprecedented upheaval in the domestic life of the states, with Kashmir, Alwar, Bharatpur, Bahawalpur, Kapurthala and Jind all experiencing major agrarian revolts and bloody communal clashes. These convulsions were in themselves distracting and unsettling. What was more; they occasioned, in two cases, heavy-handed exercise of British paramountcy. In 1932, Hari Singh of Kashmir was subjected to an imperial inquiry and made to take on an English ICS officer as his Prime Minister." Meanwhile Lord Willingdon, the Viceroy (1931-37), agreed to the appointment of E J Colvin as Prime Minister of Kashmir."

The Maharaja, seeing the Muslim leadership on the warpath dismissed the English Prime Minister and appointed a new Prime Minister, Raja Hari Kishen Kaul, who was familiar with local atmosphere. A seasoned diplomat he entered into negotiation with the Muslim agitators, and subsequently, on August 26, 1932, concluded a truce with them. But nothing could satisfy the diehard agitating Muslim masses. Their agitation continued and the Maharaja was compelled to announce Martial Law in the valley.

Canker of Communalism

Muslim fanatics were waiting for an occasion, particularly from Punjab and frontier Provinces , to invade the state by sending Ahrar Jaths to start Jihad. As per Ravinderjit Kaur,[48] "On October 4, 1931, Mazhar Ali the dictator of the Ahrar-i-Islam, who had previously been permitted to enter the State as a guest to see things for himself, set out from Sialkot for Jammu with a Jatha of sixty men. The Deputy Commissioner, Sialkot, issued an order under section 144, Criminal Procedure Code, and in the end arrested the whole Jatha. Later they were released after a proclamation of amnesty was made by the Maharaja." The British Indian Government taking a serious view of the situation impressed upon the Maharaja to make concessions to the Muslim community in the State. Meanwhile, the Ahrar community from Punjab and Frontier Province which had entered Jammu crying the slogan of Jihad got themselves involved in looting and killings in Jammu. The Maharaja had to request the British government for help to control them. However, in order to diffuse the communal disturbances, the Maharaja made, on 6 October 1931, a proclamation to the effect, "If any of my subjects desires to submit any reasonable request they will receive my sympathetic consideration." States Prem Nath Bazaz,[49] "All communities including Muslims, Hindus, Kashmiri Pandits, Sikhs etc. submitted their memorandum for Maharaja's consideration." He further states, "The Kashmiri Pandits further observed that they were as anxious as any other community for the introduction of Constitutional Government but they were equally anxious that the body politic should not be corrupted by the canker of communalism."

Glancy Commission

On 12 November 1931, Maharaja Hari Singh appointed a commission of four non-official members presided by B J Glancy, a member of the foreign political department in the Government of India. The Glancy Commission Report came in April 1932 AD. It recommended the introduction of a State Legislative Assembly. The Maharaja allowed the establishment of Praja Sabah and its first session was held in autumn of 1934 AD. The minimum qualification of a voter was fixed as middle pass. This Praja Sabah had recommender's powers and served as a platform for all the communities where they could explain their grievances. Nevertheless, the recommendations were more favourable to Muslims than Hindus. According to Prof M L Kaul,[50] "The lop-sided and biased recommendations of the Glancy Commission were prominently marked by an appeasement of the Muslim majority of Kashmir. The legitimate rights and interests of the Kashmirian Hindus were ruthlessly sacrificed and trampled upon." Maharaja Hari Singh accepted almost all the recommendations of the Commission and that cooled the political climate of the state.

Meanwhile, the Glancy Commission's recommendations seemed pro-Muslim and anti-Hindu. All the Hindu members, particularly from Jammu, resigned from the commission. But, Prem Nath Bazaz, a representative nominated by Kashmiri Pandit community continued to remain in the commission against the wishes of his community. The Pandit community became hostile to him and almost excommunicated him from their community.

The important recommendations of the commission were:

- There should be minimum qualification required for an appointment in Government services but not to make it an unnecessarily high qualification.
- To maintain the interest of the backward community of Muslims in Government service.
- Grant of proprietary rights of the agriculturists as the ownership of agricultural land rested with the State.
- Abolition of several high taxes.
- Regenerating employment for unemployed by starting new industries in the State.
- A legislative Assembly be started where people aired their grievances.

Sheikh Abdullah was the President of Kashmir Muslim Conference. He had succeeded in elbowing out Maulvi Yusuf Shah to become its President. This gave rise to hostilities between Sheikh Abdullah and

Yusuf Shah. Thereafter, the followers of Yusuf Shah were nicknamed 'Bakra' (Goats) and Sheikh's followers were known as 'Sher' (Lions). For many years till the partition of the country, there were regular skirmishes between both the parties in the State but immediately after partition Yusuf Shah opted to go to Pakistan. He went there and had to live there permanently because he was not permitted to enter Jammu And Kashmir State. Sheikh Abdullah became very vocal. His speeches were anti-Dogra and anti-Hindu—rather anti-Kashmiri Pandits, since most of the Hindus in the valley were Kashmiri Pandits. Traditionally, the Muslim community was in majority. The abject poverty forced some of them to work as wood carriers , servants, water carriers for Pandit families. Sheikh Sahib had many times expressed that he would love to see the Kashmiri Pandits as wood carriers and their womenfolk as water carriers for Muslim families. Luckily, that did not happen till he expired. It may be pointed out here that Hindu domination of Kashmir ended in the year 1339 AD when Shah Mir took over as Sultan of Kashmir. The Islamic rule remained in the valley till 1819, when Sikh supremacy started in Kashmir. It is intriguing why even during Islamic rule of more than 500 years, the condition of the majority community did not improve. Majority of them were poor and had to earn their living by doing menial jobs.

Genesis of Nationalism

There were many gradual changes, nationally and internationally, that took place before and after Maharaja Hari Singh's succession to the throne, which had, in one way or the other, affected and disturbed the smooth functioning of the State administration. For instance, a powerful movement of Indian nationalism began to assert itself during the second half of the nineteenth century.

In 1920 AD, a movement of non-cooperation with the British was started by the Indian National Congress, particularly against the Simon commission in 1927 AD. Then there was Civil Disobedience in 1930 and 1934. Finally the slogan of Quit India Movement in 1942 became responsible for inculcating the spirit of nationalism among people.

The most important step in the development of the National Movement in India was the starting of the non-cooperation movement by the Congress under the leadership of Mahatma Gandhi. The British

Government was very uncomfortable with the agitation of Congress who raised the slogan of complete independence for India. To seek favour of the Princes the British Government invited them to a Round Table Conference. Maharaja Hari Singh was also invited. According to Narendra Sahagala,[51] "His (Maharaja Hari Singh's) patriotism is testified by the way he supported total independence for India as a representative of the Chamber of Princes in the Round table Conference in London in 1931. The Maharaja said candidly, 'It is the first occasion when the Indian princes have come to discuss the political future of India with the representatives of the British Government and British India. As Indians we want our motherland to enjoy a place of honour and equality in the British Union'." This statement jolted the British Government and they became hostile towards him. The Muslim community too became hostile towards the Maharaja. Muslim leaders like Abdul Aziz of Delhi, Karamat Ali of Jaunpur and Sayyid Ahmed of Bareilly tried to reform the Islamic movement in India by introducing true Islam and not any other Islam infected by Hinduism.

Sayyid Ahmed of Bareilly, who was a religious bigot, proclaimed that India being under non-Muslim power was a Dar-ul-Harab in which Jihad or Holy War should be waged against infidels (non-believers). Some Muslims had argued that India had become Dar-ul-Harab because of British rule. They wanted to fight and change it into Dar-ul-Islam. Another development of far reaching consequences started in India and that was the growth of Muslim communalism. Indian Muslims who had enjoyed lucrative posts, places of profit and prestige and influence under Muslim rule in India had faced a severe setback during British Raj. British rulers in India preferred Hindus who were better qualified than Muslims to carry on their administration in India. Muslims were relegated to the background.

In order to establish their identity, Muslims in India laid the foundation of 'Muslim League' to counter the movement by the Indian National Congress. The Indian National Congress, under the leadership of Mohandas Karamchand Gandhi and Pandit Jawaharlal Nehru passed a resolution in 1928 at Calcutta (now Kolkata) and another in 1929 AD at Lahore asking for complete independence. This had antagonised the

British. They introduced a "divide and rule" policy and began patronising Indian Muslims by coming closer to them. Taking advantage of British patronage some Muslim leaders decided to try militant preaching of Islam started by Sayyid Ahmed and Mohammad Ismail. Both of them had started this propaganda in Punjab which became the hub of Muslim fundamentalism and Islamic militancy.

The Muslim think-tank wanted to pursue their hidden agenda to become the harbingers of Pan-Islamic-Movement. They believed that Pakistan should become the epicentre of achieving it. So the Muslim community of India supported the divisive program and the formation of Pakistan.

As already stated, Punjab became the hub of Muslim fanaticism. Muslims began propagating against the Dogra rule in Jammu and Kashmir. Even during Maharaja Pratap Singh's rule, the Punjab Muslims were against the Maharaja. Prem Nath Bazaz writes,[52] "In the beginning of 1931, the Lahore Muslim Press started a violent and venomous campaign against the Hindu Maharaja and his administration. Newspapers containing articles written in words of fire were published and sent by thousands into the state. In the name of Holy Prophet and Islam, the followers of the faith were asked to sacrifice everything for the cause of the community and join the struggle which, it was evident to everyone, was coming with great speed." Religious fanatical material was imported from outside Kashmir and that aroused very strong anti-Hindu feeling among peace loving Muslims of the State. This turned quite dangerous for the political climate of the state.

A few educated Muslim boys had started a Reading Room Party, which gradually came into the forefront to pursue the agenda of ending Hindu rule in Kashmir. The important members of this reading room party were Mir Waiz Yusuf Shah and Sheikh Mohammad Abdullah. In this scenario, they began holding religious public gatherings wherein they would criticise Maharaja Hari Singh. One of the meetings was held on 21 June 1931 at Khanqah Maulana where Muslim representatives were elected to prepare a charter of their grievances to be submitted to Prime Minister George Edward Campbell Wakefield. At the end of this meeting, "Abdul Qadir, an ugly looking, short statured butler of an European, delivered a violent speech advocating massacre of Hindus," says Prem Nath Bazaz,[53] The government took his speech as sedition to ignite communal frenzy. He was arrested. Sheikh Mohammad Abdullah had already made the state's ground fertile for communalism and soon communal riots started. Says PNK Bamzai,[54] "As an active member of the Reading Room Party, Sheikh Abdullah was responsible for organising mammoth meetings of Muslims in various mosques. He was also responsible for delivering fiery speeches exposing the hardships and the depressed condition of the people. Communal tension reached the flashpoint and it needed only a spark to explode."

Abdul Qadir was arrested. Keeping in view the law and order problem, the government decided to conduct the court proceedings in the premises of central jail. The Muslim crowd, in sympathy for the accused, came in thousands. They tried to enter the jail premises. Their ringleaders were detained, which infuriated the crowd which became violent. The police had to use arms to quell the violence; as a result about 10 people died. "The jail firing which killed several Muslims created great bitterness in the mob mind against the Hindus. So when the procession reached Maharaj Gunj, busy trade centre of the city, shops owned by Hindus, which had been closed owing to panic, after hearing of the jail incident, were broke open and looted. Serious rioting followed not only at Maharaj Gunj but also in several parts of the city, notably Vecharnag and Nowshera. Hundreds of Hindu houses and shops were mobbed and the inmates injured. Three Hindus were murdered and 163 wounded," says Prem Nath Bazaz[55].

Four

Emergence of National Conference

Mir Waiz Ahmed Ulla was the sole spokesperson of Kashmiri Muslims. He was venerated by the entire Muslim community in Kashmir. After his death in March 1931, Mir Waiz Maulvi Yusuf Shah became the sole representative of Sunni Muslims. A young man in his twenties, Yusuf Shah was an enthusiastic leader. He was one of the articulate members of the Reading Room Party. Subsequently, in December 1930, a political party by the name of All Kashmir Muslim Conference was formed. Both Sheikh Mohammad Abdullah and Maulvi Yusuf Shah were its founding fathers.

The Punjabi Muslims of Lahore had taken upon themselves to make Kashmir State Dar-ul-Islam. They hosted an annual session of All Kashmir Muslim Conference in Lahore. At this function, Jammu Muslim representatives also took part. As expected, it was decided to launch an aggressive campaign against the Hindu Maharaja of Jammu and Kashmir. To make this movement accepted among Kashmiri Muslims, they raised a slogan 'Islam is in Danger' when they found that a constable had shown disrespect to the Holy Book. Soon riots broke out. Sheikh Abdullah and Gulam Abbas from Jammu jumped into this communal riot. Hundreds of Hindu houses were looted and burnt. Some Hindus were also killed. This communal virus spread into many towns and villages. Sheikh Abdullah and Abbas were arrested and put into Hari Parbat Fort.

After his release Sheikh Abdullah tried to win over the Hindus. He advocated the secular card as he knew that time was not ripe to isolate Kashmiri Hindus. In the meeting of March 26, 1938, he stressed that communalism be ended by ceasing to think in terms of Muslims and non-Muslims. According to Tariq Ali,[1] "On their release from jail, Sheikh Abdullah and his colleagues set about establishing a political organisation capable of uniting Muslims and non-Muslims in Kashmir—mainly Hindus, dominated by the Pandits, upper-caste Brahmins who looked down on Muslims, Sikhs and low-caste Hindus alike, but looked up to their colonial masters, as they had to the Mughals."

Sheikh Mohammad Abdullah

It seems that destiny pushed Sheikh Mohammad Abdullah into Kashmir politics, where he elbowed everyone away, even Mir Waiz Yusuf Shah and became the principal leader and sole representative of Kashmiri Muslims.

Sheikh Abdullah was born in December 1905, in an ordinary, converted Kashmiri Muslim family, in village Soura. The village is about ten kilometres from Srinagar. Tracing his lineage, he says in his biography *Aatish-e-Chinar* that Gulam Rasool, his grandfather, was the son of Raghav Ram a Kashmiri Brahmin. Sheikh Mohammad Ibrahim was the son of Sheikh Gulam Rasool and father of Sheikh Mohammad Abdullah. He was a Pashmina shawl dealer who died fifteen days before Sheikh Abdullah was born. He was reared by his widowed mother and uncle. Initially, he was sent to a Madrasa where he learnt Arabic and Persian, but later on he got admission in a Government primary school. In 1911 AD, after passing Matriculation from a Government high school, he went to college and completed his FSc and subsequently went to Lahore to study further. He stayed in Punjab for two years.

Punjab was then the hub of Muslim fundamentalism and communalism. It is from Punjab that Kashmiri Muslims were instigated to Jihad against non-Muslims. Young Muslims from Kashmir were indoctrinated to annihilate Hindus and oust the Maharaja. It was while studying at Lahore that Sheikh Sahib came into contact with the preachers of Jihad. After completing his Bachelor of Science he went to Aligarh Muslim University where he completed his Masters Degree in Chemistry.

Once he returned from Aligarh, he rejected the scientific knowledge and focused on Islamic beliefs.

According to *Aatish-e-Chinar*, the Sheikh was always proud of calling himself a devout Muslim and saw no objection in reciting verses from the *Holy Quran* at political meetings or while delivering speeches of political nature. Yet, he reiterates in his biography that he feels saying of Vande Mataram in Congress meetings is in bad taste. Says Prem Nath Bazaz,[2] "Abdullah is a hater of books and no admirer of intellectual debates and discourses. He shuns the company of the learned and rarely tolerates a man with independent opinion about him." Sheikh Abdullah had learnt that faith could move mountains but never believed that knowledge could destroy the faith. Though he had attained scientific knowledge, he never talked about it nor did he try to inculcate scientific temper into his community. For the people of Kashmir he was their mentor, their protector, their Messiah, and *Sher-e-Kashmir* (Lion of Kashmir) who knew how to roar loudly. According to Tariq Ali,[3] "in a hangover from Mughal days, and to make up for their lack of real power, the Muslims of India had developed the irritating habit of giving their leaders fancy titles. So Sheikh Abdullah became Sher-e-Kashmir and his wife Akbar Jehan, Mader-i-Meharban(the kind mother)."

Meanwhile, in 1939, dark clouds of the Second World War had slowly started hovering over the European horizon. The British Government was very disturbed at having no control over Gilgit to keep watch over Russian movements. Lieutenant Colonel E J D Colvin, the Prime Minister of Kashmir and the Resident, pressurised the Maharaja so much that they succeeded in getting Gilgit on lease basis for 60 years for the British Indian government. Having attained their objective, the British Indian government stopped interfering in the state affairs. Unfortunately, this was ominous for Sheikh Abdullah who was banking on the British government's help to oust the Maharaja.

He organised religious congregations for the mobilisation of people. Ian Copland has argued that,[4] "Religion was an essential factor in the process of mobilisation, providing an avenue for organisation and propaganda and a sense of communality among Muslims which transcended the formidable barriers of class, education and religion. But the root cause of the revolt was socio-economic—determination on the part of Muslims to win for themselves a prominent position in Kashmiri society."

Looking at the popularity of Sheikh Abdullah in the valley, Punjabi Muslims stopped giving political help to Kashmir Muslims. They sent mullahs to preach Islam, but with the condition not to indulge in Kashmir politics. Sheikh Abdullah yet could not totally abandon the concept of composite culture of the land. He felt that to distance himself from Hindus and other communities at that stage would jeopardise his cause for ousting the Maharaja. He had talked many times in his public speeches about composite culture and said that all communities must join hands with him. P N K Bamzai says,[5] "The Muslim Conference Party observed a Responsible Government Day throughout the state on May 8, 1936. Sheikh Mohammad Abdullah appealed to Hindus and Sikhs to participate in the functions held in this connection. The response was most encouraging and a number of meetings were addressed by Hindus, Sikh and Muslims leaders exhorting the people to forge a common platform and party."

In his Presidential address to the sixth annual session of the Muslim Conference on March 26, 1938, Sheikh Abdullah observed, "We must end communalism by ceasing to think in terms of Muslim and non-Muslims when discussing our political problems and we must open our doors to all such Hindus and Sikhs who like ourselves believe in the freedom of their country from the shackles of irresponsible rule."

Emergence of National Conference, 1939 AD

Prem Nath Bazaz, who was initially the President of Kashmiri Pandit Conference and also a member of Glancy commission, had faith that Hindus, Muslims, and Sikhs could live together peacefully in Kashmir. He writes,[6] "A few young Muslim leaders including Abdullah began to think on non-communal lines." Abdullah and Prem Nath Bazaz met two months later on a historic afternoon in July 1932 in the Cheshma Shahi garden to thrash out the problem. This meeting proved to be of a great significance. The decision taken in it by the two after a frank, detailed and heart-to-heart discussion of the basic issues considerably influenced the state politics. It was in this meeting that Abdullah and Bazaz firmly resolved that the Kashmir Freedom Movement would be conducted on secular, progressive and democratic lines.

After a fervent appeal made to Hindus, Muslims and Sikhs by Sheikh Abdullah, a special session of the Jammu and Kashmir Muslim Conference was held at Srinagar on June 10, 1939. About 176 delegates from all over the state attended. The resolution to convert Muslim Conference into Jammu and Kashmir National Conference was passed with overwhelming majority. Only three hands rose against this resolution. As per Geraldine Forbes,[7] "Eventually, under the influence of Jawaharlal Nehru and the Indian National Congress, Abdullah, Gulam Abbas, a Muslim leader from Jammu, and Prem Nath Bazaz, a Kashmiri Brahmin Pandit, transformed the Jammu and Kashmir Muslim Conference into the secular Jammu and Kashmir National Conference."

N Gopalaswami Ayyengar as Prime Minister

In the meantime, Colonel E J D Colvin gave up the post of Prime Minister of Kashmir. In 1936, Maharaja Hari Singh appointed N Gopalaswami Ayyengar as the next Prime Minister. Ayyengar was a shrewd bureaucrat and had served the Indian Government for a long time. The change that took place in the conversion of Muslim Conference into National Conference was appreciated by him. In view of the change, he ordered the release of all political prisoners. The leaders of Indian National Congress were also satisfied. They believed it was a step of solidarity towards their freedom movement. Pandit Jawaharlal Nehru gave whole-hearted support to Sheikh Abdullah.

Quit India Movement

Field Marshal Erwin Rommel, the German General fighting the Allied forces was inflicting heavy casualties on the Allied forces in Africa. The Japanese Government also joined the war against the Allies. Her victorious army captured the countries of South-East Asia. They occupied Burma and threatened India. Political activities in India started changing rapidly. It was in the same year that the Congress passed the Quit India Resolution. The British Indian Government arrested all the Congress leaders.

New Kashmir,1943 AD

Except a few insertions, which are a rehash of fashionable slogans of Communism, this manifesto, issued by the National Conference in 1944 was named as New Kashmir. It was a revolutionary treatise advocating that all key industries were to be managed and owned by the democratic state. Big private capitalist monopoly, whether formal or virtual, should be abolished. The revolutionary aspect of this treatise was, "All students shall have the right to education; women citizens shall be accorded equal rights with men in all fields of national life—economic, cultural, political and in the state services." Had this manifesto been used as a guide line for the establishment of a popular government it would have decidedly taken the Kashmir state towards Communism.

The highlight of this manifesto, as per Prem Nath Bazaz is,[8] "This in brief is the 'New Kashmir Manifesto' of the nationalists which they submitted to the Maharaja some time after they decided to boycott the Royal commission and withdraw their nominees from it. It was an interesting though thoughtlessly drafted document, envisaging the establishment of a communist State, yet opportunistically enough, it guaranteed the perpetuation of the alien Dogra rule in Kashmir and gave the Maharaja a solemn assurance that he would continue to exercise the right of general control over the administration of the state."

It is said the 'New Kashmir' plan, which was adopted by the National Conference in 1944 was authored by an Indian Communist B P L Bedi and was painted in Communist colours, which was not suitable or acceptable to the Indian National Congress ideology. Though Sheikh Mohammad Abdullah was not communist by faith, as Islam and Communism are diametrically opposite, yet he accepted the plan for the state, the reason being that in doing so the majority community gained more than the minority.

Jinnah's visit to Kashmir 1944 AD

In 1944, Mohammad Ali Jinnah visited the valley 'for having rest'. The National Conference gave him a magnificent reception. Welcoming him the leaders roared, "We Kashmiris today receive you as a prominent Indian despite ideological differences we have with you. We hope that you, along with other leaders of India, will try to arrive at a solution which will go a long way to emancipate the teeming millions of India." To this Jinnah replied, "I am happy to see all classes and groups combined here to receive and honour me."At another reception given by the disgruntled Muslims, Jinnah said, "Muslims have one platform, one Kalima and one God. I would request the Muslims to come under one flag of All India Muslim League." This slogan did not go down well with the National Conference.

Jinnah had also made an unpleasant remark against National Conference leaders calling them a 'band of gangsters'. There was uproar in the valley. Sensing that majority of the Muslims of the valley were with the National Conference, Jinnah had to leave Kashmir disappointed.

In August 1942, after passing of the 'Quit India' resolution by the Congress, the British Government prepared to act. Almost all the leaders of Indian National Congress were imprisoned. The British Government tried to suppress this movement ruthlessly. Muslims, by and large, did not support the movement. The Muslims in India, led by Mohammad Ali Jinnah, were working for the partition of the country. This was the greatest disservice Jinnah did for the country—to break the unity of the people and then to divide the country on religious basis. In 1940, Jinnah made a statement at the Lahore Conference for a separate Muslim land. The Indian Muslim League passed a resolution asking for the creation of Pakistan as an independent state of Muslims in India.

Quit Kashmir Movement, 1946 AD

The conversion of Muslim Conference by its working committee into National Conference was welcomed by the leaders of Indian National Congress. This step made Sheikh Abdullah an outstanding personality in Kashmir as well as in India. Prem Nath Bazaz made all efforts to arrange a meeting of Sheikh Abdullah with Pandit Jawaharlal Nehru. In 1940 AD, Pandit Nehru had visited Kashmir. There was spontaneous enthusiasm among the people of Kashmir irrespective of caste or creed. Both Hindus as well as Muslims took him as a son of the soil. Nehru's personal interest in the well-being of the people of Kashmir, as a whole, had impressed both the communities.

Sheikh Abdullah's association with the Indian National Congress made him one of the most important members of the All-Indian States People Conference where he represented Kashmir.

By putting on a secular mask, he was determined to end Hindu domination of Kashmir by Maharaja Hari Singh. Taking a cue from Indian National Congress's 'Quit India Movement', on May 10, 1946, Sheikh Abdullah declared a 'Quit Kashmir Movement' whereby he asked the Dogra monarchy to go away from Kashmir. National Conference leaders in different parts of the valley made speeches propagating it. This 'Quit Kashmir Movement' was launched with the demand of transfer of power from the British Crown to Indian people. The sovereignty in the states was to be reverted to the people of the states and not to the ruler. The people would decide the future course of the state. Sheikh Abdullah submitted this demand in a memorandum to the Cabinet Mission.

This movement and this demand had sinister implications. Though he sought the cooperation and help of non-Muslims in bringing a responsible government in the state, the 'Quit Kashmir Movement' had undoubtedly communal connotations. This slogan put the Congress leaders in an awkward situation. Victoria Schofield says,[9] "Mirroring Gandhi's Quit India movement in 1942, Sheikh Abdullah launched a Quit Kashmir Movement, describing how 'the tyranny of the Dogras' had lacerated their souls."

Extract of Quit Kashmir speech of Sheikh Mohammad Abdullah, May 10, 1946

> "The tyranny of the Dogras has lacerated our souls. The Kashmiris are the most handsome people, yet the most wretched looking. It is time for action. Every man, woman and child will shout 'Quit Kashmir'. The Kashmiri nation has expressed its will. I ask for a plebiscite on this question."

This ill-conceived slogan of 'Quit Kashmir' by Sheikh Abdullah had put Hindu members of the National Conference into shock and embarrassment for they felt that the working committee was not consulted. The Indian National Congress never wanted to oust the Dogra government from the state. Ram Chand Kak, as Prime Minister, took a very strong view of this movement, as it would destabilise the Maharaja's government, a policy outlined neither by Congress nor by the Muslim League. Even right thinking Muslims did not support this movement. The government of Ram Chand Kak suppressed this movement ruthlessly. All National Conference leaders including Sheikh Abdullah were arrested. Sensing all round criticism of this movement, Bakshi Gulam Mohammad, who along with Gulam Mohammad Sadiq and Durga Prasad Dhar had escaped, issued a statement in Lahore that "National Conference demanded the establishment of responsible government in the state," and by the slogan of Quit Kashmir, "they did not desire to harm the royal family in any way." That was the end of 'Quit Kashmir' movement.

Nehru visits Kashmir, 1946 AD

Ram Chand Kak, the then the Prime Minister of Kashmir got the leaders of the movement arrested. Islamic extremists, though in a microscopic minority in Kashmir, did not join the movement. They accepted Jinnah's advice, which described the 'Quit Kashmir Movement' as an agitation carried out by a few miscreants who were out to create disorderly conditions in the state.

Pandit Jawaharlal Nehru could not tolerate the ruthless repression of the leaders of National Conference by the Maharaja. He decided to visit Kashmir. From Rawalpindi, on June 18, 1946, he reached Kohala Bridge to enter the valley. The Kashmir government had placed security forces on their side of the bridge. Rai Bahadur Maharaj Kishen Dhar, the District Magistrate was there to monitor the situation. Pandit Nehru forced his way into the valley but the security men stopped him. In the scuffle, Nehru got minor injuries. He had come to give comfort to the people of Kashmir and to bail out Sheikh Abdullah and the National Conference from the mess they had created by the 'Quit Kashmir Movement'. However, the District Magistrate allowed him to proceed only up to Domale. The Congress high command asked Nehru to come back. He, therefore, abandoned his onward journey and rushed back to Delhi. He visited Kashmir again on July 24, and met Sheikh Abdullah at Badam Bagh prison, and assured all support to him. However, Sheikh Abdullah, during discussions with Jawaharlal Nehru, admitted that it was a slip-up to have started the 'Quit Kashmir' movement. Writes Lt Col Vivek Chadha,[10] "Sheikh Abdullah is a paradoxical character. It was he who shaped the destiny of J&K on the one hand and on the other was partially responsible for degradation in the state and its virtual isolation from the rest of India."

Mahatma Gandhi's visit to the Valley, 1947 AD

Mahatma Gandhi visited Kashmir on 1 August 1946. His visit had two purposes. One was to fulfil an old pledge he had made to Maharaja Pratap Singh at Kumbh Mela in 1919. Another was to give healing touches to the injured feelings of the National Conference leaders and pledge help to Kashmiris who were repressed by the Kashmir

Government during the 'Quit Kashmir' movement. During his stay in Srinagar, he met Maharaja Hari Singh. His stay was brief and on August 4, he went back via Jammu. Rumour says that it was due to his meeting with the Maharaja that Ram Chandra Kak was removed from the premiership and Major General Janak Singh was appointed as prime minister. The National Conference leadership, and the people of Kashmir heaved a sigh of relief when he was removed.

Labour Party's coming to power in United Kingdom, 1945 AD

The 'Quit India' movement launched by the Indian National Congress had rattled the British Parliament. Various reforms introduced by them like the Government of India Act of 1919, failed to appease Indians. The three Round Table Conferences—First Conference in London from November 1930 to January 1931 AD, the Second from September to December 1931 AD, where Mahatma Gandhi represented the Congress and Jinnah the Muslim League, and the third Round Table Conference from November to December 1932, did not yield any positive agreements. Feeling helpless against the growing opposition from the Indian people, the British Government published the White Paper in 1933 AD, which became the basis of the Government of India Act in 1935. The seed of independent India had started germinating.

Clause (4) of this Act states: "The act proposes an All India Federation consisting of British Indian provinces and the Indian states. The Government of India Act envisaged the setting up of a Federal form of Government consisting of British Indian Provinces and Indian States as chose to join the Federation by executing an instrument of Accession whereby certain powers were to be surrendered by the acceding state to the centre." Meanwhile, the Labour Government in United Kingdom came to power as a result of the general election held in 1945 AD. Clement Richard Attlee became the Prime Minister.

Recommendations of Cripps Mission, 1946 AD

The political conditions in India were changing with great swiftness. On 17 May 1946, a mission of three cabinet members came to India—Lord Pethick-Lawrence (Secretary of State for India), Sir Stafford Cripps (President of the Board of Trade) and Albert Victor Alexander (The First Lord of Admiralty), to solve the constitutional problem. The Cabinet

Mission had made a road map for Indian states after India was partitioned into India and Pakistan. The cabinet mission's recommendation was clear giving an indication that India was going to be liberated.

Though the Congress and the Muslim League accepted the Cabinet Mission plan, however, the Muslim League decided to declare August 16, 1946 as a 'Direct Action Day' resulting in death, devastation and ruthless murder of thousands of innocent people. The Muslim League wanted a separate state. They had declared their wish for a separate state earlier in the year 1940. However, they now decided to launch a 'do or die' struggle for the state. The leaders of Muslim League blamed the Congress leaders for standing in their way to achieve their goal. Writes Gyanendra Pandey,[11] "Indeed, as the struggle for Pakistan reached its high point and the lines came to be drawn more and more sharply between 'us' and 'them'; the wrath of God was called down upon all those who stood in the way of the achievement of Pakistan. It was 'traitors' within the community who became the target of the most virulent and continuous attacks. 'Mahatma Gandhi' was a 'celestial quack', Pandit Nehru a 'hypocrite', Sardar Patel a 'Hindu Mahasabhite'. But it was Abdul Kalam Azad, long-term president of the Congress (until mid-1946), renowned for his Islamic learning, called 'Maulana' Azad—in reality, as League propagandists had it, no 'Maulana' at all. He was 'renegade' Azad, the guiltiest of all. He was taunted when the Bihar massacres occurred, reviled for his preaching of Indian unity, prevented from entering various mosques at prayer time, and was insulted and spat upon by students of Aligarh Muslim University when his train stopped at Aligarh railway station."

Seeing this holocaust in India, the blackest spot in Indian history, British Prime Minister Clement Attlee, declared on February 20th 1947, that the British Government would leave India by June 1947, even if no agreement was reached between Congress and the Muslim League. Subsequently, Lord Mountbatten was sent as Viceroy and Governor General in March 1947. By this time, communal passions had risen high and the atmosphere in Punjab and elsewhere had deteriorated to a great extent.

However, in June 1947, a plan popularly known as 'Third Plan' was announced by which India was to be:

- Partitioned into India and Pakistan.
- The native states were to be free to either join one of the two dominions or remain independent.
- As on August 1947, the transfer of power would take place.

Mountbatten's address to Princes, 1947 AD

With this plan the paramountcy of British Indian Government over the Indian States ended. In this connection, Lord Mountbatten spoke to the Princes in the Princes Chamber, New Delhi on July 25, 1947, and apprised them of the division of British India into the two new and fully sovereign dominions of India and Pakistan, with effect from August 1947.

Call for Independent Kashmir, 1947 AD

When it was absolutely clear that India would be divided into India and Pakistan, in Kashmir, Chowdhury Hamidulla Khan, President of Jammu and Kashmir Muslim Conference, issued a press statement on May 10 1947 that the Maharaja should declare Kashmir as 'independent'.

India awakes to life and freedom, 1947 AD

The British Government had sent Lord Mountbatten to India as Viceroy as well as the First Governor General of India. He announced his 'Third Plan', which was acceptable to both, Indian Congress as well as Muslim League. The British Parliament passed the Indian Independence Act, which was to come into force on 15 August 1947. By this act, India was to be partitioned into two countries, India and Pakistan. The common man of India became aware of the reality that soon India would be free of British Rule and the country would be divided into India and Pakistan.

According to Varghese Koithara,[12] "There is wide scholarly agreement that partition came about not because Hindu and Muslim masses had difficulty living together but because the elites of the two communities could not agree on political power sharing."

Five
Political Conditions in Kashmir

The political conditions in Jammu and Kashmir were that of wait and watch, both for the Government as well as for political parties. According to Sten Widmalm,[1] "Three days before independence, the newly appointed Prime Minister of Jammu and Kashmir Janak Singh, tried to remove the insecurity thus created by asking the leaders of India and Pakistan to sign a Standstill Agreement."

At the same time, Mirwaiz Maulvi Yusuf Shah said in a speech that Maharaja Hari Singh should declare Kashmir as an independent state. Sheikh Abdullah was still in prison. His other political activists, Gulam Mohammad Sadiq, Durga Prasad Dhar and Bakshi Gulam Mohammad went underground and escaped to Lahore. Rumour was that Gulam Mohammad Sadiq and Bakshi Gulam Mohammad had approached Jinnah and asked him for a guarantee to the effect that in the event of Kashmir's accession to Pakistan, power would be given to the National Conference and not Muslim League of Kashmir. But Jinnah refused to give any such commitment. This was a set-back for the National Conference. It became the turning point for Sheikh Abdullah and he, therefore, finally decided that Kashmir should accede to the Indian Dominion. According to Santosh Kaul,[2] "He (Jinnah) refused to give audience to the National

Conference leaders, though he instructed Khan of Mamdot (Nawab Iftikhar Husain Khan) and Pheroz Khan Noon to advise them to dissolve the National Conference and join the Muslim League to strengthen the movement for Pakistan in the State."

The Kashmir government was in a state of confusion. Under these conditions, Maharaja Hari Singh thought it fit not to join either of the two dominions and to make a standstill agreement with both. According to Jagmohan,[3] "Clearly, Maharaja Hari Singh was badly advised. Prime Minister Ram Chandra Kak and Raj Guru Swami Sant Dev had planted the idea of independence in his mind." Meanwhile, Mehar Chand Mahajan took over as Prime Minister of Jammu and Kashmir.

Sheikh Abdullah was, in fact, disillusioned with the tantrums of Pakistan. Had Pakistan recognised him as the tallest leader of Kashmir, perhaps things would have taken a different turn. Justice A S Anand writes,[4] "Sheikh Abdullah addressed a public meeting in Srinagar. He reiterated that the main demand of the Kashmiris was 'Freedom before Accession'. He, however, emphatically added, 'How can Muslim League or Mr Jinnah tell us that we should accede to Pakistan? They have always opposed us in every struggle. Even in our present struggle (Quit Kashmir), he (Jinnah) carried on propaganda against us and went on saying that there was no struggle of any kind in the State. He even termed us gundas'."

This was the time when the troubles of Kashmir started again. Perhaps Jinnah acted hastily and antagonised Kashmiri leaders and lost Kashmir for Pakistan. The National Conference leaders were disgusted with the treatment given to them by Pakistan. One wonders how Jinnah was so sure about Kashmir's accession to Pakistan. He once even said, 'Kashmir is in my pocket'. According to Syed Mir Qasim,[5] "Things were shaping in a way which much facilitated our choice. Jinnah killed the chances of Kashmir going to Pakistan by condemning the campaign against the princely rule as a movement engineered by some malcontents." He further writes, "Mr Jinnah had alleged that the Quit Kashmir Movement was foreign inspired. Yet he asked the people of Kashmir to accept his specious two-nation theory and join Pakistan in the name of Islam." Though he proferred faith in secularism as he said in the Pakistan assembly, "Muslim will cease to be Muslim and Hindu will cease to be Hindu", but to gain Pakistan he played all the religious cards.

Sheikh against accession to Pakistan

Sheikh Abdullah, though Muslim by faith and proud of being a devout Muslim, yet was against the State's accession to Pakistan. To corroborate this statement Prem Nath Bazaz writes,[6] "In a letter to a friend in Jammu which he managed to send from the Bhadarwah Jail (a report about which was published in, the *Hindustan Times,* New Delhi, June 7, 1947), Abdullah advised the Maharaja to at once accede to the Indian Union and not to remain independent as the leaders of the Muslim Conference wanted him to do."

Sheikh Abdullah was undergoing three years imprisonment. Nehru wanted the Maharaja to release him unconditionally before the Instrument of Accession was signed, while the Maharaja wanted Delhi to first accept the accession. He called Justice Mehar Chand Mahajan of the East Punjab High Court to Srinagar. Mahajan reached Srinagar on September 13, 1947. Appointing him as his Prime Minister, Maharaja Hari Singh wanted him to negotiate with Delhi to secure Delhi's acceptance of Kashmir accession. According to Prem Shankar Jha,[7] "without insisting on a referendum, or any other step of internal administrative reform, designed to bring Sheikh Abdullah into the government."

In order to feel the political pulse, the Maharaja sent his brother-in-law and Household Minister, Thakur Nescient Chand to meet Sheikh Abdullah at the bungalow where he was placed under house arrest at Badam Bagh (He had been brought from Bhadarwah to Badam Bagh). After exchanging pleasantries, both of them had a heart-to-heart talk. After the talk was over Sheikh Abdullah wrote a letter dated 26 September 1947, for Maharaja Hari Singh. This letter is of great significance.

Noting the relevant contents of the letter Prem Shankar Jha writes,[8] "In spite of what has happened in the past, I (Sheikh Abdullah) assure your Highness that myself and my party have never harboured any sentiments of disloyalty towards your Highness' person, throne or dynasty. The development of this beautiful country and betterment of its people is our common interest and I assure your highness the fullest and loyal support of myself and my organisation." The Maharaja sent Mahajan with this letter to Pandit Nehru to show that his condition was fulfilled.

Partition and after, 1947 AD

With the end of Second World War, it had become clear to the British Government that it was very difficult for them to continue to rule India. On February 20, 1947, His Majesty's Government announced their intention of transferring power to the Indian people. Writes Geraldine Forbaes,[9] "Much of the historiography on this topic has focused on whether the British withdrew from India primarily on their own initiative or whether the Indian nationalists pushed them out. Historians tend to a take middle position. Nevertheless, in order to make peaceful transfer of power, Lord Mountbatten, the Governor General of India undertook the herculean, formidable work. The job was tough, tiresome and tedious."

Lord Mountbatten's personal friendship with Jawaharlal Nehru was termed as his tilt towards India. Akbar S Ahmed says,[10] "He was there as an impartial Viceroy, a neutral referee, between two opposed parties. By becoming closely involved with one party he compromised his neutrality. He thus became not only ineffective but also morally vulnerable. The deaths and the subsequent unending confrontation between India and Pakistan are in that sense traceable to his poor implementation of what were solid and sensible ideas."

However, when Lord Mountbatten surveyed the political landscape of this country, he came to the conclusion that the Muslim League was the sole representative of Indian Muslims who wanted a separate homeland for their community naming it Pakistan. The work of the cabinet mission on framing the constitution was going on. The British Government made it clear that they did not intend to frame any constitution for India, which was the prerogative of Indians only.

The partition gave a fillip to political activities amongst the leaders of the Indian National Congress and Muslim League. Both the parties blamed one another of bribing the British. Akbar S Ahmed says,[11] "In Shimla, a few weeks before partition, Mountbatten broke all official protocol and precedence by giving a lunch. He showed Jawaharlal Nehru and V P Menon, the future division of India because they were his good friends. Nehru reacted badly, lost his temper and objected in writing. Mountbatten was stunned by the 'Nehru bombshell'. Menon, Mountbatten tells us, came to the rescue by drafting what came to be known as the Menon Plan. Nehru now gave his approval to Mountbatten. These plans were the basis for partition."

On 17 July 1947, the British Parliament passed the Indian Independence Act of 1947. Under this Act, there was provision for setting up in India, two Independent Dominions—India and Pakistan. Besides the full share of the Muslim majority provinces, Pakistan would have a part of Bengal and the Punjab. The British Government was to withdraw from the Indian soil on 15 August 1947. On August 14, 1947, Jinnah was declared the Governor General of Pakistan.

Determination of borders

With the declaration of partition, as per 'Mountbatten Plan' of June 3, 1947, and subsequent declaration of Independence for India and Pakistan on August 15, 1947, the struggle between the newly constituted states started. Jinnah wanted that the whole of Punjab, Bengal and Kashmir should become a part of Pakistan but unfortunately for him, the accession of Kashmir to Pakistan or India was not in the hands of British Government. Writes Lucy Chester,[12] "One of the most intriguing connections between the Radcliffe award and the Kashmir problem involves not the substance of the award but the possibility that Mountbatten, the last Viceroy of British India, who delayed the announcement of the Radcliffe Award until two days after independence, may have done so in an effort to coerce the Maharaja of Kashmir into acceding to India rather than Pakistan." It was purely Maharaja Hari Singh's prerogative to select the dominion to which he would accede. As regards the inclusion of Bengal and Punjab with Pakistan, neither the British Government nor Congress agreed to it. It was at this point that Jinnah had intimidated Congress leaders by declaring a 'Direct Action Day' in the country. Ayesha Jalal says,[13] "As its permanent share in the division of assets the League could have only those districts which possessed a clear Muslim majority and were contiguous to each other. Taking the logic of Jinnah's demand to its extreme, Congress now offered him a Pakistan stripped of the Punjab's eastern division (Ambala and Jullundur), Assam (except Sylhet district) and western Bengal and Calcutta—the 'mutilated and moth eaten' Pakistan which Jinnah rejected out of hand in 1944 and again in May 1946."

Fundamentally, the partition of India was unacceptable for Indian leaders. Mahatma Gandhi was shocked and stunned; Maulana Azad was astounded and dazed and other Hindu leaders were fuming. Maulana Azad, who vehemently opposed Partition, wrote in his book,[14] "When Sardar Patel was convinced, Lord Mountbatten turned his attention to Jawaharlal. Jawaharlal was not at first ready for the idea and reacted violently against the idea of partition. Lord Mountbatten persisted till Jawaharlal's opposition was worn down step by step."

It is said that even Mountbatten was against partition of India and he tried to convince the leaders of India including Jinnah. According to L A Sherwani,[15] "Besides, Mountbatten, who evolved the partition plan, was as already stated, not only personally opposed to the division of India but also developed close and friendly relations with Nehru." It is debatable whether the British Government and Mountbatten were or were not in favour of partition. People in India and Pakistan believe that British leaders instigated Jinnah to form the Muslim League and ask for a different state. According to Stanley Wolpert,[16] "Prime Minister (Clement Richard Attlee) hoped that with his famous 'irresistible charm,' Mountbatten might, within fourteen months, bring Gandhi, Nehru and Jinnah round his vice-regal table, teasing agreement from them to resolve their problems. Britain could then withdraw its troops with dignity and take credit for leaving independent India unified." However, partition became a reality. When Mountbatten's charm didn't work, the British Prime Minister employed a commission headed by Radcliffe to draw the dividing line between India and Pakistan.

Empty pockets of Pakistan

When the news of Kashmir's accession to India reached Pakistan, it was like a bolt from the blue for its leaders. They were flabbergasted and astounded. A state which they thought was just in their pockets had slipped away. The accession was the people's verdict. It was the people of Kashmir who had acceded to India. Pakistan leaders could not adjust to the new situation. In fact, the leaders of Pakistan have many a times raised queer slogans such as 'thousand year war with India', 'thousand cuts of India', 'nuclear disaster of India within 8 seconds', 'one mujahid is equal to 10 Indians.' One wonders if such absurd slogans are for their home consumption or these leaders actually believe in them. They have always believed that they are the finest martial race and can challenge any country. Having this background in mind, the news of Kashmir accession with India was a big blow to Pakistan. Their leaders began to spew out fire and started a flurry of communications, mostly in the form of telegrams to the Prime Minister of Britain, and of India.

Sir Cyril John Radcliffe Award

Sir Cyril John Radcliffe, a young gentleman, Oxford trained, with a fellowship in Law had earned an aura of brilliance, He was the son of sportsman Radcliffe. Having been considered the right person to undertake the very complex, intricate and herculean task of planning the partition by drawing the boundary lines, dividing two provinces of Bengal and Punjab, he was burdened with all informative material. As per the facts noted in the book *Freedom at Midnight*,[17] "Despite his encyclopaedic knowledge of a vast array of subjects, however, Radcliffe knew virtually nothing about India. He had never written about it nor became involved in any of its complex legal problems. Indeed, Radcliffe had never even set foot on the sub-continent. Paradoxically, it was for that very reason that he was summoned from his chambers to the office of the Lord Chancellor on the afternoon of 27 June 1947."

It was not an easy job for this young lawyer of London's Law Chamber to draw a borderline through two provinces to the satisfaction of all the concerned parties. His final Award had special importance for the future of Kashmir state. If Kashmir would not have been provided a corridor to enable her people to reach the Indian dominion, the state would have been isolated. In the words of Aurel Stein,[18] "In my account of ancient topography of Kashmir, I have endeavoured to show to what extent the great mountain barriers around the valley have until quite modern times isolated its population from the rest of India. This isolation has at all times exercised a decisive influence on the history of Kashmir."

Radcliffe's work became more onerous on two accounts. One was the setting up of frontiers in Bengal and Punjab and the other was the paucity of time to do so. On his arrival in Delhi, Mountbatten had explained to him that the Award had to be ready by August 15, 1947. He hardly had five weeks to complete the colossal task.

Radcliffe had, in fact, to preside over two commissions—one for Bengal in NorthEast India and other for Punjab in NorthWest India. The two commissions had four South Asian judges. Two judges were selected by Congress and two by Muslim League. The commission's terms of reference was to demarcate the boundaries of the two provinces of Punjab and Bengal. According to Lucy Chester,[19] "In the end, this two-versus-two format and the judges' strong political biases produced a deadlock, leaving Radcliffe with the responsibility to make all the most difficult decisions himself."

Radcliffe submitted his Award on August 12, 1947. Mountbatten announced it two days later. As per Lucy Chester,[20] "The two most controversial elements of this line involved Gurdaspur and Ferozepur. Pakistani critics interpreted Radcliffe's decision to grant most of Gurdaspur District to India as an attempt to provide India with a land link to Kashmir. As one element of the beginnings of the Kashmir conflict, this allegation remains controversial."

Radcliffe did not accept the specific criterion offered to him in drawing the lines of Partition. He was guided by his own reasoning. Larry Collins and Dominique Lapierre write,[21] "Ironically, the one specific criterion he was given was based on a totally erroneous assumption. Convinced that future relations between India and Pakistan would be friendly, the Commander-in-Chief of the Indian army, Field Marshal Sir Claude Auchinleck, authorised Radcliffe to ignore the elements which were usually the first concern of a nation in setting its frontiers, considerations of defence." It is very difficult to understand if there was any ulterior motive behind this advice. However, subsequently, the coming events showed to what extent the Pakistan authorities would go with unfriendly postures towards India.

With the announcement of the Radcliffe Award on 17th August 1947, there were accusations of official partiality towards India or Pakistan and these allegations came from all sides. In the words of Lucy Chester,[22] "Justice Munir of the Punjab Commission accused Radcliffe's top aide, Christopher Beaumont, of pro-Hindus bias. Munir claimed that Beaumont intentionally misled Radcliffe in order to achieve a result favourable to India. Beaumont rejects these charges as ludicrous." In reply to these allegations Radcliffe had said, "differences of opinion as to the significance of the term 'other factors' and as to the weight and value to be attached to these factors, made it impossible to arrive at any agreed line."

According to Tai Yong Tan and Gyanesh Kudeshia,[23] "When the Radcliffe Awards were published, there were claims, particularly from the Muslims, that the awards had been tampered and Mountbatten had a hand in this. Although he took pains to present an outward image of total impartiality when the boundaries were being decided, Mountbatten was known to have advised Radcliffe on some of the interpretations of the terms of reference, and it has been revealed that the former had also influenced Radcliffe into making last minute changes to the Punjab borderline, in favour of India. It was even alleged that Mountbatten and Nehru had a spy in the person of Rao Sahib V D Iyer, an assistant commissioner working on the Punjab and Bengal boundaries with Radcliffe." The declaration of Award was followed by mayhem everywhere. It is said that Radcliffe was so shocked that he refused to accept his wages for the job which was fixed at Rupees 40,000.

Aftermath of Partition

There is perhaps no parallel in the world, where the partition of a country consumed so many human lives. It was the greatest upheaval of the 20th century. Says Akbar S Ahmed,[24] "There could have been a more orderly, a more dignified withdrawal, a more lasting relationship between India and Pakistan if there had been a less impetuous, emotional and partisan Viceroy in Delhi than Lord Mountbatten." The partition of India left both India and Pakistan facing unprecedented destruction and devastation. Traumatised people were shattered and bartered; refugee camps had to be set up. There was mismanagement in both the countries. Killing in the name of religion was the order of the day. Train loads of dead reached both countries. Thousands of women were raped. According to Urvashi Butalia,[25] "The political partition of India caused one of the greatest human convulsions of history. Never before or since have so many people exchanged their homes and countries so quickly."

Maulana Azad, the lone Muslim voice, tried his best to bring reason to the people who were interested in partition. On one occasion when he asked Gandhiji about partition,[26] Gandhi said, "What a question to ask! If Congress wishes to accept partition, it will be over my dead body. So long, I am alive, I will never agree to the partition of India. Nor will I, if I can help it, allow Congress to accept it." Maulana Azad perhaps could smell the mood and foresee the bloodshed and carnage after the declaration of partition. He stated that he knew that fire was simmering in Calcutta, Noakhali, Bihar, Bombay and Punjab. He asked Lord Mountbatten who, without a moment's hesitation replied,[27] "I am a soldier, not a civilian. Once partition is accepted in principle, I shall issue orders to see that there are no communal disturbances any where in the country."

It is not only baffling but astonishing that a person of the calibre of Mountbatten did not envisage the carnage and massacre. Terrorised, frightened, scared and desperate, Hindus and Sikhs from Pakistan fled towards Indian Territory and Muslims from India fled towards Pakistan. According to Urvashi Butalia,[28] "By far the largest proportion of these refuges—more than ten million of them—crossed the western border, which divided the historic state of Punjab, Muslims travelling west to Pakistan, Hindus and Sikhs east to India. Slaughter sometime accompanied and sometimes prompted their movement; many others died from malnutrition and contagious diseases. Estimates of the dead vary but the figure of two million is now widely accepted. As always there was widespread sexual savagery; about 75,000 women are thought to have been abducted and raped by men of religions different from their own."

One wonders why such a situation culminated and could it not have been prevented. What was the administration of British India doing? Was there a spirit of vengeance in the British camp that they were being deprived of such a big empire? Did their frustration dissuade them, not only from performing their duty, but also led them to turn a blind eye to the gigantic spectacle of bloodshed, carnage and mayhem that was taking place.According to Maulana Azad,[29] "on one hand, communal passions were mounting, on the other, the administration was becoming lax. Europeans in the services no longer had their heart to work. They were now convinced that within a short time, power would be transferred to Indian hands. As such, they were no longer interested in their work and only marked time. They told people openly that they were no longer responsible for the administration. This led to more unrest and uncertainty among the people and created loss of confidence."

Six
War against India by Proxy

Pakistan's pressure tactics

On 15 August 1947, India attained Independence. With that, Pakistan was also born, as a separate homeland for Indian Muslims. According to Ayesha Jalal,[1] "The following morning, when the Indian leaders came together for their fateful meeting (Declaration of Partition), the Quaid-i-Azam, the spokesman of India's Muslims, the Father of the Nation about to be born, was meekly to accept the partition of Pakistan's two main provinces and when Mountbatten said: 'Jinnah has given me assurances which I have accepted and which satisfy me', Jinnah would under no circumstances contradict that, and, when the Viceroy looked in his direction, the Quaid would nod his head in acquiescence. And that is how it was to be."

Out of all the Indian States, Jammu and Kashmir assumed special significance as it had predominantly Muslim majority though the ruler was a Dogra Hindu. According to Hilal Ahmed,[2] Maharaja Hari Singh had offered a Standstill Agreement on 12th August 1947, to both India and Pakistan for giving him time to decide the future affiliation of J&K State. Pakistan accepted this proposal but the Indian Government, led by

Pandit Nehru, rejected it. While accepting the Standstill Agreement, the Government of Pakistan, out of foolishness, closed all trade and traffic, from all highways, leading to J&K State. Maharaja Hari Singh directed his Prime Minister to inform the Pakistani rulers about the problems this was creating for his country.

There were incursions too. Hundreds of hostile tribesmen dressed in Khaki dresses entered Poonch from Pakistan. They incited the local Muslims to rise and kill Hindus and Sikhs and abduct their women. Local Muslims sent their families to Pakistan to safe places and started killing Hindus and Sikhs. The soldiers of the state army abandoned their regiments and joined the looters. In retaliation, the local Hindus and Sikhs also started burning Muslims houses and abducting their women.

The Maharaja had to fight for his country on many fronts. He had requested for a Standstill Agreement with India as well as Pakistan but Pakistan's pressure tactics changed the shape of the game. And in this game, unfortunately, Maharaja Hari Singh started becoming a victim of circumstances.

As per Victoria Schofield,[3] "In the months preceding independence, Maharaja Hari Singh appeared as a helpless figure caught up in a changing world, which he was unable to keep pace with." Insufficient armed forces to quell the aggression of the raiders from Pakistan was a complication for the Maharaja. Victoria Schofield further states,[4] "As both India and Pakistan continued to court the old ruler of the state of Jammu and Kashmir, the new, diplomatic initiatives were brought to an immediate halt when news was received that a large number of raiders from the tribal territory of Pakistan's North-West Frontier province, had crossed the borders and were heading for Kashmir." G M Sadiq returned from Lahore to Delhi. According to Faiz Ahmed Faiz, chief editor of *The Pakistan Times* and an old friend of Sadiq's, when news of the tribal invasion reached Lahore, 'we could see that everything was lost.' The general belief amongst Pakistanis is that the tribesmen were incited to a Holy War by the stories of atrocities which fleeing Muslims brought with them to the market places of Peshawar.

There was complete disrespect and violation of the Standstill Agreement between the Governments of Kashmir and Pakistan. The holding back of export goods to Kashmir created a grim situation in the state. Pakistan authorities resorted to double speaking. By letters and even by telegrams they assured the Kashmir Government that supplies would be maintained but in reality they weren't. They also assured the Maharaja that armed raiders would be stopped from entering the state; but the truth is that they pushed the raiders inside Kashmir.

As per Horace Gundry Alexander,[5] "Just when it seemed as if the communal violence in the Punjab was at an end, news came that the Kashmir valley had been invaded by armed men from North-West Frontier, now a part of Pakistan." In reality, after October 18, 1947, the infiltration from Pakistan increased and the raiders came to Kashmir in hordes with modern weapons. According to Varghese Koithara,[6] "On October 22, 1947, it (Pakistan) pushed 7,000 armed Pashtun tribesmen in 300 trucks through the Domale-Mahura-Baramulla-Srinagar road. Two days later a provisional 'Azad Kashmir' government was announced in Pulandri."

Horace Alexander was sent by the British Government to India so that an attempt could be made for a reconciliation between Viceroy Lord Irwin and Mahatma Gandhi. He became a close friend of Gandhi and recalls, "I was assured by a man in authority in Peshawar that the corpses of Muslims killed by Dogras had been paraded through the Peshawar streets by men who called on the people to support a Jihad against the infidels in power in Kashmir and in India."

Pakistan brought death and devastation in the state of Jammu and Kashmir. The tribals killed, raped women, burnt houses and looted the property of both non-Muslims and Muslims. Things became unmanageable for the Jammu and Kashmir Government. According to Syed Mir Qasim,[7] "The winter of 1947 was setting in when suddenly all hell broke loose in Kashmir; blood thirsty and sex-starved invaders swarmed the State killing and raping without discriminating between Hindus and Muslims."

Jammu and Kashmir armed forces fight gallantly

Jammu and Kashmir state forces fought gallantly but unfortunately, their numbers being less they could not defeat the invaders. The heroism, valour and bravery shown by Brigadier Rajinder Singh, is still remembered by the people of Jammu and Kashmir. According to L P Sen,[8] "That Brigadier Rajinder Singh's action was gallant in the extreme is unquestionable. It disrupted the planned time-schedule of the enemy and gave the valley the hope of survival, but there is one point in connection with his action, which is inexplicable. Available to him in Badam Bagh Cantonment were 1,850 officers and men of Jammu & Kashmir state forces of whom 500 were Muslims. In view of what had taken place, he may have lost faith in the latter and decided not to put their loyalty to the test."

Brigadier Rajinder Singh went to fight the invaders with a small contingent of officers and soldiers. Though more troops were available, it seems that in view of communal riots in North India and also in Poonch, he thought is best to fight the enemy with a few trusted officers and soldiers. Perhaps he also did not envisage that Pakistan, recently born, could send so many desperados and create such a nuisance on the borders. In spite of these shortcomings he launched attacks on the enemy. He used tactical war strategy to fight them. He blocked roads, smashed the bridges and hampered their free movement and advancement to Srinagar.

M L Gupta writes,[9] "He (Brigadier Rajinder Singh) also destroyed the bridges at Uri which cut off invaders forward line from their base. Attacked from three directions, he suffered heavy losses and withdrew to Mohra and then to Rampur. Here he died of a Pakistani bullet while offering resistance to the invaders. Guarding the rear single-handed he kept up a steady fire until his men could withdraw to safety. The three days for which he held the invaders from marching on to Srinagar were very crucial and these three days enabled the accession of the State to India and dispatch of Indian forces."

His soldiers wanted to evacuate him to a safer place but Brigadier Rajinder Singh gave them different orders. L P Sen writes,[10] "Realising that any attempt to evacuate him would only hamper his men, he ordered them to leave him behind and to continue the withdrawal. His men placed him under a culvert, hoping that he might escape detection. That was the last that was seen or heard of Brigadier Rajinder Singh." He had taken over as Chief of Staff from General H S Scott. Brigadier Rajinder Singh remains a significant figure in Kashmir history.

The civilians also contributed in their own way. Committees were organised to maintain calm and communal harmony in the state.

According to Sayed Mir Qasim,[11] "The party organised an Emergency council and a peace brigade under the leadershipship of Sheikh Abdullah, Bakshi Ghulam Mohammad, Khwaja Mohiudin Qara, Maulana Masudi, Mirza Afzal Beg and Mr Sadiq to resist the invaders and maintain communal peace. To face the armed invaders we had prepared a trained militia of men and women. The women's brigade was led by Zinel Begum, Mahmooda Begum, Sajdah Begum, and Sumitra Inder Mohan. For them it was a question of life and death because women and wealth were the most coveted targets of invaders."

Maharaja Hari Singh at the crossroads

Maharaja Hari Singh was compelled to seek the help of the Indian Government. Not only the Maharaja but almost all leaders had by now decided resolutely to seek help from India. They understood the intentions of Pakistan. The Maharaja started working towards requesting the Government of India to accept the accession. The contents of his letter dated October 26, 1947 to Lord Mountbatten, the Governor General of Free India, show to what extent things had changed. He wrote about the grave emergency which had arisen in the state of Jammu and Kashmir. Reacting to the information, the Prime Minister of India, Shri Jawaharlal Nehru, immediately sent a telegram to the British Prime Minister.

Sheikh Abdullah released

Maharaja Hari Singh declared Royal Clemency on October 27, 1947. Sheikh Abdullah, who was placed in Bhadarwah Jail to undergo a three year jail term, was transferred the same day to Srinagar and kept in Badam Bagh military cantonment. With the declaration of royal clemency, Sheikh Abdullah was released from jail on October 29, 1947.

He was appointed on the same day as Chief Emergency Officer for the Jammu and Kashmir State. This was, in fact, a condition laid down by India to the Maharaja for the acceptance of accession of Kashmir to India. Justice Mehar Chand Mahajan, the last Prime Minister of Maharaja Hari Singh's government, wrote and is quoted by Prem Shankar Jha,[12] "while leaving Nehru to play his high stakes game of forcing the Maharaja to induct Sheikh Abdullah into his government before he agreed to accept the accession." To corroborate this, Prem Shankar Jha states, "Pandit Nehru was against accepting the Maharaja's accession without first obtaining an explicit commitment to bring Sheikh Abdullah into the Government."

In view of the grave emergency, Sheikh Abdullah rushed to Delhi to request the Indian leaders personally to accept the Instrument of Accession and send military help to stop the raider's assault on Kashmir. Writes P N K Bamzai,[13] "Sheikh Mohammad Abdullah flew to New Delhi to personally appeal to the Indian cabinet to dispatch armed forces to help Kashmiris repel the invaders. Meanwhile, the Maharaja alarmed by the invasion of his State and by the prospects of devastation which seemed imminent appealed to India on 24 October, for military help."

India accepts accession reluctantly

According to Iqbal Singh,[14] "He (Nehru) showed a marked reluctance in accepting the accession of the State of Jammu and Kashmir which Hari Singh 'in extremis' offered the Indian Government through Mahajan, his Prime Minister, after the invasion was already three days old and invading tribesmen were almost on the approaches to Srinagar. However, he had no other option than to accept it when Sheikh Abdullah, the leader of the main liberation movement against the Maharaja's autocratic regime, urged him and asked him to send the Indian armed forces to defend the territorial integrity of Kashmir. That might have been the reason why Jawaharlal Nehru readily agreed to Mountbatten's suggestion that the Kashmir issue had best be referred to the Security Council."

Lord Mountbatten replied to Maharaja Hari Singh on October 27, 1947, and informed him of the acceptance of the Instrument of Accession. He also assured him about the military help being rushed to Kashmir to fight the raiders. India accepted Kashmir's accession. Immediately afterwards , the Indian army was airlifted and landed at Srinagar on 27 October 1947.

When the news of Maharaja Hari Singh's accession to India flashed, Pakistan blamed a conspiracy between Britain and India against Pakistan. Prem Shankar Jha says,[15] "Within days, the Pakistan government also began claiming that the accession was the product of a long matured plot in India aided and abetted by Lord Mountbatten, to tie Kashmir to India and prevent the States accession to Pakistan. Proof of the British involvement was the Punjab boundary commission's award of three Tehseels in Gurdaspur district of Punjab to India."

Claim of Pakistan's Prime Minister

Speaking about the killings in the Poonch Sector, Pakistan's Prime Minister tried to blame the Kashmir forces. However, the ground realities were different. According to L P Sen, who retired as Major General from the Indian Army,[16] "In the early hours of the morning of 22nd October while their Dogra comrades lay sleeping, the Poonchie Muslim troops rose. They drew their weapons from the company armouries and trained light automatic and medium machine guns on the barracks occupied by the Dogras, and on their armoires so that they would be incapable of reaching their weapons. They then moved in and killed their own comrades, including Lt Col Narain Singh who had placed implicit trust in them. Then they made contact with the tribal convoy, which had arrived and lay halted on the Pakistan side of the border. With the town of Muzaffarabad open to them, the tribals swarmed in. Rape, loot and arson engulfed the town."

The false Pakistani version of the "state of affairs in Poonch and on the borders of Sialkot district where Muslims were massacred by State troops", the Maharaja communicated to the British Prime Minister in his telegram dated October 29, 1947. In this connection, Prem Nath Bazaz writes,[17] "The enraged people all over the valley and other parts predominantly inhabited by Muslims rose in rebellion against the despotic and despised foreign rule. From Poonch the disturbances spread to Muzaffarabad and some fighters for liberation provisionally founded a parallel government in the town, which subsequently became known as the Azad Kashmir Government."

Pakistan's refusal to recognise Kashmir's accession to India

It can be seen from the flurry of telegrams that shuttled between Pandit Jawaharlal Nehru, Prime Minister of Pakistan, Liyaqat Ali Khan and Prime Minister of Britain, Clement Richard Atlee that there was an outcry regarding the accession in Pakistan. The Pakistan government said that it was the outcome of secret planning by India supported by Lord Mountbatten and Radcliffe, the presiding officer of the boundary commission. As per *Dawn* newspaper of November 5, 1947, "We do not recognise this accession. The accession of Kashmir to India is a fraud, perpetrated on the people of Kashmir by its cowardly ruler with the aggressive help of the Indian Government." But the facts were different. As can be seen from para 3 of his cable to Clement Atlee, Pandit Nehru says, "I should like to make it clear that question of aiding Kashmir in this emergency is not designed in any way to influence the State to accede to India. Our view, which we have repeatedly made public, is that the question of accession must be decided in accordance with the wishes of people. It is quite clear, however, that no free expression of the will of people of Kashmir is possible till it succeeds in imperilling integrity of its territory." In his telegram dated October 30 1947, Liyaqat Ali Khan writes, "Your recent action of sending troops to Kashmir on pretext of accession has made thing infinitely worse. The whole of Frontier is stirring and feelings of resentment among tribes are intense."

Sensing an armed conflict between India and Pakistan on the Kashmir issue, the Prime Minister of UK suggested in his telegram dated November 22, 1942 to Liyaqat Ali Khan, "After full consideration, I am inclined to think that the speediest and most satisfactory way of putting this idea into practice would be to have recourse to one special organ of the UN, namely the International Court of Justice." Mohammad Ali Jinnah who was a highly reputed legal luminary knew the fate it would get at the hands of the International Court of Justice, which he was sure would go against Pakistan. He sidetracked the suggestion of the Prime Minister of UK. The accession made by Maharaja Hari Singh to India was therefore legally and constitutionally valid, which was then confirmed by the International Community at UN Security Council Resolution of 13 April, 1948 and the subsequent UN Resolution of 5 January, 1949.

India complains to the United Nations, 1948 AD

It was India's representative in the United Nation, P P Palli, who sent a letter on January 1, 1948 lodging a complaint under article 35 of the UN Charter. On January 15, 1948, Pakistan's Foreign Minister Sir Mohammad Zaffarulla Khan submitted some documents in reply to India's complaint making their own complaint against India.

In its complaint, India had assured the UN that, "It (India) had accepted the accession of Kashmir as offered by the Maharaja on October 26, 1947, as also the ruler's appeal for help against the invaders which was backed by the National Conference, the largest popular organisation in Kashmir headed by Sheikh Abdullah, But to avoid any suggestion that India had utilised the States immediate peril for her own political advantage, the Government of India made it clear that once the State had been cleared of the invaders and normal conditions restored, its people would be free to decide their future by recognised democratic method of a Plebiscite or referendum which, in order to ensure complete impartiality, might be held under international auspices."

Extracts of UN Resolution of April 13, 1948

The April 13, 1948, Resolution of UN is in two parts. In the first part, both the governments of India and Pakistan agreed to make ceasefire. The UN would send its observers to monitor the effectiveness of the ceasefire.

According to the second part, Pakistan agreed to take all the necessary steps to secure the withdrawal of tribesmen and Pakistan nationals from the State of Jammu and Kashmir. The territory evacuated by Pakistan troops would be administered by the local authorities under the surveillance of the commission. When Pakistan had withdrawn its nationals and forces from Kashmir and the UN was satisfied of their withdrawal, the Government of India would start withdrawing the bulk of its forces from the State, only after making sure that peace, law and order had prevailed. The Government of India would also ensure that peace, law and order was maintained henceforth.

According to the UN Resolutions dated January 5, 1949, and April 28, 1949, both Pakistan and India agreed to the appointment of a Plebiscite Administrator by the UN. The assurance by Pakistan was never fulfilled, and therefore, Plebiscite in Jammu and Kashmir, could never take place. In view of these developments, the UN clearly recognised that accession to India by Maharaja Hari Singh, gave India legal and constitutional right to be in Kashmir.

In support of Pakistan's conspiracy theory, pertaining to Kashmir's accession to India, one of the western historians, Alastiar Lamb wrote two books—*Kashmir, a Disputed Legacy 1846 - 1990*, and *Birth of a Tragedy 1947*. Alastair Lamb has blamed Britain and India for conniving Kashmir's accession to India. He even challenged in *Birth of a Tragedy 1947* that the Instrument of Accession may never have existed. He says that it is a mystery that the Maharaja ever signed an Instrument of Accession as this document is said to be missing from Indian records. Commenting on

Lamb's books, Prem Shankar Jha states,[18] "That there was such strategic understanding between the Indian Union and Britain came to light, Lamb claimed, when the Indian Foreign Department wrote a letter to Prime Minister Attlee on October 25, 1947, which Lamb believed was inspired by the Home Minister, Sardar Vallahbahai Patel. This justified India's decision to provide assistance to Kashmir, because Kashmir's northern frontiers, as you are aware, run in common with three countries, Afghanistan, the USSR and China."

Subsequent developments in the International geo-strategic scenario proved that the Anglo-US combine made Pakistan a front line State. Neither India nor Kashmir played any such role. According to Prem Shankar Jha,[19] "...why was Britain keen that Kashmir should go to Pakistan? The answer is that having partitioned British India on communal lines, the British were keen to make a clean job of it with regard to princely states. The real reason was that Britain had assigned a place to Pakistan in its strategic design, and Pakistan's possession of Kashmir was an integral part of it."

Importance of Kashmir for Pakistan

Pakistan tried to make an issue of a non-issue. All the leaders and generals had explained the importance of Kashmir for Pakistan. According to General Akbar Khan, "Kashmir's accession to Pakistan was not simply a matter of desirability but absolutely necessary for our separate existence." Jinnah believed it should be part of Pakistan on account of its Muslim identity. He had said that, "Kashmir is the jugular vein of Pakistan..." The stalwarts of Pakistan had given this impression to the world community that Pakistan was incomplete without Kashmir.

To give practical shape to the intimidating warning expressed by Pakistan's Prime Minister in his telegram dated 30 October 1947, about the restiveness of the 'whole frontier', Pakistan sent hordes of Pathan tribesmen and Afridis to Kashmir to join the Holy War of Jihad against so called Infidels—Hindus and Dogras. On 22 October 1947, these invaders, supported by the Pakistan army in civilian clothes entered into the State.

Tai Yong Tan and Gyanesh Kudeshia write in their book,[20] "The violence that shook Northern India in the months before and after partition was dramatic; so were the refugee movements, whose scale even at that time was described as unprecedented in human history." Truly the whole of North India was burning but, due to the efforts of Sheikh Mohammad Abdullah the people of the State, particularly of the valley, remained aloof from the Indian holocaust. To strengthen their army, Pakistan recruited many young people to join the Jihad. The Azad army was raised from disgruntled soldiers from Mirpur and the neighbouring areas. The religious fervour was ignited to the extent that even the soldiers from the regular army resigned and joined the Azad army.

Prem Shankar Jha writes,[21] "A close examination of contemporary accounts, including those of Mountbatten himself, of both the published and unpublished documents, pertaining to the transfer of power from Britain to India and Pakistan, and the records of the last eventful months of the British Raj in Punjab, NWFP (North Western Frontier Province), and Kashmir, now in the India Office Records Library in London, show that both the original Pakistani version of the events of 1947 AD, and Lamb's distinctive interpretation of them, are totally unfounded." The fact remains that while communal disturbances in British India were resulting in deaths and devastation, the people and the Government administration in Jammu and Kashmir remained peaceful and no communal freezy took place.

Describing the Azad army Prem Nath Bazaz writes,[22] "On entering the borders of the State the tribesmen did not behave like disciplined forces of a revolutionary government. Despite the strict orders of their officers, many of them committed heinous and disgraceful crimes. They looted people, sacked towns, burnt houses, killed innocent non-Muslims and raped women. Some nationalist Muslims were also done to death. Abdul Aziz the, local nationalist leader was murdered at Muzaffarabad. Among those who were killed by the tribesmen in Baramulla was Muhammad Mqbool Sherwani who, it will be recalled, had attempted to disturb the public meeting which Jinnah addressed in 1944 AD, on his way back from Kashmir. Sherwani was brutally impaled in the market place and fired upon till he was dead."

The raiders led by Pakistan military Officers, instead of quickly seizing Srinagar and capturing the airport, which they were in a position to do, stopped at various small towns to plunder, murder and rape the womenfolk. They, in fact, felt that they were invincible. Their delay in reaching Srinagar, however, lost them the valley.

Indian Army marches to Srinagar, October 1947

Meanwhile, the first contingent of the Indian army, 1st Sikh Regiment, under the command of Lieutenant Colonel Dewan Ranjit Rai, flew to Srinagar and landed at the airport on October 27, 1947. Lieutenant Col Ranjit Rai was apprehensive about landing safely at the airport. According to PNK Bamzai,[23] "when the first troops were flown for Srinagar, they were instructed to circle over the airfield before landing. They were not sure whether the airfield had fallen into the hands of the enemy. As a matter of fact, the instructions of Lieutenant Colonel Ranjit Rai were not to land if there was any doubt on the point, but to fly back to Jammu. After an interval of tense suspense, at 10.30 am a wireless flash from Srinagar announced the safe landing of the first wave of troops..."

Open trucks were made available to the Indian army by National Conference leaders, particularly Bakshi Ghulam Mohammad. The soldiers boarded these trucks and the military convoy moved from the airport to confront the enemy at Shallteng which was at a distance of seven kilometres from Srinagar. The Muslims and people from other communities of the state lined up on both sides of the roads and cheered the Indian soldiers. The soldiers responded with shouts of "Baramulla Milenge" (we will meet the enemy at Baramulla). When the Indian army set foot in Srinagar, Kashmir was agog with elation, jubilation and relief.

The National Conference leaders and workers maintained peace and discipline in the State. It will not be an exaggeration to say that during those fateful days there was not a single criminal case registered in the capital of theft. According to Vivek Chadha,[24] "Suffice to note at this juncture that this peaceful coexistence of all religious denominations in Kashmir was a result of centuries of moderate, secular and tolerant religious thought. The sufferings that the Kashmiri people had in common, bound them closer together, and led them to evolve the Philosophy of Kashmiriyat."

Brigadier Rajinder Singh, the chief of the army designated for Jammu and Kashmir had gone with a small contingent to fight the raiders. Seeing the overwhelming number of raiders with modern weapons he had thought it best to destroy the bridges of the Jhelum valley road through which the enemy was advancing towards Srinagar. This was another reason the enemy got delayed in reaching Srinagar. As a matter of fact, by sending the army by air, India fulfilled her duty to render military assistance to the State of Jammu and Kashmir, irrespective of the accession to India, as India was the successor authority after the British Government ceased to be.

The barbaric raiders

On the way to Srinagar, the raiders stopped to attack the Convent of Jesus and Mary at Baramulla. These cruel fanatic raiders raped the missionary nuns and then massacred the French, Scottish, Spanish, Italian and Portuguese missionaries of the Church. They vandalised the church. According to LP Sen,[25] "the sight that greeted us in Baramulla is one that no period of time can erase from the memory. It was completely deserted, as silent as a tomb, with not even a whimpering dog. Everywhere one looked, whether it was a house or a shop or a shed, there were signs of pillage, arson or wanton destruction. The well-equipped Mission Hospital, the most modern in the valley, looked as if it had been hit by a tornado. Nor had the mission Church escaped the wrath of the savages. The lovely image had been mutilated with axes and riddled with bullet holes. There were unmistakable signs that the patients in the hospital had been slaughtered in their beds or dragged out to meet the same fate in the compound." He further says, "It was a lovely little Cocker Spaniel that led to the discovery of the spot where the mother superior and the nuns lay butchered. They had eventually rushed out to save the patients in the mission hospital and had drawn the wrath of the tribesmen."

Dewan Ranjit Rai's martyrdom

Lieutenant Colonel Dewan Ranjit Rai was among the first Indian army officers to reach Srinagar early morning on October 27, 1947, when the Pakistani-backed raiders were almost about to capture the capital city of Kashmir. He went with the soldiers of the Sikh battalion to face the enemy at Baramulla. He personally conducted the reconnaissance and operation to fight the enemy. A fierce battle took place. The enemy incurred heavy loss of life. In this battle Ranjit Rai lost his life. He was the first Indian military officer who became a martyr while fighting the enemy and displaying his courage of the highest order. He was subsequently awarded a Maha Vir Chakra, posthumously.

According to Kuldip Singh Bajwa,[26] "A celebrated Pakistani historian says, 'Two tricks of fortune conspired to cheat the Quaid-I-Azam (Jinnah) of the Kashmir gaddi (throne); the loss of a day and half in pillaging at Baramulla, and the reckless bravery of an Indian officer, who, with no reserve of men or ammunition, made an attack on the invading forces as if he had the whole army division at his support. Col Rai, with the small detachment at his disposal, dashed down the Baramulla road. He seized the airfield, delayed the raiders advance by 36 hours, and enabled reinforcements sent by air to reach Srinagar. He saved Kashmir though he gave his life in the effort."

Another military officer who went to fight the enemy was Col Lionel Protip Sen. Sen was sent with the honorary rank of Brigadier to command the 161 Infantry Brigade in place of Brigadier J C Katoch who was hit with a bullet on his leg. Brigadier L P Sen writes,[27] "When advancing to Pattan, we found an abandoned Chevrolet Station Wagon in the vicinity of Hokar Sar. This was duck-shooting preserve of the Maharaja, and only he and his selected guests were permitted to use it. The enemy commanders were evidently at Hokar Sar shooting duck while their tribesmen and the defectors were being smashed at Shallteng. It was only when they streamed past them, in full flight towards Baramulla, that the officers must have realised what had happened and, considering it too dangerous to try retrieving their car, had abandoned it and joined the race."

The military brigades from India continued to arrive in Srinagar. The Indian army had commandeered almost all the civilian aircraft for air lifting soldiers to Srinagar. According to P N K Bamzai,[28] "The situation in the first week of operations in Kashmir can best be described as 'touch and go'." The moment the army reached Srinagar airport they had to move to fight.

Major Som Nath Sharma's heroic fight

Major Som Nath Sharma, at the head of four Kumaon regiments was engaged against well-trained Pakistan army in civilian dress, and hundreds of raiders at Budgam. Major Sharma and his battalion decided to set up their headquarters at Budgam. The battalion fought for many days. A day arrived when only a few soldiers were left. Though the Major was injured very badly, the eyes of this courageous soldier were on his target.

He repulsed all the attacks, but a motor shell burst close to him and he was laid to rest forever. When the Indian soldiers reached Budgam, they found him dead. It was by dint of his sacrifice that the Srinagar airfield was saved from Pakistani raiders. Major Som Nath Sharma, son of Major General Amar Nath Sharma, was awarded the Param Vir Chakra posthumously.

Final assault on Srinagar

The enemy had decided to make a final assault on Srinagar. Meanwhile, in the first week of November, mechanised armed cars of a squadron reached Srinagar. When the cavalcade of these armed cars, after a hazardous journey on Banihal Cart road, reached Srinagar, people greeted them with cheers. Their arrival had assured the people of the state of their safety from the ruthless raiders. Major General Kulwant Singh took charge of the command. The enemy had collected near Shallteng to make the last attempt to capture the city. But the troops of armed cars and infantry pounced upon the enemy. Some raiders escaped but more than three hundred were killed in the battle.

Winter Pause

The winter season starts in Kashmir from the first week of November. This time, the winter season was harsher than that of previous years. On both sides there was a compulsory pause in the war. Though at times, at some places like Uri, Handawara and Trihgam, raiders made feeble yet futile attempts to raid the military pickets, by and large, there was no major confrontation as such.

Civilian Suffering

The worst sufferers in the State were the civilians. Wherever the raiders reached, they indulged in wanton rape, death and devastation including scorching the houses of people of all faiths. Another suffering for the people was the scarcity of foodstuffs. The import of edible oil, salt and other consumables had stopped from August 15, 1947. A kilo of salt was sold for Rs 25. Sensing the scarcity of eatables and the deteriorating condition of people, the Indian Government lent a helping hand by sending truckloads of food with the military personnel.

Recapture of Baramulla

Clearing Shallteng from raiders, the Indian Forces found the enemy sneaking away for safety. The encouraged Indian army decided to chase them as far away as possible. The raiders ran to Baramulla. But they found the Indian Army chasing them there too. While retreating the raiders destroyed roads and bridges behind them. The Indian Army captured Baramulla. According to Brigadier LP Sen,[29] "a wireless message was flashed to Srinagar to inform Major General Kulwant Singh and the Emergency Government that the town was in our possession. Bakshi Gulam Mohammad came to Baramulla within an hour and immediately got down to calming the local population. Doubtful at first whether it was really true that they had been liberated, they were chary of venturing across the south bank of Jhelum River. However, when the news got round that Bakshi Gulam Mohammad had arrived, they flew across the bridge and rushed to meet him. Most of them were crying and denounced the quislings who had been responsible for much of their suffering."

Jamadar Nand Singh

The sons of the soil fought bravely, courageously and gallantly and the raiders had to run for their life. The daredevil officers of the Indian army used right strategy, took correct and accurate decisions for manoeuvring of the forces under their command. The nation is grateful to them for their selfless devotion to duty. However, this exercise would be incomplete without mention of the great sacrifices made by thousands of Indian soldiers, who laid down their lives to protect the people of Kashmir. One such great soldier, Jamadar Nand Singh of 1st Sikh battalion, was a Victoria Cross holder in the British Indian Army. The officers at the helm of affairs thought it best to send him to fight the infiltrators in Kashmir. Jamadar Nand Singh fought gallantly and helped to recapture important positions. While he and the soldiers were rejoicing in the victory and hoisting their victory flags, a stray bullet of the enemy hit him and this great hero, Jamadar Nand Singh became a martyr on December 12, 1947, in the Uri sector. He was awarded the Maha Vir Chakra posthumously.

Mohammad Ali Jinnah dismayed

When the news of the disorderly retreat of Pakistani raiders and soldiers reached Jinnah, (who had moved from Karachi to Lahore to be near the scene of operations) he became greatly dejected at their failure. Larry Collins and Dominique Lapierre, write,[30] "seething with anger, Jinnah defied the British commanders of his army by sending Pakistani units disguised as irregulars to Kashmir to stiffen the demoralised raiders. More tribal levies were raised, and for months in the hostile winter the war would rage on."

Heroic deeds of Brigadier Harbaksh Singh

Brigadier Harbaksh Singh had moved with his brigade to Handawara where some raiders had collected. After defeating the enemy at Handawara, he moved towards Tithwal which was not only difficult but hazardous too. However, with full determination and enthusiasm he reached Tithwal and gave a befitting fight to the enemy. The enemy moved away but Brigadier Harbaksh Singh chased them.Lt Col Vivek Chadha writes,[31] "The Indians advanced under Brigadier Harbaksh Singh. His Brigade commenced operation from Handawara on the night of May 18-19, 1948 and captured Chowkibal on May 20, 1948. At this blistering pace, they were able to take Tithwal on May 23, 1948. Thus in five days Harbaksh Singh had advanced 64 kms across very difficult terrains and captured his objective. Besides killing 67 of the enemy his brigade took a number of prisoners."

Martyrdom of Brigadier Usman

The raiders who had retreated to Pakistan were collecting at Mari Mountain on the Pakistan side. They were directed to move to Poonch area and to Nowshera, with the support of Pakistan's regular army. Brigadier Mohammad Usman was moving towards Nowshera when he faced the Pakistan forces shelling this area heavily. On the night of July 3, 1948, in a fierce engagement with the enemy he was hit by a bullet. He was the first Muslim army officer who became a martyr for his motherland, India. He was awarded the Maha Vir Chakra posthumously.

Refusing to go to Pakistan after the partition, Brigadier Usman was posted as Brigade Commander of the 50-Para brigade at Nowshera. He was also known as 'Lion of Nowshera'.He is the symbol of India's inclusive secularism.

Other Fronts

By the end of October 1948, Pakistani raiders and military personnel had panicked on account of reverses faced at the hands of the Indian army. They tried to make some gains by attempting to invade Ladakh, Kargil and other towns of the northern area. While reaching Zojila, they were surprised to find the Indian army particularly the Gurkha Regiment ready to confront them. Zojila is a hilly terrain towards Leh, Ladakh. Lt Col Sukhdev Singh confronted the raiders at Machoi on November 2, 1948. After capturing Zojila Mountain, the Indian army went to Drass, and from there they sought to capture Kargil. Lt Col Sukhdev Singh and his brave men fought the invaders gallantly and captured the Kargil area. When Kargil was captured , Pakistan realised the invincibility of the Indian Army.

Says Husain Haqqani in an article *Pakistan's Endgame in Kashmir*,[32] "Ayub Khan genuinely believed that as a general rule Hindu morale would not stand more than a couple of hard blows at the right time and place."

Incidentally, it may be stated that Pandit Jawaharlal Nehru was not at all alarmed by the presence of raiders in the valley. He had complete faith that even if the raiders had captured Srinagar, the Indian army was capable of chasing them out. In this connection Prem Shankar Jha says,[33] "The real bone of contention between the two governments was entirely different and persisted to the point where, if Mahajan's account of his second meeting with Pandit Nehru on 26 October is to be believed, Nehru was prepared to lose the valley and Srinagar to the raider and retake it later, if this was necessary to force the Maharaja to take Abdullah into the government."

Seven
National Conference as Administrator

The Indian army took charge of protecting the state of Jammu and Kashmir from outside aggression while the National Conference leaders took responsibility of internal security. Some Pakistani raiders had infiltrated in the capital, Srinagar, too. They had secretly begun to recruit young Muslims who would disturb the communal peace in the state.

Recruitment of National Militia

The National Conference, under the leadership of Bakshi Gulam Mohammad, organised a small National Militia consisting of young Kashmir recruits who helped in the maintenance of law and order and peace in the state. These recruits arrested the Pakistani intruders who had sneaked into Srinagar, and also helped people in other ways. They helped in the distribution of foodstuffs. Many recruits suffered casualties at the hands of raiders. The National Militia also rendered all possible help to the Indian Army in the form of making available transportation such as civil buses and other vehicles for their use.

Appointed as Chief Emergency Administrative Officer, Sheikh Abdullah did not fail to remember his own agenda. He was inching slowly and steadily towards achieving that. He pursued his plan very cleverly, so much so, he was able to hoodwink not only Pandit Nehru but also even the seasoned politician and administrator, the iron-man of India, Sardar Vallahbhai Patel, who was India's Home Minister. After becoming Chief Administrator in 1948, Sheikh Abdullah convinced the Central Government that there was no work left for Justice Mehar Chand Mahajan as Prime Minister of the state. The entire administration was being run by the Emergency Administration headed by him. Since the argument was reasonable, Maharaja Hari Singh was also convinced to dispense the services of Justice Mahajan as Prime Minister. Thus, on 5 March 1948, the Emergency Administration was converted into a full-fledged cabinet headed by Sheikh Abdullah as Prime Minister and Bakshi Gulam Mohammad as Deputy Prime Minister. This was another step forward for Sheikh Abdullah to realise his dream.

Sheikh Mohammad Abdullah as Prime Minister

On 5 March 1948, Sheikh Abdullah took over as the Prime Minister of Kashmir. He felt the time was ripe for fulfilling all those dreams he had developed when leading the Muslim conference. He addressed a Muslim congregation on 24 April 1948. In his address to them on Id-e-Milad, the real Sheikh Abdullah appeared in his true colours. He attacked Hindu politics, derided Hindu society and contemptuously referred to the Hindu religion.

Land to the tiller

The first thing Sheikh Abdullah did was to introduce Agrarian Reforms. Though this law—'Land belongs to the Tiller' was a revolutionary step towards the wellbeing of the people of Kashmir, he knew well that most of the land belonged to Kashmiri Pandits who had purchased it with their hard-earned money (even by selling the ornaments of their spouses) when the Kashmir government, during 1935 AD, had transferred the 'Land Property Rights' to the people. The Agrarian reforms would snatch the land from Pandit owners without paying them a penny as compensation.

Debt Cancellation Laws

In the absence of any organised government or private financial agencies or institution that could advance financial loans to peasants, which they needed for agricultural development as well as social obligations, the peasants borrowed money from Kashmiri Pandits who had taken up the trade of money-lending. Thus, there developed a section of Hindus who were known as Soodir (moneylenders). It is true that these moneylenders indulged in malpractices but overall they did provide help to the agriculture sector. By introducing 'Debt Cancellation/Reduction Law', these moneylenders could not get back the money they had lent. A large number of Hindu land owners and moneylenders were left unemployed.

Abolition of big landed estates

The abolition of 'Big Landed Estates' law passed by the Abdullah government was reasonable, and in a sense a revolutionary step. According to this law, property owners who were usually the Maharaja or his kin from the royal family were known as jageerdars. With the introduction of the new law these jageerdars had to forgo large portions of their land. Writes PNK Bamzai,[1] "The landlord was allowed to keep not more than 160 Kanals (29 acres) of agricultural land, 8 Kanals (1 acre) of land for vegetable gardening, 4 Kanals (1/2 acre) as residential site and 10 Kanals (1.25 acres) of orchards – altogether 182 Kanals (22.75 acres). The expropriated land was to be transferred in full ownership to the tenant to the maximum of 160 Kanals (20 acres). He had to pay the regular land revenue." In addition, the uncultivable land was to be transferred to the Government who would distribute it to landless tillers. However, in many cases, the tiller of the land was found to have more land than permissible under this law but the main thing was to snatch the land from the jageerdars. Some of them who had some inkling about this law distributed their estate to their children and relatives, according to the admissible area, to avoid having it taken away by the government.

Education Reforms

In the field of education, the government opened many schools and colleges in the state. With the help of the Central Government and the University Grants Commission, the Jammu and Kashmir University came into being. This facilitated imparting of education upto the university level in the state. This was a revolutionary step taken by the new government, which helped the Muslim community to get their children educated in modern subjects. All these steps taken by the new government with regard to people's economic and other problems proved of great relief to them. In these measures the new government was backed by the people of Communist ideology. Among them was Niranjan Nath Raina, a staunch follower of Communism. These comrades infiltrated into political parties of the state without starting their own Communist party.

Favouritism to Muslims of other countries

Sheikh Abdullah also tried to increase the population of Muslims in the valley. Perhaps the question of plebiscite of Jammu and Kashmir was lurking in his mind. He, therefore, consented to allow Muslims, other than that of Jammu and Kashmir, to settle down in the valley throwing the State Subject rules out of the window. According to K N Pandita,[2] "Immediately after coming to power in 1947, Sheikh Abdullah had invited in early 1950s nearly 5000 Kazakh Muslims to settle down in Kashmir ignoring the state subject rule and oblivious of manipulated demographic change in the state. In early 60's large number of Tibetan Muslims were settled in Kashmir and provided all facilities including residential quarters in Idgah locality in Srinagar." He further says, "Against this, not a single Buddhist refugee from Tibet was granted permission to settle in Kashmir; facilities like those provided to the Muslim refugees remained a distant dream. Discrimination is loud and eloquent when comparison is made with the treatment meted out to Hindu and Sikh refugees from Muzaffarabad and Domel."

India fighting on many fronts

Indian soldiers were successful in recapturing the parts of Kashmir Valley up to Uri, Keran and Kargil in the north. There was a very big chunk of the state, almost one third of the total area, under the control of Pakistan, when the UN's Security Council adopted a resolution in its 26th meeting on 21st April 1948 for the ceasefire of hostilities between India and Pakistan. The relevant excerpts of the resolution are mentioned here, on the India Pakistan question, submitted jointly by the representatives of Belgium, Canada, China, Colombia, United Kingdom and United States of America.

> "Being strongly of the opinion that the early restoration of peace and order in Jammu and Kashmir is essential and that India and Pakistan should do their utmost to bring about a cessation of all fighting, noting with satisfaction that both India and Pakistan desired that the accession of Jammu and Kashmir to India or Pakistan should be decided through the democratic method of a free and impartial plebiscite."

The resolution had issued instructions for both India and Pakistan.

> **For Government of Pakistan**"To secure the withdrawal from the State of Jammu and Kashmir of tribesmen and Pakistani nationals not normally resident therein who have entered the State for the purpose of fighting and to prevent any intrusion into the State of such elements and any furnishing of material aid to those fighting in the State."

> **For Government of India**"When it is established to the satisfaction of the commission set up in accordance with the council's resolution of 20 January, that the tribesmen are withdrawing and the arrangements for cessation of the fighting have become effective, put into operation in consultation with the commission a plan for withdrawing their own forces from Jammu and Kashmir and reducing them progressively to the minimum strength required for the support of the civil power in the maintenance of law and order."

Promulgation of ceasefire by United Nations

With this promulgation of ceasefire by the United Nation's Security Council, the most important towns inhabited mostly by Punjabi speaking Muslims remained under the control of Pakistan. They are Bhimber, Mirpur, Kotli, West Poonch, Muzaffarabad, Astor, Chillas in the North West, Gilgit and Frontier parts of Nagar, which is now called Azad Kashmir.

It was not an easy task to approach the United Nations (UN) for an honest, reasonable and unbiased decision. The Indian Government was surprised to find itself swallowed up in the international intrigues that were conspicuously visible in this international council. Indian leaders were upset and regretted their decision to approach the UN. According to Iqbal Singh,[3] "Mountbatten, in his Report of Governor-General writes that Nehru told him that he now bitterly regretted going to the UN."

Pandit Jawaharlal Nehru said that he was shocked to find that power politics and not ethics was ruling the UN organisation and was convinced that it was being completely run by the Americans. Senator Warren Austin had made no bones of his sympathy for the Pakistan cause. He thought that the UN did not intend to deal with the issue on its merits but merely to help Pakistan against India. He said that he thought that Philip Noel-Baker, the British diplomat, had been nearly as hostile to India as Senator Warren Austin, except that he had been more polite and had wrapped up his phrases in careful language. The British complicity in favour of Pakistan also became known to Indian leaders. Prem Shankar Jha says,[4] "The correspondence in the India Office Records Library shows that Britain not only expected, but wanted Kashmir to accede to Pakistan. It tried its best to persuade India not to accept the Maharaja's accession even when the raiders were a bare 17 miles from Srinagar. When Kashmir did accede to India, it did all it could to keep the doors open for the decision to be reversed. This makes it possible to understand Britain's stand on the accession, and the position it took in the UN Security Council over Kashmir, which caused great hurt to Pandit Nehru and poisoned Indo-British relations in the fifties and sixties."

The British preference for Muslims and consequently for Muslims of Kashmir started from the day Maharaja Pratap Singh was enthroned as king of Kashmir on September 15, 1855. The British started forcing the Maharaja to accept the stationing of a British Resident in the State.

During Maharaja Hari Singh's rule, the Punjabi Muslims in Lahore started vigorously propagating against the Maharaja.The Kashmiri Muslim religious leaders and landlords presented a list to the Viceroy of India for the redressing of their grievances against the Maharaja. Many young Muslims from Kashmir, who went to Aligarh like Sheikh Abdullah for higher education, came in contact with fanatic Muslim leaders who had plans of organising a 'Pan-Islamic Movement'. These fanatic Muslim organisations had the tacit support of the British Government. Curiously enough, when Maharaja Hari Singh gave the district of Gilgit on lease to the British Indian Government for 60 years, all the restrictions on the Maharaja's administration were relaxed and the Muslim Communal organisations were disregarded.

Why were Britain and America keen that Kashmir should go to Pakistan? The answer according to Prem Shankar Jha is,[5] "The real reason was that Britain had assigned a place to Pakistan in its strategic design, and Pakistan's possession of Kashmir was an integral part of it. This becomes apparent as one follows British reactions to the development of the Kashmir crisis."

Perhaps today the Anglo-US groups who had opposed Kashmir's accession to India may be feeling thankful for the Indian Government's consistency in resisting the undue pressure from them. According to *Times of India News* dated 15 April 2008,[6] "Washington now appears to have come out in the open about a country that has long being described by many analysts as the most dangerous place on the earth and the ground zero of world terror." Further it said, "The latest attempt to get a fix on Pakistan's nuclear assets is the 12th in a series of demands aimed at establishing greater US oversight on what many commentators see as a dangerously unstable country."

India faces partisanship at United Nations Security Council

It has been already stated that India approached UNSC with a complaint against Pakistan's aggression in Jammu and Kashmir. India's complaint under S-628 was formally admitted to the UNSC agenda at its 226th meeting held in New York on January 6, 1948. Allowing Pakistan's request for adjournment, the next date for the debate on this complaint was fixed for January 15, 1948. M C Setalvard was designated as representative of India, and Mohammad Zaffarulla Khan was the representative of Pakistan. For the main debate India deputed N Gopalaswami Ayyengar, former Prime Minister of Jammu and Kashmir and a Minister without portfolio in the Central M C Setalvard, the Attorney General of India, and Sheikh Abdullah, the Chief Emergency Officer in Kashmir as an alternative to Ayyengar. On 15 January 1948, the Security Council heard Ayyengar, who explained Pakistan's aggression in Kashmir. On January 16, 1948, Mohammad Zaffarulla Khan spoke and on January 17, 1948, Ayyengar replied to what Khan had said. He also explained that when India failed to make Pakistan see reason, due to her intransigence and lack of cooperation, India approached the Security Council for justice.

The first Security Council resolution was brought on January 17, 1948 by Van Langenhoven, representative of Belgium, which was not acceptable to Andrei Gromyko, Russian representative to UN, who said, "We think that this question should be studied in greater detail and that a resolution should be adopted as soon as possible on the substance of the question, in order to rectify and improve the situation in Kashmir and to settle relations between India and Pakistan."

From the Security Council proceedings it was found that India had to face stiff antagonism and hostility from some members and much partisan treatment from the Anglo-American group even though Pakistan had committed blatant aggression against Jammu and Kashmir State.

There was a flurry of resolutions submitted by various members that smacked of partisanship, and thus, were not accepted by India. For instance, a resolution was submitted by the representative of Belgium supported by China, Colombia, UK and USA and accepted by the Security Council at its 286th meeting held on 21st April, 1948. The resolution was regarding ceasefire of the fighting in Kashmir. The relevant excerpts are:

> "Being strongly of the opinion that the early restoration of peace and order in Jammu and Kashmir is essential and that India and Pakistan should do their utmost to bring about a cessation of all fighting;
> Noting with satisfaction that both India and Pakistan desire that the accession of Jammu and Kashmir to India should be decided through the democratic method of a free and impartial plebiscite;
> Considering that the continuation of the dispute is likely to endanger International peace and security."

This resolution was rejected by both India and Pakistan.

On July 8, 1948, during a three-hour meeting with the commission appointed by the Security Council, the Pakistan Foreign Minister, Sir Mohammad Zaffarulla Khan, disclosed that three brigades of the Pakistan army had been engaged in operation in Kashmir since the first week of May 1948. Having said that he further explained that the action had been taken primarily as a measure of self-defence against the spring offensive of the Indian army which constituted a grave threat to the security and defence of Pakistan. Curiously, the Pakistan Government had not brought this fact to the notice of the Security Council as by the time the Pakistan Army was moved into the State the question had been deferred by the council to the commission, which was expected to begin its work any moment. Later, the Pakistan Government made available to the commission a detailed note prepared on April 20 1948 by General Sir Douglas David Gracey, Second Commander-in-Chief of Pakistan, about the military aspects of the Kashmir situation, recommending the moving of the Pakistan army into the State. The Pakistan authorities stressed the fact that it was not their intention to re-conquer the areas captured by the Indian army but to guard their defence line.

The disclosure, to quote Josef Korbel, the Czechoslovakian diplomat "came as a bombshell, a rude shock to the commission". Although officially they did not express any opinion, the members of the commission agreed between themselves that this constituted a material change in the situation from the time the matter was discussed in the Security Council. It also emphasised the need for the commission to apply itself immediately to the task of bringing about a cessation of hostilities between India and Pakistan. The commission flew to New Delhi on July 9, 1948 to begin its discussions with the Government of India. Pandit Nehru informed the UNCIP (UN's Commission for India and Pakistan) that the confession made by Zaffarulla Khan had brought in a material change in the complaint. He insisted that Pakistan must be condemned as an aggressor. The UNCIP passed a resolution on August 13, 1948. The commission also made the appointment of a Plebiscite administrator.

The commission stated in its memorandum dated 26 August 1949:

> "As the two governments (India and Pakistan) are aware, the commission has recognised that neither government has found it possible to give to the truce-terms the unreserved acceptance recognised by the commission. However, the commission subsequently decided to seek to bring about agreement on a cease-fire line through meeting of the military representatives of the two Governments. The commission is highly gratified that these meetings, held in Karachi from 18 to 28 July 1949, resulted in the definition of an agreed cease-fire, thus completing the implementation of part I of the resolution of 18 August 1948."

This way the ceasefire between India and Pakistan came into being. The commission tried to give the Kashmir problem to arbitration but India outright rejected it in a letter dated September 15, 1949. The arbitration was rejected on the plea that the points for arbitration were not clear and accepted by either India or Pakistan.

General Andrew McNaughton Plan, 1949 AD

General Andrew McNaughton (Canada's Ambassador to UN) Plan for demilitarisation was submitted on December 22, 1949 to the UN Security Council. He had envisaged UN supervision over the Northern area and its administration and disbandment of militia from there.

Dixon's Plan,1950 AD

On March 14, 1950, the Security Council decided to appoint a UN representative to take over the functions of the UN council regarding India and Pakistan and called upon both countries to prepare and execute, within a period of five months, a program for demilitarisation. The UN representative would help both countries find an expeditious and enduring solution of the dispute over the Kashmir State.

On 12 April 1950, the Security Council appointed Sir Owen Dixon, an eminent Australian jurist, as the UN representative. Sir Owen Dixon was in Sydney, and on 13th April 1950, he left for New York to take charge as the UN representative. On April 26, 1950, he left New York for India via London. On May 27, 1950, he reached New Delhi. By the time he reached Delhi, out of five months, ten weeks had elapsed. On June 1 1950, he left for Karachi to obtain Pakistan's view of the Kashmir problem.

From Karachi, Sir Dixon left for Srinagar and reached there in June 1950. He stayed there till July. During this period he said "My purpose in going to Kashmir was to obtain a knowledge of the country, the people, the topographical features, the ceasefire line, the general disposition of the armed forces on either side of the ceasefire line and also other conditions and circumstances existing in the state which would or might assist in understanding the dispute and possible means of resolving it."

Apart from visiting various towns and districts of the state, Dixon interviewed Sheikh Abdullah more than once. His observation about the administrative structure existing on both sides of the ceasefire line was that Pakistan had two sets of administration—one on the West side administered by Azad Kashmir and one on the Northern side administered by a political agent answerable to Pakistan government. The Indian side of the line was administered by Sheikh Abdullah and his colleagues subject to the Federal System wherein decisions rested with the Indian government in respect of defence and external affairs as obtained by the instrument of accession but safeguarded from unwanted central interference by section 370 of the Indian constitution.

For Dixon, it became a tricky matter when he saw that it was India that had proposed to know the will of the people through a Plebiscite under International supervision. But India felt it necessary to have Indian military present there lest Pakistan should make armed intrusions as they had done previously. Another objection from India was that Pakistan had no locus-standi to be in Kashmir, nor did the Pakistan army, any longer, have any authority to be there during Plebiscite time as Pakistan was the aggressor.

Dixon made an attempt to arrange a meeting between the Prime Ministers of India and Pakistan, which took place at New Delhi on July 20, 1950. It lasted till 24 July, when it came to an end with mutual consent without breaking any ice. India did not accept Pakistan army on the soil of Jammu and Kashmir state. Another objection was why India should be asked to reduce their armed forces in Kashmir which was part of Indian Territory. The only thing the two prime ministers accepted was the ceasefire till the date of plebiscite.

Sir Owen Dixon formulated many alternative proposals but none of them was acceptable to the concerned parties. Nor was any feasible proposal forwarded by India or Pakistan. An area-wise plebiscite was proposed. But Pakistan did not accept this area-wise plebiscite; they wanted the plebiscite for the entire state at one go.

Sir Dixon finally arrived at the solution that the state be partitioned either outright or with partial plebiscite limited to an area which included the valley of Kashmir. He wanted the partition of the State on above mentioned lines. The Indian authorities informed Dixon that the Indian Prime Minister was prepared to meet the Pakistan Prime Minister and discuss with him the possibility of settlement of Kashmir problem based on Dixon's second plan ie Partition and Plebiscite in the valley.

He also agreed to include the Chenab River in the settlement. The Indian demand was:

- There should be a plebiscite in the valley of Kashmir. The area should include part of the Muzaffarabad district to bring in the natural geographical feature provided by the river Kishenganga and its watershed in the North.
- India considered that the following areas should go to her: The province of Jammu east of the ceasefire line, subject to minor corrections; one correction was to reduce the bulge in the ceasefire line near Gulmarg.
- The Tehseels of Ladakh and Kargil, except the area above the Suru River, should go to India or Pakistan, according to the result of the plebiscite in the valley.
- India was willing that the following areas go to Pakistan—the Gilgit Agency, Gilgit Wazarat, political districts and tribal territory of Baltistan and the Jammu province lying to the west of the ceasefire line.

Pakistan, not sure of favourable results of the plebiscite in the valley where the National Conference was more popular than Pakistan, refused to accept this plan and even refused to attend the conference. Their only condition for attending the conference was to transfer the valley of Kashmir to Pakistan without conducting any plebiscite. Seeing no possible solution to the problem, Sir Owen Dixon left Karachi on August 23, 1950 and submitted his report to the UN Security Council on 15 September 1950. His final observation was, "If there is any chance of settling the dispute over Kashmir by agreement between India and Pakistan it now lies in partition and in some means of allocating the valley rather than an overall plebiscite." He was not prepared to recommend any further course of action. "It is perhaps best that initiative should now pass back to the parties," he said. According to the Security Council resolution of March 14, 1950, Admiral Chester William Nimitz of US Navy was appointed as plebiscite administrator, which never took place.

The Security Council appointed Dr Frank Porter Graham as its UN representative as per resolution sponsored by UK and USA, on March 30, 1951 and suggested an arbitration of the dispute. But India rejected any attempt of arbitration. Dr Graham concentrated his efforts to decide the quantum of Armed Forces acceptable to both parties. The Russian delegate, Soviet Ambassador to UN, Yakov Alexandrovich Malik, made on January 17, 1952 a virulent attack on United Kingdom and United States of America. Charging them with interference in the internal affairs of Kashmir and aggressive design to convert it into a military base against USSR, he opposed the continuance of Graham's mission. He further stated that the Anglo-USA interference be avoided and the Constituent Assembly of Kashmir decide the accession of the state. But both UK and USA refuted the charges. Dr Graham's proposal was based on the terms of UN Security Council Resolution dated 13, August 1948.

Commonwealth Premier's efforts, 1951 AD

Pakistan was very dismayed by the failure of Sir Owen Dixon's efforts to resolve the Kashmir problem to the benefit of Pakistan. Meanwhile, Commonwealth Premiers Conference (CPC) was to take place in London in January 1951. Pakistan was very eager to internationalise the Kashmir issue. They insisted that Kashmir accession be raised in that forum.

Pandit Jawaharlal Nehru objected to this. Pakistan was so eager for it that Liyaqat Ali Khan, verbally threatened to boycott the conference. The Kashmir question was raised in the CPC in an informal meeting. Instead of 10, Downing Street, it took place at the Australian Prime Minister's suite at Hotel Savoy. The Australian Prime Minister Robert Menzies, British Prime Minister Clement Attlee, Indian Prime Minister, Pandit Nehru and Pakistan Prime Minister Liyaqat Ali Khan were only present. Pakistan said that plebiscite for the whole of Kashmir was acceptable to it.

The Australian Prime Minister suggested that Sir Dixon's line of approach, of partial plebiscite be accepted. In this informal meeting, Pandit Nehru explained that India did not accept the Two-Nation-Theory—partition on the basis of religion, the founding principle of the Pakistan Movement. He warned that no attempt should be made to upset the existing equilibrium that was slowly and steadily maintained between India and Pakistan. In case they resorted to solve the Kashmir problem on the basis of religion, there would be no plebiscite, but civil upheaval, not only in Kashmir but all over India and Pakistan, particularly in India where there were more Muslims than in Pakistan. He pointed out that India had all along insisted in the UN Security Council that the appeal to religion must be avoided. The meeting came to an end inconclusively. The Kashmir case in UNSC remained in limbo.

The last effort by the United Nations Security Council, 1957 AD

India had complained to the United Nations Security Council (UNSC) about Pakistan's aggression against Kashmir on January 6, 1948. The UNSC took a partisan attitude by treating Pakistan at par with India. India was in Kashmir as a result of the Maharaja's accession to India as required in India's Independence Act. However, after nine years, on January 16, 1957, the UNSC met to deliberate on the Kashmir problem to see if any solution came, particularly from India. The Indian Prime Minister, on March 29, 1955, announced in the Indian Parliament that, "Pakistan is out of court." Since Pakistan did not honour UNSC resolution of August 13, 1948, under which the withdrawal of their forces and and of Pakistani raiders from the State of Jammu and Kashmir did not take place during the period of nine years, there would be no plebiscite.

India declares Kashmir as its integral part, 1957 AD

Govind Vallab Pant, the Home Minister of India, in his public meeting in Srinagar declared that, "Kashmir is an integral and irrevocable part of India." Also, the Kashmir Constituent Assembly on 17 November 1956, ratifying the accession of the State with India declared that from 26 January 1957, the State of Jammu and Kashmir would be an integral part of India.

However, UNSC appointed on February 1957, Gunnar Jarring, a Swedish diplomat, to examine if there could be any possibility of settlement of Jammu and Kashmir State between India and Pakistan. When the proceedings were discussed in the UNSC, the Soviet delegate attacked UK-USA for their interference and "Vetoed" the resolution sponsored by Australia, Cuba, United Kingdom and United States of America on February 20, 1957. The resolution suggested the deputation of a temporary UN Force in Kashmir. Gunnar Jarring again suggested arbitration which was not acceptable to India.

Tirade against Maharaja

As stated earlier, Sheikh Abdullah, while in Lahore for his studies, was mesmerised by the venomous campaigns unleashed by the Muslim Press of Lahore during the twenties and thirties against the Hindu Maharaja. The copies of those newspapers were distributed in thousands. They contained anti-Hindu sentiments wherein the Muslims of the valley were asked to join the Jihad to save Islam. On 21 June 1931, a Muslim named Abdul Qadir delivered a violent speech inciting the Muslims to massacre Hindus. Many Hindus were killed, their shops looted, and houses gutted by the violent Muslim mobs. Muslim leaders sympathised with the man who was arrested by the government for sedition. Later on, most of the Muslim leaders including Sheikh Abdullah were also arrested.

According to Mridu Rao,[7] "Under such prompting, Kashmiri Muslims led by Sheikh Abdullah had refused to meet with the Maharaja on 6th August 1931, aiming to 'procrastinate' until 14 August which had been declared 'Kashmir Day' throughout Mohamadian centres in British India by the Kashmir Committee formed only a week after the killings of 13 July, 1931. This was an early instance of the reliance Sheikh Abdullah had begun to place on the Ahmediyas, who were prominent in the Kashmir Committee, in his struggles against not only the Dogra-Hindus but also against the Kashmiri Muslim elite led by the then Mirwaiz-i-Jama Masjid, Yusuf Shah."

It can be said with certainty that Sheikh Abdullah was influenced, rather convinced, by the Punjabi Muslim propaganda to sacrifice everything for the cause of Islam. But surprisingly, he was never in favour of using violence to achieve the objective. Perhaps, instinctively, he followed the age-old tradition of composite culture advocated by venerable saints like Lall-Ded and Noor-ud-Din whose sayings preached composite culture of Hindu-Muslim love. Mridu Rao says,[8] "The votaries of Kashmiriyat never lost sight of their religious affinities, nor were these deemed incompatible with regionally shared culture."

In 1944, the National Conference adopted its manifesto containing a program for the state and named it *Naya Kashmir*. This manifesto was based on the pattern of Parliamentary democracy with independent judiciary. Apart from some of the notable and laudable features of this manifesto, it gave the Maharaja solemn assurance that he would continue to exercise the right of general control over the administration of the state.

Some excerpts from *Naya Kashmir* are as follows

> The ruler of Jammu and Kashmir shall:
> - Convene sessions of the National Assembly twice a year; shall convene extraordinary sessions of the Assembly at his own wish or at the request of the speaker of the Assembly, and
> - Dissolve the National Assembly and fix new elections
> - Conduct a referendum upon his own initiative or upon the demand of the majority of the legislators
> - Declare general or partial mobilization
> - Ratify international treaties after the national Assembly has approved them
> - Summon the leader of the largest single party in the national Assembly to form the ministry.

On 22nd July 1944, Maharaja Hari Singh returned from his European tour. The Muslim leaders of the National Conference were very eager to participate in the public reception to express their loyalty to the Maharaja. They raised slogans like "Maharaja Bahadur Zindabad."

In 1944, Maharaja Hari Singh decided to include in his cabinet two popular Ministers from the Praja Sabha (elected members of the Kashmir Assembly), as goodwill for the people of the state, and two from the National Conference. Sheikh Abdullah and his deputy Mirza Afzal Beg joined the Maharaja's cabinet. It is true that the elected members were handicapped by the administrative non-cooperation and indifference shown to them by state administrators. But that should not have been the cause for Sheikh Abdullah to withdraw his deputy from the cabinet. Mirza Afzal Beg resigned on 17 March 1946. The decision irritated the administration and even some National Conference members. In the words of Pran Chopra, a former Chief Editor of *The Statesman* and a recognised political analyst who wrote in an article,[9] "Sheikh Abdullah was full of faults—impatience, arrogance, vanity—complexities which made him seem unpredictable, even unreliable." Sheikh Abdullah's unpredictable behaviour appeared in the open. On one hand he had hailed the Maharaja when he returned from abroad, but in his public addresses he provoked the masses to rebel.

Says Prem Nath Bazaz,[10] "Sheikh Abdullah and many of his followers have been arrested following a series of speeches delivered by him and members of his party during the last two weeks. In these speeches, people were incited to destroy the existing Government, to repudiate allegiance to 'His Highness' and force him to quit Kashmir. Unmentionable abuse was heaped upon the person of his highness and the ruling family." Sheikh Abdullah was arrested. When he had accepted Maharaja Hari Singh's accession of the state of Jammu and Kashmir to India, a very feeble protest from some Muslim Conference leaders aroused the valley's common, innocent, illiterate, Muslim community to accept the Sheikh's choice by saying in Kashmiri, *'Ye Kari Ti Kari Bub'* meaning'whatever he (Sheikh Abdullah) does let him do, he is the father'. Such was the blind loyalty of Kashmiri Muslims towards him.

Meanwhile, on the international political front, many things were changing. During the Second World War, Japan joined Germany in 1941 against the Allies. Japan's victorious armies captured the countries of South-East Asia. They captured Burma and threatened India. In order to please the people of India, in March 1942, the British government sent Sir Stafford Cripps, the leader of the House of Commons, with certain proposals, which came to be known as 'Cripps Plan'. The Cripps Plan was not acceptable to India and Mahatma Gandhi recommended the "Quit India" movement be launched. All India Congress Committee passed the 'Quit India resolution' on 8th August 1942.

The political situation in India during the Quit India movement was most distressing for the British government. In 1945 AD, in a general election in the United Kingdom, the Labour Party came to power. Clement Richard Attlee became the Prime Minister. He sent a mission of three members to India to solve the constitutional tangles which came to be called the 'Cabinet Mission' of 1946. The mission's task was to bring the political parties of India to an agreement for:

- framing of constitution for self-governing, independent India
- setting up of an executive council or interim government till the formation of the constitution.

But the mission did not succeed in bringing reason to the political parties.

Sheikh Abdullah thought it an opportune time to dent the Dogra rule in the state. He, along with his deputy Afzal Beg, left for Delhi to seek an audience with the members of the Cabinet Mission to implore them to abrogate the Treaty of Amritsar, which was signed on 16th March 1846 between Maharaja Gulab Singh and the British Government. According to this treaty, the British Government transferred and made over for ever independent possession to Maharaja Gulab Singh and his heirs all the mountainous country and the territory of Kashmir State. The Cabinet Mission did not bother to concede to the Sheikh Abdullah's request. This is mentioned in the book *My Frozen Turbulence of Kashmir* by Jagmohan,[11] "As the mission is at the moment reviewing the relationship of Princes with the Paramount Power with reference to treaty rights, we wish to submit that for us in Kashmir re-examination of this relationship is a vital matter because a hundred years ago in 1846, land and people of Kashmir were sold away to servitude of Dogra House by British for seventy-five Lakhs of Sikh rupees equivalent to fifty Lakhs of British Indian rupees. As such, case of Kashmir stands on unique footing, and people of Kashmir press on their unchallengeable claims to freedom on withdrawal of British power from India."

Frustrated and annoyed at the disinterested attitude of the mission he launched the 'Quit Kashmir' movement on May 10, 1946. Writes Jagmohan,[12] "On May 10, 1946, the National Conference, under the leadership of Sheikh Mohammad Abdullah, launched the 'Quit Kashmir' movement."

According to Vivek Chadha,[13] "Sheikh Abdullah had still not given up on the idea of Kashmir's independence. He pursued this cherished goal surreptitiously, secretly negotiating with US leaders to gauge the level of international support for, and feasibility of, his proposals. His meeting with Adlai Stevenson in May 1953 in Srinagar was viewed with alarm. As reported by *Manchester Guardian*, Stevenson had stated that the best status for Kashmir could be independence both from India and Pakistan."

However, Pran Chopra does not agree with this view. He says,[14] "Suddenly his standing was undermined by a rumour that when Adlai Stevenson called on him in Srinagar in the summer of 1953, he had offered Kashmir as a base for American operations against the Soviet Union in exchange for recognition of Kashmir as an independent state. The rumour mongers forgot that even at the height of the suspicion against Abdullah, he stood by the limited accession he himself had accepted and opposed only, but openly, the creeping expansions of it, which had been brought about by his successors. This he affirmed repeatedly to me."

Sheikh Abdullah's agenda

On 5th March 1948, the emergency administration headed by him was converted into a full fledged cabinet system on the pattern of Parliamentary democratic system with the maharaja as the constitutional head. He was conscious that the people of the valley depended on him. He was now being described as the 'Messiah' of the people of Kashmir. Some historians say that he wanted to see the valley of Kashmir as an independent Muslim country and earn glorifying praises from the entire Muslim-world for creating another Islamic country in the Pan-Islamic Commune. In this connection says Prem Nath Bazaz,[15] "It is true Abdullah occasionally stated that the alternative before the State people was not accession to India or Pakistan but they could also think of a third possiblity—to remain independent."

The real programme of this National Conference was what they had said to Jinnah, the President of Indian Muslim League. Jinnah, while speaking at Jama Masjid in Srinagar, on 14th June, 1944 and on June 17, 1944, said, "The (Muslim) leaders of National Conference have assured me that the National Conference is the party of the Muslims; that their goal, policy and programmes are the same as that of the Muslim Conference; that they fight for the welfare of the Muslims and that if the State Hindus and Sikhs co-operate with them well and good, if not they do not mind."[16]

Maharaja Hari Singh was distressed on account of the political jugglery of Sheikh Abdullah. He felt absolutely humiliated by his behaviour. Writes M L Gupta,[17] "Exasperated by the aggressive attitude of the Sheikh, Maharaja Hari Singh sent a letter to the Indian Home Minister Sardar Patel on Jan. 31, 1948 in which he expressed the following feelings, 'There is an alternative possible for me and that is to withdraw the Accession which may kill even the reference to UNO. The result may be a return to the position the State held before accession'.

It is surprising that even Pandit Jawaharlal Nehru sided with Sheikh Abdullah in his tirade against the Maharaja.[18] In another letter of May 6, 1949, to Sardar Patel, Maharaja Hari Singh wrote, "Nor would it be fair on my part to conceal, from you my own feelings that while

Sheikh Abdullah has been allowed, to depart from time to time as suited his inclinations from the pledges and written words, to act consistently in breach of the loyalty which he professed to me prior to his release from Jail and the oath of allegiance which he took when he assumed office..."

The Indian leaders were busy settling the issues of the other states. Therefore, they thought it best to leave the decision and settlement of problems of Kashmir to Jawaharlal Nehru. Nehru's intense interest in Kashmir affairs was another reason for the Indian leaders not to interfere in it. However, Nehru's aversion for the Dogra rulers was unexplainable. According to Maroof Raza,[19] "Nehru's passion for Kashmir was in contrast to the matter-of-fact and realistic attitude of Sardar Patel, who had mentally written off Kashmir following the logic of communal-country divide. Nehru had not." When there was no response and reaction from the leaders of the Government of India, the Maharaja felt belittled and shamed. In 1949, he transferred all powers to his son Yuvaraj Karan Singh and left for Bombay, with the view 'never to return' even to Jammu, his homeland.

Socio-Political conditions in the State

In 1948, the National Conference took the state's administration in their hands by forming their Ministry under Sheikh Sahib's prime ministership. The economic, political as well as social conditions of the people of the state had deteriorated. The raiders, accompanied by Pakistani soldiers in plain clothes, who had created turbulence in the state had shattered the entire economic structure of the state. Even prior to the raid , the Pakistan Government had stopped the movement of essential commodities from Punjab to the State and the movement of Kashmiri products from the State to pass through Pakistan territory. As a result, trade and commerce were crippled in Kashmir. The prices of essential commodities had risen sky-high. One kg of rock salt would cost people fifty rupees. This entire situation arose on account of the dislocation of import and export trade routes from Pakistan.

Realising this, the Government of India took immediate steps to widen the BC Road, (the only exit route for the people of the valley), constructed new highways with very long bridges , not only up to Jammu but also on Jammu Pathankot Highway, making a reliable and permanent link of the state with the rest of India. It was really one of the marvels of

Indian Roads Constructing Organisation(Border Roads). The Banihal Pathankot road, particularly the part from Srinagar to Jammu is blocked due to landslides during winter season, on account of heavy snowfall or heavy downpour. But with the constant vigil of the engineers, the roads have improved considerably and the surge of traffic has enhanced.

A considerable number of Kashmiris are engaged in tourism. During summer there is a great influx of tourists from outside the valley and abroad. With the improved roads there is an increase of tourists visiting Kashmir during winter season for winter sports. Rail links have been improved and have been extended from Pathankot to Udhampur. Rail link is also available from Qazigund to rest of the valley, connecting most of its towns. The Government of India is planning to carry the rail link from Jammu right inside the valley.

Other political personalities

Yusuf Shah got appointed as the chief maulvi after the death of his father in October, 1931. Initially, he joined hands with Sheikh Abdullah. The Muslim Conference formed by the Sheikh along with Yusuf Shah had members such as Chaudhri Ghulam Abbas, Mirza Afzal Beg, GM Sadiq etc. Soon, serious difference arose between Sheikh Abdullah and Yusuf Shah. Sheikh Abdullah refrained from inciting communal violence against Kashmiri Hindus. Subsequently, Mir Waiz Yusuf Shah and his hardcore Muslim fanatic followers held themselves back from Sheikh Abdullah and his Muslim Conference.

Yusuf Shah was an Islamic scholar but he was not intellectually proficient to face or compete with Sheikh Abdullah's political acumen. The Sheikh was a Quranic scholar while the Muslims led by Yusuf Shah were cobbled together under the barrier of Unitarian Islam. Their differences widened so much that they became political as well as religious adversaries. Young and educated Muslim gentry became Sheikh Abdullah's followers. The traditional Muslims residing around Jama Masjid were the followers of Shah. The tussle for supremacy between them continued for a long time. Many skirmishes took place. Sheikh Abdullah had a clever knack of satisfying the religious yearning of common Muslims. His reputation as an orator grew among the masses. When he addressed a Muslim congregation at Hazrat Bal, which he made this political headquarters , he recited verses from the Holy *Quran* and also explained their contents in Kashmiri language. This gave him tremendous power. Mir Waiz Yusuf Shah could not compete with him. According to Jagmohan ,[20] "During Jinnah's visit, Maulvi Yusuf Shah also came in for some sharp tongue lashing from Jinnah. He described the maulvi as a 'rotten egg'. He also told him 'I advise you to remain aloof from politics. In Kashmir we want a leader and not a Mulla'. That time Mir Waiz was the President of Kashmir Muslim Conference which was revived at Jinnah's visit to the State."

In September 1946, Muslim Conference leaders were arrested in connection with violating prohibition orders of the Government to hold any public meeting. Yusuf Shah, Prof Ishaq and Hamid Ulla ran away to Karachi, primarily to escape detention and also to hold talks with Pakistan leaders. After some time they tried to return to Kashmir but they were not allowed re-entry into the state. Since then, Mir Waiz remained in Pakistan. He made many attempts to re-enter the state and even requested the Kashmir Government. In fact, he felt completely disillusioned and frustrated at seeing events and developments taking place in Pakistan which turned into a military dictatorship.

Minority feels insecure

After Abdul Qadir's violent speech against the infidel Hindu Maharaja and Kashmiri Hindus, in 1931, there had crept a feeling of uncertainty and insecurity among Kashmiri non-Muslims, particularly Kashmir Pandits who are a microscopic minority in the state. The incident had given a very serious jolt to the age-old composite culture. Slowly and gradually, the mutual trust between Hindus and Muslims began waning. The mutual trust and faith between the two communities was so great that a Muslim man could be trusted to escort a newly married Pandit bride, wearing golden ornaments worth thousands, to safety. That trust got a severe jolt.

Formation of Yuvaksabha

A Kashmiri Pandit religious organisation named Yuvaksabha jumped into politics to ensure that the small community of Hindus was not subjected to communal carnage. Later on, this Yuvaksabha was converted into 'All Kashmiri Pandit Conference'. Prem Nath Bazaz was its president and the leader of the organisation was Kashap Bandoo. To begin with, Prem Nath Bazaz and Kashap Bandoo introduced several social reforms among

Kashmiri Pandits`. Kashmiri Pandit women were wearing very complicated 'Taranga' (headgear) and 'Pheran' (a gown). Both these leaders introduced the simple dress of sari—the normal dress of Indian women.

The role of Prem Nath Bazaz

The Pandit community had nominated Prem Nath Bazaz to the Glancy commission. But many of them boycotted the commission, once they found that it was considering the question of Hindu converts right to ancestral property. Prem Nath Bazaz remained a member until the end, and by doing so, he earned his community's wrath. It is noteworthy that he was thinking ahead about the future of Kashmiri Pandits. His warning to the Pandits as well as to Government of India that he made in 1954 AD, about the explosive conditions in Kashmir, came true in the year 1989. He wrote,[21] "It is time that they (Hindus) realise the stern reality that if the dispute is not settled amicably and peacefully between India and Pakistan the internal conditions in the State can in no way improve; indeed they will deteriorate and some day unawares something might happen which will jeopardise the life of the community." These words, written then, were prophetic. Kashmiri Pandits were hounded out of Kashmir and forced to leave their homes and hearths and take refuge outside the valley, reviving the terrible memories of bad times faced by Kashmiri Pandits during the reign of Sikandar Butshikan.

Prem Nath Bazaz wanted Sheikh Abdullah to convert the communal politics into a secular and democratic system. It was because of his reasonable and lucid persuasion that Sheikh sahib accepted to convert the Kashmir Muslim Conference into Kashmir National Conference; by implication it can be stated that he helped Kashmir's Accession to India.

Influenced by the views on religion held by Pandit Nehru and Jinnah, Prem Nath Bazaz used his *Hamdard* newspaper for the cause of democracy, secularism and nationalism. In a reply to his letter dated June 24, 1936, Pandit Nehru wrote to him a letter dated July 7, 1936,[22] "Viewing this larger struggle in true perspective, we see that the communal problem in India, bit as it seems today, is a passing phenomenon. The real issues are national and economic. You see an identical development in other oppressed countries (Egypt, Syria, Palestine etc.) The religious aspect is going into the background and nationalist aspect is becoming far more important and behind it, and influencing it, is the economic urge of the hungry and unemployed or partly employed masses and lower middle classes."

Pandit Nehru further wrote, "In Palestine today the Arabs, both Muslim and Christian are jointly struggling for independence. They are always stressing the fact that theirs is a national struggle and not a religious or a communal one. So also are Syria and Egypt. From this point of view, the communal question in India recedes into the background, important as it is today. All talk of the Pan-Islam and Pakistan is the veriest nonsense. Every single Islamic country has shed this idea and thinks along nationalistic lines. Pan-Islam cannot obviously flourish in north-west India alone. The whole idea is an absurdity but some publicity is given to it by Anglo-Indian newspapers."

Similarly, when Prem Nath Bazaz met Mohammad Ali Jinnah in1944, in Srinagar and wanted his views on religion and communalism, he was given the same views, which Jinnah later spoke on August 14, 1947, addressing the Pakistan Constitution Assembly. "We are starting with fundamental principles that we are all citizens and equal citizens of one state. We should keep that before us as our ideal and you will find that in course of time Hindu would cease to be Hindu and Muslim would cease to be Muslim not in the religious sense because that is personal faith of each individual but in the political sense as citizens of the State."

Soon Prem Nath Bazaz was disillusioned with the activities of Sheikh Abdullah. He began criticising the unhealthy role of the National Conference. For instance, he writes,[23] "The speeches delivered in these congregations were hardly creditable to Abdullah, the sponsor of nationalism. In his characteristically demagogic manner, he attacked Hindu politics, derided Hindu society and contemptuously referred to Hindu religion. In one of these public utterances he made an unwise remark that Islam was the sun and other religions were stars."

Other prominent Kashmiri Pandits

However, after Prem Nath Bazaz left the membership of Yuvaksabha, its working committee members were elected from the lawyer fraternity with the exception of Shiv Narayan Fotedar. Amar Nath Kak, Jia Lal Kilam, Janardan Teng, Shamboo Nath Dhar and Sri Kant Chaku were elected as working committee members. All these members had intellectual maturity and were well educated. Among them, Srikant Chaku was a rational thinker. He was very well read and had attained his Master's Degree in Oriental Philosophy, and Law from Lucknow University.

The problems facing the Hindu community that these Kashmir Pandit leaders wanted to find solutions to:

- Security from the majority community violence against the minority community and the safety of their life and property.
- To secure safety of their womenfolk who unlike Muslim women had come out to secure proper education and employment.
- The criteria for employment to be based only on merit. Since this community was educated and had for thousands of years taken up Government Service that should continue to be provided to them.
- Also, admissions in educational institution be based on merit.

These leaders, in a deputation, met Jawaharlal Nehru who visited the valley in May 1940. The Yuvaksabha apprised Pandit Nehru about their grievances against Sheikh Abdullah's communal politics as well as about their own future, and also safety of their life and property. Nehru advised them that Kashmir Pandits should cooperate with the National Conference. They were also assured that with the passage of time the situation in the state would stabilise and their condition would improve. Pandit Nehru particularly explained to them that their economic problems were not that problematic. Since Kashmiri Pandits were well educated, they could find employment anywhere in India, in the industries that would develop after independence.

Sensing that the National Conference was coming closer to the Indian National Congress, large numbers of Hindus joined it to cooperate and show solidarity with them. Jia Lal Kilam, Chief Justice of High Court of Kashmir, joined the National Conference. Shiv Narayan Fotedar became the Chairman of the Legislative Assembly of the State. Srikant Chaku, an eminent criminal lawyer, was repeatedly elected as Municipal Commissioner of Srinagar Municipal Committee. Slowly, Yuvaksabha, headed by Srikant Chaku, lost it relevance. However, he made a niche for himself by devoting most of his time to the success of Vishva Bharti Institute as its Chairman. This institute was running a High School, a College and a B Ed college, where hundreds and thousands of students got educated. Srikant Chaku expired in 1989 AD. This was the political, social and economic scenario of the State of Jammu and Kashmir when Sheikh Abdullah became its Prime Minister.

By 1939 AD, the international political situation was slowly turning explosive. The crusading idealism of the First World War had given way to nations self seeking aggrandisement, and the peace treaty signed between the Allies and Germany at Versailles, while it brought to many small countries opportunities for political and economic self determination, was so harshly punitive, that it contained within itself a dangerous seed for World War II. In India, the British Government had enacted the Government of India Act 1935 containing instructions for the princes of the Indian States on how to act in the event of India becoming independent and partitioned. In view of the extraordinary situation in India and the world as a whole, Sheikh Sahib thought to convert the Kashmir Muslim Conference into Kashmir National Conference to give it a secular shape in1939. This was his wisest step to modernise the party and with that the people of Kashmir. By this time, his popularity, his reputation and prestige in Kashmir and India had attained a unique place which went to his head. "He could do wonders, provided, he could maintain his clarity of thought, the magnanimity of his heart and boldness in action," laments Prem Nath Bazaz.[24]

Pakistan, after coming into being, wanted to annex Jammu and Kashmir State to it, either by force or by any other means. Sheikh Abdullah had sent a message to Maharaja Hari Singh that he should accede to India. The Maharaja acceded to India in October. 1947. According to a report of October 16, 1948,[25] Sheikh Abdullah said, "The pledge I gave to Pandit Nehru last year that Kashmir will be a part of India has now become an eternal bond. We can never forget the help rendered by Indian army and the people of India at a time of grave crisis in the history of our State." Further, he said, "Our decision to accede to India is based on the fact that our program and policy are akin to those followed by India."

He wanted, if not whole of Jammu and Kashmir, at least the valley, predominantly Muslim populated, to become independent. According to B Krishna's article, appearing in *Kashmir Sentinel*, dated January 31, 2004,[26] "First the alien Maharaja's exile, thereafter independence of his people from India, and finally to become Sheikh in the Sheikhdom, was his ultimate goal." He made good use of Pandit Nehru's weakness for him. He prevailed upon Pandit Nehru and sought his help in ousting Justice Mehar Chand Mahajan from the post of Prime Ministership. He then convinced both Maharaja Hari Singh and Pandit Nehru and prevailed upon them that the National Conference needed to form its own National Government. On March 5, 1948, Sheikh Abdullah became the Prime Minister of Jammu and Kashmir.

Sheikh Abdullah decided not to antagonise Maharaja Hari Singh. According to B Krishna's article in *Kashmir Sentinel*, on January31, 2004, "Abdullah went a step further in assuring the Maharaja in writing; 'In spite of what has happened in the past, I assure Your Highness that my party and I have never harboured any sentiment of disloyalty towards Your Highness's person, throne or dynasty." That was mere pretence to camouflage his hidden aspirations.

Article 370 and its necessity

The decision regarding the provision of Article 370—grant of special autonomous status to Jammu and Kashmir in the Indian Constitution was raised by Sheikh sahib. It was an unattainable and impossible task as long as Sardar Vallahbhai Patel was in charge of the State of Jammu and Kashmir. The Sardar treated Sheikh Abdullah like the leaders of other states of India. Sheikh Abdullah circumvented this in four ways; first by Nehru taking away Kashmir affairs from the States Ministry—and thus out of Patel's hands—placing it under the charge of his yes-man, Gopalaswami Ayyengar. This was his second victory, which paved the way for his third and fourth—sending the Maharaja into an indefinite exile, and securing Kashmir's independence through Article 370 of the Indian Constitution.

"Article 370 (originally Article 306 – A), drafted by Gopalaswami Ayyengar in close consultation with Sheikh Abdullah, proved most controversial, poisoning relations between those who administered the State and the rest of India. It conveyed wrong signals to the valley's Muslims: a 'separate' people within Democratic India. Article 370 was clandestinely manoeuvred by Abdullah with Nehru."[27]

By getting Article 370 included in the Indian Constitution, Sheikh Abdullah had betrayed the trust India had reposed in him, when he had written to Pandit Nehru in 1948, "We have made our choice and linked our destiny with India and nothing can separate us now." Though Sheikh Sahib considered the inclusion of Article 370 as his victory he did not see its side effects. The Indian leaders were shocked to know about it and they began suspecting him of a separatist agenda .

Permit System for Kashmir

With the formation of his government in Kashmir, the National Conference prevailed upon the Government of India for a separate Constitution and separate flag. Introduction of 'Permit System' ie nobody could enter the State or leave it without a permit was yet another step to isolate the state from the rest of India. As all these steps were favouring Sheikh Sahib's agenda, the Indian people began wondering what type of 'accession' Maharaja Hari Singh had made with India; that too on Sheikh Abdullah's persistence and insistence.

The exercise of framing the separate constitution started, to finalise the form of administration of the State, and decide the future of the ruling family. But even before the finalisation of the constitution, the bills regarding future of the Royal family and acquisition of land without payment of compensation were hurriedly passed in the assembly. It passed the abolition of monarchy and decided to have an elected 'Sadar-i-Riyasat'. Sheikh Abdullah did not think it proper to submit the reforms and resolutions passed by the Constituent Assembly to the Maharaja for his signature.

During May 7 to 14, 1952, the National Conference celebrated Independence week from Dogra Rule. During these celebrations, Sheikh Abdullah openly declared in public speeches, "The Dogra Rule is dead and Maharaja has ceased to have any authority," writes Prem Nath Bazaz.[28] Also wrote M L Gupta in his book, *Kashmir A Wailing valley*,[29] "Maharaja Hari Singh had been humbled to such an extent by Sheikh Abdullah and his friend Nehru that he on June 20th 1949, issued a proclamation vesting all the King's powers in his son Yuvaraj Karan Singh and left for Bombay never to return to the State."

After Maharaja Hari Singh's exit from Jammu on June 20, 1949, Sheikh Abdullah came out openly advocating limited accession and subsequently declaring Kashmir as an independent State. States Vivek Chadha,[30] "The rumbling of discontent emerging from the valley, along with demonstration and occasional bomb blast rocked the administration out of their stupor.The writing was well and truly on the wall."

To quote Mohan Kishen Teng,[31] "While the Indian leaders decided to remove Maharaja Hari Singh from the State, Sheikh Mohammad Abdullah threw a bombshell amidst them. In a press conference with Michael Davidson, editor of an influential English newspaper, he pleaded for independence of the State, which he claimed would ensure friendship of the State with both the Dominions and economic cooperation with them."

Similarly, Victoria Schofield writes,[32] "Although overtly Abdullah was loyal to India, he never lost sight of what has become known as 'third option'—that of independence." When he visited the United States as one of India's representatives at the UN in January 1948, he spoke openly in favour of Kashmir's accession to India. But in private, he met Warren Austin, the US representative at the UN. According to a telegram sent to the US secretary of state, Austin reported that Abdullah had been anxious to point out 'that there is a third alternative, namely, independence.' He had not wanted his people torn by dissensions between Pakistan and India. It would be much better if Kashmir were independent and could seek American and British aid for the development of the country. Austin, however, assured the secretary of state: "I, of course, gave Abdullah no encouragement on this line and am confident that when we left he understood very well where we stand on this matter." Sheikh Abdullah's discussion with Louis Anderson, Ambassador to America from 1947 to 1948 AD, about Kashmir becoming an independent country had alarmed the Indian Government, particularly when the Anglo-American lobby favoured the accession of Jammu and Kashmir to Pakistan.

The Indian media gave headlines like "Betrayal of Nehru", "Friendship Squandered" etc. Such reactions from the media did not bother the Sheikh. But the working committee members of the National Conference were taken aback by the Sheikh's outburst against accession to India. They under Bakshi Gulam Mohammad's guidance discussed this new line of politics and Sheikh Abdullah could not convince them as to what prompted him to revise the accession issue. According to

PNK Bamzai,[33] "The whole question was thoroughly discussed in a marathon session of the Working Committee extending to three weeks held in Srinagar in May. Sheikh Abdullah failed to convert the members to his point of view and the resolution endorsing the accession to India and supporting the Delhi Agreement was passed with majority of fifteen against four votes."

Dr Shyama Prasad Mukherji

The Delhi Agreement between India, and State of Jammu and Kashmir was formalised. According to the Agreement, Kashmir was given a special status in the Indian Constitution and complete autonomy was accepted for the state. This was a victory for Sheikh Abdullah.

In Kashmir, people organised themselves in the Praja Parishad under the leadership of Prem Nath Dogra, who started an effective agitation against unreasonable activities of Sheikh Abdullah. The Praja Parishad submitted their charter of demands :

- The Jammu and Kashmir State should be fully integrated in the Indian Union.
- The State should be brought within the constitutional organisation of the Indian Union and the application of the Constitution of India should be extended to the State in its entirety.
- The jurisdiction of the Supreme Court of India should be extended to the State without any reservations.
- The customs barriers between the State and the Indian Union should be abolished.
- The division of powers between the State and the Union should be determined by the Seventh Schedule of the Constitution of India.
- Free and fair elections should be held to the Constituent Assembly of the State.
- An impartial tribunal of enquiry should be instituted to investigate into the corruption charges against the Interim Government.
- In case the State was not fully integrated into the Indian Union and its constitutional relations with the Union continued to be based upon limited accession, Jammu province and Ladakh should be fully integrated with the Indian Union.

The Praja Parishad had affiliation with Bhartiya Jana Sangh, a political organisation, started by Dr Shyama Prasad Mukherji. Dr Mukherji also participated in this agitation. He explained that Sheikh Abdullah was advocating a separate independent Kashmir. India was a federal country consisting of different provinces, with different customs, religions, language, castes, creed and ideology. For all practical purposes, these provinces were enjoying provincial autonomy, under the jurisdiction of the Election Commission, Supreme Court, Comptroller and Auditor General, Defence, Foreign Affairs and Communication.

"If Kashmir has acceded to India why separate flag, separate Constitution, inclusion of Article 370 in the Indian Constitution etc. The introduction of Permit system shows that Kashmir is not a part of India," said Dr Mukherji. He had also alleged, *"Ek desh me do vidhan* (two constitutions), *do pradhan*, (two prime ministers) *aur do nishan*, (two flags), *nahi chalenge* (will not do)," meaning that we cannot tolerate two Constitutions, two Prime Ministers and two Flags in our country. To test Pandit Nehru's statement that Kashmir was hundred percent a part of India, Dr Mukherji decided to enter Jammu without a Permit. He said that as a citizen of India he had the full right to visit any part of the country including Kashmir, which had acceded to India. The people of Jammu, along with the people of India, greeted him with support.

The Deputy Commissioner of Gurdaspur had assured Dr Mukherji that he could enter Jammu province without a permit, but when he crossed over the Jammu border along with his associates in May 1953, the Kashmir Militiamen stopped him on the Ravi Bridge. A Superintendent of Police directed him not to proceed any further into the state. Dr Mukherji refused to accept these directions and subsequently was arrested under the Security Act. Before he was taken away from there, he said in a message to the people of India through Atal Bihari Vajpayee, "I have defied the prohibitory orders and entered into Jammu and Kashmir State, without a permit but in the capacity of a prisoner." This message ignited an upheaval that was already rumbling in the minds of the people of India. Satyagraha started with people coming and courting arrest near the Jammu, Kashmir border. Meanwhile, Dr Mukherji was taken to Srinagar and kept under 'House Arrest' near Nishat Bagh. Unfortunately, on the

43rd day of his detention he was declared dead. On June 23, 1953, Dr Shyama Prasad Mukherji attained martyrdom in fighting separatism of Kashmir advocated by Sheikh Abdullah. In view of the resistance from everyone, the Permit System crumbled and was abolished.

Dr Mukherji, born on July 6, 1901, was the son of an illustrious father Sir Ashutosh Mukherji, the noted educationist and Vice Chancellor of Calcutta University. His mother's name was Smt Jogmaya Devi. After attaining a first class degree in Law he joined Calcutta High Court as an advocate. In the year 1923, he married Sudha Devi. He then went to England to study law and became a Barrister. After a brief practice in the Courts he joined politics and is known as the founding father of Bhartiya Jana Sangha, a political party, now Bhartiya Janata Party.

Demand for separate constitution for Kashmir

Sheikh Abdullah tried to delay the drafting of the Constitution of Jammu and Kashmir. He might have thought that the undertaking of the exercise would be futile as the independence of the state was a few steps away. After attaining independence a new Constitution would have to be shaped. Meanwhile, the government of India started monitoring his activities. His speeches ignited communal passions. They were recorded and analysed. Pandit Jawaharlal Nehru listened to the tapes and was hurt and pained. It was decided to cage the 'Lion of Kashmir'. Nehru had no option left but to give his consent to arrest Sheikh Sahib.

Sheikh Abdullah's arrest

Power and success had gone to Sheikh Sahib's head. He did things without discussing them in the cabinet and without consulting his cabinet colleagues. Many National Conference leaders mistrusted him . Only Mirza Afzal Beg actively supported him. Instead of being anointed as Sultan of Kashmir, Sheikh Abdullah was sent to Kud Prison on August 9, 1953. The immediate cause was that Sheikh Sahib, on August 7, 1953, asked the lone Kashmiri Pandit Minister Shyam Lal Saraf to submit his resignation. Shyam Lal Saraf refused to resign unless the whole cabinet was dissolved and a new government formed. According to PNK Bamzai,[33] "Finally on August 7, the three members, led by Bakshi Ghulam Mohammed, accused Sheikh Abdullah in a memorandum, of making arbitrary decisions, of being responsible for deterioration in the administration, despotism, inefficiency and wanton wastage of public resources. The memorandum informed Sheikh Abdullah that the cabinet had lost the confidence of the people." A copy of this memorandum was submitted to the Sadar-i-Riyasat which suggested an emergency meeting of the cabinet to be held under his presidency wherein the differences would be sorted out and a solution found. Sheikh Abdullah did not accept the suggestions of Sadar-i-Riyasat and in the afternoon of August 8, left on a weekend holiday to Gulmarg.

Sadar-i-Riyasat was faced with a grave threat to the unity, prosperity and stability of the State. No doubt at the instance and support of the Central Government, they issued an order on August 8, 1953, dismissing Sheikh Abdullah from the Prime Ministership of Jammu and Kashmir, and dissolving the council of Ministers headed by him. On August 9, Sadar-i-Riyasat invited Bakshi Ghulam Mohammad to form a new government.

Sheikh Sahib, it seems, had never done any self analysis. He accused everyone, including Pandit Nehru, Sardar Patel, Gopalaswami Ayyengar, D P Dhar, J N Zutshi and many others in his biography *Aatish-e-Chinar*.

Bakshi Ghulam Mohammad as Prime Minister, 1953-1963 AD

On 9 August 1953, Bakshi Ghulam Mohammad took the oath administered by Sadar-i-Riyasat, and assumed prime ministership of Jammu and Kashmir. Immediately after the oath taking ceremony, the new Prime Minister addressed the state on Srinagar Radio for broadcasting his message to the people.

Being a man of practical thinking, he explained to the people that "it was due to exigencies that were confronting the state that necessitated the taking of this unfortunate and painful decision to part with the leader under whom we have worked so long." His theme was that "personalities come and go but when there is question of millions of people's lives at stake, neither personalities nor personal relations have any value." Explaining the geo-strategic position of the state, an Independent Kashmir would become a source of intrigues, violence and physical involvement by all the countries that surrounded the state. If that happened the state would be involved in international conspiracies, that would turn the state into a battleground. He explained to the listeners that, "India has constructed a democratic and secular constitution and is now a Federal Republic consisting of various provinces with full provincial autonomy. These states, with diverse castes, religion, customs and languages enjoy full freedom. For Kashmir, a special provision has been provided in Indian Constitution by inserting Article-370, which guarantees us perfect freedom." Explaining about economic conditions of the farmers, Bakshi Sahib said, "Our agrarian reforms, though sound on principle, do not seem to have aroused the enthusiasm of the masses and the cooperative movement which might have inspired the people towards voluntary efforts for the reconstruction of our national economy have become a symbol of tyranny in the courtyard."

He assured the people of the remedial steps his government would take to ameliorate the hardships of the people. He declared the abolition of 'Mujvaza' (levy) forthwith. He declared the price of paddy at Rupees two per 'Khirwar' (80 Kg), and opening of cooperative and competitive essential commodities retail shops where subsidised essential items would be available to the people. He declared free education up to Masters Degree to the people. He assured people of the abundant availability of goods at reasonable prices. During Sheikh Sahib's administration, Ladakh was virtually ignored. But Bakshi Sahib made it a point to take care of the people of Ladakh. He made Kushak Bakula, the Buddhist Lama of Ladakh, a Deputy Minister of the State.

After Sheikh Abdulla's dismissal, the majority of his cabinet colleagues joined Bakshi sahib who took them in his cabinet. According to Prem Nath Bazaz,[34] "It was not surprising therefore that most of those men who had seemingly supported throughout summer the line adopted by Abdullah promptly changed sides immediately after the Lion of Kashmir had been put inside the cage at Udhampur. The desertion was unseemly no less than an eye-opener. Those prominent nationalists unabashedly raised full throated slogans to support Bakshi." Feeling fully secure of the cooperation from people who mattered, Bakshi sahib expanded his cabinet giving representation to all sections of the people. His cabinet ministers were: Gulam Mohammad Sadiq (Education), Girdhari Lal Dogra (Finance), Mir Qasim (Revenue), Sham Lal Saraf (Development).

Seeing the wholehearted support of the people of the state including the members of Kashmir Constituent Assembly, Bakshi Sahib called the session of the Constituent Assembly in the first week of October, 1953. On 5 October 1953, out of 74 members, 60 were present. The assembly recorded, "its deep appreciation for the timely action taken by Sadar-i-Riyasat by its order dismissing Sheikh Mohammad Abdullah and "thereafter inviting Bakshi Gulam Mohammad to form the Government." The Assembly assured its full support to Bakshi Sahib and expressed full confidence in his government. It unanimously passed the resolution confirming the Accession of the State of Jammu and Kashmir to the Republic of India on February 6, 1954.

During Bakshi Sahib's rule, people, by and large, were fully satisfied with the way the new administration was working. Food was in abundance and even people below the poverty line could afford to purchase it. The whole state was humming with satisfaction. When he saw the hoarders and black-marketers doing their mischief, he administered a strong warning to them, to sell all commodities at reasonable prices else he would deal with them harshly. Prem Nath Bazaz wrote,[35] "The new Prime Minister of the State introduced reforms that could catch imagination."

Bakshi Sahib earned praise from all quarters. Dag Hammarskjold, Secretary General of the UN, while praising him said, "Kashmir has conquered our hearts and you, Bakshi Ghulam Mohammed, have contributed most to this conquest." Pandit Nehru said, "Situations throw up a man to deal with them and the great Prime Minister of Kashmir, Bakshi Ghulam Mohammed is a person who has undoubtedly shown quite remarkable qualities of organisation and leadership." Writes Jagmohan,[36] "Bakshi Ghulam Mohammad was an effective administrator. He firmly dealt with the disturbances following Sheikh Mohammad Abdulla's detention. In these disturbances 70 persons lost their lives." He further writes,[37] "Bakshi Ghulam Mohammad understood that to build a workable relationship between the Union and the State, closer constitutional links had to be forged between the two. He put an end to the obstructive attitude of the State Government in regard to the implementation of the Delhi Agreement."

The Special Correspondent of *Sunday Times London* wrote, "A four-day tour of the Kashmir valley in company with the Prime Minister, Ghulam Mohammed Bakshi, brought home to me the notable change since I last visited Kashmir two years ago. The Prime Minister moved unescorted among crowds who garlanded him, and peasants showered lumps of sugar, signifying a sweet welcome, on his car while everywhere there were shouts of "long live Bakshi Sahib" and women sang, "Our bread-winner has come". The *Manchester Guardian London* commented that the relations between Bakshi Ghulam Mohammed, Prime Minister of Kashmir and his people are unique in India.

Bakshi Ghulam Mohammad, remembered as the 'Architect of Modern Kashmir', was born in 1907. He did his schooling fromTyndale Biscoe School at Srinagar. He started his career as a school teacher in far-flung area of Skardu in Ladakh. He then took service in the Kashmir branch of All India Spinners Association. In 1927, he joined Sheikh Abdullah in his struggle to secure civic and political rights of Muslims of the State.

Bakshi Sahib ruled over the State for eleven years. He proved an able administrator and is remembered by people of all regions and religions of Kashmir. He was popular among all communities—Kashmiri Pandits, Dogras and Muslims—who fondly remember him as a real secular Prime Minister and architect of modern Kashmir. Meanwhile, in 1955, Sheikh Abdullah's followers started a new organisation and named it 'Plebiscite Front'. They intimidated the Central Government by supporting plebiscite in the State. This organisation made a very effective and stiff challenge to Bakshi Sahib's government. Bakshi Sahib, being a shrewd personality, could withstand the political onslaught , and remained in the Prime Minister's chair until 1964. His personal style was a combination of excellent administrative skill, exemplary courage, robust commonsense, ready wit and compassion.

In 1963, the Indian National Congress introduced the 'Kamaraj Plan' under which all Congress governed Chief Ministers were asked to submit their resignation to the Congress President Pandit Nehru. Bakshi Sahib also submitted his resignation, which was finally accepted and he had to head the opposition to the Sadiq Government. The same year, a majority of legislative members provoked him to move a vote of no-confidence against the Sadiq government, but before he could do so he was arrested and detained under Defence of India Rules. He was later released on health grounds.

Bakshi Ghulam Mohammad was not without faults. Kashmiri Pandits believed he was pro-Muslim. Their grouse against him was that he would go out of the way to help Muslims. For instance, the State Public Service Commission, functioning under Chairmanship of General Yadava Nath Singh, conducted the first Kashmir Civil Service Examination for the selection of the candidates to fill up the slots in the State Administration. Not a single Muslim candidate could pass the test and those who were cleared for appointments were Hindus. But Bakshi Sahib subverted the Kashmir Civil Service recommendations and that became the general trend when it came to helping the Muslim candidates.

His cabinet ministers like Sayed Mir Qasim and Ghulam Mohammad Sadiq were also not happy with the treatment he gave to Sheikh Abdullah. Syed Mir Qasim writes,[38] "One day, Mr Sadiq and I were in Gandhi Nagar, Jammu, when Bakshi suddenly appeared from nowhere. We pleaded with him not to spurn all the opportunities of reconciliation with Sheikh Sahib. He replied, 'You have taken a wrong stand. I must make it clear to you that firstly Sheikh Abdullah will never reform himself; secondly, even if he does , it will be political illusion, and I do not want to see that'. Bakshi Sahib then took out a letter for us to see. It was addressed to one Ghulam Rasool of Pakistan. The letter said: 'We are sending you a pair of scissors and other implements for pruning trees. Do good pruning in the garden with these implements.' Bakshi read in it a conspiracy to assassinate some of us." At another place, he writes, "Our differences with Bakshi Saheb had started while we were working hard on drafting the Constitution. He was losing trust in us. He was suspecting me, Sadiq, D P Dhar and Dogra Saheb of plotting against him. The same complex had overtaken Sheikh Sahib before his fall. The loss of confidence had made both unreasonable, authoritarian and suspicious of colleagues." He also writes, "Our differences with Bakshi Sahib had started in 1955 when we began to realise that he was taking the State to the very inhuman and tyrannical conditions which characterised the Maharaja's rule before 1947. There was full freedom to indulge in corruption and anti-social activities but no freedom to breathe as a law-abiding citizen."

Sheikh Abdullah in his biography, *Aatish-e-Chinar,* has a caption, 'Bakshi Brothers Corporation'. He writes that Bakshi sahib with his brothers amassed great wealth and was asked to explain the source of this wealth by the Ayyengar commission.

As per Prem Nath Bazaz,[39] "Bakshi has become notorious for his atrocious behaviour as the Deputy Prime Minister (during Sheikh Abdullah's Prime Ministership) in charge of law and order. He is a scowling, big shouldered, six foot bully who is frequently seen with a danda (stick) in his hand. He has publicly belaboured, insulted and disgraced persons who disagreed with him."

According to Jagmohan,[40] the coterie around Bakshi Ghulam Mohammad built a system of personal and political patronage and indulged in gross nepotism and corruption. He further states, "The tempo of hostility against him and his supporters increased and this found expression in what is known as the Moe-e-Muqaddas—theft of the hair of Prophet Mohammad—the Holy Relic."

In 1967, he stood for parliament membership and his popularity was so remarkable that he defeated the ruling Congress candidate by a big margin. He remained a member of the Lok Sabha till 1971. By this time his health had deteriorated to a great extent. He expired in July 1972, leaving behind the foundation of modern Kashmir and vast goodwill among the people.

Khwaja Shamsuddin, 1963-1964 AD

Bakshi Gulam Mohammad resigned from the Prime Ministership of Kashmir on 12 October 1963. In his place his crony Khwaja Shamsuddin was made the Prime Minister. Though he remained in office only for four months till February 1964, an extraordinary event took place that shook the entire valley. It was the theft of the Holy relic *Moi-Muqaddas* which disappeared on December 27, 1963.

Mischief with the Holy Relic

This Holy relic of Prophet Mohammad was enshrined at the Hazratbal Mosque in Srinagar. It was on a cold morning of December 27, 1963, that it was found missing from its place in the mosque. The news of the loss of the Holy relic spread like wildfire. The window of the room where it was kept was broken. The news plunged the whole valley into grief, anguish and anger. The people felt that doomsday was near. There were violent processions all around. Kothi Bagh Police Station and Bakshi Sahib's cinema house was set ablaze.

The administration of the state, headed by Khwaja Shamsuddin, was benumbed. Not knowing what to do and how to find it, he sought the help of the Central Government. The Government of India realised the significance and urgency of the matter. They sent a team of Intelligence Officers from Delhi to help the Kashmir Police trace the Holy relic. The Central Intelligence Officers believed that someone from the Mosque itself stole it. They advised the mosque be kept without guard so that the thief would replace the relic. The Hazratbal Shrine was kept without watch up till January 1964. As expected, on January 4, 1964, the Holy relic was replaced. Sayed Mir Qasim writes,[41] "This was an intelligence operation, never to be disclosed. Later when G M Sadiq became Chief Minister in 1964, we asked B N Mullick (Director, Central Bureau of Investigations) but he replied: 'This secret will remain with me till my death. One person came to talk to me in private. He disclosed who stole the relic. I recorded his statement'." After this episode, Khwaja Shamsuddin had to vacate the chair of Prime Minister for Gulam Mohammad Sadiq.

The genuineness of the relic was certified by Sayyid Mirak Shah who headed a team of fifteen divine Muslim cleric. The State and Central Governments heaved a sigh of relief. But till date the mystery of removing and bringing it back has not been disclosed. According to Syed Mir Qasim,[42] "the theft of the Holy Relic was an act of the conspirators who believed that without generating an anti-Government religious movement, they could not achieve their political objective in Kashmir. The people of Kashmir are deeply religious, but not communal."

Moi-e-Muqaddas, the Holy Relic

According to Giriraj Shah,[43] "The Holy Relic (Moi-e-Muqaddas) kept in a gold-embroidered bag in a walnut box is a single hair of Prophet Mohammad, said to have been brought to India by Sayyid Abdullah, who claimed to be a descendant of the prophet, some 350 years ago." Sayyid Abdullah was living in Medina. He was Chief Keeper of the mosque in Medina where the relic was kept. There arose a family feud and he had to flee from his house. However, he travelled from Medina to India and settled in Bijapur. The Sultan of Bijapur understood the value of the relic. He offered him a place to live peacefully along with his family. After a stay of about 20 years, he died. His son Sayyid Hameed inherited the relic. Sayyid Hameed was spending his days in abject poverty. One day, a Kashmiri trader by the name of Noor-ud-Din Ishbari visited him. Sayyid Hameed gave the Holy relic to Noor-ud-Din Ishbari, with the request that it to taken to Kashmir. Noor-ud-Din promised to do so.

It was the time when Aurangzeb invaded Bijapur. He came to know about the Holy relic. He ordered the arrest of Noor-ud-Din who by then had left Bijapur to travel to Kashmir via Lahore. When Noor-ud-Din reached Lahore, he was imprisoned there. Thus the relic passed on to Aurangzeb, who in turn, decided to enshrine it with Khwaja Moinuddin Chisti at Ajmer.

The legend: One day Prophet Mohammad appeared in Aurangzeb's dream and advised him that the relic should go to Kashmir. When he woke up, he instantly issued orders for the release of Noor-ud-Din from the prison. Alas! It was too late as Noor-ud-Din was dead by that time. Nonetheless, the holy relic was sent to Kashmir along with the exhumed body of Noor-ud-Din. According to Syed Mir Qasim,[44] "The holy relic reached Shupiyan in Kashmir along with the exhumed body of Noor-ud-Din in AD 1700. It was kept in a place, which is now known as the Hazratbal Shrine. The descendents of Noor-ud-Din alone had the right to exhibit the relic on special occasions. These descendants are now known as Nishan Deh." Inayat Begum, the daughter of Noor-ud-Din Ishbari became the first custodian of the holy relic.

Release and rearrest of Sheikh Mohammad Abdullah

Sheikh Sahib was in prison for five years. Pandit Nehru was not happy at his incarceration. He had developed a friendly relationship with him. Prison life did not soften Sheikh Sahib; invariably he would express rage over being implicated by his adversaries and enemies. From prison itself he came out openly against Kashmir accession to India by asking Mirza Afzal Beg, his trusted follower, to intimidate the Central Government by establishing a new political party with the name 'Plebiscite Front'. The Central Government had discarded the Plebiscite plan due to Pakistan's refusal to comply with the UN Security Council's resolution of August 13, 1948. However, It took a very lenient view of this Plebiscite Party. The Kashmir Government under Bakshi Sahib allowed this new political party to launch itself with full propaganda. The front, therefore, tore off the secular mask put on by Sheikh Sahib and the party began advocating Muslim interest in Kashmir. They never talked about the difficulties the other people of Kashmir faced.

Because of Pandit Nehru's disapproval of keeping Sheikh Abdullah in prison, the two Cabinet Ministers of the State, namely, Syed Mir Qasim and G M Sadiq began openly advocating Sheikh Abdullah's release. As per Syed Mir Qasim,[45] "In 1958 we began to openly demand Sheikh Sahib's release. Bakshi sahib, shrewd as he was, would not let Sadiq or me take the credit for the release. Therefore, before our campaign for his release could gather momentum, he (Bakshi Gulam Mohammad) released him on his own in January." He further writes, "We wanted the Sheikh to work with us and revert to his old political philosophy. Mr Sadiq sent an emissary to him in Sura with the message that the accession was not a disputed matter and that the slogan of plebiscite had become meaningless. The emissary, Motilal Misri was engaged in a long conversation with Sheikh sahib, when Vijayalakshmi Pandit made her appearance to keep a lunch appointment with him. The conversation was discontinued. But Mrs Pandit's visit to the Sheikh filled us with the hope of an eventual Nehru-Sheikh meeting. But Sheikh Sahib was rearrested on April 30, 1958, following riots on the occasion of Maraj-un-Nabi in Hazratbal."

Though released from prison in January 1958, Sheikh Sahib was kept under surveillance. He began propagating aggressive communalism. At every public meeting that he addressed, he started igniting communal fire. The first speech he delivered at Hazratbal was anti-India. Rioting broke out after the speech. One person was killed and many wounded. Though shadowed by intelligence sleuths, he was given complete freedom. His speeches were again recorded.

Conspiracy case against Sheikh Abdullah

The Kashmir government had collected all the necessary proofs and evidence to show Sheikh Abdullah's links with Pakistan to destabilise Kashmir and the Indian Government. The entire case was submitted to Pandit Nehru along with his recorded speeches. It is said that Nehru was dismayed while listening to the tapes and on perusal of the letters Sheikh Sahib had written. He thus, reluctantly, approved launching a conspiracy case against him in connection with his indulging in treason against India. Sheikh Abdullah was arrested again on 30 April 1958. With his consent, some of his followers started a 'War council'. Huge amounts of money flowed in from Pakistan. The Plebiscite Front began preparing for waging war against India.

Unprovoked aggression by China, 1962 AD

India has two potential adversaries as her neighbours, China and Pakistan. Both these are by design as well as by faith, expansionist. Curiously enough, both these neighbours dub India as expansionist. Pakistan has illegally usurped one-third of Kashmir territory and wanted to take the whole of Kashmir by force. As far as China is concerned, they made an unprovoked attack on 20 October 1962, over the sovereignty of the widely separated Akashi-Chin and Arunachal Pradesh, both border regions. India claimed Akashi-Chin as part of Jammu and Kashmir, China claimed it belonged to Xinjiang as it contains an important road link that connects the region of Tibet with Xinjiang. China also constructed a road connecting Xinjiang with Tibet, which runs through Indian territory and this became the point of conflict between India and China. China also claims Arunachal Pradesh naming it as South Tibet—also a point of dispute between the two countries.

India shares a long border with China. This border is sectioned in three stretches. It starts from former Burma, goes from Bangladesh to Pakistan in the West. It also runs through the Himalayan mountain range. Akashi-Chin stands at its western end. The Eastern stretch comes between Burma and Bhutan. In between lies India's Arunachal Pradesh (Formerly known as North East Frontier Agency/ NEFA). Both these regions were overrun by China in the 1962 conflict.

When the Sikh Confederation, to oblige British forces in 1846 AD, parted with the whole of Jammu and Kashmir including Ladakh area to Maharaja Gulab Singh, a British commissioner contacted the Chinese officials and negotiated the border between Jammu and Kashmir including Ladakh boundaries that connected with Chinese territory. The borders at the two points of Pongong Lake and Karakoram Pass were well defined. But Akashi-Chin remained undefined. Maharaja Gulab Singh appointed a British surveyor known as WH Johnson in 1865 AD, to carry out the survey of Karakoram and Pongong. While doing that Johnson proposed a boundary line under which Akashi-Chin comes within the boundary of Jammu and Kashmir. China had rejected the Johnson line. At that time the British Indian Government also became doubtful about the Johnson line and deferred the matter for a future date. Meanwhile China erected boundary markers at Karakoram pass on the ancient caravan route between Xinjiang and Ladakh. This was disputed by the British Indian Government.

As a result of the Anglo Burmese war in 1913 AD, India and China gained a common border including the area of what is now called Myanmar. In order to make a well defined border the British Government, China and Tibet attended the meeting in 1913 at Shimla. An agreement was made by the three parties but later on China objected to the proposed boundary between area of outer Tibet and inner Tibet, and did not ratify the Indo-Tibetan boundary. This proposal known as McMahon Line was drawn by Foreign Secretary of the British Indian Government, Henry McMahon. He then decided to get this boundary line passed between the authorities of Tibet and India, overlooking the Chinese. Tibet was an autonomous independent territory. With its independence in 1947, India stuck to the Johnson Line as border on western side of India China border. That made Akashi-Chin a part of India. The McMahon line lay south of the boundary, the area that India was claiming. India's claim was that the border between India and China runs traditionally through the Himalayas from ancient times.

India had cordial relations with China. With the change of Government in China, the Indian Government revived the traditionally friendly relations with them also. But the new government of China entertained suspicions about Indian intentions. China believed that India was expansionist and would soon annex Tibet with its territory. The new government of China announced its intention to reclaim Tibet from the British. In 1950, the Chinese People's Liberation army invaded Tibet and defeated the Tibetan army and established sovereignty over Tibet.

Independent Tibet was a buffer between India and China. With annexation of Tibet by force and violence, China's army came nearer the Indian border. Even then, India did not object . With this annexation, there was a huge exodus of Tibetans who came to India for asylum. Among these migrants the Tibetan head—Dalai Lama also migrated to India. Dalai Lama being a spiritual head of Tibetan Buddhism, India received him with honour. China misunderstood this Indian humanitarian action of offering asylum to fleeing Tibetan people and Dalai Lama and termed it as a conspiracy against China. According to Rob Johnson,[46] "The Chinese occupation of Tibet in 1950 brought to an end the buffer state policy exercised by the British and it was met with considerable protest in India amongst the educated elite. Nehru, who was eager to win over the Chinese, was accused of weak acquiescence. The Deputy Prime Minister, Vallahbhai Patel, suggested that the Indian army should be redeployed to meet this new threat, but Nehru would not be deterred and continued to support China at the UN."

Pandit Nehru advocated the principles of co-existence—Panchsheel, (five principles of peaceful co-existence), by which two nations agreed to the settling of disputes by peaceful negotiations. Curiously China continued to keep India in good humour all the time humming 'Hindi Cheeni, Bhai-Bhai'. But the fact is that they were meticulously planning, preparing and getting ready for an attack on India. M L Gupta observes,[47] "Chinese intentions became clear when it launched a large scale attack on India in both the sectors. Indian forces, ill-equipped and ill-clad for high altitude warfare were overwhelmed by the Chinese, supported by heavy mountain guns. There were wide condemnations of China, nationally and internationally."

The Chinese started annexing Indian territory, part by part, slowly and gradually. They constructed a road through Akashi-Chin connecting it with Tibet. Then suddenly they started to lay their claim over Arunachal Pradesh. During early 1962, China resorted to military skirmishes.

The Chinese army was very well trained . On the other hand, India had won independence by non-violence and the Indian army remained ill equipped and untrained for mountain warfare. Taking advantage of these deficiencies China occupied Akashi-Chin and issued a map showing the North East Frontier Province as Chinese territory. It refused to accept the McMahon Line between the two countries.

Apart from annexing some parts of Indian territory, China had other reasons to start a war in 1962, against India. It wanted to assess the Indian's strength. Also, since India had good relations with Russia and USA, China wanted to see if those countries would come to Indian 's help. Writes Rob Johnson,[48] "Within days of the battle at the Thag La Ridge the Indian army had been driven out of the North East Frontier Province and every formation had been destroyed. In the plains, there was something approaching panic as evacuation of towns and villages in the path of the Chinese offensive got underway. Hundreds of kilometres to the west, the Chinese had also overwhelmed Indian forces in and around the town of Leh in Ladakh." On October 24, 1962, The People's Liberation army of China captured the territory previously administered by India and that gave diplomatic superiority to China . On October 27, 1962, Chou-En-Lai announced unilateral ceasefire and Pandit Nehru accepted it for the maintenance of peace between the two countries.

Pakistan watched with interest how China was daunting and humiliating India by their unprovoked aggression.

Pakistan blackmails India

Meanwhile, India decided to enter into a discussion with Pakistan for political reconciliation and to extend a hand of friendship. Pakistan thought this an excellent opportunity to blackmail India on the Kashmir issue. Pakistan's condition for friendship with India was that India should vacate Jammu and Kashmir and hand it over to Pakistan. "Nehru agreed to hold talks with Pakistan on Kashmir. Shaken by the military debacle and dependent on the goodwill of Western powers, he was hardly in a position to act otherwise. The talks opened in Rawalpindi on December 27 1962. Zulfikar Ali Bhutto represented Pakistan and Sardar Swaran Singh, India. The first round was ill-fated. Just as the talks were about to begin, Pakistan announced a border agreement with the People's Republic of China. Under the terms of this agreement, Pakistan ceded 2059 square miles of territory in northern portions of the State of Jammu and Kashmir to the People's Republic of China."[49] India termed Pakistan's proposal, handing over the whole of Jammu and Kashmir State to Pakistan, as a disgraceful demand and brought the negotiations to an end.

Gulam Mohammad Sadiq, 1964-1971 AD

On February 29, 1964, Khwaja Shamsuddin was removed from the premiership of Jammu and Kashmir, and in his place, Gulam Mohammad Sadiq headed the government, initially as Prime Minister but on March 30, 1965, his designation was changed to Chief Minister of Jammu and Kashmir. Though the new Chief Minister and Pandit Nehru were not in favour of Sheikh Abdullah being tried for sedition although the State

Government agencies had prepared a foolproof conspiracy case against him, yet the conspiracy case continued for six years. There were open discussions on all the charges against Sheikh Sahib. The government spent three crores on this case. On behalf of Sheikh Abdullah, Mridulla Sarabai incurred all the expenses. However, ultimately, Sadiq Sahib, on April 8, 1964, under the instructions of Pandit Nehru, ordered the withdrawal of the case.

Sadiq was representing the Indian National Congress but had leanings towards communism. He never became a die-hard communist. The political uncertainty created by Sheikh Sahib's speeches against India and Kashmir's accession to India, made everything unsettled in the valley. Everything came to a standstill. All the work of progress and prosperity came to a stop. No one was prepared to invest in the state. No capitalist from India came forth to start a big industry. In one of his speeches in Ganderbal, Sheikh Sahib admitted, "It is impossible in the present conditions of uncertainty to raise the economic standard of the masses or even to give people an honest and efficient administration, which finds itself subjected to insurmountable internal-external tensions." This was the economic, administrative and political scenario of the state when Sadiq was the Chief Minister.

Sheikh Abdullah's visit to Pakistan

After his release Sheikh Abdullah expressed his desire to visit Pakistan. On May 24, 1964, he along with Mirza Afzal Beg, Maulana Masood, Khwaja Mubarak Shah, with the blessings of Pandit Nehru, visited Pakistan. According to Sayed Mir Qasim,[50] "Sheikh Abdullah went to Pakistan on May 24 1964, along with Mirza Afzal Beg, Maulana Masudi, Khwaja Mubarak Shah and a few others. He talked of his confederation proposal to President Ayub Khan. The latter rejected the proposal and described it in his autobiography *Friends Not Masters* as 'absurd.'

Nehru's Death

A great tragedy struck India when Sheikh Abdullah was still in Pakistan. Pandit Jawaharlal Nehru breathed his last on May 27, 1964, and Sheikh Sahib and his companions had to cut short their visit to Pakistan and rush back to India. *The Pakistan Times, Lahore* of 28 May 1964 wrote, "Nehru's death came close upon the announcement by Sheikh Abdullah, the veteran Kashmir leader, who at that moment was on a special mission to Pakistan, that President Ayub and Premier Nehru would meet in June 1964, to solve the seventeen-year old Kashmir question. After Nehru's death, the hope of the success of the Abdullah mission, which was expected to improve Indo-Pakistan relations, receded still further."

Sheikh Abdullah goes for Hajj

Sheikh Sahib and his wife went on Hajj pilgrimage in February 1965. It seems the pilgrimage was only an excuse. The real objective was to propagate his political agenda on Kashmir.

During Hajj, he tried to foster International opinion against India through foreign journalists and foreign newspapers. When he reached Cairo (capital of Egypt) he made an appeal through a press conference to use his international political influence for merging divided Kashmir into one Independent Kashmir. In 1965, he demanded that Kashmir issue be raised in Afro-Asian Conference. India tolerated Sheikh Sahib's meetings with the heads of Cairo, Egypt etc. But during middle of March 1965, he held meetings with Chinese Prime Minister Chou En-lai. Sheikh Abdullah was aware that India had snapped her diplomatic relations with China after China's unprovoked aggression on Indian soil in 1962. According to Sumit Ganguly,[51] "These persistent demands alone would have created no problems for him with the government of India, but his decision to meet with Chou En-Lai, the Chinese Prime Minister, while in Algiers and to seek assistance for 'self-determination' was more than any regime in India was prepared to countenance. On his return to New Delhi on May 8 1965, Abdullah was arrested under the Defence of India Rules and whisked off to the southern Indian hill resort of Ootacamund."

It is very difficult to say what conspired between the Chinese Prime Minister and Sheikh Abdullah. Writes Victoria Schofield,[52] "Abdullah says that he sent summary of his conversation to the Indian ambassador to China, but news of Chou En-Lai's invitation to Abdullah to visit China upset the Indian authorities." In view of Chou En-Lai's invitation, on 8 May 1965, Sheikh Abdullah was arrested on his return.

The arrest was not to the liking of the Central Government or of the Kashmir Government. He was, therefore, released on December 8, 1967. From his subsequent activities after his release, it seemed that prison life had enabled him to do a little self-analysis and to some extent, he seemed to have been chastened. The first thing he did was to write a letter to his friend Khwaja Gulam Ahmed on December 11, 1967. From that letter one can get an insight into his mind.

The next thing Sheikh Sahib did was to undertake a journey to many parts of the country where he made public speeches. From his speeches what emerged was his awareness that there were more Muslims living in India than in Pakistan. He could not understand how when millions of Muslims could live with dignity and comfort in India, why a few Lakh Kashmiri Muslims could not do that. Why then Kashmir's independence? However, according to Prem Nath Bazaz,[53] "Abdullah had the habit of occasionally describing the plight of Kashmir to which he had himself been instrumental in reducing it. But we are not ignorant and unaware of the difficulties of the Indian Muslims." Thereafter, the Kashmir as well as Central Government left Sheikh Sahib alone.

Eight
Events in Pakistan

"We are starting with the fundamental principle that we are all citizens and equal citizens of our state. We shall keep that in front of us as our ideal. Hindu will cease to be Hindu and Muslim will cease to be Muslim, not in religious sense because that is the personal faith with each individual, but in political sense as citizens of the nation." These were the sentiments expressed on 14 August 1947, by Quaid-e-Azam Mohammad Ali Jinnah, founder of the new State of Pakistan, in his message at the opening session of the Constituent Assembly of Pakistan. Jinnah must have felt a rude shock when Pakistan's Constituent Assembly decided:

- The name of the State shall be the Islamic Republic of Pakistan
- The head of the State of Pakistan should be a Muslim
- No legislator should enact any law which is repugnant to the Holy *Quran* and Sunna
- An organisation shall be set up in Pakistan which will make known the principals of Islam to the people.

From the decision arrived at in the Assembly it was evident that disregarding the sentiments of the father of the Nation (Pakistan) , the administrators were determined to build it as a Muslim theocratic state based on the principles of Sharia laws. This was the great blunder that

Pakistan committed in mixing religion with politics even in Government administration. Instead of preparing people for the 21st century, the Pakistan leaders pushed her back to medieval times where religion was the sole activity of the people. The head of Pakistan state had to constitute a board of five mullahs who would scrutinise the bill passed by the legislator. This way the new Muslim country of Pakistan introduced Mullah Raj instead of a democratic system.

Mohammad Ali Jinnah died on Sept 11, 1948. His death may have been a great loss for the true lovers of democracy in Pakistan. He was ailing even before Pakistan came into being. His Hindu doctor had kept his ailment a closely guarded secret. Otherwise, the news could have prejudiced the division of India.

The other architect of Pakistan was Liaquat Ali Khan, who was the Prime Minister of this new state. To administer a new country was not easy for him. On October 16, 1951, he was scheduled to make an important policy announcement at a public meeting of the Muslim City League at Company Bagh at Rawalpindi. Suddenly he fell to the bullets of an assassin who was sitting in the crowd only fifteen yards away from the stage. The assassin's name was identified as Saad Akbar Babrak, an Afghan, a professional assassin from the Hazara tribe. There was some misunderstanding between the tribe and Liaquat Ali Khan that seems to have been the motive for his assassination.

With the death of these two architects of Pakistan, the political scenario worsened day after day. One of the greatest temptations the Muslims had to form a separate Muslim state was an expectation of Pakistan becoming the centre for achieving the idea of Pan-Islamism. Writes Arif Hussein,[1] "Jamalud-Din Afghani was the modern prophet of Pan-Islamism. To him Islam was primarily a political concept. The Western powers were trying by all methods, both peaceful and warlike, to break the political backbone of Islam. Witnessing the ever-increasing encroachment of the West upon Dar-ul-Islam, Afghani saw in the Christian offensive a political monster whose aim was to devour the heritage of the Prophet. Consequently, there was but one way of combating the menace: all Muslim nations must unite."

With Kashmir's accession to India, Pakistan started sabre rattling against India. Pakistan's perception of India as an enemy nation overshadowed the possibility of amiable relations between the two neighbours. According to Rafiq Zakaria,[2] "the creation of Pakistan as an Islamic state, put them on the horns of a dilemma. Gandhi's India overnight was painted as Hindu Raj. A religious barrier instantly was sought to be created between their people and India. It misled many Arabs by trying to exploit the idea of a predominantly Muslim state of Kashmir." He further says, "Despite the pressure exerted by Pakistan and the false propaganda unleashed by it, they (Arab Countries) refused to be swayed." Further, he mentions, "I have had the experience of seeing how cleverly Pakistan used the Kashmir issue to prejudice the Muslim representatives in the UN. In the wake of the Indo-Pakistan war of 1965, the then Prime Minister of India, Lal Bahadur Shastri sent me as India's representative to rebut and confute the pernicious propaganda of Zulfikar Ali Bhutto."

On October 7, 1958, the Pakistan President Sikandar Mirza staged a coup. He abrogated the 1956 Constitution and imposed Martial Law in Pakistan. General Mohammad Ayub Khan was made Martial Law Administrator. In fact, it was General Ayub who had engineered this coup. As expected, on October 27, 1958, General Ayub deposed Sikandar Mirza and declared himself the President of Pakistan. Thus came the end of democracy, nay, Islamic democracy, in Pakistan. Thereafter, Pakistan formalised the militarisation of its politics. After three and a half years of Marshal Law, President Ayub Khan introduced his constitution in May 1962 to give his authority a constitutional mask. He remained as President till March 25, 1969, when he abrogated his own constitution and gave way to commander-in-chief Agha Mohammad Yahya Khan. General Ayub Khan, who usurped Pakistan rule by force wanted to perpetuate his illegitimate grip on power by blaming India for all Pakistan ills. Encouraged by successful aggression of China against India in 1962, he believed that the time was ripe to defeat India and annex Jammu and Kashmir with Pakistan.

War of 1965

Pakistan had entered into a military pact with western countries and also with USA. It tried to acquire as much military equipment from them as possible. Having armed itself to the teeth, it embarked on a massive attack on India. By 1964, America had supplied 1.5 billion dollars worth military hardware to Pakistan. When India protested to USA against such huge military aid to Pakistan, the USA President Dwight Eisenhower announced that USA would supply military hardware to Pakistan but assured India that the equipment would not be used against them.

To humble India militarily, Pakistan raised an army of more than two and a half Lakh trained soldiers. It also raised a very strong Air Force consisting of more than twenty thousand officers to man nearly 300 fighter aircrafts. General Ayub Khan alienated Pakistan from power blocks that had formed during the coldwar with Soviet Union. This action on the part of Pakistan was to counteract Pandit Nehru's non-aligned movement. Pandit Nehru wanted to stay away from the cold war as participation in it would disturb India's efforts for development. However, Pakistan brought this cold war to the border of India by joining SEATO. According to Victoria Schofield,[3] "Pakistan had been permitted to receive weapons only after joining the two Western military alliances, CENTO and SEATO; in addition, Pakistan had been obliged to allow the Americans to install surveillance equipment on Pakistani soil, which had displeased the Soviets and potentially impaired Pakistan's relations with the Russians." The next step Pakistan took was to become the member of CENTO. By this membership, Pakistan entered into an agreement between USA, Turkey, and Iran. This agreement was signed on 5 March 1959.

General Ayub wanted to assess the fighting capacity of the Indian army so he decided to make a 'Test Case' at Rann of Kutch in Gujarat province. They also arranged guerrilla warfare in Jammu and Kashmir and named it Operation Gibraltar. According to Wikipedia,[4] "However, the strategy (Operation Gibraltar) went awry from the outset as it was not well-coordinated and the infiltrators were soon found. The debacle was followed by an Indian counterattack that resulted in the 1965 War." Also according to Hassan Abbas,[5] "The plan of this operation (Gibraltar) was finalised by General Malik and approved by Ayub Khan.It was to infiltrate a sizeable armed force across the CFL into Indian Kashmir to carry out acts of sabotage in order to destabilise the government of the state and encourage the local population to rise up against Indian occupation."

In the Rann of Kutch, the Pakistan and Indian forces clashed in the summer of 1965, a clash which resulted in favour of Pakistan. The Indian forces took defensive action. Prime Minister Lal Bahadur Shastri spoke to the nation that, "Our neighbours, both China and Pakistan, have chosen to adopt an attitude of aggressive hostility towards India. They seem to have joined hands to act in concert against us."

The western countries were not happy with this war between India and Pakistan. The British Prime Minister Harold Wilson took the lead to defuse the war . He started negotiations with both Prime Ministers, Lal Bahadur Shastri and General Ayub Khan. Both leaders reached London in connection with the Commonwealth Conference held on June 17, 1965 and met each other and agreed to maintain peace in Kutch. On 13 June, 1965, ceasefire was announced. According to Victoria Schofield,[6] "A ceasefire was mediated in the name of British Prime Minister, Harold Wilson, facilitated by the two British high commissioners in Islamabad and Delhi, Morrice James and John Freeman."

Pakistan was determined to fight India and weaken her so that she would come to the negotiating table where Pakistan would have an edge over her. Thus they gave priority to Operation Gibraltar. Infiltrations by a specially trained force of some 40 thousand men, highly motivated and well armed were sent to the valley. According to Victoria Schofield,[7] "The Pakistani strategists believed that the discontented population would support their invasion. After seizing the Radio Station and Srinagar Airport, a Revolutionary council would issue a declaration of Liberation, proclaiming it was the only legitimate government of Jammu and Kashmir." It was reasoned that this conflict would be confined to Kashmir valley only where local Muslims would join them and enable them to 'defreeze' the Kashmir problem. It was assumed that the weakened Indian military would not respond to the disturbances created by these Pakistani mujahidin infiltrated into the valley. However, Pakistan's strategy misfired . The people of the valley saw the cold and sinister game in this operation and they co-operated with the Government and helped the army to locate the infiltrators who were rounded up. The army killed some of the infiltrators while many escaped through dense forests. Yet Pakistan continued to infiltrate more. They began to cross the ceasefire line, destroyed bridges, tunnels and highways, disrupting communication, logistic installations and aerodromes.

India accused the Pakistan Government of sending and aiding the infiltrators but Pakistan denied any role in it.

The Indian population was angry with Pakistan at their aggression against India. Pakistan forces tried to encircle Jammu by invading Akhnoor. Had they succeeded in reaching Akhnoor,that would have given them an edge in controlling the communication and roads—disabling Indian forces and forcing them to move the Nowshera and Rajouri sectors. It would have been easy for Pakistan army to take control of Gurdaspur territory and break the communication link between Kashmir and India. The Indian defence planners realised the grave situation and took the challenge seriously. On 6 September 1965, the Indian army crossed the Punjab border and reached Lahore. They inflicted heavy causalities on the enemy. Pakistan army's pressure at Akhnoor slackened. The Indian army's tactical manoeuvring was successful and earned a great victory against Pakistan. According to P N K Bamzai,[8] "The capture of Burki by the Indian forces was a feat of bravery and tactical superiority over the better-equipped Pakistanis." The Operation Gibraltar forces faced humiliating defeat. According to Wikipedia,[9] "These troops, called 'Gibraltar Force', were given different code names, mostly after historically significant Muslim rulers. The operation's name, Gibraltar, itself was chosen for the Islamic connotations. The 8th century Umayyad conquest of Hispania was launched from Gibraltar, a situation not unlike that Pakistan envisaged for Indian Kashmir, ie conquest of Kashmir ."

The Indian soldiers hoisted the national flag atop a peak in the Hajji Pir Pass, which was captured soon after the infiltrators were defeated. The mujahidin sent to the valley were none other than Azad Kashmir forces. According to Hassan Abbas,[10] "Having no reserves for the purpose, General Malik decided that the only option for him was to simultaneously train a force of Azad Kashmiri irregulars (mujahidin) for this purpose.

Tashkent Agreement

The conflict between India and Pakistan reached the Security Council which passed a resolution on 6 September 1965, directing the Secretary General of UN, U Thant, to make the necessary endeavour so that Indo-Pakistan war was brought to an end and ceasefire announced. In order to diffuse the tension, U Thant visited Pakistan to impress upon them the futility of continuing the war. Though Pakistan was in a state of defeat, yet it laid down conditions with the Security Council for declaring a ceasefire. The conditions were:

- Withdrawal of all the Indian forces including those from the Indian State of Jammu and Kashmir.
- Foreign troops be inducted into the State who would replace Indian and Pakistani troops as UN Peacekeeping Force.
- To undertake plebiscite within three months.

The Indian Prime Minister Lal Bahadur Shastri announced that not a single condition laid down by Pakistan was acceptable to India. On the battlefront, Pakistan was being routed. President General Ayub Khan was so exasperated that he sought help from USA. But they refused to intervene and advised that the Security Council was capable of taking care of the issue. Meanwhile, U Thant continued his efforts and ultimately Pakistan Foreign Minister announced at a special Security Council meeting that Pakistan accepted the ceasefire resolution. Thus from 3.30 am on 23 September 1965, ceasefire came into effect. Since Pakistan failed to annex Kashmir by force and ceasefire came into effect, Russian Prime Minister, Alexey Nikolayevich Kosygin offered his good offices in hosting the peace talks between India and Pakistan. General Ayub very reluctantly accepted the offer. Since India wanted to maintain peace in the Indian sub-continent, she gladly accepted the offer. India believed that peace in the Indian sub-continent was essential for development.

Soviet Prime Minister Kosygin made all efforts to bring the two Asian leaders to the negotiating table. On 4 January 1966, the meeting between the two rivals took place and continued for one week. At one stage, the talks reached a dead end, and there was every likelihood that the deadlock would lead to a failure. But Kosygin made determined efforts and on 10 January 1966, both leaders signed the Tashkent Declaration.

As per the Tashkent Declaration, it was announced by the two leaders that the two countries would maintain peaceful relations with each other. Both agreed to inculcate neighbourly relations among the people of their countries, which was most vital for progress and development. They also agreed to withdraw their armies back to the position they held prior to August 5, 1965. It was also agreed that a joint committee would be appointed which would suggest improvements in the relations between the two countries.

There was jubilation on the successful conclusion of the talks in India, Pakistan and in Soviet Government circles also. Suddenly the jubilation in India turned into gloom and sorrow when Lal Bahadur Shastri unexpectedly passed away at Tashkent. This news sent a wave of shock and disbelief throughout India. Flags were brought down to half-mast and three days mourning was announced.

President Ayub Khan went back from Tashkent to Pakistan. On March 25, 1969, he abrogated his own constitution and handed over power to General Yahya Khan. General Ayub Khan was a heartbroken man on account of the crushing defeat in the 1965 war. Zulfikar Ali Bhutto had accompanied him to Tashkent. He betrayed him by telling the people of Pakistan that President Ayub had made a secret treaty with India and sold the honour of Pakistan. However, Soviet Union *Tass* rescued General Ayub by denying Bhutto's allegations.

Sheikh Mohammad Abdullah's wait and watch policy

Sheikh Abdullah returned from a foreign tour where he met the Chinese Premier Chou-En-Lai. On his return he was arrested and subsequently released. For nearly six years he remained in wilderness. Meanwhile, age also started catching up with him. Pran Chopra, in his article, *Who Shaped India*, for *India Today* wrote[11] "When the time came to move the State Assembly, he was no longer able to move himself. Heart, diabetes and other ailments had laid him low."

Indian plane Ganga hijacked

On January 30, 1971, at 13:05 hours, an Indian airplane, named Ganga was en-route to Jammu from Srinagar. This plane, carrying twenty-eight passengers and four crew members, was hijacked by two Kashmiri Muslim terrorist cousins named Hashim Qureshi and Mohammad Ashraf Qureshi at gunpoint. Hashim Qureshi went into the cockpit and ordered the crew to take the plane to Lahore.

A Kashmiri young man, Maqbool Bhatt, resident of Trihgam in Kashmir valley masterminded the hijacking of this plane. He was amongst the founding fathers of Jammu and Kashmir Liberation Front (JKLF), a separatist organisation initially formed in Birmingham, England under the chairmanship of Amanullah Khan. Later, Mqbool Bhatt joined the armed wing of Plebiscite Front. He attacked Amar Chand, Inspector of Local Crime Branch and killed him. Then he, along with other terrorists, engaged in an encounter with security forces. A terrorist, Aurangzeb of Gilgit got killed and Maqbool Bhatt along with other members Amir Ahmed and Kala Khan were arrested. In view of their involvement in the shootout, Mqbool Bhatt was sentenced to death. However, he along with two others managed to dig a tunnel under the Srinagar prison and escaped to Pakistan.

While in Pakistan, Maqbool Bhatt masterminded the hijacking of the Indian plane with the help of the two young Kashmiri boys . According to Kishin R Wadhwaney,[12] "NLF activists Hashim Qureshi and Arshad, forced the pilot to take the plane from Srinagar-Jammu to Lahore."

The plane started from Srinagar. While it was flying over Nagrota, 13 km from Jammu, the two hijackers got up from their seats. Hashim Qureshi took out his revolver, went into the cockpit and told Captain G S Oberoi and Captain KK Kachru (co-pilot), "Divert the plane to Lahore without making any fuss." Ashraf took a bomb in his hand and facing the passengers told them, "Do not move from your seats. The plane has been hijacked and the flight will go to Lahore. If you make any fuss this bomb will destroy the plane and also all of us." Once the plane landed at Lahore, the hijackers conferred with Pakistan authorities. They laid a condition for the safe return of the plane with the passengers and the crew back to India —the Indian Government should release 36 prisoners who were languishing in various jails in India. The hijackers also requested the Pakistan Government to grant asylum to them.

The Indian Government was worried regarding the safety of the passengers and the crew. They at once entered into negotiations with Pakistan authorities and were able to secure the release of all the passengers as well as the crew who were under the custody of Pakistan authorities. Pakistan did not allow another Indian plane to land at Lahore Airport to airlift the passengers and the crew back to India. After two days they were allowed to come back to India by road.

The entire Pakistani population rejoiced. Zulfikar Ali Bhutto, who was leader of the majority party in West Pakistan, came to Lahore airport personally to felicitate the two hijackers and hugged them enthusiastically and declared them true champions of Pakistan. A few days later, he said in a statement that the two hijackers were brave men and their deed demonstrated that "no power on earth could stifle the Kashmir struggle for liberation." Since the Indian government refused to accept the hijacker's conditions of releasing 36 prisoners, the Indian plane was consigned to flames on February 2, 1971. Aftab Ahmed Khan, who was holding the Indian Desk at the Pakistan Foreign Office, informed a journalist after his retirement that the plane was set on fire by ISI.

The burning of the Indian plane caused great annoyance and hostility in India against Pakistan Government. According to N S Saksena,[13] "The two criminals Mohammad Hashim Qureshi and Mohammad Ashraf were made heroes by Pakistan. When this plane was destroyed at Lahore, the people in India were angry. The Government of India took strict measures and stopped Pakistani flights over Indian territory. While this made us wise about Pakistan motives it was not taken as a sufficient warning to be prepared to meet terrorism."

This hijacking of the Indian plane gave rise to a very strange situation quite beneficial to India and most disadvantageous for Pakistan. Since Pakistan's eastern part was in East Bengal, which was geographically unconnected with West Pakistan, India's embargo for Pakistan flights over its territory proved very expensive and disastrous for them. To maintain regular contact and administrative supervision over East Pakistan became most cumbersome, time consuming and costly, as they had to go either by steamer or by road through other countries to reach East Pakistan. Soon Pakistan realised the folly of burning the hijacked plane. They began suspecting that the two hijackers called 'Champions of Pakistan' by Bhutto were Indian spy agents. The Government of Pakistan appointed a commission of enquiry headed by Justice Noor-ul-Arfin. The commission declared these two hijackers as Indian spy agents and the hijacking episode as India's mastermind. Both hijackers, including their mastermind Mqbool Bhatt were arrested in Pakistan. Hashim was only seventeen years old. Both Hashim and Ashraf were sentenced to fourteen years rigorous imprisonment. After his release, Ashraf remained in Pakistan but Hashim returned to India where he was arrested and lodged in Tihar Jail.

Meanwhile Mqbool was also released after two years. In June, 1974 he was re-arrested in India, after his return from Pakistan. His earlier sentence awarded by the courts was still valid as he was found guilty of a shootout in Srinagar. He petitioned the President of India for clemency.

Pending the decision on the petition for clemency, Amanullah Khan, a hardcore terrorist, kidnapped Ravinder Mhatre, a member of the Indian Diplomatic Corps in Birmingham, United Kingdom. The ransom condition laid by Amanullah Khan for Mhatre's release was the release of Mqbool Bhatt. The Government of India rejected the condition and Amanullah Khan killed the hostage Ravinder Mhatre on February 6, 1984. In view of this, the clemency petition was rejected by the President of India and Mqbool Bhatt was executed on February 11, 1984, in Tihar Jail, New Delhi.

The 1971 war and creation of Bangladesh

With the partition of Indian sub-continent in 1947AD, two dominions, India and Pakistan came into being. Pakistan consisted of two distinct and geographically unconnected parts —East Pakistan and West Pakistan. East Pakistan had a majority of Bengali speaking population, by and large homogeneous, linguistically as well as culturally.

Eastern Pakistan was more populous than the Western wing. The political power, since independence remained with the Western wing. For a long time, from 1947 to 1971AD, for twenty-four years, the people of East Pakistan were seething at the high handedness of West Pakistan leaders. This resentment reached a boiling point when in 1970, Pakistan held general elections in which East Pakistan, under the charismatic Bengali leader Sheikh Mujib-ur-Rehman, won the majority of seats. He was a very articulate political leader, who had organised a political party by the name of Awami League. Sheikh Mujib-ur-Rehman, after winning the majority, should have been the Prime Minister of Pakistan. But West Pakistan leadership refused the premiership to him.

When Mujib-ur-Rehman asked General Yahya Khan for autonomy for East Pakistan, he was arrested. As soon as he was put in jail the entire population of East Pakistan rose in revolt against the high-handed. Pakistani leaders.

General Yahya Khan sent his junior General Tikka Khan to negotiate with the Bengali people and pacify them so that the peace was restored in East Pakistan. Instead of pacifying the people, General Tikka Khan ordered on March 25, 1971, a crackdown on unarmed innocent Bengali civilians. This crackdown left thousands dead. The Pakistan authorities in West Pakistan than began air lifting a few divisions of the army to East Pakistan so that they could disarm the Bengali army personnel. The Pakistan army did not succeed. Bengali resistance fighters in different parts of East Pakistan organised themselves under the banner of 'Mukti Bahini' and engaged Pakistan army in guerrilla warfare. The well-armed Pakistan army, for a full week, from March 25, 1971, began massacring retired soldiers . Many soldiers deserted the Pakistan army and joined Mukti Bahini. The Pakistan army attacked many parts of East Pakistan. Many civilians were gunned down by machine guns. The Pakistan army tried to bribe the Bengali Muslim peasants by appropriating the land of Hindus and donating it to them. That did not lessen the anger against the West Pakistan forces.

It led to a huge exodus from East Pakistan. More than eight million refugees, an equal number of Hindus and Muslims, moved to India, particularly to West Bengal. This created great economic and administrative problems for India. India made repeated appeals to Pakistan as well as to the International community but there was no response. Exasperated by the indifferent attitude of the International Community, the Indian Prime Minister Indira Gandhi decided to lend a helping hand to Mukti Bahini, so that they could succeed in achieving their autonomy and eventually India would get rid of the huge refugee burden.

Pakistan threatened that, "should India continue to help Mukti Bahini there would be total war against India." An all-out war between India and Pakistan would necessitate a lot of defence planning. India had to fight on two fronts—in East Pakistan and in the Western sector. Another problem for India was not only to guard the border with China but also be vigilant about their movements. On December 3, 1971, Pakistan launched air strikes on several Indian airports. Surprisingly, Pakistan missed the targets and most of the airports were functional or could be repaired soon. Prime Minister Indira Gandhi addressed the Nation at midnight on December 3, 1971, informing her countrymen that Pakistan had declared war against India and India was forced to react and retaliate.

On the Western front Pakistan made a successful thrust in the Chumb sector. Major General Iftikhar Khan who was leading 23rd Pakistan

Division and 2nd Infantry brigades completely overwhelmed the forward Indian Defence Divisions commanded by Major General Jaswant Singh. The Pakistan army captured Chumb village and began advancing towards Jammu. The Indian Division commanders, realising the grim situation in this sector, launched a heavy attack against Pakistani forces and pushed them back to a non-threatening position. During this battle, Pakistan commander Major General Iftikhar Khan was killed in a helicopter crash.

In the western sector Pakistan forces aimed to capture as much territory from Jammu and Kashmir as possible. They, therefore, launched a major attack on Poonch sector. The Indian forces were able to repulse the attack. Then the Pakistani army indulged in small skirmishes at Fazilka and Hussaniwala in the Punjab sector. But when confronted by the Indian army, the Pakistani forces could not sustain their advance. They turned towards Rajasthan. But the Indian army was successful in stopping them.

In the Eastern Sector, the Indian army chief, General Sam Manekshaw had a very difficult problem to tackle. He had to keep a watchful eye on the long borderline that divides India and China. He had to act smartly so that the Indian objective of installing an interim government in East Pakistan was done expeditiously.

General Manekshaw, a Parsi by birth, was an experienced army general and had earned the Military Cross in World War II. Lieutenant General Jagjit Singh Arora, a Sikh by birth, held the Eastern Army HQ. The Chief of the Staff was Major General J F R Jacob, a Jew by birth. All these men proved invincible for the Pakistan army. They planned the military offensive so skilfully that at one end they gave potential help to Mukti Bahini and on the other they successfully advanced. The Pakistan General Amir Abdullah Khan Niazi had almost fortified the approach to Bangladesh. However, Vikrant, the aircraft carrier of the Indian Navy, moved towards East Pakistan's port of Chittagong. This made a difference.

The war ended with the surrender of the Supreme Commander of the Pakistan army, Amir Abdullah Khan Niazi along with approximately 90,000 prisoners of war. Pakistan's defeat and the creation of a new country, Bangladesh, dismayed Anglo-US combine who had backed Pakistan politically as well as financially. President Richard Nixon and Henry Kissinger had tried to reason with Indira Gandhi not to make haste in dismembering Pakistan by creating Bangladesh. America's support for

Pakistan was also due to the fact that Pakistan had facilitated a meeting between US and China. America feared that India's victory would enhance Soviet influence in the region. Against all these odds, the Indian victory over Pakistan in the 1971 war is commendable. In the words of Shamim Ahmed Shamim, an esteemed member of Indian Parliament , "Indira Gandhi did not make history only but also geography." According to Verghese Koithara,[14] "On Kashmir, a major gain for India was that a Line of Control replaced the 1949 ceasefire line that had stood through the 1965 war. The territories captured by the two sides in J&K stayed with them, unlike the case in 1965. The new LoC gave India not only a net gain of 283 square miles but also several key strategic features including the Kargil area. By 30 December 1972, withdrawal of troops behind the international border and the new LoC was completed. Repatriation of prisoners began in September 1973 but was completed only in April 1974."

Ceasefire and after

After achieving the objective of the liberation of East Pakistan from Pakistan bondage, and naming it as Bangladesh, the Indian Prime Minister Indira Gandhi unilaterally declared ceasefire on December 17, 1971. President Yahya Khan was shattered and devastated by the creation of Bangladesh but he accepted the ceasefire. The war ended with the surrender of Pakistan army. In his book, a Pakistan based author Tariq Ali writes,[15] "Pakistan lost half its Navy, a quarter of its Air-Force and a third of its army." With the end of the war there was a change in the government in Pakistan. The military dictator General Yahya Khan resigned and Zulfikar Ali Bhutto took charge of the government. Sheikh Mujib-ur-Rahman who was in detention in West Pakistan, was released. On his arrival in Dhaka he received a tumultuous reception. On January 2, 1972, he assumed power as Prime Minister and then President of Bangladesh. India entered into consultation with the Bangladesh government. The refugees from Bangladesh started returning to their homes by the end of February, 1972. The Indian army returned to India during the month of March 1972.

American policy in this war was primarily dictated by a desire to prevent the dismembership of Pakistan. Nixon's administration had ignored reports of genocide of East Pakistan civilians. When Nixon saw

Pakistan's defeat he sent USA-Enterprise to the Bay of Bengal to intimidate India with a nuclear threat. To neutralise the American bullying, the Soviet Navy dispatched ships armed with nuclear missiles from Vladivostok on December 13, 1971, and they trailed the US task-force into the Indian Ocean on December 18, 1971 and January 7, 1972. USSR also sent a nuclear submarine to ward off the threat posed by American Enterprise. Many years after the Indo-Pak war of 1971, the American think-tank criticised Richard Nixon's policies as being badly flawed and against American interest.

After the end of this war, India was not in favour either of UN or a Third Party mediation in peace talks between the two countries. Therefore India informed the UN Secretary General on February 14, 1972, that India and Pakistan would hold mutual peace talks without any third party. Initially, lower level negotiations started with the Pakistan Government to prepare the ground for direct talks between Indian Prime Minister Indira Gandhi and Zulfikar Bhutto. Finally, the summit meeting took place at Shimla from June 28 to July 3, 1972.

There were many problems that required solutions. The first was repatriation of 90,000 war prisoners to Pakistan and then the conditions for peace between the two countries. The Shimla Agreement was signed on July 2, 1972.

However, the general feeling in India was that what the Indian armed forces won on the battlefield, the leaders lost on the negotiating table. One wonders what transpired between Indira Gandhi and Zulfikar Ali Bhutto—why India could not settle an effective agreement with Pakistan. It is believed that when Indira Gandhi asked Bhutto to declare the LoC as international border, he begged her that the declaration would jeopardise his prime ministership . Mrs Gandhi relented. According to some she felt that since India had torn Pakistan into two countries, declaring LoC as an international border would have jeopardised democracy in Pakistan and the international community would have blamed and maligned India for that. Therefore, she did not stress forcefully for the settlement of the Kashmir issue.

According to an officer who was present at the deliberations, Bhutto disclosed that he was personally prepared to consider a settlement of the Kashmir question along the ceasefire line but his political enemies and military bosses would denounce him for what they would consider surrender of their vital interest. That would endanger Pakistan's fragile democracy after fourteen years of military rule. He assured Mrs Gandhi that as soon as things settled down, he would personally settle the Kashmir issue and declare LoC as the international boundary.

After signing the Shimla Agreement, India transferred the Pakistan territory gained in the war and repatriation of 90,000 war prisoners took place. After achieving these objectives Bhutto began showing his true colours by stating that the Kashmir Question was not resolved and "we have to fight for the same."

Syed Mir Qasim, 1971-1975

On the Kashmir front, Chief Minister Gulam Mohammad Sadiq passed away on December 12, 1971. He was succeeded by Syed Mir Qasim on the same day. Mir Qasim remained Chief Minister of Jammu and Kashmir from 1971 to 1975 when he, to the surprise of all concerned, willingly offered to quit , to make way for Sheikh Abdullah.

Mir Qasim was born on 17th March, 1919, in Mir Mardan Duru. He was the youngest of four brothers. Sayed Ahmedullah, his father was a teacher by profession. Mir Qasim traced his ancestry from Prophet Mohammad. He said,[16] "Sayed Shah Mohammad Syedullah, descending from the line of Prophet Mohammad was my first ancestor to arrive here in 1664 from Baghdad." He further wrote,[17] "As a student of the Hanifa School, I was impressed by Sheikh Abdullah's progressive politics and was getting into the company of like minded students."

Married at the age of twenty, he studied in Sri Pratap College and thereafter went to Aligarh Muslim University for post-graduation. He jumped into politics during India's freedom struggle and took part in the Quit Kashmir movement, as a result of which he was arrested and imprisoned. He was leader of the non-sectarian movement. Mir Qasim drafted the Kashmir Constitution and served many important assignments in the state as well as in the centre. He was respected as a politician, a statesman and noted for his "tenacious courage and cool sagacity". Indira Gandhi described him as a "great nationalist who worked selflessly in public interest for peace and devotion in Jammu and Kashmir."

Mir Qasim acquired the attitude and habit of tolerance, mutual respect and goodwill. His humanistic feelings dissuaded him from repression of any political person. He had a lot of respect for Sheikh Abdullah, in spite of the fact that he had differences of opinion with him. He very willingly offered to resign to make way for him.

Syed Mir Qasim breathed his last in an ambulance carrying him to a hospital near India Gate in Delhi. In accordance with his wishes, he was buried in the remote village of Duru in Kashmir where he was born. He was posthumously awarded India's highest civilian award by the Indian President APJ Abdul Kalam in 2005. What distressed Kashmiri Hindus is that in order to make himself popular among separatist elements he patronised them by methods which made it possible for the separatist organisation Jamat-i-Islami to win five seats in Kashmir's assembly election. The separatists wanted to infiltrate the government and then fight for autonomy.

Reappointment of Sheikh Mohammad Abdullah, 1975-1977 AD

After his arrest in 1953, Shiekh Abdullah had given his consent to float a new political party by the name of Plebiscite Front, perhaps with the idea that Pakistan, under the presidentship of General Ayub Khan could wrest Kashmir valley from India in the 1965 war. But the result of the war had left him disappointed and disillusioned. Sheikh Sahib did not give any kind of observation, remark or comment on the result of Pakistan's defeat in 1965. He continued regularly to address Friday gatherings of Muslims at Hazratbal Shrine.

Then the 1971 war was thrust upon India by Pakistan resulting in the creation of a new and independent country, Bangladesh. With this war, India emerged as the dominant power in the sub-continent. Seeing no future hope for Pakistan to wrest the valley from India he decided to cease hostility and asked Indira Gandhi for his rehabilitation.

His enthusiasm for Pakistan diminished. There was change in Mirza Afzal Beg too. According to Jagmohan,[18] "they started making conciliatory speeches. Indira Gandhi also thought it was expedient to arrive at some settlement with Sheikh Abdullah. Negotiations started between the two parties in 1972. After three years of protracted talks between G Parthasarthy and Mirza Afzal Beg, an agreement, known as the Kashmir Accord was signed on February 24, 1975."

Sheikh Sahib was chosen as the leader with the support of the Congress party of Jammu and Kashmir. He was sworn in again as chief minister on February 25, 1975. The change in the attitude and behaviour of Sheikh Sahib was more of expediency than a real change of heart. He dissolved the Plebiscite Front and revived the National Conference. This change, and removal of other small irritants he resorted to , had created a rumpus in the Congress Party particularly when he had invited Congress members to join the National Conference. He seemed to be pursuing his own agenda without caring for the susceptibilities of the Central Government.

No doubt Sheikh Abdullah was a great leader and messiah of the people of Kashmir. He could have helped solve the problem of Kashmir. Yet he left a legacy of uncertainty and insecurity. He fostered distrust, mistrust, and suspicion amongst the peoples of Kashmir, India and Pakistan. He was autocratically assertive and relied upon absolute obedience of all, including the Indian authorities.

Even wars have not settled the issue. Thousands of Hindus, Sikhs as well as Muslims have died in the strife, and thousands become homeless. The Kashmir problem stands today where it began. And, in future too there is no tangible solution in sight.

State of Emergency in the country

Meanwhile, there arose very serious political turmoil in India. On June 26, 1975, Indira Gandhi clamped Emergency in the country. There was a massive anti-Indira movement in the country. Jai Prakash Narayan, the venerable Indian leader, was at the head of this movement. The Government put thousands of protesters under preventive detention. However, in March 1977, Parliamentary elections were announced. The Congress Party headed by Indira Gandhi was completely routed and an amalgam of many parties named as Janata Party came to power. This change in the central government provoked Sheikh Abdullah to break relations with the Congress Party. Seeing this the Congress party in Kashmir withdrew support to him. As a result, there was Presidents Rule in the state. However, on June 30, 1977, in the Assembly election in the state, the National Conference won 39 out of 42 seats. With the Janata Party wave prevailing in India the Congress party got only two seats and it was wiped off.

With the National Conference achieving overwhelming success in the Assembly elections, Sheikh Abdullah was sworn in as the Chief

Minister of the State. However, on September 8, 1982, he passed away. With his passing his son Farooq Abdullah succeeded as Chief Minister. According to Jagmohan,[19] "Because of the behind-the-scene support of Indira Gandhi and Governor B K Nehru, the transition was smooth."

Dr Farooq Abdullah, 1982-1984

The Janata Dal government in the centre became vindictive towards Indira Gandhi. Mutual bickering among Janata Dal leaders was the cause of people's lack of support to them, and eventually the Congress party came back to power again in 1980. The relations between Farooq Abdullah and Indira Gandhi, due to misunderstandings during Assembly election of 1983 between National Conference and Congress resulted in the dismissal of Dr Farooq Abdullah Ministry on July 2, 1984 by Governor Jagmohan.

Farooq Abdullah was born in Soura on October 21, 1937. After completing his early education, he became a doctor of medicine. He was destined to serve the people of Kashmir but not as a doctor as he chose to join politics. He is married to Ms Mollie who is of British origin.

Farooq Abdullah inherited the Chief Ministership from his father. Sheikh Abdullah had nominated him as his heir. Parmanand Parashar says,[20] "Sheikh Abdullah fought against the Dogra dynastic rule and abolished monarchy. But, instead he wanted to impose his own dynastic rule on the State." He further says, "Sometime in March 1981 he held the Seerat Congress in Srinagar where religious representatives of several Muslim countries including Imam of Kaaba came to participate. Sheikh Abdullah brought in the issue of his successor in the meeting at Hazrat Bal Shrine soon after recovery from a heart attack in June 1981 and in the presence of the audience nominated his son Dr Farooq Abdullah as his successor."

Farooq Abdullah has been the most controversial Chief Minister of Kashmir. He is, to a great extent, answerable for some of the problems of the State. Hari Jaising in the book *Jammu Kashmir, Ladakh* writes,[21] "Abdullah dynasty has been responsible for the ills of Kashmir. We seem to have learned little from our experience of the past 47 years." He further says, "Rigged elections, manipulative politics, blatant corrupt practices, all these only throttled the legitimate aspirations of the people and the democratic machinery in the state." It is believed that he is amongst the founding fathers of JKLF. However, how far that is true has not been confirmed. According to Ramesh Chandra,[22] "Farooq Abdullah, who had once travelled to the UN with a Pakistani delegation and on a Pakistani passport, is today acknowledged as a nationalist."

However, his interest in performing arts is enormous. He patronised many art performances and performers especially from Bollywood. He also enjoys dancing and singing himself.

Gulam Mohammad Shah, 1984-1986 AD

Gulam Mohammad Shah, popularly known as Gulshah was the son-in-law of Sheikh Abdullah. He assumed the office of Chief Minister on July2, 1984. His rule was quite brief and Governor Jagmohan dismissed his cabinet on March 6, 1986.

Nine
Birth of Terrorism

United States of America and Pakistan were responsible for creating the Frankenstein monster of terrorism by liberating Afghanistan from Soviet occupation. The Soviets continued to work in Afghanistan in spite of guerrilla warfare by the terrorists, in which Pakistan and Iran played an active part and other Muslim countries contributed with men and material. The USA viewed the Soviet invasion of Afghanistan as an integral part of the Cold-War struggle and the Central Intelligence Agency of USA provided assistance to Pakistan's Inter-Services Intelligence in fighting Soviet invasion. In this fight, Osama-bin Laden also joined but had no connection with USA- Pakistan combine. It is estimated that more than 4,000 training centres were set up with their headquarters in Pakistan. Thousands of Mujahidin were made available for the terrorist activities. The USA supplied the most modern weaponry. Ahmed Shah Masood led the terrorist activity with 10,000 trained troops. He also established his political control in Tajik dominated area. The Soviet Union starting losing control and gradually the war reached its fag end.

During the war against Soviets miserable conditions were created for the Soviet-Afghan combine. The guerrilla tactics destroyed most important installations like water pipelines, radio station, power lines, government buildings, terminals, hotels, cinema houses, civilian areas, bridges and military installations .

In these terrorist activities Pakistan was the sole beneficiary. United States, Saudi Arabia, United Kingdom, and other western countries, who were main financial contributors, pumped in more than thousand million dollars per year for Pakistan to punish the non-believers like USSR. It was the time when General Zia-ul- Haq was president of Pakistan and the entire financial aid went to him for its onward disposal.

The USSR began withdrawing its forces from Afghanistan in 1988. The first Soviet contingent withdrew around 15/16 August 1988 and by 15 February 1889, Soviet withdrawal was complete.

Establishment of Taliban government in Afghanistan

For their leaders, the Taliban had a large number of madrasa trained mullahs. These mullahs had not even an iota of modernism in them. Mullah Mohammed Omar, had fought as a guerrilla with the Harkat-i Inquilab-i Islam faction of anti-soviet Mujahidin under the command of Nek Mohammad. The members of the command were also madrasa trained or madrasa teachers who had specialised in religious scholarship from Pakistan. Consequently, in the formation of the Taliban government , the ISI of Pakistan had a great role. According to Rizwan Hussain,[1] "Religious students, educated in Pakistani Deobandi Madrasas, formed the core of the Taliban." He further says, "The military, with the cooperation of the Ministry of Interior, was again successful in cultivating hundreds of Afghan Pashtun religious students to form the core of the Taliban from the same refugee camps."

Mullah Mohammed Omar and Taliban

Mullah Mohammed Omar, born in Nodeh, was an ethnic Pashtun from Hotak tribe of Afghanistan. The Taliban movement constituted an overwhelming majority of Pashtun tribes though some volunteers from other countries like North Africa, Middle East, from Muslim community of Soviet Union also joined them.

After the Soviet withdrawal, the Taliban established their government and the Afghan people gave them overwhelming support, as they were fed-up with the corruption, brutality, nepotism of the Mujahidin workers who were fighting against the Soviets. Mullah Omar, worried about this uncertainty prevailing in Afghanistan, vowed to bring to an end the unsocial activities of these bandits. Another problem for him was to control a mafia group known as Afghanistan Transit Trade, who were Pakistan based, and had also made the life of the common Afghan insecure. They were known as 'Extortionist Bandits'. In order to eliminate these criminals, Mullah Omar got enthusiastic cooperation from the Afghans. In October 1997, after Kabul fell to Mullah Omar and his followers, they named the country as Islamic Emirates of Afghanistan. The supporters of Mullah Omar bestowed on him the title of 'Amir al-Muminin'.

As time passed, the contradictions in the administrative functioning of the Taliban government appeared due to the clash between medieval system of governing assumed by Taliban, and the modernism required in 21st century. The Taliban ideology was based on Sharia. Also, influenced by hard-line fundamentalists, the Wahabism of Saudi Arabia, Jihadism and Pan-Islamism advocated by Pakistan, the creed of violence advocated by Osama-bin Laden, the Taliban government, therefore, became anti-modern, anti-women and anti-humanist.

According to Murad Ali Baig,[2] "Mohammad Abd Al Wahab (1703 – 1794 AD), redefined Islam in a narrow and intolerant way and injected into it such a virulent cult of hatred that though repeatedly put down, it has risen to become the single threat to the world peace today."

The Taliban were against the democratic system. They believed that Sharia does not recognise any modern system of having political parties and fighting elections. They did not give salaries to officials and Jihadists. They gave them only food, clothes, shoes and weapons. They did not issue any policy of state through press statements and conferences. The government had banned photography, films, beauty parlours etc. Cabinet Ministers and high officials were only mullahs without modern education. Health ministers and State Bank governors were not chosen from trained personnel in their respective subjects—they were chosen from mullahs. There was no modern type of yearly budget proposal. They had also banned clapping as an act of applause. Disobeying of law and orders was punishable according to severity of the crime, that is either by beheading or by flogging by lashes. Women in Afghanistan were the most besieged and harassed lot. Apart from covering themselves from head to toe, they were not allowed to move in markets without family escorts. They were not permitted to undertake any job or to join any educational institute. They, if poor, at the most, could go for begging.

In order to bring some modernity as well as rationality into the Afghan government, the UNO sent their representatives for training them to get them acquainted with UNs directives for preserving 'human rights' and for conducting efficient administration. The Taliban Attorney General Maulvi Jalil-ullah-Manbozada observed that, "what UN wants us to do is un-Islamic. The UN policy is the policy of infidels, which gives freedom to women." He further advised non-Muslims and by implication NGO workers, "The Holy *Quran* cannot adjust to other people's requirements, people should adjust themselves to the requirements of Holy *Quran*."

Farooq Abdullah succeeded Gulam Mohammad Shah

Farooq Abdullah succeeded Gulam Mohammad Shah on November 7, 1986. This was the time when Pakistan was chalking out its strategy to infiltrate terrorists in the valley of Kashmir. Backed by Pakistan, the terrorists' infiltration and radicalisation of local youth started in 1988 AD. Soon lawlessness prevailed in the valley. Something was happening in the valley almost every day. In view of the prevailing conditions the Govt of India decided to impose President's rule in the valley. In January 1990, Farooq Abdullah resigned. Governor V K Krishna Rao was replaced by Jagmohan who took over as the Governor on January 19, 1990. On May 26, 1990, Jagmohan dissolved the Legislative Assembly to facilitate new elections.

President's rule in Kashmir

Imposition of President's rule in the state did not stop terrorists from creating mayhem. Attacks on minority, army camps and government buildings continued. Mirwaiz Maulvi Farooq, a very well read religious preacher and chairman of the Awami Action Committee, was gunned down on May 21, 1990. Some unidentified gunmen barged into his residence and shot him point blank. People all over the valley, as well as the secessionists held the security force responsible. A furious crowd accompanied the funeral procession and there was commotion and disturbance near Islamia College. To control the crowd security forces had to open fire resulting in the death of sixty people. A high level enquiry was constituted and it was found that the militants included Muhammad Ayub Dar, one of the gunmen who had shot at Mirwaiz. Mirwaiz was considered as belonging to the moderate faction. Hurriyat leaders also accepted that security forces had no role to play in this murder. With Mirwaiz's assassination and subsequent killing of sixty people, the Government of India decided to replace the Governor. On May 26, 1990, Jagmohan was replaced by Girish Sexena. Kashmir this time remained under governors' rule for about seven years.

During this period secessionists came out in open and created chaotic conditions. The terrorists continued to be on a killing spree. In March 1994 AD, they killed 13 Army Officers including a Major General. In May 1995, the terrorists burnt down the Charar-i-Sharief sanctum-sanctorum of Hazrat Sheikh Noor-u-din Wali (Nund Rishi). They also gutted around 800 houses and 500 shops of the town. Overjoyed Pakistan press also commented in *Nation,* "The Kashmiri Muslims' struggle for freedom is at crossroads and a historic opportunity awaits them to transform it into decisive assault for breaking the shackles of Indian bondage."

Pakistani terrorists in Kashmir

The Pakistan army fought many wars with India, including the one in 1971. It lost all the wars. It knows that trying to wage another could further dismember Pakistan as they lost East Pakistan. The army, therefore, is losing its relevance. The fear of army generals is that of civil dominance over their military authority. By keeping tensions with India alive, they promote their own political power and importance. The army takes help from terrorist organisations, whom it terms as strategic assets. It believes that by fostering these it is creating additional forces without straining the taxpayers of Pakistan, since their expenditure comes from contributions.

When Zia-ul-Haq was the President of Pakistan, the ISI had provided necessary logistics to the Afghan authorities, in the fight against Soviet Union, with the help of America and other Western countries. Encouraged by this success the Pakistan army began believing that they could apply the same yardstick to the Kashmir problem and get the Indian forces withdrawn from Kashmir. They found political conditions quite favourable as Sheikh Abdullah had sown the seeds of separatism among Kashmiri Muslims by getting Article 370 incorporated in the Indian Constitution. He had flown a separate flag and prepared a separate constitution for Kashmir. He had also not accepted the designation of Chief Minister but had designated himself as Prime Minister instead.

According to Prem Shankar Jha,[3] "The Indian government has consistently maintained that the armed insurrection in the valley was not spontaneous, but carefully planned and nurtured from 1986, and sustained after 1990, by Pakistan. Pakistan has poured more than 30,000 modern weapons into the valley and trained and armed more than 20,000 militant youth." It was decided that all Mujahidin fighting in Afghanistan be slowly infiltrated into the State of Jammu and Kashmir. Gradually they should build communication and friendship with local Muslim Jihadists who were trained in handling sophisticated arms and fomenting insurgency.

The Jihadists would start disturbances in the State and the Mujahidin would join them in killing non-Muslims and Indian defence personnel. The local Jihadists would indulge in sabotage and arson against the non-Muslims. According to Jagmohan,[4] "There were at least 44 terrorist organisations operating in the valley at that time." He further says, "Important among them were the Jammu and Kashmir Liberation Force, the Hizab-ul-Mujahedeen, Jammu and Kashmir Liberation Front, the People's League, the Allah Tigers, the Hizbi Islami, the Hezbollah, the Operation Balakote and the Al Khomeini. An apex body coordinating the activities of eleven major organisations, under the chairmanship of Mian Quoyum, a local advocate, also existed. But the real guidance and direction to almost all these organisations came from Pakistan-occupied Kashmir and Pakistan." These terrorist organisations began actual operation of their activities from 1988. Pakistan had set up training camps in Azad Kashmir for to new Muslim recruits from Kashmir valley. They were trained militarily and indoctrinated in religious fundamentalism in Pakistan by Taliban and Al-Qaida organisations. They were taught to have zero tolerance for non-Muslims as preached by Abdul Wahhab. According to Murad Ali Baig,[5] "He (Mohammad Abdul Wahhab, a zealous preacher of twelfth century) urged followers to mercilessly exterminate 'infidels' 'blasphemers', 'idol worshippers', 'Christians' and even 'Muslim apostates' like the Shia and Sufis."

In Kashmir, the terrorists instigated the people to come out openly in processions and spout hatred against non-Muslims through the loudspeakers of the mosques. The slogans included:

"*Aay Zalimon, Aay Kafiron, Kashmir Hamara Chodh Do*"
(You cruel, Infidels, Kashmir is ours, leave it)
"*Bharat Kay Aiwanu Ko Aag Lagado, Aag Lagado*"
(Burn Bharat's establishments)
"*Kashmir mein rehna hai to Allah-o-Akbar Kehna hai*"
(If you live in Kashmir, you have to say Allah-o-Akbar (accept Islam)
"*Yahan Chalega Nizam-e-Mustafa*"
(What is needed here is rule of Mustafa)

The militants wanted to terrorise the non-Muslims, particularly Kashmiri Pandits, so that they would go away from the valley. They started killing important and respectable Kashmiri Pandits. Neel Kant Ganjoo was killed by firing upon him on 22 September 1988. He was a retired Session Judge who had sentenced Mqbool Bhatt to death. Similarly, Tika Lal Tapiloo, Vice President of Bhartiya Janata Party, Jammu &Kashmir was gunned down outside his house on September 14, 1989 This ethnic cleansing made the Pandit community refugees in their own country

The next step the terrorists did was to start blasting government offices. In October' 89, a bomb was planted in the Song and Drama Division of the Ministry of Information and Broadcasting of the Government of India. The office consisted of three flats in the Munir Manzil complex at Lambert Lane. There were about 20 staff members inside the office. The militants planted a bomb in the first flat of the office and then locked the door from outside. The staff saw the militants planting the bomb and in panic rushed to another flat. After a few seconds, there was a big bang. The whole flat turned into a heap of rubble with no ceiling, no windows, and no doors. Fortunately, no one was hurt.

Some of the prominent people killed brutally were:

Tika Lal Tapiloo	Lawyer, President BJP Srinagar	18.09.1989
NK Ganjoo	Retired Session Judge	04.10.1989
PN Bhatt	Advocate	03.12.1989

Lassa Kaul	Director Doordarshan	13.02.1990
PN Handoo	Asst Dist Information Centre	01.03.1990
Sarwand Kaul Premi	Writer and Social Worker	10.04.1990
Kundan Lal Ganjoo		04.05.1990
NN Wanchoo	Human Rights Activist	05.12.1992
Som Nath Pujari	In charge, Durganag Temple	30.05.1995
Vijay Kumar	Session Judge	05.12.2001

June 4, 1990	A teacher from Bandipora was abducted, raped, and cut into pieces by a sawmill.
March 22, 1997	Sangrampora massacre — the terrorist kidnapped seven Pandits and killed them.
March 20, 2000	Thirty- five Sikh villagers were killed in Chattisinghpora.
March 24, 2003	Twenty-four Kashmiri Pandits were massacred. These included 11 women and two children.

The state security forces remained mute spectators. Farooq Abdullah was the Chief Minister. From the government's disinterestedness in maintaining law and order by bringing the Pakistan trained terrorists to book, it seemed as if the Kashmir Government too was a party to the chaotic situations in the State.

Jagmohan took over as Governor of Jammu and Kashmir on 26 April 1984, from Brij Kumar Nehru who was governor from 22 February to 26 April 1984. His second term as governor started in January 1990 when he took charge from V K Krishna Rao (governor from July 1989 to 19 January 1990). As governor of Jammu and Kashmir, during his second assignment, Jagmohan writes,[6] "A few days later, three Central Ministers had met the President and complained that the secessionist forces were enjoying official patronage under chief ministership of Dr Farooq Abdullah, and these anti-national elements were dominating the valley. On the other hand Dr Farooq Abdullah was threatening that if the Congressmen did not behave there would be a bloodbath."

Processions were taken out and these stretched for miles. People were shouting the slogan '*Azadi Azadi*' (freedom). Watching helplessly, the non-Muslim community, particularly Kashmiri Pandits, felt absolutely insecure. Then started the killing spree of Pandits, through barbaric methods. One by one their houses were looted, the loot being considered as *Mal-i-Ganim*at (acceptable as looted articles were of infidels). The Pandit community were confused and baffled. The Jammu and Kashmir Government security personnel responsible for enforcing law and order were looking the other way. The non-Muslims, therefore, decided to migrate to safer places like Jammu and other parts of India leaving their homes behind. Initially, the Pandits were thinking of temporary migration but it turned out to be permanent. Before leaving their homes they handed over the keys of their houses to the Muslim neighbours with the message, "if we return give us back the keys, otherwise the house is yours." The Government, instead of helping them, set up migrant camps at many places, the prominent ones in Jammu being : Muthi Migrant Camp, Migrant Camp Transport Nagar, Purkhoo Migrant Camp, Stadium Migrant Camp, Hhiri Migrant Camp, Nagrota Migrant Camp, Mishriwala Migrant Camp. Others were Battalbalian Migrant Camp Udhampur, Nandnagri Migrant Camp Delhi, Sultanpuri Migrant Camp Delhi, Kailash Colony Migrant Camp Delhi, Aliganj Migrant Camp Delhi, Bapu Dham Migrant Camp Delhi, Amar Colony Migrant Camp Delhi, Begampura Migrant Camp Delhi, etc.

End of Composite Culture

The composite culture was the mainstay of society in Kashmir for ages. It had evolved through thousands of years of Kashmir history through the hard and pious work from ancient times by revered philosophers of many faiths like Hinduism, Buddhism, and the Trika teachings of Shaivism (Islamic saints who contributed in cultivating a composite culture). But, concerted efforts by those who represented communalism and fundamentalism completely toppled the edifice of that composite culture. Their strategy was aimed at the establishment of a theocratic state. They were trying to enforce Pan-Islamism. According to Wajahat Habibullah,[7] "The new mosques are designed with domes and minarets in what has become the standard Muslim design across the sub-continent. In that way they convey their own message of Pan-Islamism."

This movement was started by Jamal-ud-Din Afghani, who felt that western powers were trying, by peaceful means as well as by violence, to break the backbone of Islam. Arif Hussain writes,[8] "Jamal-ud-Din Afghani was a modern prophet of Pan Islamism." He further says, "Fired with Pan-Islamic idea, Abdul Hamid despatched emissaries all over the

Muslim world to rally all believers behind their caliph. The Muslims of India responded favourably." Kashmir, having tremendous scenic beauty and salubrious climate had attracted hordes of scholars, thinkers, artists, architects, and builders. Kashmiris had studied almost all the branches of knowledge like philosophy, religion, medicine, astrology, astronomy, literature, poetry, grammar, logic, engineering, sculpture, painting, dramatics, music, dancing and even sexology. It was these scholars and thinkers who had contributed to the noble doctrine of composite culture. Many Hindu and Muslim monarchs also made efforts not only to preserve this humane culture but they tried to contribute to its preservation. Shahab-ud-Din, the Muslim king of Kashmir in 1354 AD was a great preserver of humanist composite culture. But kings like Sikandar, in his mad zeal for conversion, looted temples, broke images of deities and demolished structures. In this he was assisted by his newly converted Brahmin adviser Suha Bhatt. Mir Mohammad Hamadani did warn him against desecrating the deities and pointed out to him the well- known verse of the Holy Quran (II-256) which says:

'Let there be no compulsion in religion'

Luckily Sikandar died at the age of 32 in 1413 AD, before he completely destroyed the composite culture though he had made a serious dent in it. Then came another Muslim King Zain-ul-Abidin who preserved the culture and contributed to it .

It was strengthened by saints like Lalleshwari and Noor-ud-Din. From their sayings it appears that they had understood the divine commands contained in Hindu scriptures and Holy Quran. Both these saints were harbingers of Rishism and Sufiism. The Rishi order and Sufi cult believed in co-existence. Their message was that Hindus and Muslims could live together in love and harmony, peace and tolerance, religious piety and brotherhood and compassion for humans as well as for flora and fauna. That was their real service to religion and their sayings exhibited the glory of Hinduism and splendour of Islam.

The Dogra ruler Maharaja Ranbir Singh, though a devout Hindu, was tolerant of the Muslim community. He allowed them to worship according to the teachings of Holy Quran. This religious freedom was seen during the rule of Maharaja Pratap Singh also. But during Maharaja

Hari Singh's time, the monarch had to face extraordinary hostility from Muslim community.

P N K Bamzai writes,[9] "An extensive and fierce propaganda campaign against Maharaja's (Hari Singh's) rule was let loose from Lahore and other cities of the Punjab by the Muslim press."

Encouraged by the defeat of the Soviet Union by compelling them to evacuate Afghanistan, the emboldened Osama-bin Laden attacked United States in their own country. On September 11, 2001, his Jihadists destroyed the two tall buildings of the World Trade Centre. In this destruction more than three thousand innocent people perished. The whole world was shocked, disgusted and appalled to see the twin towers crumbling.

The American President George Bush declared war against terrorism and in the process destroyed the Taliban government and Al Qaida in Afghanistan. The Jihadists, including Mullah Omar and Osama-bin Laden, escaped to the caves of Tora Bora. However, the Afghan people, particularly the womenfolk got rid of Taliban rulers who were cruel, rapacious, intolerant, bigoted, uncivilised and incorrigible fanatics.

In this war, Pakistan had long lent support to the Taliban and Al-Qaida terrorists and their government in Afghanistan. Sensing the repercussions of annoying America, Pakistan suddenly opted to become its ally in the war against terrorism. Eventually Pakistan became an enemy of these Mujahidin. Admiral Michael Mullen, an American military commander, is quoted by Amit Baruah in his article,[10] "These two nations (Pakistan and Afghanistan) are inextricably linked in a common insurgency that crosses the border between them. We can hunt down and kill extremists as they cross over the border from Pakistan. But until we work more closely with Pakistan government to eliminate safe havens from which they operate, the enemy will keep coming." This way USA intruded into Pakistan territory, which the people of Pakistan did not like but could not stop. Pakistan's need to ally with USA was due to their dependence on the aid they were receiving, otherwise the economy of Pakistan would crumble .

Muslims outside Kashmir

It has been observed that a Muslim, by and large, howsoever modern, moderate, and educated he may be, dislikes living in a secular, democratic ambience. Some of the hardliners among the Muslim educated term secularism as 'Kafirism' and democracy as un-Islamic. The people under the separatist organisation of Hurriyat Conference declare strikes and take out processions in the valley almost daily. They are questioning the legality of Jammu and Kashmir's accession to India. According to UN Security council's resolution dated August 13, 1948, Para II of Part 2, reads,

> "Pending the acceptance of the conditions for the final settlement of the situation in the State of Jammu and Kashmir the Indian Government will maintain, within the lines existing at the moment of ceasefire, the minimum strength of the forces, which in agreement with the commission are considered necessary to assist local authorities in the observance of law and order. Also the legal adviser of the commission came to the conclusion that accession was legal and could not be questioned."

On the basis of this the Times Network has stated in the *Times of India*,[11] "Kashmir is an in-alienable element of India's identity and symbolises the fundamental principles on which the modern Indian state has been built." It further impresses upon the Central Government that, "No responsible government can ever compromise the country's territorial integrity by even contemplating the secession of Kashmir. This is not a trifling issue. If the Indian state is seen as weak enough to let Kashmir go, other states and the affected groups within India will only get emboldened."

On 20 September 2008, Khushwant Singh became tired of the frequent noises made by Kashmiri separatists for Azadi. He suggested in his article,[12] "The situation has been going out of hand since 1990. Basharat Peer (a journalist from India) tells us that thousands of Kashmiris have crossed over to Pakistan to get military training and arms and sneaked back into the valley to create mayhem and murder. The locals give them shelter and food." All non-Muslims believe that all Muslims are, if not terrorists, undoubtedly terrorist sympathisers. It is true that not all Muslims are terrorists. But the terrorists have brought Islam into this controversy. They defame the nobility of Islam which means peace and purity.

Collapse of law and order in the Valley

In 1989, the terrorist insurgency in the valley increased. The local press advised the Kashmiri Pandits to leave Kashmir immediately. This message was conveyed through Public Address Systems from each and every mosque, telling non-Muslims to get away from the valley as Kashmir belonged to Muslims only. On 4 January 1990, there was a press release in *Aftab* and *Al Safa,* (local Urdu newspapers issued by Hizb-ul Mujahedeen) asking Hindus to pack up and leave . The Kashmiri Pandit community started their exodus from the valley. With Kalashnikov rifles dangling over their shoulders, the militants roamed quite freely in the city of Srinagar. The dead bodies of non-Muslims they killed in broad daylight remained unattended for days. Dr Farooq Abdullah was the Chief Minister, yet no action was taken against the militants. The law and order had collapsed.

Jagmohan writes[13], "Throughout Pakistan, strike was observed on February 5, to express solidarity with the Kashmiris. It was a government-sponsored strike in which all political parties participated. Huge placards were displayed which read: 'Kashmir will be in Pakistan." He further says[14] "The people, almost all of them, believed that Kashmir was going to be either independent or become a part of Pakistan in January 1990 itself. In fact, January 26 was promised by the militants to be a day of supposed deliverance when the new People's Republic of Independent Kashmir was going to be declared and foreign correspondents invited to be witness to the birth of the new State."

Jagmohan was governor of the state of Jammu and Kashmir in those days. He has described quite vividly the day to day development of subversion and the people responsible for that in his book *My Frozen Turbulence in Kashmir.*

Operation Tupac

Operation Tupac was named after Tupac Amaro, who was the ruler of Inca, a state in Peru, during 1571 – 1572 AD. He was executed in 1572 AD, in Cozco by a Spanish officer. He was the fourth son of the Inca Emperor Manco Capac. To provide resistance to Spanish domination, Tupac Amaro became the operational name of the fight.

Operation Tupac was a very well planned terrorist activity that would intensify the internal subversion in the valley and then planned attack would follow from Pakistan. It was left in the hands of Pakistan ISI who were asked to chalk out a plan and co-ordinate insurgency in Kashmir. The ISI were already supporting and fomenting insurgency through Pak mujahidin in Kashmir. This Tupac operation was a proxy war which India had to fight in Kashmir against Pakistan.

In this proxy war, the Indian forces were combating with, apart from forty-four militant organisations, most of the terrorist groups based in Pakistan administered Kashmir, known as Azad Kashmir. The notable terrorist groups are Lashkar-i-Taiba and Jaish-e-Mohammad. These groups get material help from Taliban and Al-Qaida. After the ban declared by USA and UK, these terrorist groups have changed their name and are now working under the names Al-Mansurin, Al-Nasrin and Harkat-ul-Mujahidin, formerly known as Harkat-ul-Ansar. All these groups are now operational from Muzaffarabad in Pakistan. The foolproof plan to make Kashmir a part of Pakistan through Operation Tupac was directed by Zia-ul-Haq, President of Pakistan. In his address to ISI in April 1988, he said, "In brief, our plan for Kashmir, which will be codenamed as 'Op Tupac' will work in a phased manner."

Pakistan termed this planned subversion in the state as the indigenous outburst of freedom fighters. The expenditure involved in this operation was so huge that Pakistan alone could not carry the financial burden. Says Rakshit Puri,[15] "In 1995, according to the *Indian Express* (September 28, 1996) a secret report compiled for the government by the Joint Intelligence Committee (JIC), which included data supplied by the Intelligence Bureau, the Research and Analysis Wing and the Directorate of Revenue Intelligence—identified sources and recipients of funds coming to terrorist groups and leaders in Jammu and Kashmir. Pakistan, Syria, Iran and Libya were listed as selecting terrorist groups worldwide, while Saudi Arabia, UAE, Bahrain and Bangladesh backed militant Pan-Islamic activities. Much of the funding in Kashmir was linked to 'drug money' generated in Pakistan. The J I C reported that the drug mafia in Pakistan used local couriers from the Islamabad-controlled part of J & K to run a Rs 5,000crore traffic in drugs through India." Lisa A Curtis, a senior research fellow for South Asian Studies Centre at the Heritage Foundation, reported to the US House Committee, "Pakistan needs to demonstrate an unambiguous commitment to severing any remaining links to terrorism in the region and to uprooting the Al-Qaida and Taliban's safe havens., Militant groups freely meet, train, and raise funds throughout Pakistan."

The conditions in Kashmir on account of Operation Tupac were so chaotic that Pakistan thought it better not to support the terrorists. Adds Rakshit Puri,[16] " Pakistan decided to drop its pretence of giving only moral and no other support to terrorist insurgency in Jammu and Kashmir. Wide coverage was given in the Pakistan and Indian Press to the visit of Islamabad's Information Minister Mushahid Hussain, along with Governor Shamas Hamid of western Pakistan (Punjab) and some provincial ministers to the headquarters of Lashkar-i-Taiba in Muridke, not far from Lahore. The Lashkar is run by the Markaz-i-Dawa al-irshad (Centre for Preaching), whose head Hafiz Mohammad Sayyid, welcomed Mushahid Hussain with remarks that 'After liberation of Kashmir the organisation will launch a Jihad for the liberation of India's 20 crore Muslims'."

This was the scenario in the state of Jammu and Kashmir till the end of December 1989. Apart from security personnel like Police Department and Home Guards, every civilian department—hospitals, advocates, some Judges, educational institutes and Revenue department who worked in villages were also infected by terrorist activities. These departments worked openly under the command of 44 terrorist organisations. People in the valley had lost faith in the law and order. It was in such conditions that Jagmohan was again sent as Governor in January 1990 for the second time.

As Governor of Jammu and Kashmir in 1984, he had earned the reputation of being quite successful. On his way to valley in 1990, he knew that the challenge for reclaiming the valley for India was really daunting. Jagmohan writes,[17] "All the time, however, I was conscious of the fact that 1990 was not March 1986. The spirit of the latter could not be transplanted in the body infected by terrorism. Subversion had gone deep into the organs of the power structure." He further writes, "While we were battling against heavy odds and dealing with manifold problems of internal and external conspiracy, Dr Farooq Abdullah and his partymen were playing a highly destructive even unpatriotic role." He also writes,[18]

"Subversion had convinced the people that their victory was certain. This conviction had to be replaced by counter conviction that it was the State Administration that was going to succeed and succeed rapidly."

In Pakistan, Benazir Bhutto, for the second time took over as Prime Minister in October 19, 1993. She promised the world that she would make Pakistan prosperous and a moderate Islamic state. However, the Pakistan army did not want to stop militancy. According to Rizwan Hussain,[19] despite Benazir Bhutto's pronouncements regarding Pakistan's role as a moderate Islamic state, the military continued to regard the militant Islamic parties as a tool for furthering Pakistani interests in Afghanistan and Kashmir.

Emergence of Hurriyat Conference

When the terrorists operating under Operation Tupac realised that their success in achieving their goal was only an illusion they became frustrated and desperate. They began accusing one another. They went into disarray. But the Kashmir separatists tried to save the movement by forming an organisation under the name of 'All Parties Hurriyat Conference' (APHC). This organisation is an amalgam of 26 secessionist parties and was formed on March 9, 1993. It is working as a front to further the cause of Kashmir's separatism and has taken a stand similar to Pakistan's claim that the Kashmir State is 'unfinished agenda of the Partition', which can only be decided by the right of self-determination under the supervision of the Security Council. Both Pakistan as well as Hurriyat Conference argued that Kashmir is a disputed territory and India's claim on it is not justified. They ignore the UNSC resolution of August 13, 1948, under which the plebiscite will take place only when Pakistan hands over illegally occupied one third portion of Kashmir. Otherwise, there will be no plebiscite. According to Maroof Raza,[20] "The all-party Hurriyat leaders are largely a collection of religious clerics, who are deeply divided over political issues. Some of them have already amassed wealth and funds, questionably well beyond their earlier means."

It is true that the entire Kashmir Muslim population is not with the separatists. The Muslim governed countries have accepted Hurriyat Conference as the representative of Kashmiri Muslims, which it is not. It enjoys the observers status in the Organisation of Islamic Conference (OIC). Mirwaiz Maulvi Omar Farooq, a young man, is the leader of the Hurriyat Conference. Though his father, Mirwaiz Maulvi Farooq, a cleric by profession, was assassinated by terrorists for his moderate approach to the Kashmir problem, yet the son accepted to preside over this separatist organisation . He wanted Kashmir to become independent. Another faction of Hurriyat is headed by Yasin Malik who also wants an Independent Kashmir. Sajad Lone, whose father was also killed by the Kashmir militants, wants the Kashmir problem decided once and for all.

All these factions of Hurriyat Conference indulged in militancy and violence and when they found that they were unsuccessful, they started civil disobedience method of pressing for secession of Kashmir from India.

Why Kashmiri Muslims want to separate from India is a question that every Indian—both Muslim or Hindu asks. What Muslims face in other countries where they live is appalling and humiliating. For instance, China, a very close ally of Pakistan, has tightened rules for Muslims in offering their prayers and religious practices. Writes Admand Wong, "In Khotan (China) the grand mosque that draws thousands of Muslims each week to kneel in prayer are greeted by large signs posted by the front door, listing edicts of the Communist Party than Quranic doctrines. The Imam's sermons at Friday prayers must run no longer than half-an-hour, the rules say. Prayer in public areas outside the mosque is forbidden. The resident Muslims are not allowed to worship at mosques outside town. One rule on the walls says that government workers and non-religious people may not be forced to attend the services of the mosque." This is the religious freedom the Muslims in China enjoy and yet they do not rise in rebellion against China like Kashmiri Muslims do in India.

In comparison to other countries where Muslims face discrimination and religious restrictions, India is a multi-religious, multilingual, multiracial and multicultural country. Its founding fathers framed a magnificent and secular constitution. The preamble of this constitution secures to all citizens, Justice, Liberty, Equality and Fraternity, without consideration of caste, creed and religion. Similarly, Article 15 provides that there will be no discrimination against citizens on ground of religion, race, caste and sex. Article 16 (1) ensures equal opportunity for all citizens in matter of employment opportunities.

One thing the separatists, should know is that there is no third option provided in the 'Indian Independence Act' of 1947, under which each princely state had the choice of joining either India or Pakistan. *Azadi* (Independence) for the Kashmiris is not permissible under the law and cannot be achieved through armed struggle either. Legally, militarily and politically, independence cannot be an option for the Kashmiri Muslims. Some western and Indian writers, though claiming that independence is an option, are not aware of the legality.

To ask for secession from India for either acceding to Pakistan or remaining independent merely on religious basis is not sufficient reason for any authority, regional or international, to accept such demands. Pandit Jawaharlal Nehru, the Prime Minister of India, spoke at the Commonwealth Premier's Conference in January 1951 at Hotel Savoy, London. He had warned that "no attempt should be made to upset the existing equilibrium that has been slowly and steadily maintained between India and Pakistan. In case we resort to put the Kashmir problem on the basis of religion, before and during the plebiscite, there is bound to be no plebiscite but civil upheaval, not only in Kashmir but all over India and Pakistan, particularly in India where there are more Muslims than they are in Pakistan."

One problem with the Kashmiri Muslims is the lack of good leadership after the death of Sheikh Abdullah. Among the present leadership, we have Sayid Ali Shah Geelani, a hardcore fanatic Muslim fundamentalist who wants Kashmir's accession to Pakistan. The other name is Yasin Malik who is chief of JKLF. He wants independence for Kashmir.

Among separatists, both Mirwaiz Omar Farooq and Sajad Lone lost their fathers who were killed by terrorists for being moderate politicians, and both leaders are known as moderate in politics and abhor violence. Omar Farooq, along with Yasin Malik made his first formal visit to Pakistan Occupied Kashmir and subsequently, unsanctioned by Indian authorities, went to Pakistan and met Pakistani leaders. Unofficially it appears that they asked the Pakistan leaders to let Kashmiris have a chance for peace, as the people were exhausted by violence.

Farooq Abdullah's third term as chief minister

President's rule in the state was a matter of anxiety for the leaders of India. It was decided to hold elections in the state. These were held in September-October 1996 AD. The National Conference won more than 50 seats out of 87 seats. Once again Farooq Abdullah became Chief Minister of Kashmir. This time he ruled for more than six years. The National Conference rule lasted till November 2002. Earlier Farooq Abdullah was Chief Minister of Jammu and Kashmir from 1982 to 1984 AD, then 1986 to 1990 AD.

Terrorism during this period continued with people becoming fed up with the activities of secessionists. Killing of innocent men and women appalled people. Frequent hartals (strikes) in the valley affected their business. The government could not do much. In spite of the fact that high level meetings between India and Pakistan were going on the terror activities continued in the state. During March 1997, fanatic terrorists pulled out seven Kashmiri Hindus from their houses in Sangrampora village and shot them. In June 1998, 25 Hindus were massacred in the mountainous district of Doda, while they were attending a marriage function. Hurriyat Conference leaders were frenetically trying to internationalise the Kashmir issue. They met the Pakistan High Commissioner, Pakistan Foreign Minister and also Iranian Diplomats in New Delhi. During this period something happened which caught international attention. In May-July 1999, one of the bloodiest battles took place between India and Pakistan—the Kargil War. Meanwhile, in 2002 AD, elections were announced. The National Conference lost and People's Democratic Party and Indian National Congress alliance formed the government.

Kargil War, May-July 1999

Quaid-e-Azam Mohammad Ali Jinnah, who fought for the creation of Pakistan, would have never thought that social and political conditions in Pakistan would degenerate to this extent. He would have never conceived that military involvement in Pak politics and administration would be so great that almost all the civil departments would be infiltrated by the army personnel.

In July 1977, General Zia-ul-Haq had overthrown the ruling Prime Minister Zulfikar Bhutto in a bloodless coup to become Chief Martial Law Administrator. Subsequently, he installed himself as sixth President of Pakistan. After his death, Pakistan decided to have a democratic form of government and Benazir Bhutto was sworn in as Prime Minister in

December 1988. She tried to minimise the army role in the affairs of the Government. Nawaz Sharif was elected as Prime Minister in 1997. Fearing an army coup he appointed his own trusted officer, General Pervez Musharaf as Chief of the army Staff in October 1998.

The Pakistan army had tasted power and so could not sit quiet. It started giving effect to 'Operation Badr,' similar to 'Operation Topaz'. Operation Badr was in fact planned by Benazir Bhutto when she was the Prime Minister of Pakistan, but when she was ousted, it was shelved. However, during Nawaz Sharif's premiership, the army thought it was the right time to reassert their importance in the eyes of Pakistani people by restarting Operation Badr, without informing the civilian Prime Minister. As already stated, the Pakistan army is not answerable to any civilian authority in the country, not even to the Prime Minister.

That was the time when the NDA (National Democratic Alliance) was in power in India. Prime Minister Atal Bihari Vajpayee had gone personally to Lahore to meet Nawaz Sharif to initiate bilateral peace talks aimed at improving confidence-building measures. It was a sincere effort to boost the peace process and resolve all outstanding disputes including Kashmir. In Jammu and Kashmir State, the Pakistan army started crossing the LOC (Line of Control) in May 1999 at Kargil. This shattered the confidence building measures between India and Pakistan.

District Kargil which was part of Gilgit Baltistan, is inhabited by many ethnic, religious, and linguistic groups in many isolated valleys among high mountains, But with the partition of India in 1947, Kargil remained with India and Gilgit and Baltistan, though part of Kashmir, were taken by Pakistan. In the Ladakh region, Kargil is the only place where there are Muslims in a majority. The National Highway runs through Kargil from Srinagar to Leh or Ladakh.

The Pakistan army sent their mujahidin and Para-military troops into Kargil to cut the road link of Kashmir with Ladakh. Pakistan declared that the operation did not have the consent of the civilian government. Prime Minister Nawaz Sharif said, "It was not known to me. All this was done without my knowledge."

In early May 1999, the Pakistan army occupied Kashmir post with about 125 personnel. They were supported by four battalions of Northern Light Infantry. In addition to this they were assisted by Kashmiri, Afghan and other foreign mercenaries whom Pakistan declared as Kashmiri freedom fighters. Initially, these incursions were not detected by the Indian army because during winter season, in extreme cold weather, Indian and Pakistan armies abandon some forward posts. India, therefore, was not aware of what was happening at the LOC near Kargil. Tashi Namgyal, a local shepherd accidently met an Indian patrol team and gave a tip-off about the movements of Pakistani troops. The Indian army came to know about Pakistan army's encroachment. The Government of India realised the seriousness of the situation and responded with 'Kargil Operation Vijay'. The Indian army consisting of two divisions numbering 2,00,000 and some thousand personnel from the Para-military forces supported by air force were deployed in this conflict. Pakistan had provided all modern weapons to the Mujahidin including anti-aircraft guns and had spread a net of landmines to stop the Indian army's advance. In this war it is estimated that nearly all infiltrators were killed. The Indian army succeeded in vacating the Kargil territory from the Pakistan army. Nawaz Sharif later said that over 4,000 Pakistani troops were killed in the operation and Pakistan had lost the battle.

India won the Kargil war because of its brave sons . Captain Vikram Batra 13 JAK RIF was awarded Param Vir Chakra posthumously. Lieutenant Manoj Kumar Pandey 1/11 GR was also awarded Param Vir Chakra posthumously. The others who got the highest honour of bravery were Grenadier Yogender Singh Yadav, 18 Grenadiers, and Rifleman Sanjay Kumar, 13 JAK RIF. Others who sacrificed their lives for the country were Squadron Leader Ajay Ahuja, Squadron Leader Rajiv Pundir, Flight Lieutenant S Muhilan, Sergeant PVNR Prasad, and Sergeant Raj Kishore Sahu. In the Kargil war more than 1,000 Indian bravehearts lost their lives.

The international community admonished Pakistan for provoking India into a war. They were closely watching this conflict lest Pakistani's foolish leadership should use nuclear warheads. Pakistan Foreign Secretary made a statement that escalation of this war could lead Pakistan to use any 'modern mass destructive weapons' available in their armoury. That was a clear indication that Pakistan intended to use nuclear weapons. Pakistan said "The purpose of developing W M D (Weapons of Mass Destruction) becomes meaningless if they are not used when they are needed."

The United States of America got very perturbed when intelligence reports reached them that nuclear weapons in Pakistan were being shifted to the border. President Bill Clinton tried to dissuade Nawaz Sharif from making such a foolish move and even chided Pakistan by explaining its grave consequences. On the Indian side too Nuclear Weapon Systems were moving towards the border. Nawaz Sharif was shaken to know this. To avoid the catastrophe of nuclear war, he at once ordered Pakistan army to vacate Kargil area. He later wrote in an official biography that General Pervez Musharaf had moved nuclear warheads to the border without informing him.

Pakistan's violation of Line of Control by intruding into Indian Territory was disliked by the international community. When in July 1999, Pakistan Prime Minister went to USA to seek support, President Bill Clinton rebuked Nawaz Sharif for this ill conceived operation of Kargil and admonished him to, "rein in the militants, and withdraw Pakistan soldiers from Indian Territory." The G-8 Nations also supported India and condemned Pakistan at the 'Cologne Summit'. The European Union also supported India. China too did not appreciate Pakistan's role in this conflict. Pakistan felt internationally isolated and that affected her status as well as her economy, which was already in shambles. The Pakistan Government was so demoralised by the outcome of the Kargil war that they refused to accept the dead bodies of their soldiers from Indian authorities. Pakistan's Prime Minister had disassociated himself from the Kargil operation and had left it to General Musharaf. The whole blame fell upon General Musharaf. Benazir Bhutto, the opposition leader in Pakistan called Kargil war, "Pakistan's greatest blunder." Many ex-army officers of ISI, and army too, called Kargil Operation a "waste of time." Lieutenant General Ali Khan criticised it as, "A disaster bigger than the East Pakistan tragedy."

Hijacking of Indian Airlines plane, Flight 841

The failure of 'Operation Tupac' and 'Operation Badr'had frustrated the Pakistani rulers. To divert the attention of the people they planned Indian Airlines Flight 841 to be hijacked on 24 December 1999.

This plane took off from Kathmandu for Delhi with Captain D Sharan, Flight Engineer Jogia and Flight Purser Anil Sharma who were Delhi-based. In addition, there were co-pilot Rajinder Kumar, Flight Purser Sateesh and airhostesses Rajni Shekhar, Kalpana Majumdar,

Sabita Khalkho, Tapa Debnath, Sapna Ravi Menon and Kavita Mukherji. There were 178 passengers on board. The plane took off from Kathmandu and attained a good height. At 4.53pm, a few young Muslim men got up from their seats and announced that the plane was hijacked. They threatened the passengers and the crew that they had explosives with them and would destroy the aircraft along with everyone in it. The hijackers asked the crew to take the aircraft to Lahore. When the plane reached Lahore airport, the authorities there did not allow it to land. Then, as directed by the hijackers, the aircraft was taken to Amritsar (India). The plane landed at Amritsar airport at 7 pm. The hijackers asked the plane be refuelled. The hijacked plane parked at Amritsar airport had shaken the Government of India. They could not precipitate any action against the hijackers while the aircraft was at Amritsar. Meanwhile, a newly wedded Rupin Katyal, one of the passengers, who had objected to a hijacker's behaviour was stabbed and killed in the plane.

This gruesome murder of Katyal had shaken the crew and the passengers. The hijackers threatened that the passengers would be killed one by one unless the craft was refuelled. At Amritsar refuelling of the plane was intentionally delayed. The delay had made the hijackers nervous. Sensing some plotting by the Indian authorities against them, they threatened the crew to take off the plane from Amritsar without refuelling of the aircraft. When the aircraft reaching Lahore from Amritsar, the Pakistan authorities again refused them permission to land but the pilot had no choice due to depleted fuel and the plane landed at Lahore Airport at 8:07 pm However, after great persuasion by the crew the Lahore authorities allowed the refuelling of the aircraft. The plane took off from Lahore for Kabul but as there was no night landing facility available, the plane was directed to go to Dubai. Thus the plane landed at Dubai airport at 1:32 am on 25 December, 1999.

According to J N Dixit,[21] "Other aspects of Pakistani reaction to the hijacking need to be mentioned. The first reaction of the Government of Pakistan could be described as farcical but for its tragic implications. Pakistani authorities decided that the hijacking was organized by the Indian intelligence agencies, particularly the research and analysis wing (RAW), to put Pakistan in a bad light as a terrorist state, with the specific objective of sabotaging President Bill Clinton's visit to Pakistan. When this idea did not find any takers, Pakistani authorities claimed that they had no personal knowledge of the hijackers and that they were indigenous militants from Indian Jammu and Kashmir." He further says,[22]"The involvement of the Pakistani authorities in the hijacking is further proved by the fact that just before the departure of IC-814, from Kathmandu, Mohammad Arshad Cheema, First Secretary Consular of the Pakistani Embassy in Kathmandu, accompanied by other officials arrived at the airport, went into the departure lounge and apparently had some last minute discussions with the leaders of the hijacking group."

At Dubai, after negotiations with the Dubai authorities, the dead body of Katyal was offloaded and with that the hijackers released 25 ailing passengers. The plane was again refuelled at Dubai and the aircraft took off for Kandahar and landed there on December 25, 1999, and with that the negotiations started with the hijackers. It was then that the Government of India became aware of the people who had hijacked the plane and their purpose for doing so. The hijackers were identified. J N Dixit writes,[23] "They were Ibrahim Athar, Sunny Ahmed Kazi, Shahid Akhtar Sayid, Mistri Zahur Ibrahim and Shakir. Ibrahim Athar, the chief hijacker, was resident of Bahawalpur in Pakistan and the brother of Maulana Masood Azhar. Shakir was resident of Sukkur in Sind, Pakistan. The remaining three were from Karachi." Abdul Rauf, the brother-in-law of Masood Azhar was another mastermind of this hijacking operation, who had sent Rs. 78,000 twice to the hijackers. The hijackers demanded the release of Masood Azhar, the Chief of Harkat-ul-Ansar, (later named as Harkat-ul-Mujahidin). Kandahar, in Afghanistan , was Taliban governed country. Though the Taliban government provided necessary items of food for the passengers but their sympathy was with the hijackers. The hijackers initially talked tough but subsequently became reasonable and reached a final stage when the government of India agreed to release Masood Azhar, Mushtaq Zargar and Omar Sheikh, who were in Indian jail.

Meanwhile, UNs officials including Erik de Mul, looking after the coordination of humanitarian efforts in Islamabad, reached Kandahar airport on Sunday morning. He met Abdul Wakil Muttawakil, the Afghan Foreign Minister, and Mullah Akhtar Mansur, the Afghan Civil Aviation Minister. This resulted in the Taliban Government providing the passengers with breakfast. A diabetic patient Anil Khurana was released and admitted to the UN army hospital in Kandahar.

The Taliban Government had warned the hijackers to desist from killing any passenger and declared their demand for 200 million dollars as an un-Islamic act. Meanwhile, the Government of India made the necessary preparations and India's Foreign Minister Jaswant Singh took the three terrorists personally to Kandahar and exchanged them for all the passengers and the aircraft and with that ended the hijacking drama.

Mufti Mohammad Sayeed as chief minister

The 2002 elections made way for P D P and Congress to form a coalition government. They decided by a power sharing agreement that the leader of each party would hold office of the Chief Minister by rotation for three years. Mufti Mohammad Sayeed became the first Chief Minister.

Born on January 12, 1936, in Bijbihara, Kashmir, he started his political career as a member of Indian National Congress party in 1987. Then he quit Congress and joined the Jan Morcha of V P Singh. In 1989 AD, Mufti Sahib became the first Muslim Union Cabinet Minister of India as Home Minister. However, when V P Singh lost the vote of confidence in Lok Sabha in November 1990, he had to resign. Mufti Sahib thought it best to work in his state. He, along with his daughter Mehbooba Mufti, formed his own party in Jammu and Kashmir known as People's Democratic Party (P D P). However, in view of the power sharing agreement, Mufti Sahib, after three years in office as Chief Minister, made way for Congress leader Gulam Nabi Azad.

Ghulam Nabi Azad as chief minister

On October 27, 2005, Ghulam Nabi Azad took over as Chief Minister of Jammu and Kashmir. Born in Doda district of Jammu and Kashmir on March 7, 1949, he graduated from Government College Bhadarwah. He started his political career from District Doda as Block Committee Secretary. As Congress worker he held many important positions such as President of the All India Youth Congress, General Secretary of the Congress etc. He also held many ministerial berths whenever Congress was in power. It was during his tenure that Government of India and the State government of Jammu and Kashmir reached an agreement to transfer forest land to Shri Amarnath Shrine Board. This became a contentious issue even between the coalition partners, Congress and P D P. Azad Sahib was blamed by P D P for the row. The Minister who headed the forest department and belonged to P D P insisted that he was not shown the forest land transfer files. There were protests in whole of Jammu and Kashmir. On June 29, 2008, Mehbooba Mufti declared the withdrawal of support to Congress, and therefore, Azad Sahib had to relinquish the chief ministership. Ghulam Nabi Azad, appears to be a moderate and gentle person who loves the performing arts. He is married to Shamima Dev, the celebrated singer of Kashmir.

Amarnath row

Amarnath has the most auspicious Hindu religious sanctum -sanctorum, situated at the end of Lidder valley at a distance of 140 km from Srinagar. This holy cave of Amarnath is at 3,888 meters above sea level and is situated in a narrow gorge in the Himalayan range of mountains. According to a legend which is popular among the people of Kashmir the sanctum-sanctorum of Amarnath cave is the secret meeting place of Shiva and Parvati [God and Goddess] where they conversed about the secret of immortality, The Shrine was discovered by a Muslim.

Every year lakhs of pilgrims come to this holy shrine of Amarnath for pilgrimage from July to early August. For the benefit of the pilgrims, the Kashmir Government provides tents at different stops of pilgrimage. The tents are provided from Pahalgam onwards to make available shelter during heavy downpours. But due to the increased number of pilgrims, the tents were inadequate. Thus on 26 May 2008, the State Government in consultation with the Central Government decided to transfer about 100 acres of forest land to S A S B [Shri Amarnath Shrine Board], from the Kashmir valley for the purpose of setting up a temporary shelter for the pilgrims. Kashmiri Muslims under the guidance of separatists organisations especially Hurriyat Conference vehemently opposed the transfer of the valley's land to Amarnath Shrine Board. They organised violent processions and strikes destroying government and public property to the extent that it became a major law and order problem. In these demonstrations, six people were killed and hundreds injured. To protect the law and order in the valley, important separatist leaders like Shabir

Shah, Sayid Ali Shah Geelani, Mirwaiz Umar Farooq and many other Hurriyat leaders were placed under house arrest.

One of the arguments put forth by the separatists was that because of the transfer of land for shelter of the pilgrims, the region would suffer from ecological imbalance, ignoring the fact that acres of forest land was used in road building and for expanding village boundaries. This opposition by Muslim separatists had very grievously hurt the Hindu sentiments. They saw an anti-Hindu stance in this opposition. When the Kashmir Government revoked the transfer order under pressure from the Muslims of the valley, Hindus got united in Jammu region and made a strong protest. The protest at Jammu was so determined and so effective that the movement of vehicles from Jammu to Srinagar came to a standstill.

In Kashmir, Auqaf, a Muslim religious organisation holds a lot of land for mosques and Muslim shrines. Amarnath Shrine also could own, though temporarily, a hundred acres of forest land.

At that time, the Indian National Congress Party led by Gulam Nabi Azad and People's Democratic Party combine was ruling the state. Gulam Nabi Azad was the Chief Minister. The Hurriyat Conference was motivating the entire Muslim community to fight as one man against this transfer order. So much so, that Mufti Mohammad Sayeed, the leader of P D P, and an ally in the government said that if the transfer order was not revoked it would withdraw the support to Congress rule in the state. They subsequently withdrew their support to show solidarity with the separatists. Mufti Mohammad and Mahbooba Mufti, joined the opposition processions.

The opposition organised by the Muslim separatists in the valley provoked Hindu sentiments and Hindu organisations like Bajrang Dal and V H P [Vishva Hindu Parishad] protested in front of Kashmir House in Delhi and a determined protest was carried on in Jammu which became a serious law and order problem. One person even committed suicide as a protest against the revocation of transfer order of the land. In Jammu, vehicular movement to Srinagar was stopped which resulted in the economic blockade of essential items from India to the valley. The people of the valley asked for permission to use the Jhelum valley road for export of Kashmir fruit and import of essential commodities from Pakistan. The

Indian government allowed it initially but them withdrew the permission as it did not work smoothly. Subsequently, the movement of vehicles was allowed by the protesters in Jammu which eased the situation of import and export of items from the valley to other states and vice-versa.

Kashmiri Pandits continue to suffer

Terrorism created an overwhelming sense of insecurity amongst Kashmiri Pandits. They left the valley in 1989-90, with the hope of returning to their place of birth some day. These Pandits, even after 20 years still long to go back to their native place. The Government has provided some relief but it has been very meagre and inadequate. Many of them are suffering from depression and other related diseases. Once prosperous landowners, they now have no place even to build homes. Their condition worsens in the hot weather of the plains. Kashmiri Pandits are grateful to Bala Sahib Thackeray who opened the doors for Kashmiri Pandits and their children. In 1990, he ordered the then Chief Minister Manohar Joshi to allow displaced Kashmiri Pandit students to get admission in every college in Maharashtra. Subsequently Bhartiya Janta Party leadership also took up the initiative and it is by their efforts that displaced Kashmiri Pandit students are getting admission for higher studies. Seeing this other states have also followed suit.

Once there was a proposal by the central government that composite townships for Kashmiri Pandits may be created in the valley. However, the proposal sparked widespread uproar by both separatists and mainstream politicians. They expressed that such settlements would create a chasm between Pandits and Muslims. But Pandits are reminded of the brutalities and carnage by the terrorists against them in the massacres of Sangrmpora (1997), Wadhama (1998), holocaust of Nadimarg (2003) and other killings, which send a chill down their spine. They want to have some place in the valley which could guarantee them complete safety.

Omar Abdullah, the youngest chief minister

On the political front in Kashmir, when Mehbooba Mufti, President of Jammu and Kashmir People's Democratic Party, declared the withdrawal of support to Congress on account of Amarnath row, Gulam Nabi Azad had to resign in June, 2008. President's rule was imposed from July 2008 till Jan 2009. Meanwhile, elections were again announced and this time

National Conference and Indian National Congress joined to form a coalition. The National Conference declared Omar Abdullah as their Chief Ministerial candidate. In this coalition it was agreed upon by both parties that the Chief Minister would not be by rotation and Omar Abdullah would continue to be Chief Minister for the entire session. Thus Omar Abdullah became Chief Minister in January, 2009.

Among the young Muslim leaders, Omar Abdullah appears to be emancipated, liberal and secular. He, decidedly, is not a religious zealot. Born on March 10, 1970, in Essex, United Kingdom, he did his schooling from Burn Hall School and Lawrence School Sanawar. He later joined St Stephen's College. He joined politics in 1998 as a Lok Sabha member. He became Union Minister of State, Commerce and Industry in 1999 AD.

Omar Abdullah left the central leadership to concentrate on party work. He was elected as President of National Conference in 2002. Initially he had a set-back as he lost his Ganderbal seat in Kashmir Assembly election in the year 2002. However, in the year 2009, he was sworn in as the 11th Chief Minister of Jammu and Kashmir State.

Armed Forces Special Powers Act

The security forces stationed in Kashmir have been under great stress as as the terrorist organisations are asking for their removal. It is surprising that even the ruling parties in Jammu and Kashmir want the Armed Forces Special Powers Act to be repealed. The National Conference, P D P and various organisations have reached a consensus in this regard. The manifesto for the 2008 election, issued by National Conference states that in case they win the election, the Armed Forces Special Powers Act would be withdrawn.

There are many reasons for the application of AFSPA. The Pakistan Army and its intelligence agency I S I (Inter-Services Intelligence) have greatly contributed to the nurturing of the Jihadist terrorism which has created militancy in Jammu and Kashmir. It is estimated that I S I has direct links with more than 60 militant groups and utilises their services, when and if needed. Former Pakistan Army Chief and President General Pervez Musharaf recently admitted that Islamabad trained groups like the LeT (Lashkar-e-Tayyiba), headed by Hafiz Saeed and Zakiur Rehman Lakhvi, in 1990 to carry out militancy in Kashmir. Musharaf also said that Hafiz Saeed and Zakiur Rehman Lakhvi are their heroes.

There are hundreds of terrorists training camps in P O K (Pakistan Occupied Kashmir) and the terrorists operating there are armed with sophisticated and hi-tech modern weapons. These infiltrators cross the border from Pakistan with the help of Pakistan Army. Though most of the infiltrators get killed by the Indian security forces, some who succeed sneak in and create havoc on Indian soil. To counter this it is important to strengthen the hands of security forces.

The Armed Forces Special Powers Act was passed by Parliament in the year 1990, where in the area which is proclaimed disturbed, an officer of the armed forces has special powers. In this connection the areas close to Line of Control were declared disturbed. When insurgency began in the valley, the whole of Jammu and Kashmir was declared disturbed in 2000. Indian Armed Forces have utilized these powers with caution. Any misuse of power by anyone has been severely dealt with.

Historic 16th Lok Sabha election

Bhartiya Janata Party, under the leadership of Narendra Modi, created unprecedented history by winning absolute majority in the 16th Lok Sabha Election, in which the party got a massive mandate and won 282 seats. The National Democratic Alliance, including Bhartiya Janata Party won more than 336 seats. The elections took place between April 7 and May 12, 2014. The results were announced on 16th May 2014. Narendra Modi became the prime minister of India on May 26, 2014. In this election Indian National Congress was decimated to just 44 seats and including its allies under U P A (United Progressive Alliance), they could not cross 60 seats.

Unprecedented floods in Kashmir

In September 2014, heavy rains created havoc in Jammu and Kashmir. Large areas were inundated by floods including Srinagar. Just within four days, from September 3 to 7, 2014, the state received about 558 mm rain which is termed as excess by Indian Meteorological Department. In Kashmir more than 2500 villages were affected; 390 villages were completely submerged. More than 200 people died in the floods. The rains submerged even the capital of the state—the Government Secretariat, High Court, Radio Kashmir, Reserve Bank, Lal Chowk, Raj Bagh, Jawahar Nagar, Gogji Bagh, Wazir Bagh etc. In Jammu area more than 1000 villages were affected. More than 50 bridges were reported to have been either damaged or washed away by the floods. In this grave calamity, the Indian Army did a commendable job of rescuing people. It is estimated that about 15000 people were evacuated to safer places by them. They also carried essential items such as food, water and blankets to the needy. Prime Minister Narendra Modi undertook an aerial survey of the state on September 7, 2014. He termed it a national level disaster.

Kashmir is a place of lakes and rivers, big and small. It is estimated that for the last 100 years more than 50 per cent of the lakes, ponds, wetlands and small rivers have been encroached upon. Where there was a small river where people were being ferried in boats, now there is a road where trucks and cars are running. In fact, these lakes, ponds, wetlands and small rivers would absorb most of the excess rainfall. Another reason for the floods is the ecological degradation—cutting of trees, creating concrete jungles, etc. After the Prime Minister's aerial survey, the central agencies rushed to the state and started relief work. Though Jammu and Kashmir has still not completely recovered, it is limping back to normalcy.

2014 Assembly elections in Jammu and Kashmir

The year witnessed an unprecedented turn of events. B J P/N D A got majority of seats in Lok Sabha Election. The Jammu Kashmir State Assembly election was held from November 25 to December 20, 2014, in five phases. The leaders of the Tehreek-e-Hurriyat Conference, Syed Ali Shah Geelani and other separatist leaders had appealed to people of Kashmir to boycott the Assembly election, but people did not bother to heed them. Surprisingly the voter turnout was more than 60 % which is the highest recorded in the last 25 years. The world was closely watching the election and the European Union congratulated India on the Kashmir election by praising its vibrant democracy.

In this election all the parties fought independently. Congress had broken its alliance with National Conference and P D P also fought independently. The results were astounding as it was a fractured verdict with no party getting full majority. P D P, the dominant party won 28 seats, B J P got 25 seats, National Conference got 15 seats and Indian National Congress had to content themselves with 12 seats. There were two options for forming the Government—either P D P would join B J P or P D P could join National Conference. After a lot of deliberations and considerations, P D P and B J P decided to align with each other.

It was agreed upon by both the parties that Mufti Mohammad Sayeed would hold office of chief minister for a full term. So Mufti Mohmmad Sayeed, once again, became Chief Minister of Jammu and Kashmir.

Conflict over Siachen

There are some important glaciers which fall within the jurisdiction of Ladakh, and Jammu and Kashmir such as Biafo Glacier, Siachen Glacier, Baltoro Glacier, Hispar Glacier and Nubra Glacier. Among these, Siachen glacier is the world's highest battleground. The word 'Siachen' ironically means 'the place of wild roses'. Siachen is a high altitude place located in the Karakorum Range of mountains. It is the second highest glacier in the world about 5,472 meters above sea level. With a glaciated expanse of about 700 sq km spread over the Karakorum mountain range, Siachen is highly inhospitable with an environment unfit for human habitation. During winter there are snowy winds, as a result the temperature goes down to -50 degree centigrade.

From the very day Pakistan came into being there ensued confrontation between India and Pakistan. Since Siachen is a part of Kashmir, it became a bone of contention between the two countries. The story of Siachen conflict is quite different from that of Kashmir dispute. Pakistan fought four wars to expand Pakistan territory into Kashmir valley but failed altogether. The first conflict between India and Pakistan took place with the accession of Jammu and Kashmir with India in 1947 AD. With the UNISCO's efforts, a standstill agreement came into effect, which subsequently became the line of control. No line of control was marked in the Siachen area due to the inhospitable environmental conditions.

The conflict over Siachen started nearly twenty years ago, to be precise on April 13, 1984. Due to inhospitable conditions there was no habitation so no security personnel were kept by India or Pakistan. The place was almost neglected, except for mountaineers who sought permission from Pakistan to go for an expedition. In 1972 AD, the Shimla agreement was signed between Prime Minister Indira Gandhi and Prime Minister, Zulfikar Ali Bhutto, where a vague demarcation of this territory was made but no specific instructions were noted as to who would have authority over the Siachen glacier. Since 1972, both India as well as Pakistan claimed the ownership of this territory. According to

Kent Bringer and Air Marshall K C Cariappa in the book *Peace Parks*,[24] "The Siachen Glacier region thus became a 6,000 meter high battleground between India and Pakistan. Although many troops have been killed in the skirmishes that have occurred on this highest battleground in the world, more fatalities and causalities have been caused by the inhospitable terrain and environment."

Meanwhile, Pakistan continued to allow mountaineers of different countries for their expeditions to the Siachen glacier area. A Japanese expedition who wanted to climb some important peaks in this glacier got permission from Pakistan in 1984. The peak they climbed was located on the Eastern side of the glacier overlooking Aksai Chin, which is at present occupied by China but is claimed by India as its territory. At this point it seems India awakened from its slumber and decided to exercise her control over this barren, inhospitable glacier area to link it with Kashmir territory. Thus the Indian authorities forbade any expedition to visit the Siachen glacier though permitted by Pakistan. India, decided to send an army to this area to get it under their control. However, India selected some troops from the Ladakh region who were already acclimatised as a result of their mountaineering expedition to Antarctica with proper outfits imported from Germany. Pakistan lacked expertise in acclimatising their soldiers and had no proper outfits for them.

Islamabad, feeling apprehensive about Indian occupation of Siachen, decided to send their army before Indian forces could have occupied it. They approached a London Company for the supply of outfits suitable for Antarctica climate. This information s reached Indian authorities who sensed Pakistani intentions and immediately sent Indian troops on April 13, 1984 to occupy the Glacier area under 'Operation Meghdoot'. Pakistan had to launch their Siachen operation on 17 April 1987. The four days difference proved a disaster for Pakistan. When they reached there they found the Indian army had already occupied the major portion of Siachen.

In this assault India's brave Subedar Bana Singh, (honorary captain) in June 26, 1987, in spite of inclement weather and heavy snow, along with his men attacked the Pakistani picket. The strategic peak was captured and all the Pakistani soldiers were killed. Subedar Bana Singh was awarded Param Vir Chakra.

According to General Pervez Musharaf's, memoirs, "Pakistan lost 2,331 km area in this territory." It is not that Pakistan has accepted defeat and left her claim on Siachen territory. Pakistan army is present and has occupied some part of the area. The skirmishes between Indian army and Pakistan forces do take place but they are few and the fatality of the security forces is more due to the inhospitable climate than use of weapons.

The glacier`s melting waters are the source of the river Indus, a vital water source for both India and Pakistan. Global warming has had its worst impact in the Himalayas with the Glacier melting at an unprecedented rate.

Ten
Lakes, Springs, Rivers and Bridges

The Kashmir valley is encircled by the splendour of the mighty Himalayan mountain ranges. These mountains, with lovely glades, glaciers and forests give it a unique identity. These mountains also used to guard the valley from any outside attacks. The unique charm of these mountains and the valley gave it the sobriquet of 'Switzerland of the East'.

The people of the valley are heavily dependent on the natural resources such as jungles and meadows for their subsistence. Over the years, there have been environmental changes and therefore some of the glaciers have vanished. One can recall that hardly 50 years ago, some people of Srinagar would earn their living by bringing glacier ice in a basket, during summers, from the nearest mountains. They made their livelihood by selling it to the people in the towns. To attract the attention of the people they would sing in praise of the ice and say:

Wai Yakho! Kamyu Van Volmakho Ha yakho—Andrei Kyazi Golkho Yakho'

'Wow! You the rock Ice! Look I brought you from the glacier of the rear forests—why do you melt within?' With the vanishing of these glaciers, this songs have also vanished. Gradually the jungles are being reduced and the lakes are drying. Once the masters of the jungles, animals have now entered human habitation.

God has bestowed Kashmir with lakes. These beautiful lakes in the valley are facing the threat of being silted up due to soil erosion and formation of 'Floating Gardens' and other contaminations. There are other factors which are contributing to shrinking of these lakes, such as flow of municipal and industrial wastes, encroachments for cultivation etc. Boatmen, tourists and others, who are encroaching on these lakes, are contributing, to some extent, towards their extinction. If the lakes like Dal Lake become polluted or dry up, no tourist would like to come to the valley. This Switzerland of the East will be lost. It will be a loss not only to the people of Kashmir but to humanity. It is, therefore, the responsibility of each and every inhabitant of Kashmir—Government officials, industrialists, the boatmen, even the tourists who enjoy the beauty of the lakes to protect them from pollution and extinction.

Famous lakes of Jammu and Kashmir

Wular Lake

Wular Lake is India's fresh water lake and one of the largest in Asia. It is mentioned as Mahapadmasaras in *Nilamatapurana*. Al-Baruni named it Bolor. It was also called Ullola as it has high leaping waves. At a distance of about 60 km from Srinagar, it is situated in Baramulla district towards northwest of Kashmir near Sopore and Bandipora area. It is 16 km long and 9.6 km wide. It plays a significant role in the Hydrographic system of the Kashmir valley by acting as a huge absorption basin for the annual floodwaters. Its economic importance for the valley is that it provides 60 per cent of the fish yield of Kashmir region. It is also a haven for the migratory birds. The lake once covered over 200 km but is now reduced to only about 80 km. The rivers that join it are the Bohnar, Madamati, and Erin rivers. From the mountain ranges, river Jhelum, and Ningal from the South also join it.

The famous King Zain-ul-Abidin constructed an Island-palace and a resort house in the middle of the lake in 1444 AD. Before taking up such a stupendous task he consulted the wise men of his time who encouraged him to take up the task. According to R C Kak,[1] "The island was named Zainalanka after its builder, and still retains that name."

Manasbal Lake

Manasbal is a fresh water lake covering an area of about 2.81 km and, is located about 30 km north of Srinagar via Shadipur, Nasim and Ganderbal road. The name Manasbal is derived from the Lake Mansarover. It is surrounded by villages such as Kondabal, Karokbal and Gratbal. It is considered the deepest lake in Kashmir valley. It is used by the locals for drinking water and fishing. There are legends woven around the lake. It is said that it is bottomless. There is no source of the lake water except rain, snow and about 1,200 to 1,500 springs that feed it.

Manasbal is also known for its lotus (Nelumbo Nucifera) and delicious lotus-stem (Nelumbo Lutea) growth. According to R C Kak,[2] "The lake is an ideal abode for the happy lotus-eater, who dreams away his days reclining under the shady Chinar trees, and passes his evenings in watching the long streaks of moonlight flitting across the mirror-like surface of the water."

Naranbagh Lake

Naranbagh Lake covers a 0.24 km area and is situated in Baramulla district. It is a small, shallow lake on the floodplain of the river Jhelum. It also produces a little fish for the local people.

Gangabal Lake

Gangabal Lake is cradled by the Haramoukh Mountain at a height of about 12,000 feet and is approximately five km in circumference.

Sheshnag Lake

The legend goes that while on his way to Amarnath cave, Lord Shiva left his snake on the way. The place is therefore known as Sheshnag Lake. It is situated near Vavjan, en-route to Amarnath cave about 30 km from Pahalgam at a height of 11,800 feet.

Vishansar Lake

The snow-bound Nichnai Pass, is the vintage point from where to ascend to Vishansar valley where we find the Vishansar lake at a height of about 12,600 feet. This lake is situated in the vicinity of Sonamarg.

Hokersar Lake

Hokersar Lake is situated in Badgam district. It supports a small fishery industry. It also provides water for irrigation.

Sukh-Dukh Lakes

These two lakes, according to legend, are two teardrops of Goddess Parvati, depicting two sides of life such as happiness and grief. These frozen lakes are cradled at Haramoukh Mountain.

Pashakuri Lake

The Pashakuri Lake occupies 0.10 km area. It is a rural valley lake near Pampore. It does not have any inflow or outflow but depends on springs.

Valley's City Lakes

Dal Lake

The beautiful Dal Lake is a gift of God not only to the people of Kashmir but also to the whole world. Its beauty gives new life to the hearts of the people who come to Kashmir. Hassan, a celebrated historian of Kashmir, described the water of the lake as sweet and delicious. He said it was so clear that one could see the fish down below. Hassan has mentioned in *Tehreek-e-Hassan* that the present Dal lake was a plain desert which was known as Vitaalini Marg. King Pravarasena closed the River Behat (now River Jhelum) from Nowpora side and brought the river into the city by way of the Koh-i-Maran (also known as Hari Parbat Hillock). After a great deal of time, the river Jhelum rose in spate and as a result of the deluge, during the reign of King Durlabhavardhana (625-661 AD), this desert became a lake. Sultan Sikandar (1389-1413 AD) constructed a very strong bund upon it from Nayidyar to Nishat Bagh along with six bridges — Chowdhury Bagh Bridge, Dood Phokhri Bridge, Tulkhan Bridge, Gani Bridge, Oont Bridge and Nishat Bridge. Another bund from Khwajayarbal to Aishabad (presently Ashai-Bagh) on Sodrakhun lake, (now the Nageen Basin), was constructed by Saif Khan, Governor of Kashmir who ruled the valley in 1647 AD.

Almost all the people at the helm of affairs in the history of Kashmir have enjoyed the matchless beauty of the Dal Lake. Legend says that Dewan Kirpa Ram, Governor of Maharaja Ranjit Singh, used to sail on the Dal Lake in a big boat, which was rowed by one hundred women, nude up to their chest and dancing girls used to dance in the boat. Dal Lake has two parts, the Lakut Dal (small Dal) and the Boad Dal (big Dal), separated by a swampy bund. There are two artificial islands in the lake known as Rupa lank and Sona lank. Surrounded by enchanting mountains on its three sides, it is undoubtedly one of the most beautiful lakes of the world. It is also the second largest lake in the State of Jammu and Kashmir, with numerous gardens and orchards all along its shores. House boats and Shikaras add to the beauty of the lakes.

Sir Walter R Lawrence, who was Resettlement Commissioner of Kashmir, in 1887 AD, wrote "Perhaps in the whole world there is no corner as pleasant as the Dal Lake. The water of the Dal is clear and soft as silk, and the people say that the shawls of Kashmir owe much of their excellence to being washed in the soft waters of the lake."

Nageen Lake

Nageen Lake is an offshoot of the Dal Lake. It is located at the east of Srinagar city at the foothill of the mountain Zabarwan.

Harvan Lake

Harvan Lake, the main source of water to Srinagar city is situated at a distance of about 21 km from Srinagar. It is connected with river Jhelum by a canal near Sumbal. The ancient name of Harvan is 'Sadarhadvana' meaning 'grove of six saints'. According to Kalhana, the great Buddhist scholar Nagarjuna lived there during the period of Abhimanyu-I, who ruled over the valley.

Harvan is famous because Vasugupta, the greatest thinker, philosopher, teacher and the father of Kashmir Shaivism, is said to have lived near Mahadeva Mountain, which is near the valley of the Harvan stream behind the Shalimar Gardens near Srinagar. Tradition goes that he (Vasugupta) received a command from Lord Shiva, who appeared to him in a dream and instructed him to go to a certain rock on which he would find teachings inscribed. This rock called 'Shankaropala' is still visited by devotees.

It is an artificial lake which takes water from the Marsar Lake. It is about five km long and one kilometre wide.

Other Lakes

Mansar Lake

Mansar Lake is in Jammu region. It is situated about 62 km from Jammu and is fringed by forest covered hills.

Tarsar Marsar Lake

Tarsar and Marsar Lakes are situated near Nagberan village of Pulwama district. These lakes are about five kilometres away from each other.

Sruinsar Lake

Sruinsar Lake is about 42 km away from Jammu.

The Rivers of Kashmir

Vitasta- Veuth-Kashur Darya-Jhelum

"Sangarav gaash heuot lolieh lalvunayeh
Veuth aayee maharin sonuyyeh"

Dina Nath Nadim

The mountain tops have started cuddling the sun rays in their lap

Lo and Behold here comes bride Vitasta to her own Kashmir. (Translation K Mota)

Most civilisations, all over the world, have developed on the banks of rivers. In fact civilisations would get all their basic needs from the rivers, which helped them in forming the settlements. In Kashmir too, civilisation began on the banks of Vitasta, now Jhelum. Therefore, River Jhelum has been witness to, good or bad, all events of the collective past that have made the people of Kashmir what they are today. It is a witness to the history of Kashmir.

The legend: According to the scriptures, Kasyapa Rishi requested God Shankar and Goddess Sati to purify Kashmir. Goddess Sati gifted the land with the sacred River Vitasta. According to the *Nilamatapurana*,[3] "O father of the world, I shall assume the form of a river in the Netherworld. Make a stroke with your spear near the abode of Nila, where, O lord, while breaking the mountain, was placed the point of the plough. By that stroke of the spear, I shall come out of the Netherworld and shall follow the way made with the plough up to the place where there is the great river Sindhu."

God Hara did this[4]. "Sankara himself named her as Vitasta. Because Hara had excavated with the spear a ditch measuring one Vitasta, through which the good river, gone to the Netherworld had come out, so she was given the name Vitasta by Svayambhu." Agreeing to his request, Lord Shankara struck his trident and out surged River Vitasta from a spring near Nilanag. Once the river was born, the people of the land thronged to have a sacred bath to purify themselves. The legend goes that while she started moving towards the city, an evil Brahmin saw it moving and instantly the river vanished. However, Kasyapa Rishi once again prayed and requested her to reappear.

Vitasta alias Vyeth is a sacred river for the Hindus of Kashmir. All the Hindus, rich or poor, celebrate 'Vyeth-i Truwah', as its birthday. They light lamps and float them on the river. Emperor Akbar and emperor Jahangir also participated in this festival. According to *Tuzuk-i Jahangiri*, on this day, whoever has a house on the bank of the river should light lamps on the Shab-i-Baraat.

History of the name

Jhelum has many names. In the Vedic period, the river was called Vitasta. It was one of the mighty rivers of 'Sapta-Sindhu' as mentioned in Rig-Veda. From Kashmir it enters Pakistan. As it enters the territory of Pakistan the river is called 'Kashur Darya' (Kashmiri River). A great battle between Alexander the Great and Raja Porus was fought on the banks of Hydaspes in 326 BC, hence River Jhelum was also named as Hydaspes by ancient Greeks.

Source

This 203 km long river—Vitasta, Vyeth or Jhelum, is the life-line of the people of Kashmir. It rises from a spring at Verinag in Shahabad Pargana, situated at the foot of the Pir Pantsal Range on the left of Kazi Nag Range, in the south-eastern part of the valley of Kashmir, in India. This spring was known as Nilakunda or Nilanag, the serpent king.

Tributaries of River Jhelum

- At Khannabal it is joined by three rivulets known as Arpat, Bring and Sadrin. Vishva is a small river (earlier known as Visoka), which joins Jhelum below Bijbihara at Sangam. This tributary is fed by the Kausarnag Lake.
- Romushi stream is another tributary that flows from Kharmarg which rises from Pir Paschal. This stream joins the Vitasta at Kakapora.
- Dudhganga stream flows from Ludurmarg from Pir Pantsal and joins Jhelum. The junction is known as Sangam. In olden times it was called 'Gambhira Sangani' (Gambhira literally means deep).
- Lidar is one of the largest tributaries, which joins river Jhelum. It flows from Sheshnag Lake to the east of Pahalgam.
- Ferozepur Nullah originates from the mountains of Baramulla-Gulmarg area and then joins the Jhelum.

- Sind Nullah that joins River Jhelum originates from the inner Himalayas at Drass and is fed by Gangabal Lake of Haramoukh Mountain.

At Khannabal, it becomes a complete river and proceeds to Srinagar from where it goes to Baramulla and to Wular Lake, the delta of Jhelum. From the northern range of the Great Himalayas at Chowkibal it enters Pakistan through a deep narrow gorge. It assumes the name of Kashur Darya and then enters District Jhelum.

District Jhelum of Pakistan has great significance for India. Many great personalities of India have born here, such as Dr Manmohan Singh, Inder Kumar Gujral, the erstwhile Prime Ministers of India, Sunil Dutt, the great thespian and politician, Gulzar Sahab, the distinguished poet, lyrist and film director. Gulzar Sahab has expressed his love for the river Jhelum and said that he has mentioned this enchanting river in many of his poems.

Ferry through seven bridges of Srinagar

The river Jhelum flows gently through Srinagar, carrying on its chest the houseboats—Lare Nav/Dunga, (a kind of houseboat for personal living of the boatmen and family), Shikara boats etc. There are various types of water transportations like 'Dembhnav', which is a flat bottomed small wooden boat for ferrying vegetables, flowers and fish from the place of production to the market. There are boats like 'Khuch' and 'Bahatch'. These are meant purely for carrying heavy articles like stones and construction material, wood and grains. While 'Khuch' is roofless, 'Bahatch' has a straw roof for the protection of grains from rain, wind and snow. Khuch can carry 200 maunds of cargo while Bahatch can carry 800 to 1,000 maunds of cargo. It has an accommodation of one room for a small family. One can see these boats on their move to earn their living.

This river in Srinagar is a great source of revenue to Kashmir. On the banks of this river, thousands of hotels and shops, attract tourists and locals. The small shikarawala (boatman) also earns his living by ferrying people from one bank to another. They also carry tourists on joy trips to the seven bridges.

River Indus

River Indus is one of the largest rivers of the world. It belongs to three countries—China, India, and Pakistan. Its length is approximately 3,200 km. Its source is the holy lake of Mansarover in Tibet and the glaciers around that feed the river. It begins at the confluence of the Sengge and Gar rivers that drain the Nganglong Kangri and Gangdise Shan mountain ranges. From Tibet it flows northwest through Leh where it is joined by Zanskar River. At Kargil it is joined by Drass River. Then it travels to Kashmir and on to Punjab province of southwest Pakistan.

According to Rig Veda, Indus was known as Sindhu. In fact, there is a mention of Sapta Sindhu—the seven sacred rivers of Hindus . The rivers are Sindhu (Indus), Vitasta (Jhelum), Chandrabhaga/Ashkani/Asuhi (Chenab), Purshini (Ravi), Vipasa (Beas), Satadru (Sutlej) and Saruri (Saraswati, now vanished). Sindhu, according to *Mahabharata* was a kingdom on the banks of the river. Jayadratha, brother-in-law of Duryodhana was the king of Sindhu. Indus River, when it flows through Kashmir, is joined by Jhelum at Shadipur. The place is very sacred for Hindus and they celebrate a festival on a particular day there. The lower Indus was also called 'Mehran' in Persian language.

The great Indus Valley Civilisation, the excavations at Harappa and Mohenjo-Daro tell us, was flourishing as early as about 3,500 BC. Paleolithic sites have been discovered in Pothohar near Pakistan's capital Islamabad, with the stone tools of the Soan culture. In ancient Gandhara, near Islamabad, evidence of cave dwellers who lived 15,000 years ago have been discovered at Mardan.

The River Indus has as many as 14 tributaries and for the people of Ladakh and Pakistan it is their lifeline. When in Pakistan, it is joined by Chenab, Ravi, Sutlej, Jhelum and Beas. It widens and becomes a magnificent river and at last it submerges into the Arabian Sea.

Chenab River

River Chenab, (a lifeline of Punjab in India) is formed by the confluence of the Chandra and Bhaga rivers, in Lahul Spiti District of Himachal Pradesh. It enters Pangi valley of Chamba District and then flows through southern Jammu and Kashmir to Kishtwar, Doda and Akhnoor, from where it moves to Punjab and finally to Pakistan where it unites with Jhelum and then with Sutlej. During the Vedic period this river was known as Chandrabhaga. Chenab in Punjabi language is in fact, 'water of the moon' Chan (Moon) Aab (Water). It is also known as 'Ashkani' or 'Iskmati' in Sanskrit language. The Greeks named it 'Acesines'.

Famous springs of Kashmir

A spring in Kashmiri language is known as Nag. The word has another meaning that is a snake. The people of Kashmir worshiped both. Tradition says that great snakes lived in these great springs to protect them. *Nilamatapurana* also gives us legends about Nags. Nilanag had his abode in Nilakunda, the modern Verinag. Nilanag, for a long time was considered a serpent that got transformed into human form. There are many more legends woven around Nags (springs and serpents). With the spread of Buddhism, people left worshiping the Nags. According to Kalhana,[5] when the traditional customs were broken in the land, the Nags, who had lost their oblations, sent down excessive snow, and thus destroyed the people.

According to Walter R Lawrence,[6] "The whole valley is rich in superstitions, and there is not a mountain, river, or spring which has not some quaint legend attached to it." Further he writes,[7] "It is dangerous to discuss a great mystery as the Hindu religion; yet I cannot help noticing the important part which water-springs and snakes play in the Kashmir mythology." There are innumerable springs in the valley and some of them are known worldwide.

Verinag

Verinag is one of the largest and finest springs in Kashmir. According to *Nilamatapurana*, Nilakunda was the abode of Nilanag, the king of serpents. The spring is said to be the source of the River Vitasta. According to the legend, Goddess Parvati had promised Kasyapa Rishi that she would appear near Nilakunda. Another view is that the spring has clear blue water. In Kashmiri language blue is 'niul' and that is why it is named as 'blue spring', Nilanag.

Jahangir, in fact, fell in love with this spring and he ordered the place be beautified. In 1620 AD, he got stones for this purpose from Iran. He constructed a small palace with Turkish baths. The banks of this spring were constructed in octagonal shape. A beautiful garden with Chinar trees was also laid around the spring with an outlet for the water. Seven years later, Shah Jahan, the son of Jahangir, constructed cascades and fountains in front of the spring. According to Abdul Majid Mattoo,[8] "In 1636, Shahjahan visited the garden, but he did not like the layout and the buildings of the garden. Malik Haider was appointed as Daroga Bayutal and directed to remodel the whole plan."

Jahangir was not only happy to see the valley but was passionate about it. In the year 1627 AD, he fell ill. He decided to visit Kashmir to recoup his health and remained till the end of summer. He was advised to move to the plains in the winter. Says P N K Bamzai,[9] "Reluctantly, he (Jahangir), accepted the advise but on reaching Behramgala, the disease took a serious turn, and on November 7, 1627 he breathed his last. While on his death bed, he had expressed the wish that his body be carried back to Verinag and buried there. But this was not thought expedient and instead he was buried at Lahore."

Kukarnag

As per revenue records the real name of Kukarnag is Bindoo Zalangam. According to *Ain-i-Akbari*,[10] "There is also another spring called Kukarnag, the water of which is limpid, cold and wholesome. Should a hungry person drink of it, his hunger will be appeased, and its satisfaction in turn renews appetite." According to the official website of the Anantnag District, there is a famous legend. "A saint (Gushwami) came here from some unknown place along with his bucket. As he rested some womenfolk came from the nearby densely forested areas in search of water. They failed in their search. They saw the saint in a deep sleep with his bucket in front of him. In order to kill their thirst, the women opened the lid of the bucket and found a big snake in it. The snake escaped from the bucket and suddenly changed into a 'Kukar' (chicken in Kashmiri language). It dug the soil with its claws at many places and water gushed out from these places. Water started gathering up slowly. Suddenly the saint opened his eyes and with his magical powers stopped the overflow of the springs. Had he not awoken the gushing water would have transformed into a big lake." The spring is famous for rearing Trout fish.

Cheshma Shahi

Cheshma Shahi's actual name given by Shah Jahan was Kauser-e-Shahi.[11] According to an inscription said to have been put up at the gateway, the garden was constructed in the reign of Shah Jahan, probably by the emperor himself. The exact wording of the verse which contained the date is as follows:

Guftamash Bahr-I Chasma Tarikhe — Guft Bar Go Kausar-I Shahi.

I enquired of him regarding the date of the spring; he replied, 'says Kausar-i Shahi'

(R C Kak)

Among the Mughal gardens of Kashmir, Cheshma Shahi fascinated Shah Jahan. It is said that once Mumtaz Mahal fell ill and the physicians were unable to cure her. Tradition says that a physician told her to drink water from Cheshma Shahi only. Shah Jahan preferred to stay at the place where Pari Mahal stands now, and Mumtaz Mahal used to drink water from the Cheshma Shahi. She had a miraculous recovery.

Shah Jahan had appointed Ali Mardan Khan, the famous architect and statesman, to look after the construction of the garden. However, according to Abdul Majid Mattoo,[12] "Dara Shikoh was impressed by the natural setting of the place. He laid out a garden and built a few houses and mosque on its site." He further writes, "Subsequently, Jahan Aara Begum laid out a beautiful garden around the spring and called it Cheshma Shahi."

It was not only the Mughals who visited the garden but the Dogra Rulers and even Pandit Jawaharlal Nehru were fascinated with it. Cheshma Shahi is located about eight km from Srinagar city, north of Pari Mahal and south of Nishat Bagh. There is a small garden around the spring. The spring is laid out as a rectangle, measuring about 108 by 38 meters. Cheshma Shahi commands a fascinating view of the Dal Lake.

Tradition says that it was Rupa Bhawani, the poetess of Kashmir, who discovered the Cheshma Shahi.

Vecharnag

The word Vecharnag consists of two words — 'Vechar' (deliberation) and Nag (spring). The place has remained a seat of learning from times immemorial. Legend goes that Lord Shiva at the time of creating this universe counselled with other gods at this place. Vecharnag is a spring receiving its water from Gangabal Range of mountains in the north of Kashmir. In the centre of the spring there is a round stone which is known as 'Baderpeeth'. Great thinkers such as Adi Shankaracharya, Abhinavagupta, and Hiuen Tsang visited the place. It is said the Janthari (Kashmiri Almanac) was compiled here. Vecharnag is also called Sath Ras

Nag because seven springs existed at this place. Now only four springs are active.

Sukhnag

Sukhnag, previously known as Sokhanag, is a beautiful spring which is located near Tosamaidan in Budgam District. Moving like a serpent through the mountains it suddenly dives from a height of 20 feet and transforms into a beautiful waterfall at Kanj Zubji.

Vasaknag

Vasaknag is about 12 miles from Verinag. The spring flows for six months and runs dry for the next six months. A legend goes that when the water starts flowing from this spring the weather becomes rough and harsh. Its water is also used for irrigation.

Matan Spring

The spring of Matan consists of one of the oldest temples of Kashmir. It is believed to belong to the 8th century. This place owes its name to Martand Temple which is nearby. It is enroute to the famous health resort, Pahalgam. The tourists who are going to Pahalgam visit the sanctum sanctorum. The spring has crystal clear water and lots of fish. People treat the fish as holy and therefore do not eat them though the fish can be caught with ones bare hands.

Khirbhawani

Khirbhawani is one of the holiest religious places of the Hindus of Kashmir. It consists of one spring, which usually changes colours. Sometimes it is greenish, then everything is calm and tranquil; but if the colour changes to black, the legend goes that some catastrophe will befall.

Nagbal Spring

Nagbal has been one of the famous religious places of Hindus in Kashmir since medieval times. The place is in Anantnag district. The Nagbal temple houses the image of Ananta Bhagwan which is set up at the outlet of the spring. The temple was built by Dogra ruler Maharaja Ranbir Singh in 1830 AD. Another temple of Lord Shiva adjacent to it was constructed by Maharaja Pratap Singh. It is on the eastern side of the city of Anantnag. This spring rises from the foot of a small hillock. The ponds are full of fish. Hindus and even the Muslims do not eat the fish found in these ponds. There is also a Sulphur spring in which people take a bath to get rid of their skin ailments.

Panzath Nag

Panzath Nag is in Anantnag district near Larikpora. It has lots of fish in it. Its water joins the Jhelum River.

Goutam Nag

This is another spring in Anantnag and the name is dedicated to Gautama Rishi.

Gardens of Jammu and Kashmir

Nishat and Shalimar gardens were constructed in the valley when Kashmir came under Mughal domination. Even today these gardens are known as Mughal gardens.

Nishat Bagh

Parallel to Shalimar Bagh, Asaf Khan, elder brother of Noor Jahan, constructed a magnificent garden, with a variety of fruit trees. It is named Nishat Bagh (Garden of Joy). This garden is designed as per Persian Chahar Bagh (Four Gardens), which takes inspiration from the Quranic description of heaven. With a splendid view of the Dal Lake and Zabarwan mountain at the back, the magnificent Nishat Bagh, which is about 11 Km from the city of Srinagar, is not considered a royal garden because no King was involved in its construction.

Nishat Bagh has twelve terraces. Each terrace is a garden in itself. Like Shalimar garden it also has a canal about four meters wide and 20 meters deep, running in the centre of the garden, decorated with fountains. It is divided in two parts — the lower Pleasure Garden and the upper Zenana Garden. The Zenana level is densely planted. A two story baradari is also constructed on it.

Asaf Khan started its construction during the reign of Jahangir. It commands a splendid panoramic view. The garden was completed when Shah Jahan became the emperor. Nishat Bagh had become more popular than Shalimar. Asaf Khan hosted a feast in honour of Shah Jahan on his arrival in Kashmir. When Shah Jahan saw the garden he was delighted. Many a time he mentioned his admiration of it to Asaf Khan hoping that Asaf Khan may offer the garden to him as a gift. But that did not happen and Shah Jahan was disappointed. His anger was visible when he ordered that the supply of the water to the garden be stopped. Water was stopped and the garden started losing its sheen, lustre, and grandeur. This upset Asaf Khan. He began to remain depressed. One of his loyal servants could not bear this. Without telling anyone, he restored the water supply of the garden. Writes RC Kak,[13] "One day, lost in a melancholy reverie, he at last fell fast asleep in the shade by the empty water-course. At length a noise aroused him; rubbing his eyes, he could hardly believe what he saw, for the fountains were all playing merrily once more and the long carved water chutes were white with foam. A faithful servant, risking his life, had defied the Emperor's orders, and removed the obstruction from the stream." This did not amuse Asaf Khan and he at once got the flow of water stopped. The news spread like wildfire and ultimately reached Shah Jahan. Instead of punishing the servant, the king praised him for his devotion towards his master and bestowed him with the robe of honour. Shah Jahan then issued an official order and restored the water supply to the garden.

Shalimar Bagh

In Sanskrit Language, Shalimar means 'Abode of Love'. It is one of the most fascinating gardens of Kashmir. The laying out of the Shalimar garden was started in 1619 AD by Jahangir and his wife Noor Jahan. It is difficult to say if it was Jahangir or his wife who had the taste for building gardens. However, both of them created a unique pleasure place and splendid marvel in the form of Shalimar. Jahangir dedicated this abode of love to his wife Noor Jahan.

According to MA Stein,[14] "The whole mountain-ridge which stretches to the south of Triphar and along the Dal Lake bore in ancient times the name of Sridvarv , situated opposite Mahadeva hillls. On the opposite side of the valley rises the bold peak of Mahadeva to the height of 13,000 feet. Numerous references to it in the Nilamata, Sarvavatara and other texts show that it was in old times just as now frequented as a Tirtha." However, there is no mention of Shalimar garden in the ancient scriptures.

Some of the chroniclers have mentioned that Shalimar Bagh was initially constructed by Pravarasena-II, who built a city in his own name which was ultimately renamed as Srinagar. Truly he was a great builder of temples and gardens. However, there is no mention that he named any of his gardens as Shalimar.

"The garden then became a royal residence and the court seems to have indelibly imprinted its spirit of decorum upon it. As the garden was probably designed by the Empress Nur Jahan...,"[15] says RC Kak. It must have been on the insistence of Jahangir that certain sentences were written in Persian language in the summerhouse of the Shalimar.

The famous couplet:

"*Gar Firdous Bar-Ru-e- Zameen Ast*
Hamin Ast-O Hamin Ast-O Hamin Ast."
(Firdous if at all there is a heaven anywhere
It is here, It is here, It is here,)

According to Bandu Desh,[16] "This garden is divided into three parts. The out-part containing a pavilion and used by Jahangir for his audience was similar to Diwan-e-Aam of Mughal buildings. The second part was exclusively used by Emperor himself similar to Diwan-e-Khas." Situated in the lap of Mahadev Mountain, the garden was originally known as Farah Bakhsh meaning 'delightful garden'. Shalimar Bagh is influenced by Persian gardens that have harmonious amalgam of design and creative use of landscaping. The garden has four terraces. It has a pleasant canal in the centre which runs down from the hills. This stream has a line of fountains in the centre. The canal receives its water from Harvan Lake. When Shah Jahan took over the reigns of the country he made various additions and alterations in this garden.

Achbal Bagh

Achbal Bagh is about 70 Km southeast of Srinagar, situated in Anantnag district, in the town of Achbal. Achbal was known as 'Akkshavala'. This town was built by King Aksa, son of King Nara II of the Gonanda Dynasty. It was famous for sacred pond known as Kapateshvara. This was a pilgrimage spot for the Hindus of Kashmir. Gushing water from this magnificent spring and the water of Kapatesvara flow into the Arpat river (ancient name Harsapatha). Arpat is a tributary of Jhelum River.

During the Mughal period, a beautiful garden was laid down by Queen Noor Jahan in 1920 AD. It was her favourite garden. However, Princess Jahan Aara the daughter of Shah Jahan redesigned it in the year 1634 AD. According to Abdul Majid Mattoo,[17] "The garden was called Sahibabad. In 1662, Aurangzeb assigned the garden to Zeb-un-nisa begum." The upper portion of the garden is called 'Bagh-i-Begum Abad'.

Achbal is located on a hillside and the garden was much bigger. Today it is only about 247 meters long and 155 meters wide. Writes Bernier Francois,[18] "The spring gushes out of the earth with violence, as if issued from the bottom of some well, and the water is so abundant that it ought rather to be called a river than a fountain. It is excellent water, and cold as ice. The garden is very handsome, laid out in regular walks, and full of fruit-trees, apple, pear, plum, apricot, and cherry."

Bagh-i-Zaffar Khan

Zaffar Khan was the governor of Kashmir during Jahangir's rule. He replaced Itiqad Khan. However, after Jahangir's death Shah Jahan replaced him with Zaffar Khan . Zaffar Khan was very efficient and had a flair for construction. He constructed a garden on the banks of Dal Lake and named it as Bagh-i-Zaffar Khan. According to Abdul Majid Mattoo,[19] "Zaffar Khan offered the garden as a 'peshkash' (offering) to Shah Jahan during the latter's visit to Kashmir. On account of its vastness, it was named 'Bagh-i-Tulani'." With the end of Mughal rule it was not looked after and it is now extinct.

Bagh-i-Sadiqabad

Emperor Shah Jahan's governor, Sadiq Khan, laid out a fascinating garden and constructed a palatial building known as Ishrat Mahal. However, Emperor Shah Jahan, during his visit in 1634 AD ordered the building to be converted into a prayer house. In its place stands the sanctum sanctorum of Hazrat Bal.

Bagh-i-Naseem

Naseem Bagh (garden of breezes) is the oldest garden laid down by Mughals in Kashmir. It is situated on the western side of the Dal Lake. In 1589 AD, Akbar laid down the beautiful garden. It is full of Chinar trees and has camping facilities for visitors. It is said that at some point the garden had about two thousand Chinar trees but now only a few remain. The unique combination of lake and mountain scenery view from this garden is fascinating.

Nehru Park

Nehru Park, at Gagribal Point of Dal Lake was laid down after partition by the Government of Jammu and Kashmir in 1951. Named after the first Prime Minister of India, it is a small garden with a building which has been made a restaurant. This is a great attraction for tourists.

Other Gardens

The other gardens laid down are either in ruins or have been affected by encroachments—Noor Bagh by Noor Jahan in the vicinity of Idgah,

Bagh-i-Iradat Khan at Nowapora and Bagh-i-Ilahi by Yusuf Khan Rizvi in the vicinity of Batspora.

Famous Resorts of Kashmir

Pahalgam

Pahalgam is a premier resort of the Kashmir valley. It is situated about 7,000 feet above sea level. Prior to its development, it was a village of shepherds. It is about 96km away from Srinagar. It is in the district of Anantnag. It also cradles the wonderful river Lidar which flowes gushing, frothing, and crashing on rocks and boulders creating musical sounds. Tourists can enjoy their stay in this exotic place with beautiful pastures of Baisaran, thickly populated charming pine forests and the beautiful picnic spot of Hajan, where there is an ancient fifth-century temple of Lord Shiva in the nearby village of Mamal. Pahalgam is also the gateway to the Amarnath cave temple.

Gulmarg

Gulmarg means 'Meadow of Flowers'. This is one of the finest and premier hill and health resorts of the country. Originally Gulmarg was called `Gaurimarg` named after Lord Shiva's wife. Later on the present name was given by Sultan Yusuf Shah in the 16th century. He visited this exotic place frequently and must have made his amorous advances towards his beloved Habba Khatoon here. He was also inspired by the magnificent beauty of its grassy slopes emblazoned with wild flowers. Towering trees on the mountains around and the lush green valley is a feast not only for the eyes but the soul as well. It must have been here that Habba Khatoon composed her Maqam Ragas and songs. Nature has bestowed the place with abundant variety of flowers. It is said that once Emperor Jahangir collected about 21 varieties of flowers in the meadow. Situated at about 8,700 feet above sea level, it is at a distance of about 57 Km from Srinagar. One travels by bus upto Tangmarg and from there one walks through fir covered hillside or takes a pony ride up to Gulmarg. During the winter months Gulmarg acquires a new persona when it wears a thick blanket of snow and tourists enjoy skiing here. It also cradles the highest golf course in the world.

Yusmarg

Yusmarg is about 50 Km away from Srinagar in district Budgam. This picturesque place is encircled by dense forests full of pine and fir trees, with the breathtaking landscape backdrop of fascinating snow clad mountains. Yusmarg is known as miniature Gulmarg. It is situated in Pir Panchal range.

Only about 13 Km away is the symbol of Kashmiriyat, ' Chrar-e-Sharif', the resting place of the famous sufi saint, Sheikh Noor-ud-Din (Nund Rishi).

Sonamarg

Sonamarg (Golden Meadow) is gateway to Ladakh. Situated at a distance of about 85 Km from Srinagar, it is about 9,100 feet above sea level. In summer the place is flooded with flowers. It is surrounded by high mountains with a variety of tall trees such as fir, pines, and silver birch. The snowy peaks of the mountains reflect the golden rays of the sun. The effect is awe inspiring, mesmerising and bewitching. According to Desh Bandu,[20] "In ancient past the traders from Central Asia wondered at the mighty glaciers and silent lakes of this place and very often camped here." Sonamarg is yet another route to Amarnath Cave Temple. Zojila Pass is only 20 km away. Another pass near Sonamarg is Nichnai Pass which offers a spectacular view of the lakes such as Kishensar, Vishansar and Gangabal. From here one can also trek to Thajiwas Glacier. According to Desh Bandu,[21] "The scenery here presents a grandeur and beauty similar to Alps in Europe." For people going from Srinagar to Ladakh, Sonamarg is the first halt.

Daksum

Daksum is known as a walker's paradise. It is surrounded by huge mountains densely forested. It is situated, in the district of Anantnag, at the foot of a mountain with a row of majestic Chinars. It is a place where one can really enjoy the music of the silence or the murmurs of Bringhi River which runs in its midst.

Patnitop

Patnitop is about 112 Km from Jammu City. It is famous hill resort. At an altitude of about 7,000 feet above sea level, it has thick forests around. It is on the highway of Jammu and Srinagar, in between Kud and Batot. It gives us a fascinating view of the River Chenab.

Pari Mahal

Pari Mahal, an architectural attraction with seven terrace gardens is situated on the Zabarwan hills, west of Dal Lake and near Cheshma Shahi.

It is 10 km from Srinagar. It was re-built by Dara Shikoh, eldest son of Shah Jahan. He was a philosopher and had faith in Sufism. He built the school of astrology and a residence for his spiritual mentor, Akhund Mulla Shah. He also built a mosque for him just below the Makhdoom Sahib Mosque. Pari Mahal was initially a Buddhist monastery. The building has a baradari facing the Dal Lake with a reservoir fed by a spring. It is said that when Mumtaz Mahal fell ill, both Shah Jahan and she stayed in Pari Mahal because Mumtaz Mahal had to drink water from Cheshma Shahi. According to RC Kak,[22] "Its interior is the most highly decorated of all the rooms in Pari Mahal."

The Great Seven Bridges

There were only seven famous bridges on the river Jhelum. However, now many more have come up. According to Kalhana, the first bridge was built by Pravarasena and named 'Brhatsetu'. The bridge was a boat bridge and built at Maksikasvamin (Present Maisuma). Harsa also constructed a bridge, which came up somewhere near the second bridge Habba Kadal. However, Zain-ul-Abidin constructed the first permanent bridge, which owes its name Zaina Kadal to him.

Amira Kadal (Amir's Bridge)

Amir Khan Jawansher was appointed as Governor of Kashmir by Ahmed Shah Abdali, the Afghan King in 1770 AD. Jawansher was a Shia by faith. Pravarasena II had constructed a wooden bridge and named it Brhatsetu near Maisuma, but with passage of time it was washed away by floods. Amir Khan reconstructed the remains of the bridge and thus it got its name Amira Kadal Bridge . He also constructed a fort at Shergarhi and built a summerhouse in the middle of Dal Lake. Some of the authors have mentioned that Raja Amar Singh, brother of Maharaja Pratap Singh and father of Maharaja Hari Singh constructed the Amira Kadal.

Habba Kadal

Habba Kadal is also known as the second bridge of Srinagar. There are some conflicting views about it. Some historians say that Habib Shah originally constructed Habba Kadal. Habib Shah was the king of Kashmir in 1557–1561 AD. Perhaps Sultan Yusuf Shah Chak who ruled Kashmir (1580–1586 AD) got the bridge reconstructed and named it after his queen Habba Khatoon.

Fateh Kadal

Fateh Kadal is the third bridge on River Jhelum. Fath Shah was an important king of Kashmir. The tug of war between Mohammad Shah and Fath Shah is very interesting. Fath Shah lost and regained the throne of Kashmir three times, between 1486 to 1517 AD. During one of his terms he got Fateh Kadal Bridge constructed.

Zaina Kadal

Zaina Kadal, the fourth bridge is certainly in the name of Zain-ul-Abidin. This great king of Kashmir constructed many famous buildings and bridges. He felt the need to construct a bridge so that his forces could have free movement and conquer other areas.

Ali Kadal

Ali Kadal is the fifth bridge. After the rule of Sikandar But-Shikan, Ali Shah took over Kashmir in 1413 AD. Some chroniclers say that he was the son of Sikandar and some say that he was the general of Sikandar. However, Ali Shah got the bridge constructed.

Nawa Kadal

Nawa Kadal is the sixth bridge on River Jhelum. On its right side , Ram Joo Dhar constructed a temple. It is here that Kota Kol, a stream enters the river. Tradition says that the bridge was constructed by Ram Joo Dhar. However, no historian has confirmed this.

Safa Kadal

Safa Kadal is the seventh bridge. During Sikandar Butshikan's period, a Hindu minister known as Suha Bhatt got converted to Islam. He was named as Saif-ud-Din. He wanted access to his residence from either side of the river. He therefore got a bridge constructed in his name as Safa Kadal.

Other Bridges

Later on, during the period of Bakshi Gulam Mohammad, a few more bridges were added—Padamgam Bridge, Zero Bridge and Budshah Bridge. These bridges were constructed in 1955.

Eleven
Flora, Fauna of Kashmir

Kashmir, the Switzerland of Asia, is described as an emerald in a necklace of pearls. The lush green valley is encircled by snow clad mountains. It can also boast of a wide variety of flora and fauna. Thus it can be termed as a biological paradise.

This diversity of Kashmir's flora and fauna continues to decline on account of human onslaught, pollution, global warming, and habitat destruction due to human encroachments and deforestation. Steps will have to be taken soon to prevent such degradation .

The concept of forest and wildlife conservation is very ancient to Kashmir. Since time immemorial, wildlife here has enjoyed privileged protection through religious philosophy. The worship of Nags (snakes/springs), from ancient time shows the commitment to protect flora and fauna. Even the saints stressed the need to protect forestation. The great Sufi saint of Kashmir Hazrat Sheikh Nur-ud-Din Wali Noorani had said,

'*Yali Wan Poshi – Tali Ann Poshi*'

(When the jungles be sufficient, then alone food will suffice)

The people of Kashmir had great reverence for nature. They even named some of the places after fruits — Chunth Var (Apple Garden), Tangdar/Tangmarg (Pear field), and Ailchi Bagh (Sour Cherry garden).

Planting trees and plants was considered a very sacred act. The great King of Kashmir, Sultan Zain-ul-Abidin got many fruit grafts from Central Asia.

Domestic crops

Rice, wheat and maize are the most important crops. Many pulses, such as mung, (Seed of Vigna Radiata), maha, muth, razmah, (variety of pulses) and 'teelagogule' (Musterd Seed), til (Sesame), are also grown though their production is meagre. According to Sir Walter Lawrence,[1] "the rices of Kashmir are infinite in variety. In one Tehseel I have found fifty-three varieties." Other crops such as cotton, tobacco, barley, and rapeseed including tromba, pingha, sholl (seeds) and Ganhar (medicinal plant) are also grown at certain places.

Different kinds of vegetables are grown such as turnips, pumpkins, cucumbers, tomatos, chillies, egg-plant, beans, knoll kohl. There are a few varieties of vegetables mostly produced in Kashmir but less available outside Kashmir, such as 'haak/munja' (leafy broccoli) knoll kohl, (a variety of brassica oleracea). It is grown in abundance because it is the staple food for all people of Kashmir, be it Hindus or Muslims. Lotus roots are also grown in abundance.

Dry vegetables

During summer, vegetables were dried so that they could be used during severe winter like bottle gourd, tomatoes, turnips, and egg-plants. Kashmiri mirch (chillies of Kashmir), are hotter and redder, and are famous for colour and taste in India and many parts of the world.

Saffron

Saffron is one of the sweet-smelling herbs. It has a long history of spiritual and magical use. It is a spice derived from the flower of the saffron crocus (*Crocus sativus*). The word saffron originated from a 12th-century old term, which is derived from the Latin word Safranum. Safranum (meaning yellow) is also related to the Arabic Zafferano. The history of saffron cultivation goes back more than 3,000 years. It was first documented in seventh century BC in Assyria located in North Mesopotamia. Traditional Kashmiri and Chinese accounts date its arrival anywhere between 900–2500 years ago.

The legends: The famous Kashmiri physician of Pampore, Vagbhatta is said to have planted the first saffron crocus bulb for medicinal use in Kashmir. Legend says that he got the bulb from a Takshaka Nag. Once

Takshaka Nag, the serpent king had a problem in his eye. He tried to cure it but was unable to do so. Vagbhatta came to know that he was a Nag (Snake) and he treated him accordingly. Takshaka Nag recovered from his illness and he gave Vagbhatta a bulb of Saffron.

According to Buddhist legend, Majjhantika, a Buddhist missionary came to Kashmir in the fifth century and planted the first Saffron crop.[2] Some historians believe that saffron first came to China with Mongol invaders by way of Persia. But a medical expert Wan Zhen, (Third century AD), of China, reported that the habitat of saffron is in Kashmir where people grew it principally to offer it to the Buddha.

Daniel Lac writes,[3] "Two wandering Sufi holy-men (Khwaja Masood Wali and Hazrat Sheikh Shariffudin) apparently arrived in Kashmir about 800 years ago, carrying flower bulbs from Asia Minor. After a local chieftain cured one of the Sufi saints, who was ill, the chieftain was given a bulb in payment." However, the claim has been termed as a legendry story and rejected by Kashmiri intellectuals. Their claim is that saffron was in Kashmir much earlier than that.

There is another legend from the time of Alexander the Great, It is said that when he arrived in Kashmir, he pitched his tent in a field full of green pasture. When he awoke in the morning he found the field full of delicate purple flowers with yellow filaments which had made his clothes yellow. He was awe struck and said, "It is magic." Legend says that he called off the battle.

In Greece also saffron has found its place in their mythology. Krokos is the Greek name of the crocus. Legend says that Zeus and Hera were making love so passionately that the heat of their ardour made the bank on which they lay burst open with crocuses. It is believed that the plant took its name from the youth Krokos. Another story is that the youth Krokos fell in love with a beautiful nymph called Smilax. She felt weary of his advances and transformed him into a saffron flower.

Saffron also became very popular in Britain. According to a legend, when Edward III was king of Britain, a person from Middle East came to England, to the town of Walden. He had a bulb of saffron in his stick. The bulb was grown and it gave prosperity to the town.

The plantation

The saffron crocus thrives in climate where hot, dry summer breezes blow across arid and semi-arid lands. Nonetheless the plant can tolerate cold winters, surviving frosts as cold as –10 °C and short periods of snow cover. Though, if not grown in wet environments like Kashmir (where rainfall averages 1000–1500 mm annually), irrigation is needed.

Each of the violet saffron flowers gets three stamens. These three yellow filaments hang out of the flower and are saffron. It takes about 8,000 to 10,000 flowers to yield about 18 ounces of fresh saffron. After it is dried only 4 ounces remain.

Saffron plants grow best in strong and direct sunlight. Most of the saffron is grown in a belt from the Mediterranean in the west to Kashmir in the east. Annually, around 300 tonnes of saffron is produced worldwide. Iran ranks first in the world production of saffron, with more than 81 per cent of the world yield.

Saffron as medicine and spice

Saffron, world's most precious and expensive spice is used almost all over the world in Iranian, Arabian, European, Indian, Turkish, Moroccan and Cornish cuisines. Egyptians used Saffron as medicine to heal a wide range of ailments of the kidney, bladder, and liver. It also helps to improve digestion and soothes gastro intestinal colic and acidity. Saffron is considered a blood purifier and anti inflammatory. Queen Cleopatra used saffron in her bath as she had belief that saffron would make lovemaking more exotic and pleasurable.

In Kashmir, it grows in Pampore. Kashmir has produced saffron for more than 1,000 years. Even when the militant insurgency was at its height a few years ago, people still flocked to the fields for the annual harvest. The harvest of saffron crop begins with picking of the blossoms and separating the stamens from them. The harvest period is traditionally from late September to late December. The process should begin early in the morning before sunrise, and the period within which the blossoms are at their last is from 15 to 20 days.

According to *Tuzuk-e-Jahangiri*,[4] "Perhaps there is no other place in the world where Saffron is so abundantly produced." It further says, "As the saffron was in blossom, His Majesty (Akbar) left the city to go to

Pampore, which is the only place in Kashmir where it flourishes. Every part, every field, was, as far as the eye could reach, covered with flowers. The flower has five petals of violet colour and three stigmas producing saffron are found within it and that is the purest saffron."

Damodaragupta, a litterateur of Kashmir of ninth century has also mentioned in his classical masterpiece *Kuttanimatam* that Kesar (saffron) was used for toiletry purposes by women of class and taste. He further says that men used to apply the paste of Kesar on their scalp to dye their grey hair.

Bilhana, one of the greatest poets of eleventh-twelfth century Kashmir, said, "the poetry and the saffron are the two beautiful creations of Sarada Desha (Kashmir), which I never found elsewhere." He mentions in his epic poem *Vikramankadevacarita* that the beautiful women of Kashmir used to bathe in Vitasta and anoint their bodies with Kesar. Lal Ded has also mentioned saffron in her Vaks.

Kong or Kong Posh means saffron or saffron flower in Kashmiri language. Many pretty women of Kashmir inherited this name. From time immemorial, the fascinating saffron blossoms have always been a great attraction for the visitors to the Valley. This exotic spice has travelled the world over through religious practices, eg the anointing of Lord Gomateswara statue with saffron paste and milk every twelve years by the Jain followers, during Mahamastakabhisheka. Its voyage has culminated into a beautiful blend of personal stories, myths and legends, history, quotations and citations, ancient remedies, and modern recipes of Mughlai and Wazwan dishes.

Yaar me gomut pampure wate
kong poshav rut naalmatye
(My beloved goes away en-route Pampore
The Saffron blossom entices him for a hearty cuddle.)

Fruits of Kashmir

"Kashmir is country of fruits, and perhaps no country has greater facilities of horticulture", wrote Walter R Lawrence. "Most of the fruits have their own varieties—Chunth (Apple), Tang (Pear), Shah Toot/Tul (Mulberry), Chaer (Apricot), Glass (Cherry Sweet), Ailichi (Cherry Sour), Aer (Plum), Peach, Badam (Almond), Bum Chunth (Quince), Strawberry, Doon (Walnut), Kharbuz (Musk Melon), Hendvend (Water-Melon), Dain (Pomegranate), Dach (Grapes) are available in Kashmir."[5]

Apple

Kashmiri apples are famous for their colour, taste and flavour all over the world; it is one of the most important fruits in Kashmir and is grown in abundance. Though it is said that apples originated in the Middle East some 4000 years ago, however, the apples of Kashmir have developed a taste and charm of their own. The aroma, the sweetness is in comparable. These apples have many varieties such as Ambru/Amri apple, Delicious apple, American Apple, Golden Apple, Kuddu Sari apple. Then there are smaller apples known as Trel and Maharaji. The smaller apples also have variety such as Jambasi Trel, Nabdi Trel etc.

Cherry

Cherries have many varieties such as Aval Gillas, Double Gillas, Goole Gillas, Makhmali Gillas, Mishri Gillas, (Sweet Cheery) Tontal Gillas and Ailchi (Sour Cherry usually used to make ketchup). There is a mention in *Tuzuk-e-Jahangiri* that cherry saplings were brought by Muhammad Quli Afshar, one of the commanders of the Mughal army during Akbar's reign, from Kabul and planted in Kashmir.

Dry Fruits

Kashmir is famous for its dry fruits such as Almonds, Walnuts, Apricot, Anardana (sour dry promegranate seeds), Chestnuts, Water Nuts etc.

Medicinal Plants

Kashmir also produces a lot of medicinal plants which are used by the local Hakims for Unani treatment of patients. This system came into practice in the Mughal rule in Kashmir. The treatment prevalent in Kashmir, prior to the system of Unani, was Ayurveda. However, both these systems are vanishing. There are some plants such as Isband (Peganum Harmala Linn) which is used to ward off the evil eye. Some plants are used by many pharmaceutical companies for manufacturing medicines.

Narcotic Plants

Kashmir also produces narcotic plants which are used in medicines,eg Dhatura and Bhang (Cannabis/Hemp). These have natural wild growth.

Sericulture

Silkworms: The mulberry cocoon reared is of superior quality . In addition to the production of silk, a superior quality of silk known as Chinon is produced in Kashmir. The wispy Chiffon, Chinon and Silk fabric is used for making saris. On these saris, traditional hand-embroidery is done and then these elegant, embroidered saris become bridal saris. Thomas Wardle, a silk businessman from Britain was all praise for Kashmir craftsmen. He said, "I have never seen a people so marvellously clever with their fingers as the Kashmiris." Silk thread is also used in designing Persian style carpets which are of high knot density reaching up to 400 to 1600 knots per square inch.

Silk was being woven since long but in a haphazard way. It was being produced as a pastime or for the kings and queens. In 1891 AD, Thomas Wardle discussed the matter with the British Indian Government and Maharaja Pratap Singh gave the silk production an industrial shape. Thomas Wardle's major achievement was to introduce an Indian Tussur silk into production in Britain. It was with his efforts that the silk production in Kashmir gave employment to thousands of people. Kashmir silk became famous all over Europe. Writes Brenda M King,[6] "By 1904, he (Thomas Wardle) conveyed much pleasure in the fact that, mainly due to his (Thomas Wardle's) unstinting efforts, the Kashmir silk industry was reinvigorated and enormous numbers of people had gained employment."

Apiculture

Collecting honey from wild bee colonies is one of the most ancient human activities. In Kashmir honeybees are domesticated and beekeeping is done on commercial scale for the production of honey.

Sheep Husbandry

Animal husbandry or domestication of animals for commercial purposes forms an integral part of Kashmir's economy. Sheep farming provides earning to the farmers by way of products like meat, wool, and also milk. Sheep husbandry in Kashmir is looked after by tribes known as 'Gujjars' and 'Bakarwals'. They rear the sheep and goats at mountain heights where they find greener pastures and then sell them in the local market.

Flora

The Kashmir valley has earned the sobriquet of 'Valley of Flowers'. It is said that Emperor Jahangir collected about 21 varieties of flowers in the meadow of Gulmarg. Blessed with salubrious climate and suitable soil there are numerous variety of exotic flowers. There are about 3,000 species of flora in Jammu and Kashmir State, about 880 in Ladakh District and about 506 in Jammu District.

The Spring season presents a bewitching and breathtaking sight of flower blossoms. Everywhere there are trees such as cherry, almonds, apples full of blossoms. The winter makes the trees absolutely barren,but, as the spring comes, the first thing to appear are shoots of flowers. It culminates into a festival for the people. Hordes of people come out of their homes to enjoy the spectacular, panoramic, and stunning floral iandscapes. Once the leaves start appearing the beauty of the blossoms starts fading away.

In the gardens of the valley, one can find flowers like Roses, Tulips, Lilies, Gladioli, Marigold, Carnation, Cornflower, Daffodils, Cockscomb, Daisy, Sweet William, Poppy Flower, Dalia, Indigofera, Heterantha, Desmodium, etc.

Forests

The mountain ranges in the valley have dense Deodar, Birch, Maple, Hazel, Kael, Wild Oak, Pine, Fir, Walnut, Willow etc. One can find thorny bushes in the plains and Alpine, Maple, Silver Fir, Birch etc. in the mountainous areas. There are other trees such as Veer (Willow) and Frest (Poplar). Boun (Chinar) has been termed as 'plant of aesthetics'.

'Frest' the Poplar tree

Frest (Poplar Tree) is a fascinating tree found in Kashmir. It is usually planted on two sides of a road and when they grow, these trees look like tall soldiers, standing at attention, holding their guns for a Ceremonial Guard of Honour for the visitors. It looks like these trees are welcoming the guests. Francois Bernier, a French physician who visited Kashmir in 1664 along with Emperor Aurangzeb, has mentioned these trees in his travel diary,[7] "The Lake is full of islands, which are so many pleasure grounds. They look beautiful and green in the midst of the water, being covered with fruit trees, and laid out with regular trellised walks. In general they are surrounded by the large-leafed aspen, planted at intervals of two feet. The largest of these trees may be clasped in a man's arms, but they are as high as the mast of a ship, and have only a tuft of branches at the top, like the palm- trees." 'Frest' wood is used for construction of houses. The logs of wood are submerged in the water to season them and then used.

Boun/Chinar

Chinar, (Platanus Orientalis) tree belongs to 'Platanaceae' family. They are also known as Planes in Europe. The tree is also known as tree-palmate as the leaves resemble a hand with the fingers. It is believed that the tree owes its origin to Greece.

The Chinar is one of the most attractive trees of Kashmir. Because of its gigantic size, it attracts attention . Most of the foreign travellers to Kashmir have mentioned this tree in their travel memoirs. This king of the trees has strange characteristics. A full-grown tree grows up to 100 feet in height. It has huge roots entering the earth and has a huge trunk. Sir Walter Lawrence says that he found a Chinar tree having a circumference of 63 feet. The most remarkable aspect of this tree is the leaves. A typical leaf is spread out like a human palm and has fingers like a human hand. It is an interesting and enthralling sight to view the Chinar changing its colours corresponding to the changing seasons. During the autumn, the tree leaves become very spectacular like a burning flame.

The Chinar's Persian name is 'Chenar'. In Kashmir, Chinar is known by the name of 'Boun' and the people have reverence for the tree as for their elders. The Boun owes its name to Goddess Bhawani, the mother goddess, who is widely worshiped in Kashmir. It is interesting to note that wherever we find a temple of the Goddess we see a cluster of Chinars in the premises. Some of the Hindu and Muslim saints found the Chinar, which becomes hollow after some time, the best place for renunciation and worship. Abul Fazal states in *Akbarnama*,[8] "On the 23rd, when the hour was favourable, Srinagar the capital was brightened by his advent. On the way the soldiers who had gone on in advance paid their homage. In accordance with orders, thirty-four persons entered into the trunk of a 'Cenar' (Chinar) tree which had been hollow for ages. If they had sat closer some more might have been accommodated."

As per tradition, even the existence of Chinar is attributed to the Mughals. Mention about Chinar is made in *Akbarnama*,[9] "On the 28th he went to visit Shihab-ud-Dinpur (Now known as Shadipur). This is a delightful spot on the bank of the Bihat (Jhelum). The planes (cinarha) there raise their heads to the sky, and the verdure enchants the eyesight."

Kalhana has not mentioned the name of the tree as Chinar, but 'Vata' tree. However, according to Pathik Jyoteesh,[10] "The most magnificent of the Kashmir trees is Chinar, which is also among the most splendid in the world. Chinar and poplar are said to have been introduced in Kashmir by Mughals. But this is now contested as the Kashmiri name of Chinar figures in verses of the poetess Lall Ded, who lived in Kashmir much before Mughals."

The Chinar is a gigantic tree which attains height of 20 to 25 meters and the trunk gains the circumference of 50 to 60 feet. Its fruits resemble raw chestnuts. Godfry Thomas Vigne who visited Kashmir in 1835 AD writes,[11] "The plane-tree, the species termed the Platanus Orientalis is commonly cultivated in Kashmir, where it is said to arrive at a greater perfection than in other countries." He further says,[12] "A chunar will grow from seed, but it will not thrive unless it be transplanted. I suppose them to have been transplanted into the Nazim Bagh when they were only five inches in diameter, and that this was done in the year 1590. Two hundred and forty eight years have elapsed up to the year 1838 AD, and I found the average to be about four yards and a foot."

This majestic tree symbolises massiveness, enormity, and magnanimity. It has very tough wood. It is used only for wood carving in a limited way. It is also used by the butchers as wooden block to chop and mince meat.

Wildlife

Kashmir can boast of an amazing variety of wildlife. With the passage of time the state has developed many wildlife sanctuaries which offer exciting wildlife.

Hangul

The great 'Hangul' (Kashmir Stag/ Cervus Elaphus Hanglu), is the most endangered species of red deer in the world. Hangul is the only surviving sub-species of the red deer family. This animal can be found in Dachigam National Park. It is a social animal and is found in groups. In herds these stags migrate into the higher regions of Dachigam during summer season. Its main diet is leaves, twigs, and grass. It lives approximately 20 years.

The other animals found are: Snow Leopard, Shapu (a kind of deer), Bharal (a kind of mountain goat), great Tibetan Sheep, Ibex, Musk Deer, Rhesus macaque, Serow (a kind of antelope) and wolves . Black bear are also found in the state.

Wildlife sanctuaries of Jammu and Kashmir

Dachigam National Park, Gulmarg Biosphere Reserve, Hemis National Park, Jasrota Wildlife Sanctuary, Kishtwar National Park, Nandini Wildlife Sanctuary, Overa-Aru Biosphere Reserve, Overa Wildlife Sanctuary, Ramnagar Wildlife Sanctuary.

Insects

In Kashmir we find a great and rare variety of about sixty species of butterflies.

Twelve
Crafts, Arts of Kashmir

Craft tradition of India can be traced to 3000-1700 BC, the dawn of Indus Valley Civilisation. Some of the motifs found there show that people had developed talent for handicrafts. Since then, the craft tradition has survived and flourished in the whole of India and in Kashmir too.

The crafts of Kashmir, in the present form, date back to 1375 AD, when Shah Hamadan visited Kashmir. He was accompanied by 700 Sayyids who had mastery over various crafts and trades. He wanted the people of Kashmir to learn the crafts. The tradition of handicrafts got a great fillip during the period of the king Zain-ul-Abidin (1423-1474 AD). To add to the list of crafts, Sultan Zain-ul-Abidin brought some carpet weavers from Samarkand. People started learning the trade and gradually the carpet industry of Kashmir became very famous. Subsequently, the Mughal Emperor Akbar also tried to induce the people to learn these trades.

Shawls of Kashmir

Yuri Borev writes,[1] "Art awakens man's creative potential, fosters his ability to find the inner measures of objects and correlates their properties with his social needs." Therefore, shawl making is not manufacturing a product but creating an object of art. Each and every shawl, with its natural sheen, is an aesthetic delight.

Shawl making has been one of the main profitable trades of the people of Kashmir. Every visitor, be it a traveller, explorer, or a tourist has had a desire evoked in him to purchase a shawl from the valley as a gift for someone. According to William Moorcroft and George Trebek,[2] "The manufacture for which Kashmir is celebrated throughout the world is the light, warm, and elegant article of dress which, from its native appellation, is known as Shawl."

The origin

Though there is no official record as to when the industry came into being, the weaving of the fabric must have started during ancient times. The fabric was used in making dresses, such as Pherans, as a winter wear. During the 15th Century when Persian language replaced Sanskrit, the word Shawl was derived from the Persian word 'SAL' meaning 'Expensive Woven Fabric'. Shawls had been a fashion statement among women for ages. These shawls were basically designed to impart a feeling of warmth and to complement a dress for symbolic reasons. They could be used for added warmth in a cold environment or for fashion at outdoor or indoor evening affairs.

Shawl manufacturing as a cottage industry can trace its history as far back as 11th Century. Initially it was one man completing one shawl from weaving the raw fabric to a finished one. However, because of the enormous demand, the manufacturer had to find ways and means to produce more. The length of the shawl was varied from time to time. At one stage its length was nine yards which was cut into pieces and distributed to many men for embroidery. All of them embroidered the same pattern as per the trace printed on paper. At the end, all the pieces were joined by invisible, very fine darning by an expert darner known as 'Rafugar'. Surprisingly, the joints were not discernible to the naked eye.

Most of the travellers who have penned their travels have mentioned the production of shawls. Says George Forster,[3] "But the wealth and fame of Kashmir have largely arisen from manufacture of shauls (shawls), which it holds unrivalled, and almost without participation. The wool of the shaul is not produced in the country, but brought from districts of Tibet." He further says, "A portion of the revenue of Kashmir is transmitted to the Afghan capital in Shaul goods."

During early nineteenth century Kashmir Shawls woven in Paisley pattern were the craze for Europeans. When the British made a treaty with Maharaja Gulab Singh wherein he was granted the kingdom of Kashmir, the British had made it a point to write about the presentation of shawls from the valley, as a tribute to them from the Maharaja. According to the treaty, Article 10 states:

> "Maharaja Gulab Singh will acknowledge the supremacy of the British Government and will, as a token of such supremacy, present annually to the British Government one horse, twelve perfect goats of approved breed (six male and six females) and three pairs of Kashmiri shawls."

Baron Charles Hugel writes,[4] "The English had begun to aspire to universal domination in India; the sums of money yearly expended for the shawls of Kashmir had not escaped their attention."

Owning a Kashmiri, Paisley pattern shawl became a matter of prestige for every European. The attraction of Kashmiri shawls was so great that Empress Eugenie, the Consort of Emperor Napoleon III, had collected as many as 150 of them. She was envied by the wives of other generals for her luxurious shawl collection.

Shahtoosh

Shahtoosh shawls are the king of shawls. This shawl has superb warmth, light weight and long lasting life. The fabric is made from Chiru fur. Chiru is a kind of antelope found at the height of about 5,000 meters, in Tibet. A Chiru is layered with two fur coatings. The outer fur is coarse and the inner is soft. Shahtoosh is made of the inner fur. Since the the Chiru has been killed to get the inner layer of the fur, the animal has become almost extinct. Shahtoosh is now internationally banned; hence there is some protection for the Chiru.

According to Alexander Cunningham,[5] "Another species of wild goat is the Tibetan 'ibis', or skyin. In Ladakh they are snared at night or shot in the grey dawn of the morning when they venture down to the streams to drink. They are killed for the sake of the soft under-fleece, which, in Kashmir is called 'Asli Tus'. This is an exceedingly fine and soft wool of a light brown colour, which is exported to Kashmir, where it is used as a lining for shawls, woollens, stockings, and gloves."

Shawl weaving

Shawl weaving is a musical melody. The Kashmiri loom has been termed as a little orchestra since the weaving of colourful threads creates a symphony of colours. The loom-woven shawls are known as Kani Kar. (Kani is the Kashmiri name given to a wooden bobbin, which works while weaving a shawl on the loom). The embroidered shawls are known as Amlikar. The Paisley pattern tapestry is made with a fine needle which works on Pashmina cloth. It is a very intricate and cumbersome job done manually which makes it so special.

According to D N Saraf,[6] "Let us remember the landscape, its generosity of seasonal colour, the texture of sky and water, the richer texture of autumn leaves of Saffron, of Lotus and willow and pale spring flowers or mellow summer fruit. The poetry of these influences can be seen in the fines Kani Shawls, in Carpets, in embroidery."

Pashmina Shawl

The word Pashmina owes it name to Pashmineh, a Persian word. Pashmina wool is taken from Chagnthangi goats which are found in the Ladakh area. These Changra goats are locally reared and then they are fleeced to get the wool which makes Pashmina. Pashmina is lightweight and soft.

Raffal Shawl

Raffal shawl is the simplest kind of fabric. It is inferior compared to Shahtoosh and Pashmina. But the shawl has elegance and warmth. It is not lightweight and after embroidery its stylishness can be termed of a high order.

The Needle Work

Needle work was introduced by a Kashmiri master craftsman Hamid Ali Baba. The shawl is known as Sozen Kari. This kind of work was introduced during Afghan rule.

Sozni/Sozankar

Very fine embroidery done on Pashmina Shawls is known as Sozni/ Sozankar.

Chickandozi

Medium fine needle work is known as Chickandozi.

Rezkar

The stitches are broad but multi-coloured and are known as Rezkar.

Watchikan

In this embroidery the petals or flowers are raised in a floral design in golden thread on a Raffal shawl. This is known as Watchikan.

Jalakdozi

This technique is used on shawls, the embroidery being in staple yarn is known as Jalakdozi.

The intricate embroidery on the shawl is really subtle poetry or a masterpiece painting on the cloth. Its unmatched beauty gives pleasant warmth, physical and spiritual upliftment. The shawals speak a lot about the social fabric of Kashmir—the artistic culture, the intellectual capacity and spiritual upbringing of its people.

As per William Moorcroft and George Trebek,[7] "The wool that is employed in this manufacture is of two kinds—the fleece of the domestic goat, Pasham Shal (or shawl wool), and that of the wild goat, wild sheep, and other animals named Asali Tus. The wool of sheep is not regularly, but sometimes clandestinely imported, being loaded with the same heavy duties as that of the goat."

Keeping in view its popularity, people in England, too, tried to copy Shawl manufacturing there. Both Edinburgh in 1790 AD, and Norwich in 1972, began to imitate Kashmiri shawls. But they could not produce the excellence of the Kashmir shawl. The rich water of Jhelum or Dal Lake or any other lake is of high quality and most suitable for shawl washing. Most people attribute the richness of the shawls to this water. However, as soon as manufacturing of shawls at other places started, it reached the common woman and soon shawls fell out of fashion. Many manufacturing units were closed. Kashmiri shawls are still the craze today. In view of the popularity of Kashmiri shawls, in 1827 AD, Dewan Kirpa Ram, the Sikh Governor in Kashmir imposed a 26 per cent tax on every shawl and it became a great revenue earner for the rulers of Kashmir.

Bernier Francois wrote,[8] "Great pains have been taken to manufacture similar shawls in Patna, Agra, and Lahore; but notwithstanding every possible care they never have the delicate texture and softness of Kachemire shawls, whose unrivalled excellence may be owing to certain properties in the water of that country."

Write Suresh K Sharma[9] "Wherever you turn in Kashmir this breath of softness meets you in various forms; a universality of satin-texture in the Himalayan setting of stark grandeur. Indeed, is it not worldwide news that its water softens a shawl better than any other water whatsoever. You should see the Kashmiri women washing their shawls in the silvery Dal Lake." Bandhu Desh writes,[10] "It is said that the Kashmir woollen shawls owe much of their excellence to being washed in the clear and soft waters of Dal Lake."

Writes William Henry Knight,[11] "Passing through the town of Islamabad (earlier known as Anantnag), on our return, we went into some of the houses to see people at work at the loom-made shawls. Very hard-working and intricate business it seemed to be."

According to Walter R Lawrence,[12] "the shawl industry is now unfortunately a tradition—a memory of the past. The trade received its death blow when war broke out between Germany and France in 1870. I have been told by an eye witness, of the intense excitement and interest with which the Kashmiri shawl-weavers watched the fate of France in that great struggle—bursting into tears and loud lamentation when the news of Germany's victories reached them. If there had been any hope that the industry would revive, and that shawls would again became fashionable, this hope was dashed when the famine of 1877-79 visited the valley."

Dr Ananda K Coomaraswamy says,[13] "Of all Indian textiles none excels in beauty, colour, texture and design as the famous Kashmir shawl. The intricately embroidered shawls, prepared by the agile hands of artisans of Kashmir, are a reflection of the culture of Kashmir. Initially Zain-ul-Abidin gave a boost to manufacture of crafts of Kashmir; nonetheless, Mughals also patronised the crafts including the shawl manufacturing in Kashmir."

Carpets of Kashmir

The Kashmiri carpet is a connoisseur's delight, representing aristocracy and providing an aura of elegance. Carpet weaving started from the period of Sultan Zain-ul-Abidin, but soon the trade became more or less extinct. Akbar the Great had tried to introduce carpet weaving in Agra and Lahore. After Akbar, Jahangir came to Kashmir and once again he tried to introduce the craft of carpet weaving but with little success. However, according to D N Saraf,[14] "It is said that in the time of Ahmed Beg Khan (1615 – 1618 AD), one of Jahangir's governors, a Kashmiri Muslim named Akhun Mulla Hussain Rahnuma went to perform Hajj pilgrimage via Central Asia. On his way back he visited Andijan in Persia where carpets were manufactured. There he picked up the art and restarted an industry in Kashmir."

Gradually carpet weaving picked up. For weavers, it became a passionate work of art. Though the designs were Persian, yet they could distinctly be seen as carpets from Kashmir. The weavers added the beauty, scenic splendour, nature and music of colours and majestic appeal of Kashmiri art in it. These carpets became world famous.

The weaving of a carpet is intricate and dramatic. The weavers are guided by the master weaver. He recites the weaving of number of knots, and making of design, pattern and colour through recitation of a coded script known as 'Talim' which is fixed in the 'wrap' thread. Sometimes the 'Ustad' or 'master weaver' recites without script. It is dramatic to see the master singing the script and the others repeating it with their hands, choreographing the salsa and dance of the carpet weaving.

Designs

Since the art was inherited from Persia, therefore, the Persian designs named after Iranian cities were used such as Kum, Tabriz, Hamadan, Bukhara, Kashan, Kirman, Ardebil, Isfahan, and Heart. Birds and animals frolicking on them carried them closer to nature. However, the typical Kashmiri design is the 'Tree of Life'.

Generally silk carpets are made up of 80 per cent of silk yarn and 20 per cent of cotton yarn, having more than 400 knots per square inch. However, depending on the quality of the carpet, the knots can vary between 400 to 1,600 per square-inch. Though very rare, carpets with 3,600 knots per square inch have also been created in Kashmir by the master craftsmen. Some of these have adorned the walls of rooms of the elite as wall decorations.

With the passage of time and users becoming very eco-friendly, there has been a change in the dyes being used for the weaving of carpets—-a shift from chemical dyes to vegetable eco-friendly dyes, the use of which has given new dimensions to the colour-design concept in the carpets. The weavers of Kashmir were the first to adapt to such desired changes.

One can feel the excellence of the Kashmiri carpet from this small story. Maharaja Ranjit Singh desired to visit Kashmir as he had heard many stories of its beauty and charm. But he could not visit the valley. According to Vitoria Schofield,[15] "Ranjit Singh once wrote to one of his governors, Colonel Mian Singh: 'Would that I could only once in my life enjoy the delight of wandering through the gardens of Kashmir, fragrant with almond-blossoms, and sit on the fresh green turf'. To please the Maharaja, he, the governor, ordered a special Kashmiri carpet to be woven with a green background dotted with little pink spots and interspersed with tiny little pearl-like dots. When he received it, Ranjit Singh was delighted and rolled himself on it as though he were rolling on the Kashmiri grass."

Papier Mache

Papier Mache is a delicate decorative art. It is a French word meaning 'paper pulp' or mashed paper. Papier Mache craft was actually known as 'Kar-i-Qalamdan' or 'Kar-i-Munaqqash' (ornamentation of pen boxes). It is believed that Papier Mache started during the time of Sultan Zain-ul-Abidin who brought experts from Central Asia. There is another version that Sultan Zain-ul-Abidin, as a young prince, was a captive in the city of Samarkand and it is from there he brought this art to Kashmir. However, with the introduction of the manufacturing of paper pulp, the art of painting of articles made of this pulp also thrived.

During Mughal period, this art got a fillip as many articles began to be made using this technique. Doors, window frames and panels were painted. Palanquins were painted as also boxes utilised for other things. It is said that furniture, Papier Mache painted, for Mughal courts was brought from Kashmir.

The designs used for decorating Papier Mache are flowers and birds. Popular designs are 'Hazara', 'Gul-ander-gul', 'bird in foliage', etc. According to Moorcroft, the design of Sabzkar was selected by Aurangzeb. Traditionally the ground layer of the painting on an object is gold, white, black, red and blue.

Papier Mache objects produced in Kashmir today vary from Christmas ornaments, incense stands, napkin rings, photo frames, ring boxes, napkin boxes, bangles, toy animals, Easter eggs, coaster sets and boxes and vases of every imaginable size and shape. These objects are not only beautifully decorated, but are surprisingly light and strong. The paintings are generally of motifs like Chinar leaves, Shikara, Hangul, houseboats etc.

Wood Carving

Perhaps, nowhere in the world except Kashmir, the finest quality of Walnut wood artefacts are produced. This wood is hard and durable. Strangely enough the quality of wood differs even in one tree. The root portion of a walnut tree is more or less blackish and very expensive. The trunk is of light chocolate colour, and the branches are still lighter. However, its colour, grains and sheen are unique and matchless compared to any other wood.

The artisans who create the intricate carving patterns are the masters of this art. They create various items of furniture, bowls, jewellery boxes, trays, photo frames, caskets, cigar or handkerchief boxes, screens, table lamps, wardrobes etc. The art is about 300 years old. The art of crafting, chiselling and engraving may have been inherited from the 'Khatumband' ceiling designs used in rooms of houses and in houseboats.

There are two types of walnut trees which grow in Kashmir. One that bears fruit and is known for its wood and another which is not fruit bearing. The latter is known as 'Zangul'. This wood is not used for fine wood work.

It is possible this art may have come from Samarkand. But some Europeans say that the art of wood carving may have originated from the suggestions given by some Europeans. The fine quality and intricacy of woodcraft of Kashmir can be judged from the fact that there are only three centres in India designated as 'Towns of export excellence'; two of these are Srinagar and Anantnag, the third being Jaipur in Rajasthan.

According to D N Saraf,[16] "there is another interesting historical fact. The carved gate of the façade during the coronation durbar of King George V in Delhi was presented to him by Maharaja Pratap Singh. Maharaja Pratap Singh was instrumental in popularising Kashmir wood carving outside India besides attracting the Indian nobles and princely society."

Houseboats

Houseboats form an indispensable part of the tourism industry in Kashmir. Floating on the enchanting Dal Lake these houseboats are always ready to take tourists for a romantic and peaceful ride on the lake. They also offer some of the most enchanting and exotic views of the splendid scenery of the historical places of Srinagar.

The king of the houseboats is known locally as 'Lare Nav'. There are many factors that necessitated the construction of the houseboats. One was the influx of Westerners who were not allowed to own immovable property during Maharaja Ranbir Singh's rule but they were eager to own some sort of residential accommodation. These people decided to own movable houseboats instead, on which there was no bar for outsiders. The credit of the construction of these movable houses goes to a Kashmiri Pandit, Pandit Naraindas who was one of the first English speaking Kashmiris to open a store to cater to Western gentry's needs. He got a Donga and converted it into a Houseboat-cum-shop. His idea was later on improved upon by Colonel R Sartorius, VC, Sir R Harvey Bart, and Martyn Kennard. Many Europeans owned houseboats in Kashmir and used them during the summer months for their residence. There are two-bedroom, three-bedroom and even four-bedroom houseboats. These are approximately 65 to 95 feet long and 14 feet wide. These houseboats have even been transformed into three, four or even five-star hotels. These flat bottomed houseboats have beautiful ceilings. They are fitted with small wooden tiles in an intricate design known as 'Khatumband'.

The bedrooms in these houseboats are furnished with beautiful Kashmiri carpets of various designs. The walls and the windows are covered with Crewel tapestry. Walnut wood furniture makes the bedrooms fit for royalty. The rooms have toilets fitted with exquisite sanitary wear. These boats have small boats shikaras attached to them for ferrying the guests from the Lake shores to a houseboat and vice-versa.

Khrav of Kashmir (footwear)

Earlier the Pulhoore (footwear) was totally made of grass. However, it was replaced by wood. This wooden footwear was called Khrav. It was about three inches high and was a bigger size than the foot as it was used to walk in the snow. This footwear was made in various designs A poor rustic peasant would buy cheaper footwear named as 'Dande Khrav' (bull's footwear). People who could afford would buy a better designed one with colours known as 'Ranga Khrav' (coloured footwear). There was a custom especially with the Hindus of Kashmir that they would give wooden footwear to their daughters as one of the items of the dowry. This footwear was termed as 'Maharen Khrav' or 'Ronye Khrav' (jingling bell footwear for brides). This footwear was specially designed, painted and decorated.

Namda of Kashmir

Namda (a woollen rug) is made up of wool and cotton, which is moistened with special chemical solution and pressed and 'felted' by beating and applying pressure. Namda originally came from Yarkand. It is said that when the Mughal emperor Akbar came to Kashmir, a man known as Nubi created the first Namda to protect the Emperor's horse from severe cold. Nubi decorated the Namda with fine embroidery and the Emperor was very impressed.

After the felt for Namda is prepared, then the embroidery is done in chain-stitch style. Patterns such as animals and birds on a tree, nursery rhymes, stories and alphabets for children are created by using embroidery. Namdas of various sizes and shapes are made—oval, square, rectangle or round. These are used as floor covering.

Gabbas of Kashmir

Kashmir can boast of making indigenous furnishing material called Gabbas. Nowhere in India or abroad can one find Gabbas. These are made of woollen blankets (Loiees), which are woven in Kashmir itself. They are made in bold designs embroidered with the same style and appliqué design (dal-guldar). According to D N Saraf,[17] "The origin of the appliquéd or 'dal-guldar' Gabba is not known but there are several interesting theories. One of them is that a refugee from Kabul, Abdur Rahman, prepared for his host, Kamal Butt of Restson village near Traal, a saddle piece in appliqué technique. This was found very interesting and the idea caught the imagination of the Anantnag Gabba makers."

Crewel Embroidery

Crewel embroidery of Kashmir is known for its excellence. This Jacobean floral embroidery has earned appreciation the world over.

Though the origin of this art is unknown, it is believed that traders from Syria travelled to Kashmir and they brought this craft to the valley during the thirteenth century. It is said that the technique is at least a thousand years old. It is not 'counted-thread embroidery' but the style is of 'free embroidery'. It is worked on a closely woven fabric such as cotton.

Crewel embroidery is done with the aid of fine needles/hooks known as Ari. These are needles of varying sizes and holes. Some are straight while others are curved. Crewel embroidery is mostly done on cotton cloth known as Dusooti. But now this embroidery is also done on silk. Master craftsmen living in remote villages stitch the blossoms, vines and leaves on the cloth. Crewel embroidery gives extraordinary beauty to the cloth. It requires tight base fabric. Use of frames like hoops is very important. The embroidered cloth is used for drapery and upholstery, bags, table covers, cushion covers, bed covers, and wall hangings etc. The cost of the cloth depends on the amount of embroidery, patterns and colours and amount of work done on the cloth.

Other Embroidery

Kashidakari

The other embroidery, Kashidakari, is like Talibar (gold work), satin stitch, cross-stitch, shadow embroidery, Kashmir embroidery, appliqué tapestry, Zalakdo (chain stitch), vatachik (buttonhole stitch), Romani etc.

Ornaments/Jewellery

Dejihoor

Kashmiri women love to wear ornaments. The designs of the ornaments are traditional and stylish. Dejihoor is an important ornament of Kashmiri Hindu women. It is made of gold and symbolises that the woman is married. Dejihoor is made of three things. The chain is Talaraz and the pendulum type hanging is known as Athoor. In a marriage, the Talaraz and Athore are give by the in-laws of the bride. It has great religious sanctiy for the Hindu ladies.

The other ornaments are 'Gunus', 'Toulsi/Halqaband', 'Kundals' etc.

Copper and brassware

Copper is part of many rich stories and legends. In ancient India, copper was used in the holistic medical science Ayurveda for surgical instruments and other medical equipment somewhere in 1,000 BC. In Kashmir, copper was used for making coins during Kushan period in the second century BC. In the year 1987, Jammu and Kashmir State Archaeology Department came across three copper pieces of the Kushan period at village Maidan Chagul in the frontier district of Kupwara.

Copper, therefore, must have been in use in the valley. During the Sultanate period, copper was also used lavishly in Kashmir. The artisans earned appreciation for making copper artefacts that lasted for years.

In addition to making the traditional utensils, craftsmen made a variety of objects such as bowls, plates, trays, flower vases, chandeliers, table lamps, lemon sets etc. Samovar is one of the important items which has attracted the attention of tourists. Engraving is done by hand aesthetically and that makes it beautiful. The price of the object is determined by the amount of engraving on it.

Samovar

Samovar literally means 'self-boiler' and is an essential part of Kashmiri life. This metal container is used to make tea and hot water. It may have travelled from Russia to Kashmir, as it used in Russia, Iran, and Turkey. It is also used in European countries and East Yemen . Samovar is of Russian origin and is connected with tea. Tea was delivered to Russia from the territory of West Mongolia in the seventeenth century and was used as medicine among the nobility. The samovars became the symbol of Russian hospitality and family comfort as well as a sign of prosperity.

The Kashmiri Samovar has two cylindrical pots, one with big and another with small circumference. The smaller one is attached inside the bigger pot. It is this smaller cylinder which works like magic. When burning charcoal is put in the smaller cylinder, it makes the water or tea in the bigger cylinder boil. Both the cylinders have openings. The smaller cylinder opening is for putting in the charcoal while the bigger one is for pouring the tea or water. The bottom of the smaller cylinder is perforated so that air passes through it. These cylinders are placed on a vessel which is also perforated so that the ash from the small cylinder collects in it and does not fall on the floor. The Kashmir Samovars are very handy and it is interesting to see that when Kashmiri folks go for a picnic , the families cluster around it and enjoy the tea prepared in it.

In Kashmir, brass was also used for making utensils especially thals (big brass plates) for Hindus. The Muslims would use copper wares for cooking and eating.

Other Crafts of straw, grass

Waguv

The waguv (mats) made of straw/grass are very common in Kashmir. They vary in sizes and are used as mats throughout the house. Waguv are found in almost all the houses of Kashmir, even today. These mats protect people from the icy coolness of the floor.

The Pulhoore footwear

Previously even footwear was made of grass. There were two types of Pulhoore—one of fine quality decorated with colourful threads and jingling bells, which, as a custom was gifted to newlywed brides. The other was a poor man's footwear. People could not afford leather shoes. Only rich people could buy leather footwear. Therefore, most of the people used Pulhoore. It has now become extinct.

Willow cricket bats

Kashmir willow is known around the world and is second only to the famous English willow. Willow wood is now used to make cricket bats, which are made in Bijbihara, Sangam, Hallmullaha, Sethar, Pujteng, Mirzapor and Charsoo areas of Anantnag district.

Wicker baskets of Kashmir

Wicker craft is also famous in Kashmir. One of the important items— the Kanger (Kashmir fire pot) is made of this material.

Kanger—The famous fire-pot of Kashmir

Kanger is a typical Kashmiri heater. It continues to be the main inexpensive source of keeping an individual warm during extreme winters. It acts as an individual,personal heater for every Kashmiri, irrespective of caste, creed, religion etc. It is made of two parts. One is an earthenware bowl of terracotta, of a quaint shape, which is called Kondul. A frame of willow or wicker, basket like, is made and the terracotta pot is put inside. Then burning charcoal dust 'Haq' of driftwood is put inside the earthen bowl. With its two side handles attached to the basket, it is put under the pheran. Slowly and gradually the fire simmers within and keeps the person warm. A spoon known as 'Tchalan' made of wood or iron or silver, is used to stir the charcoal, which gradually gets covered with ash.

The 'Tchalan' removes the ash and the glow of the burning charcoal is refreshing and warm.

Kanger for Kashmiri people is named as 'Sheena Maharen'—the snow bride. It is their bosom friend and benefactor. Sir Water R Lawrence has given a lucid description of Kanger in his book. At one place he writes,[18] "There is a proverb 'What Laila was on Majnus bosom so is Kanger/ Kangri to a Kashmiri'." Kanger is so important for a Kashmiri that they have developed many songs for it. On one particular auspicious day known as 'Teela Ashtami' after the end of winter and beginning of summer, the Kanger is burnt like a bonfire on the festival of Holi. Boys tie a rope to the Kanger, ignite it and swing the rope in a circular manner. It creates a spectacular spectacle of fireworks.

The origin of Kanger

It is difficult to say when the Kanger was invented. It is believed that the locals probably, learnt its use from Italians who used to visit the valley during the rule of Mughal Emperors. This may not be totally true.

Earlier a Kanger was totally made of terracotta clay. It was called Mannan. This Mannan was difficult to handle. Subsequently, by further innovations, the earthen bowl was encased in a wicker basket and we got the Kanger of today. It is said that the word Kanger is derived from Sanskrit 'Kut Angara' or 'Kashthangarika'. M A Stein has mentioned,[19] "In his (Kalhanas) description he refers to the burn marks left by the Kanger or brazier, which has been in general use in Kashmir since early times."

Types of Kangers

Tchrar Kanger is very beautifully decorated. The Kangers from Chrar-e-Sharif are famed for their beauty and strength as they are made from superior willow wickers. Then there is a Maharen Kanger (Bridal Kanger). It is used by the brides during the marriage ceremony. Anantnag, Shahabad, Bandipora also manufacture Kangers, which are known after the places where they are made. The peasants who work in fields use somewhat bigger Konduls and that Kanger is known as Grees Kanger (Peasant's Kanger). The finely worked ones of the elite are known as the Khoja Kanger.

While Kanger is a saviour for the people of Kashmir in winter season it has its disadvantages. Frequent use of Kanger gives burn marks on the thighs. In the year 1835, G T Vigne visited Kashmir. His observations about Kanger are,[20] "The common people usually carry abroad with them in the winter season an earthen stove, which hanging near the thigh, gives it a scorched appearance."

It is interesting to know that most Kashmiri families have patched mattresses. The reason being that while they sleep, a Kanger is kept in the bed to warm it. Sometimes sleep engulfs the man, and the Kanger overturns resulting in the burning of bedding. There have been many casualties with burns.

The Kanger has not escaped the spontaneous flow of powerful feelings of poets. Its warmth has stirred their hearts. These lines show the importance of Kanger in Kashmiri society.

ma:g o:y dra:g vothuy, ka:gri:,
Came (Magh) winter and you were scarce
pha:gun o:y za:gun tso:y, ka:gri:,
Came (Phagun) you were under observation

Terracotta

Use of Terracotta must be very old. Even Lall Ded has used Toak (Plate) in her verses. There are many proverbs in Kashmiri language wherein Toak has been used. It was important initially as a plate to be used for eating till the advent of metal plates. The use of Toak is still prevalent in wedding ceremonies and even death rituals. The smaller plate was known as Toak and the bigger as Tabchih.

Math, a huge big cylindrical jar was used to store rice and other grains. A smaller one Lej, was used for cooking. Mini pots of terracotta were used for getting milk and fermenting curds. The other important item was 'Sanipotul'. Images of god, shivlings and goddesses were made of terracotta and were worshiped during Shivratri and other festivals.

Stone Carving

Stone carving has been an ancient art of Kashmir. In most of the temples, sculptures of gods and goddess are made of stone. The 'Gratta' (Grinding Machine), was used to grind flour and the Kanz (Rice Mill) was previously used to remove the outer husk of grain with the help of a log known as 'Muhul'. It is interesting to see two women simultaneously crush the grain with the help of logs (Muhuls) creating a musical rhythm. .

Handicrafts from Jammu

Jammu has its typical handicrafts. It produces brassware which caters to home needs, woodwork such as spoons, containers, carved godly figures etc. Jammu also produces fabric of cotton and wool. However, most of the things produced are used by the people.

Handicrafts of Ladakh

Ladakh is a picturesque land of gigantic mountains, monasteries, and lamas. It has a unique place for its exquisite craftsmanship. The handicrafts of Leh, Ladakh project the exclusive art and cultural heritage of the region and serve the needs of the local people. For many it is the main source of livelihood. The dresses of local people are distinctive in craftsmanship. The monasteries are full of art treasures. The local handicrafts include handmade carpets, copper and silver jewellery, baskets, Thangka paintings, masks, shoes etc. Ladakh also excels in woodwork. They produce low tables, jugs, and stands for Gompas.

In the village of Chiling, 19 km away from Zanskar most of people are metal workers. These workers are considered to be the offspring of artists from Nepal. They produce articles such as Khorten (Prayer Wheels) for religious purposes and utensils for domestic use made of copper, silver and brass. One can find hookah-bases, tea cup stands, and bowls. Sometimes they sell Chorten (Stupa) for domestic shrines and temples.

One can see the best of metal and woodwork in the wealthier Ladakhi homes and kitchens. They proudly display big and ornate iron stoves decorated with precious stones made by the deft hands of craftsmen. Exquisite woodwork can be seen in the form of beautifully carved large wooden shelves and low curved tables. The artistic skills of local artisans are also projected on the wooden beams or pillars in monasteries and even in some hotels. Actually, craftsmanship in this region has not gone beyond producing items of daily use. Another signature style craft of Leh-Ladakh is Pattu. Pattu is a warm and rough woollen fabric.

The carpets of Ladakh are indigenous to that part and have not been introduced to the outside world. The Buddhists inhabiting Ladakh mainly prepare carpets for their personal use. People of this area have been weaving carpets from very early times. A carpet is the main furnishing, used for sitting during the day and sleeping at night. People also seat their guests on it, and spread it for ceremonies and feasts. Women dominance is widely felt in weaving of the carpets. A vertical wooden loom, light in weight is the sole base on which it is made. A 3×6 ft carpet is known as Khalidan. These carpets are woven by the method of looping knots, known as 'Khabdan' in local parlance.

The designs woven into the carpet are generally derived from religious myths. The motifs are inspired by the Mahayana Buddhist symbolism. Dragon motif is quite common. A few more designs like Guanakchagri (Chinese wall), Khorlo (Three Wheels), tashi stak gyat (Eight Lucky Signs), Mentok (flower) and cha (Birds) are also used. The eight lucky signs or symbols are those of lotus, wheel of religion, conch-shell, banner of victory, holy-vase, endless knot, pair of golden fish and umbrella in Buddhism.

There is one more type of carpet woven in Ladakh. This is called 'Tsukdan' in local dialect.

Thirteen
Music, Dance and Drama

Yuri Borev writes,[1] "Dance is an echo of music, a melodious and rhythmic sound translated into melodious and rhythmic movements of the human body revealing the characters of people, their feelings and thoughts about the world."

Music is found in every known culture of the world. Music and dance are influenced by all other aspects of culture, including social and economic. Kashmir also evolved its own music and dance. It is difficult to determine the precise origin of performing arts of Kashmir. However, keeping in view the great cultural heritage of Kashmir, we find that the dance, music and dramatic performances seem to have been an important part of the social fabric of ancient Kashmir. The music, dance and drama must have been passed on from the Vedic tradition and probably can be attributed to *Samveda.*

Interestingly, Kashmir has produced one of the most famous musicologists, Sarangadeva (1210 – 1247 AD) whose monumental work on music and dance titled *Sangeeta-ratnakara/ Sangita-Rahlakara*, is considered a very important work after the treatise on music, *Natyashastra.*

The traditional ethnic music of Kashmir, its dance and drama have had musical influences from various parts of the world especially from

Central Asia. Performing artists, men and women from Kashmir were employed in the Mughal court and were highly thought of. According to *Ain-i-Akbari*,[2] "There are numerous musicians at court, Hindus, Irani, Turani, and Kashmiri, both men and women. The court musicians are arranged in seven divisions, one for each day in the week."

According to *Natyashastra*

In the literary world, one cannot say authoritatively but tradition says that Bharat Muni who wrote the great treatise *Natyashastra* (The Science of Drama) belonged to Kashmir. It is believed that the work may have been written between 200 BC to 200 AD, while some authors have put it around the fourth century. The treatise takes into account every aspect of theatrical relevance, including theatre architecture, costumes, make-up, properties, dance, music etc. Many of the scholars in Kashmir, including the great Abhinavagupta, also wrote commentaries on *Natyashastra*. Abhinavagupta wrote *Abhinavabharti*, a commentary on Bharat Muni's *Natyashastra*. Lollata Bhatta, who flourished in ninth Century in Kashmir, is famous for interpretation of Bharata's *Rasa Sutra*. Also Matrgupta, the king of Kashmir is said to have written a commentary on the *Natyashastra* of Bharat Muni.

According to *Nilamatapurana*

Nilamatapurana is the most valuable ancient Sanskrit manuscript. This sacred book of Hindus of Kashmir throws light on the ancient history of Kashmir. In addition to the historical background, it describes the people, their way of living, their habits, their recreation, their food, their sports etc.

Says Ved Kumari Ghai, who has translated *Nilamatapurana*,[3] "The Nilamata says that the land of Kasmira was thronged with ever-sportive and joyful people enjoying continuous festivities. Living amidst scenes of sylvan beauty, they played, danced and sang to express their joys, to mitigate their pains, to please their gods and to appease their demons." It is evident that Kashmir in ancient times must have had a vibrant culture where performing arts were a part of social life.

According to *Rajatarangini*

There are many references in *Rajatarangini* that music, dance and singing was prevalent in ancient Kashmir. It mentions that there was a tradition of devdasis who performed ritualistic dances in the precincts of temples. King Jalauka was a lover of music. King Harsa was a great singer and composer himself. His father Kalasa, while dying, requested some of the singers to sing the songs composed by Harsa, since Harsa was kept under arrest by his brother. There are many such examples that tell us that performing arts in ancient Kashmir flourished. Abhinavagupta, the great Shaivite scholar, was himself a musician.

Music during Zain-ul-Abidin's period

During Zain-ul-Abidin's reign, art and craft got tremendous fillip. Music, singing and dance too got patronage. Srivara writes in his *Zaina Rajatarangini* that,[4] "the Sultan showered gold in the courtyard of the palace which was resounding with all the local melodies in vogue in Kashmir, the progeny of sage Kasyapa." A circular shaped theatre hall was constructed at Bijbihara. Open air stages were improvised in the gardens and performances were given just as *apsaras* would perform before god Indra. The Sultan would also invite rulers from adjoining places to witness and enjoy the festivity.

The most accomplished performing artists were Khuja, the disciple of Abdul Qadir, Mullah Zada the flute player, Mullah Jamal a vocalist, Srivara the composer, and Jaffar and Srivara, the singers. A famous poet Yodha Bhatta wrote a play named *Zaina Prakasha* depicting details about the Sultan. According to *Ain-i-Akbari*, musicians from Persia and Turkestan flocked to his court ; among them Mulla Uudi, the pupil of the famous Khwaja Abdul Qadir arrived from Khurasan. Mulla Jamil was outstanding among his contemporaries in singing and painting. Two schools of music were founded in Kashmir during the period of Zain-ul-Abidin. Iranian musicians founded these schools.

Position of performing arts during Mughal Period

"The folk theatre called Bhand Pather is probably the oldest theatre in the subcontinent, if not in the world," says Javed Iqbal Bhatt.[5] Amongst Mughal Kings, Emperor Akbar was very liberal towards music, to the extent that he appointed Tansen as his minister as he was the greatest musician of his times. However, when Aurangzeb visited Kashmir, he witnessed a performance of Bhand Pather. He was appalled and shocked to see the performance and immediately issued orders to stop them. In spite of his orders, the Bhands of Kashmir continued to practice and perform their art and that is the reason this vibrant art form is to some extent still alive. He even issued orders that the instruments of the artists be confiscated and destroyed. It is said that once Aurangzeb was sitting in his window where he would give audience to the people. Suddenly he heard the screaming and wailing of women. When he enquired, he was informed that the teacher of the dancing girls was dead and she was being taken to the burial ground. He said loudly that she should be buried deeper under the earth so that no sound or echo of her rises again.

Bhand Pather

The word Bhand Pather is a corruption of Bhana Patra. However, it owes its origin to the Sanskrit language. Bhana means 'actors' and Patra means 'playing some character'. According to Javed Iqbal Bhatt,[6] "The word Bhand with its origin in the Sanskrit 'Band' meaning comical behaviour or imitation is found in most of the north Indian languages." Pather in Kashmiri language is acting and Bhand is the actor. Hence 'actor performing'.

Bhand Pather is a traditional folk drama of Kashmir. It is, in fact, a powerful combination of drama, satire, dance and music. The form is traditionally passed on through generations from father to son. Previously, there used to be no script and everything was improvised. M K Raina says,[7] "Bhand Pather though is not a monologue but a social drama incorporating mythological legends and contemporary social satires." The performances earlier used unwritten scripts and often the plots would speak of the days of kings, when land was with the landlords and the poor peasant was oppressed by them.

The form has tremendous mass appeal. The group selects an open space and improvises almost everything for the performance, such as the stage, the script, the costumes, the properties etc. The performance starts with a ritualistic dance Chhok. The dance is accompanied by music played on Swarnai (Pipe), Dhol (Drum), Nagara (Percussion Instrument) and Thalij (metal plate). After the dance, the actual play starts. Maskharay (Jesters) enter the stage. The essential property in their hand is a Koodar/ Chabuk (Whip) and a bamboo stick. The music used to be based on the classical ragas of Kashmir known as 'Maqam'. It is these Maskharas (Jesters) who begin the play and end it with a message.

The leader of the group is called Magun. Even Sheikh Nur-ud-Din, the great Rishi of Kashmir had praise for him, "*Pather byon byon ti akoy Magun.*" There are different kinds of plays and different characters in the play but Magun is unique. He is found in every play. According to R K Braroo,[8] "The advent of Islam, however, destroyed both temple and Court Rangmandapas (Royal Court Theatres) – the source of inspiration and sustenance of folk theatre, and thus started the distortions in folk art. Magun, the pivot of Bhand Pather is, in fact, the deformed name of Mahaguni, the Sutradhara of classical drama."

The play, whatever may be the storyline, usually revolved around kings and their rule, but serious messages, including the current problems were orally transmitted. According to Sir Walter Lawrence,[9] "It is said that Maharaja Gulab Singh acquired a very intimate knowledge of village administration from the Bhaggats (Bhands)) performances, and I have picked up some hints from them as to the method of the Patwari, the village accountant."

There are various kinds of Pather—Darza Pather,Watal Pather (Play on sweeper), Angrez Pather (Play on Englishman),Shikaargah (Play on animal hunt),Gosain Pather (Play on ascetic), Grees Pather (Play on villager),Raaza Pather (Play on king), Haanz Pather (Play on boatman),Bakarwaal Pather (Play on Bakkarwal Tribe),Mughal Pather((Play on Mughals) etc. Though these Pathers are different in name they have a striking resemblance to each other when performed.

The Bhands of Akengam, Mohuripora and Wathura are highly skilled. They are mainly Muslims. Subhan Bhagat of Akengam contributed a lot for its revival. Many Kashmiri Pandit thespians such as Moti Lal Kemu, M K Raina, and Radha Krishan Braroo did a lot of experiments for reviving this art form. The form was nourished by the monistic concept of Kashmir Shaivism and Sufi mysticism of Muslims, giving it a secular concept. However, it is sad that this form is gradually getting extinct.

Ladishah

Ladishah is a unique, witty, and satirical form of singing in Kashmir. It is performed by only one man who relates a legend or a folk tale or the present social and political conditions. The singing of Ladishah Ballads can be done with just a few notes, even two notes. The minstrels move from village to village and sing a story that they create on-the-spot, lampooning social lapses or issues relating to that village. The music in the background is an iron rod striking on the bangles of iron worn on their hands. Previously the singers would move to villages after harvesting, but that form is also now extinct. According to Mohiud-Din Hajini,[10] "Major portion of this form is lost in verbal transmission by the illiterate bards; nevertheless we still possess some very fine pieces in the Ladishah. Hakeem Habibullah (1905), Munawer Shah of Kulsoo (1925), and Lala Lakhman (1947) are recognised masters of this form."

Chakri

No important festival of Kashmir is complete unless Chakri, the most popular genre is sung. It is a peculiar style of singing. The group consists of six, seven or eight artists, headed by a leader. The leader initiates the song and the others follow him in choral responses. Write James Porter,[11] "Chakri is sung in responsorial style; vocal solo sections alternate with choral responses and instrumental interludes."

Chakri is a real symbol of the very essence of artistic genre of Kashmir, which depicts a long tradition of folk music that evolved many decades back in the valley. It is difficult to find the origin of Chakri. However, the form of singing has upheld the heritage of the culture of Kashmir.

The group consisting of singers and instrumentalists sits in a semi-circle, the leader in the middle. The Instrumentalists consist of a Sarangi player and a Rabab player. According to Sunita Dhar,[12] "The most popular instrument used in folk music is Rabab, which was borrowed from Persia."Other instruments used are Nout, a percussion instrument, a Tumbaknari, (percussion instrument made of terracotta clay that has at one end a bulge covered with goat skin) and a Harmonium. In Chakri, the initial song composition starts with a low rhythm but it gradually picks up. As soon as one composition of slower beats finishes it is accompanied by another composition with a fast rhythm. This part of the Chakri is known as Rouf but is different from the 'Rouf' which is performed by women on festive occasions.

Sufiana Kalam

The word Sufiana is derived from Sufism, which means devotional, and Kalam is poetry. Thus, Sufiana Kalam is rendering of mystic poetry, the song of Sufi saints. It is attributed to have travelled from Iran to Kashmir during the fifteenth century. The lyrical language used is Persian and Kashmiri dialects. Sufiana singing is known as 'Saazandar Geawun' and it has attained the form of classical rendering of Ragas known as

'Maqam'. There are approximately fifty-four Maqam (Ragas). Sufiana Kalam/Mauseqi is also like Chakri choral singing. All seven to eight participants, in addition to their playing some instrument, sing in unison following their leader. The poems sung are those of mystic Sufi saints, such as Hafiz, Jallauddin Rumi, Jami Omar Khayyam, Amir Khusro, Rasul Mir, Neame Seah and other Sufi Saints. The singers sang in Persian and Kashmiri languages.

The instruments played in this art form are Santoor (a hundred string instrument),Kashmir Saz (A bow instrument which has three prominent strings),Wasool/Dokra (Percussion Instrument)Tabla (Percussion) and a Sitar/Sehtar (A miniature version of the original Sitar). Describes Sunita Dhar,[13]"Kashmiri Sehtar or Sitar is said to be the original model of Indian Sitar. The instrument is now, however, comparable to Indian Sitar of these days and it has retained its originality. The Kashmiri Sehtar is the original instrument accompanying Sufiana Kalam or Mauseqi which came to Kashmir from Central Asia."

Tradition says that during fifteenth century a musician Hayat Joo came from Iran and settled in Kashmir. He started imparting training of his art to his disciples. Zain-ul-Abidin, the king of Kashmir was a great admirer of music. It was during his period that Sufiana music got a major boost.

Wanvun

Wanvun is the Kashmiri Hindu's oldest form of singing. It is chorus singing usually sung at various festivals such as marriages, yagnopavit (Thread ceremony/ Hindu baptism), child birth etc. On these occasions whenever the elderly ladies get together, the Wanvun starts. The singing gets a boost when an elderly woman takes the Kangri and puts in it the 'Isband', a kind of seed (Peganum Harmala). The process emits smoke. Tradition says that it is to ward off the evil spirits. She takes a pinch of Isband, goes to other relatives, touches their forehead with it and then drops it in the Kangri .

Wanvun of Hindus of Kashmir is in fact a prayer to God. The elderly ladies bless the groom or the bride praying to Lord Shiva to protect them and bless them. The name of Shiva and Parvati or Devi (Mother Goddess) is recited repeatedly.

The rendering of Wanvun

On auspicious days when relatives and friends meet, the elderly ladies extend their helping hand in doing the household chores, such as cleaning the rice or pruning the vegetables for the chef. They sit in a circle and the music session starts. One lady leads and starts the song. Hardly has she finished half a line when the other ladies join her and together they sing the melodious Wanvun. Writes Sunita Dhar,[14] "Among Hindus, Wanvun performers sit in a circle, pentagon, hexagon or nonagon form and sing Wanvun, suiting the ceremony."

Wanvun of Muslims

Muslims also sing Wanvun during festive occasions such as weddings, betrothals or circumcision of a young boy. However, in the Muslim community singing of Wanvun by women is performed in two groups. One group leads by singing a couplet and the other repeats after it. Then the second group takes the lead and the first follows.

Rouf Dance

Tradition says that Rouf is the oldest dance of Kashmir. It is essentially a fascinating spring dance and is performed in marriages and on religious festivals such as Eid by women dressed in exquisite zari embroidered pherans (Gowns) and glittering jewellery. They move with their hands holding one another and their steps move to and fro creating a charming choreography, which is a feast for the eyes. The dance culminates in Hiket (A kind of dance step wherein girls in pairs hold one another's hands and swing in a circular form, with joy and gay abundance). The dance is performed at almost all the joyful events. The songs are full of joy and romanticism.

Hafiz Nagma

Hafiz Nagma is a dance performed by women known as Hafiz. The dance dates back to antiquity. In the medieval period, Hafiz was very popular when it was danced with Sufiana Kalams.

Bache Nagma

Bache Nagma is a dance where boys dress themselves as girls, like Gotipua dance of Orissa. However, Gotipua is based on classical music and movements of dancers are structured but in Bache Nagma, one can be innovative on the spot. Tradition says that the dance was ushered into the performing arts of Kashmir during Pathan Rule.

Hiket

Hiket is the corrupt version of Raas Leela. According to Sunita Dhar,[15]"Hiket is an inseparable part of 'Raas' prevalent in Kashmir." Raas is a traditional form of dancing. In Sanskrit, it is known as 'Kreeda'. Raas Leela was the favourite pastime of God Krishna. It is said when he performed in full moonlight, the gods would witness this divine performance. Hiket is performed when two dancers make a pair and create various love plays.

Habba songs

Some of the Habba songs which became very famous have transformed into folklore. The songs sung and composed by the famous songstress Habba Khatoon. in the sixteenth century, are so popular even today that these songs are sung as legendry songs. They seem to echo the love life of every woman irrespective of caste and creed. Every women of Kashmir finds her own story in these songs.

Zyin Mazoor

This is a fascinating story/ballad of Zyin Mazoor (woodcutter), written by Akbar Lone. A woodcutter goes to the forest for collecting wood. Suddenly he decides to go to Hazrat Suleiman, and pray to him for financial help. He bestows the woodcutter with a jewel. As he hides the jewel in his turban it accidently falls in the river and is lost. Lamenting, mourning and dejected he again goes to Hazrat Suleiman who gives him another jewel. While he is on his way home, the jewel this time is stolen by a thief. This happens many times and ultimately there is a happy ending to the story. This folk song has many musical variations.

Niyand Gyavun

It is a typical singing form. The farmers, while ploughing, sowing the seeds or saplings for the next harvest, or extracting the unwanted weeds from the fields, sing in unison and the choral songs reverberate into the hills and produce lilting melody.

Bombur Yemberzal

Bombur (Bumblebee) Yemberzal (Narcissus), is a Kashmiri opera written by Dina Nath Nadim. It is about the symbolic triumph of spring over autumn. The opera was produced in 1953 AD. It was directed by the famous Music Director Mohan Lal Aima.

Gulrez

Gulrez is a love poem written by Maqbool Shah. It is said that originally the poem was written by Zia-ud-Din Nakhshabi, a Persian scholar. However, Maqbool Shah translated his works and they are famous in Kashmir.

Kraal Koori

Kraal Koori is a song written in praise of a potter's daughter.

Doub Bai

The song depicts praise for the work of a washerwoman.

Fourteen
Fairs, Festivals and Food

Kashmiri Pandits

Kashmiri Pandits are a unique community. They are a peace loving, non-violent, intelligent race. According to Sir Monier Williams,[1] "The Kashmiri Pandits are among the finest types of the Aryan race." About the characteristics of Kashmiri Pandits, Anand Kaul writes,[2] "The Pandit is truly of 'simple breed'—simple in food and simple in dress. Patience and resignation are writ large on his behaviour. Give him a slap on the right cheek and he will turn the left but will never provoke you to a quarrel. So law-abiding he is that he regards a state official as a 'fiat of destiny'."

Kashmiri Brahmins who later gained the title of Kashmiri Pandits trace their history from the Vedic period. According to Michal Witzal,[3] "The history of the Kashmir Brahmins may even go back all the way to the Vedic period as the valley and the surroundings were already known in Vedic times." A highly accomplished community, Kashmiri Pandits are the original inhabitants of Kashmir with a long history, even earlier than the Mahabharata period.

Kashmiri Pandits belong to Saraswat division of Brahmin cult and are seekers of knowledge and wisdom. Saraswat Brahmins are spread over northern India, Gujarat, Maharashtra and many other Indian states. According to Michael Witzel,[4] "They were regarded as belonging to the most Brahminical group of Northern India, the Saraswat, and are thought to originally have come from the Saraswat area in Kurukshetra (now in Haryana)."

Kashmiri Pandits belonged to the Aryan race; when they settled in Kashmir is not known. However, their name appears in the oldest scripture '*Nilamatapurana*'. Some of the descriptions appear in another treatise known as *Kuttanimatam* written by Damodaragupta in the 7th century. In *Kuttanimatam* it has been mentioned that Kashmiri Brahmins were permitted to eat meat and fish which they enjoy even today.

Seeing the exquisite natural scenic beauty and salubrious climate of Kashmir these Saraswat Brahmins made Kashmir their permanent abode. They were intellectually superior and and had thirst for knowledge regarding astrology, astronomy, medicine, architecture, philosophy and even sexology. They also contributed to the development of these subjects. They devoted their time towards meditation and, asceticism. They also believed in physical fitness. George Campbell wrote, "The figure of an ordinary working Kashmiri is strong and athletic. They rule by the brain and the pen and not by the sword." Francois Bernier says,[5] "It left no doubt in my mind that there are as handsome faces in Kachemire as in any part of Europe."

Though, initially, Kashmiri Pandits formed only a single group but with the passage of time some focused on Shastras and religious practices, forming a Purohits(priests) group. The remaining took to activities such as government jobs known as Karkun (Service Class). Both these classes of Kashmiri Pandits enjoyed the royal patronage and respect of the common citizens.

For Kashmiri Pandits, rather for Kashmiri Hindus, the Muslim rule in Kashmir turned out to be most tragic. Rinchan, a Tibetan prince ran away from his country, came to Kashmir and sought asylum which Suhadeva the ruler of Kashmir at that time granted. Many Muslims also came to Kashmir. Among them was a holy man, Bulbul Shah who converted many Kashmiri Hindus to the Islamic fold.

Rinchan became the King of Kashmir and married Kota Rani, the daughter of Prime Minister Ram Chandra. Bulbul Shah converted Rinchan to Islam. This way Rinchan became the first Muslim ruler of

Kashmir. After his death, another Muslim, Shah Mir who had come from Swat, usurped the throne of Kashmir. Gradually Muslims began to rule Kashmir. Though Islam became the court religion, yet the Kashmiri Brahmins continued to handle the administration.

During the reign of Shahab-ud-Din (1360-1378 AD) Kashmiri Pandits had expressed their resentment against the special privileges granted to Muslims. According to Jia Lal Kilam,[6] "A feeble rising on behalf of the Brahmans was the result. The other castes do not seem to have participated in the rising in any large numbers. The king, in order to break the upheaval amongst Hindus, turned his attention towards their temples which must have provided a meeting place for them. Hassan, the Kashmiri historian, says that almost all the temples in Srinagar including the one at Bijbihara were greatly damaged. It seems that the kings of Kashmir had by now become completely muslimised as a result of their contacts with the Sayyids." In the process many Hindus got converted to Islam mainly for fear of the onslaught or to gain royal favours. Savage methods and brutal force were used to convert the innocent locals to Islamic faith. In the reign of Sikandar Butshikan, in order to please the king, one Kashmiri Hindu convert Saif-ud-Din alias Suh Dev, planned the liquidation of all Hindus in Kashmir. On the bank of Vitasta an ancient Hindu temple named Kalishri (built by Lalitaditya) was destroyed and converted into Khankha-i-Maula. According to Anand Kaul who quotes Hassan, the historian,[7] "this country possessed, from the times of Hindu Rajas, many temples which were like the wonders of the world. Their workmanship was so fine and delicate that one found oneself bewildered at their sight. Sikandar, goaded by feelings of bigotry, destroyed them and levelled them with the earth and with their material built many mosques and Khankhas."

The helpless Kashmiri Pandits had either to convert to Islam or migrate to other parts of India. Some accepted death and gave their lives for their faith. Tradition says that Sikandar's persecution of Hindus continued till there remained only eleven Hindu families in the valley. Prem Nath Bazaz writes,[8] "At the death of Shahab-ud-din's successor Qutb-ud-Din, in 1389 AD, there came to the throne of Kashmir a ferocious begot, a cruel fanatic and religious zealot who brought the noble tradition of the Kashmir culture and the fair name of Islam into disgrace." Many times they had to leave their homes to escape the brutal persecution. They were taxed, humiliated and killed. According to E F Knight,[9] "Kashmiri Hindoos are always known as pundits—why I am unable to say for it is an utter misuse of that term, which is supposed to imply learning, a quality very scarce among these people."

With the passage of time—with the Sikh rule in 1819 and then Dogra rule in 1846 AD, their political and social conditions began becoming better. Their quest for learning made their community join schools and colleges and make themselves available for jobs in government and other institutions.

By the time India became independent and Pakistan came into being in 1947, the Kashmiri Pandit community had become a microscopic minority.

According to Sir Francis Younghusband,[10] "Kashmir Pundits are well known over India for their acuteness and subtlety of mind, their intelligence and quick-wittedness. They prefer priestly, literary and clerical occupations." All other economic activities in the state—agriculture, trade, construction, transport, forest timber trade, have been totally in the hands of the Muslim community. The lucrative industries like tourism, handicrafts and artefacts have also been in their hands. Therefore, being reasonably educated, it was due to their efficiency, honesty and hard-work that they manned the administration, of course at the lower level of the State for centuries under successive rulers of Muslim Sultans and then the Mughals followed by Pathan rulers and also under Sikhs and Dogra rulers. But after Kashmir's accession to India the doors of employment for this community during the National Conference's so called secular government were totally closed.

Reeling under the distress of unemployment and realising that there would be no end to the discrimination against them by the State Government, thousands of Kashmiri Pandit families migrated to India during the first five years of the secular rule of National Conference. It is unbelievable that Pandit Nehru, the Prime Minister of India, was made to issue instructions to the effect that no Kashmiri Pandit should be taken in the Indian Government service. It was Sardar Vallahbhai Patel, India's first Home Minister, who got the order amended and Kashmiri Pandits got the opportunity to join various Indian Government offices outside the state of Jammu and Kashmir.

The agrarian reforms, debt reconciliation laws were enforced without any consideration for the Kashmiri Pandits. They became second class citizens in their own homeland. Ultimately, came the holocaust in 1990. After plundering their belongings the terrorists torched their houses.

Mekhal/Yagnopavit (Sacred thread ceremony)

Yagnopavit, also called Upanayanam/Yajnopavitam in Sanskrit language, is one of the most significant ceremonial festivals of the Hindus of Kashmir. The male child of the family is inducted into the Hindu fold by baptising him with the sacred thread in a function known as Yagnopavit. The thread ceremony is a ritual referring to the boy's taking shelter with his guru (spiritual teacher).

Livun/Garnavai (House cleaning)

In a traditional Kashmiri family, the rituals of thread ceremony are more or less the same as those of a marriage ceremony. The family priest is asked to find an auspicious day for the function. The day is fixed and the preparations start well in advance. Close relatives and elderly ladies of the neighbourhood visit the house a few days prior to the function and help the family in readying the house, which is known as Livun/ Garnavai (House Cleaning). During the process they sing traditional songs such as 'Wanvun'. The next step is 'Mainziraat' when Henna is put on the boy's hands. On the morning of Mainziraat, there is an important function, Krool Kharun, when the door of the house is painted with dots and floral designs. This is done to ward off the evil spirits. On this occasion, a salted rice pudding 'Ver' is prepared and distributed.

Mainziraat is usually performed a day before the actual Yagnopavit day. It is celebrated with a lot of gaiety. There is a music and dance programme and the function continues the whole night. Elderly women burn some seeds 'Ishand' to create smoke to ward off the evil eye from the family. Then the 'Pouph' (father's sister) applies henna to the boy and other relatives. She is paid in cash for this.

The next step is Devagon. It is one of the most sacred ceremonies. It literary means Dev Agaman meaning visit of god. The boy has to take a sacred bath known as 'Kani-Shraan'. After the bath new clothes are worn. This ceremony, is observed in wake of the transition of the boy from childhood to boyhood.

Main function

A group of priests come and light the holy fire. They recite shlokas from the holy books. Ladies are supposed to wear Narivan (Colourful threads/ Moli) and at the back of their heads they attach Tekpooch (Painted, colourful paper). Then the boy's head is tonsured. He is made to wear a yellow gown and a rope is tied around his waist. He is given a stick from the Mulberry tree in his hand and the sacred thread is worn. The whole day he is made to beg alms from the relatives and friends and visitors to the function, while reciting the shloka '*Boo Bikhyam Dehyam....*' (Please give me alms).Relatives offer him money, which is offered to the Guru—the priests who are there to perform the rituals. The parents and close relatives observe a fast while other guests enjoy milk, tea, fruits etc.

In the evening, the boy is made to wear expensive clothes and a turban so he looks almost like a bridegroom. He and the relatives visit a temple where they offer prayers. Once he is back there is a feast which is strictly vegetarian. Dal and Nadru (pulses and Lotus stem) are a must.

Kashmiri Hindu Marriage

The Pundit weddings rely mainly on matching of horoscopes. At the outset, the boy's family sends the bio-data of the boy and details of the family (Kolavali), along with horoscope of the boy known as Tekni. The boy's family also get the Kolavali of the girl. Once the priest declares that the horoscopes are matching, the families meet and if they like each other the marriage is fixed.

Kasam-Driee

Both the families meet and pledge in a temple before the idol that they agree to the tying of the knot between their children. The elders from the family exchange garlands. This lays the foundation of a new relationship. The commitment of both the families is known as 'Vainee'. The eldest aunt of the boy prepares a special salted pudding in which dry fruits, especially walnuts, and meat bits are added. The pudding is distributed to the relatives and neighbours. The bride's family offers money according to their capability , and then traditional Kashmiri food is served by the girl's side.

Gandun

After the first ceremony is over, the family priest is asked to fix a date for the Gandun ceremony which is to reaffirm the promises made previously. On this occasion, the girl's family gives a grand feast for the boy's family and relatives. Once again, an exchange of presents takes place. The boy's family carries an elegantly stitched expensive pheran, along with 'Pooch', (a long cloth attached to the headgear), 'Dupta', another piece of cloth put on the headgear and 'Loongi' (yet another cloth tied at the waist) . The traditional costumes are ethnic wear, now getting extinct; this attire has been replaced by the saris. Taranga is a complex headgear, which takes hours to arrange and is decorated on the head of the bride. According to Sunita Dhar,[11] "In Vedic period, when Goddess Sinnavali's marriage was performed, God Pooshan had prepared a beautiful headgear to decorate her head. This was called Kapal–Apush (The Kalpush) in Sanskrit. Lord Indra beautified it further by wrapping a white strip of cloth around it."

Lately, an exchange of rings has found place in the ceremony. At the bride's house the groom's family feeds the girl cream which is presented in a silver cup and fed with silver spoon.

Elderly women of both families sing 'Wanvun'. Says Prof Sunita Dhar,[12]"Wanvun is a prayer in the form of folk music. It commences with a prayer to God. The subjects of Wanvun also refer to the events of the Vedic period." While singing, women pray to God for the prosperity of the bride, groom and their parents. Lilting melodious tunes are sung in harmony by a group of women. This singing continues until the end of all the ceremonies of the marriage.

On this occasion, the boy's family requests the girl's parents to fix the day of marriage. Accordingly, the family priest decides the day and then he is sent to the groom's family to inform them of the date.

Livun

Livun is the traditional cleansing of the house before the marriage takes place. This cleaning is done by both families.

Dapan Bata

Dapan Bata is to extend invitation to the relatives. The parents of the prospective groom and the bride go to their relatives and invite them formally and personally. The relatives offer money or gifts to the groom and bride and then accept the invitation.

The auspicious day, Mehndiraat

The Mehndiraat is observed a few days before the marriage. On this occasion an important function is 'Krul Kharun'. The main door of the house is painted and a kind of tapestry drawn. The purpose is to beautify the door and also traditionally to ward off the evil spirits. Ver, is prepared and walnuts are added to it. Mehndi (henna) has been in use since ancient times. (Archaeologists have found 5,000-year-old mummies with traces of henna on their fingertips)

Mehndiraat can be performed within seven days before the date of marriage. On this occasion, there is a get together of all the relatives. Dancing and singing continues the whole night. At the appropriate time of the night, the father's sister applies henna paste to the bride or groom.

Kanishraan

After Mehndiraat is over comes Devagon. But before Devagon, the boy or the girl have to take a sacred bath known as 'Kanishraan'. After the bath, new clothes are worn.

Devagon

Devagon is a ceremony observed for the transition of the boy or the girl from an unmarried state to a wedded one. Houses are cleaned, doors painted, the salted rice pudding Ver is again prepared and distributed. Then the boy and the girl perform puja for a prosperous wedded life.

Duribata

The maternal grandparents of the girl or boy offer presents to them.

Lagan, wedding rituals of the Baraat day

The bride's house is agog with activities. The whole area is decorated so that it gives a festive look. Earlier, married women were approached and were requested to lend their brocade saris for decorating the place, especially for designing the entry gate and the place where the groom would sit. Then traditional vegetarian Kashmiri food is prepared, which includes, Dumaloo (potato dish), Choukwangan (Brinjal/Eggplant) dish, Nadiryakhin (Lotus Stem cooked in yogurt), Mujchetin (Crushed Radish with yogurt), Nadurchurma (fried Lotus Stem),—the staple food of the Kashmiris. The girl's side make a design of with colours at the entry of the house termed as 'Vyug'. Before the procession starts from the boy's house, the groom has to stand on the Vyug and an elder lady blesses him and feeds him Nabad (Sugar Candy).

Shankh Naad (Blowing Of Conch Shell)

The Hindus of Kashmir are mainly Shaivites and therefore they use Shankh Naad on festive occasions. Shankh Naad is a call to God Shiva, praying to him to bless the groom.

Procession of Baraat

Then the procession of guests starts from the boy's house. Once they reach near the girl's house, all the relatives of the bride stand with reverence to greet all the guests from the boy's side. The groom is made to stand on the 'Vyug'.

One of the older ladies offers Nabad to the groom. Meanwhile, the other guests proceed to enjoy the spicy Kashmiri food .

The Sacred Fire

The groom and bride move to the place where the family priests of both families perform the rituals. The sacred fire is lit and amidst the chanting of shlokas, the ceremony of marriage begins. The bride and groom have to perform many rituals.

Poshpooza (The floral worship)

All the relatives are invited for 'Poshpooza' (Floral Worshiping). The bride and groom are covered with a shawl or decorated cloth, and all the relatives shower flower petals on them amidst chanting of shlokas by the priests. The bride and the groom are treated as Lord Shiva and Goddess Parvati. The relatives worship them with devotion.

While the bride and the bridegroom are busy performing rituals, usually the younger sister of the bride stealthily steals the shoes of the groom. The boy's family has to pay for the shoes. The payment is sometimes much more than the cost of the shoes. This has become more or less a part of the celebrations.

Bidayee (The parting)

The Groom has once again to stand on the Vyug. The maternal uncle of the bride carries the bride until the 'Vyug' and she also joins the groom. One of the elders of the bride's family offers Nabad to the bride as well as the groom.

Bidayee (parting) is the most painful part of the marriage ceremony when the groom and his relatives prepare to take the bride to their house. The bride is accompanied by her younger sister or brother.

The celebrations at the girl's house come to an end, but at the boy's house they continue.

Satraat

In case the marriage takes place during the day then in the evening the bride, along with her groom, visits her parents. This is termed as Satraat. If the ceremony is performed at night then the next evening the girl visits her parents along with her groom and a young sister-in-law or brother-in-law. Both the bride and the groom are given new clothes.

Phirlath

Phirlath means the groom and bride visit her house once again and have a meal. The boy is given gifts and then both leave to begin their journey of life.

Roth Khabar

After a few days, the bride's parents send someone, usually her brother, to know the welfare of their daughter. On this occasion, they send sweet Nan (baked bread cakes) along with dry fruits. The bride accompanies her brother back to her parents house and stays there for a few days.

Muslims of Kashmir

The spread of Islam in Kashmir began towards the end of Hindu rule. With the advent of Islam in 14th century there were very few changes in the social and cultural milieu of Kashmir. People, in spite of accepting Islam, continued to observe some rituals of Hindus as most them were converts. According to Walter R Lawrence,[13] "It is a generally accepted fact that up to about the beginning of the 14th century, the population of the valley was Hindu and about the middle and the end of this century, the mass of the people were converted to Islam." It is not that before the 14th century there were no Muslims in the valley. Many Muslims had visited the valley and many had even settled there permanently.

During Muslim rule in Kashmir this community enjoyed special status, as a result they occupied most of the places of prestige and influence. But the British government in India followed a policy of relegating them to the background. They were not given plum jobs as the British government preferred Hindus to Muslims. So they too were subjected to discrimination.

The reason for pushing the Muslim community to the background was the fact that Indian Muslims had taken an active part in the Mutiny of 1857 and the government did not trust them. The Muslim community in the state of Jammu and Kashmir was a neglected lot. Although during Maharaja Hari Singh's rule, they were not subjected to discrimination but as Muslim communalism in India had raised its head, Kashmir too was influenced. Another factor for Muslims backwardness was that they had preferred to take up trades such as agriculture or handicraft as their profession and avoided going to school or universities. They preferred to study the Holy *Quran*.

During Sikh and Dogra rule, the Muslim community suffered. The rulers introduced 'Begar' (Forced Labour). A story goes that a Muslim youth whose wife was pregnant and had developed labour pain went to get a midwife. But before he could do so, he was forcibly taken by the government agency for Begar. At home his wife, waiting for the midwife, perished.

From 1931 AD, Sheikh Mohammad Abdullah gave political lead to the Muslim community and finally brought awakening among them. While he changed their political scenario, Bakshi Gulam Mohammad enlightened them in the field of education. After Sheikh Sahib's death some religious zealots brought Punjabi Muslim culture from Pakistan. During the holocaust against Kashmiri Pandits, the Muslim community could not save the helpless Hindus from death, devastation and migration.

The Muslim community has various sects that are enemies of one another. As already stated, by the end of 14th century majority of people in Kashmir were converted to Islam. According to Abdul Majid Mattoo,[14] "New Sufi Order like Naqashbandi, Chistia and Suharawardi were introduced." In this process those orders which were already in the valley like Rishi (Mystic) order, Kubrawi order and Nurbakshia order (which was followed by Shia community) got a setback after Chak dynasty was thrown out by Mughals in Kashmir. But with the passage of time Shia community survived. Naqashbandi order was spread by Khwaja Bahau'd Din Mohammad Naqashband in Persia and in Kashmir it was spread by Sayid Hilal who came to Kashmir during Sikandar's period.

The Sufi order too made tremendous progress in the valley. According to Abdul Majid Mattoo,[15] "The influence of Shaiva ideology resulted in the foundation of an indigenous mystic order. The founder of the order was Sheikh Noor-ud-Din Rishi. Due to his efforts and favourable circumstances the order gained adherence in almost the entire kingdom." Further, he writes, "In the course of time they even did not take the basic fundamentals of Islam into consideration." Many sects like Suharawardi order, Naqashbandi order, Chisti Silsilah, Kubrawi order, Qadiri Silsilah, and Nurbakshian Silsilah were found among Muslim community. There were some in which both Hindus and Muslims had full faith. These were Rishi Peer Pandit Padsha, Roopa Bhawani, Noor-ud-Din Rishi and Mishah Sahib of Rainawari.

Almost all the sects had faith in the Holy Quran, Prophet Mohammad and other holy scriptures. The only difference was the approach which varied from one sect to another. With the passage of time, there grew great enmity between Sunni and Shias. The Shia order was introduced by Mir Shamas-ud-Din Iraqi and his son Damyal in Askardu and Kargil. The enmity between Sunni and Shia followers existed even when Mirza Haydar conquered the state in 1541 AD. He destroyed the only Shia holy place at Zadibal. Today, this enmity has taken a very destructive turn in Punjabi Muslim dominated areas of Pakistan. The original Muslims after conversion called themselves Bhatt, Dar, Pandit and Bamboo. Those who had come from outside Kashmir were Sayyids, Sheikhs, and Pirzada.

Muslim Marriages

Marriages in a Muslim family have undergone tremendous changes. Previously it would be a simple affair. Some of the customs the Muslims have inherited from Hindus are dowry and extravaganza of ceremonies. Marriage is an occasion of festivity be it a Kashmiri Hindu marriage or a Kashmiri Muslim marriage. Many ceremonies are common to both.

Wanvun

For a week before the wedding, festivities such as singing and dancing are organised in both families. The women finish their household chores and assemble in the groom's or bride's house and sing and dance till the wee hours to express their joy.

Mainziraat

The day before the marriage, Mehndi is sent to the bride's house. She paints her hands and feet with it. On this occasion all the relatives anoint the mehndi on their palms. There is a Ladies Sangeet (program of song and dance) with the women singing traditional songs. This occasion is celebrated in both families.

Baraat

On the wedding day, the groom's family goes to the bride's house. The groom visits a neighbouring shrine and then visits the graves of his ancestors. Then they move in a procession to the bride's house, where they are welcomed with songs sung by the women of the family. A lavish feast of a thirty-six course meal (Wazwan Kashmiri Cuisine) awaits the people.

Nikah

The Nikah or wedding ceremony can be conducted at the home of the bride or the groom, or at any other convenient venue. A maulvi (priest), in the presence of close family members and relatives, conducts the ceremony. In orthodox Muslim communities, the men and women are seated separately. The fathers of the bride and groom play an important role in the ceremony. The maulvi reads selected verses from the Quran and the Nikah is complete after the Ijab-e-Qubul (Proposal and Acceptance). The boy's side proposes and the girl's side conveys her assent. The mutual consent of the bride and groom is of great importance in a Muslim marriage for it to be legal. On the day of the Nikah, the elders of the two families decide the amount of Mehar, which is a compulsory amount of money given by the groom's family to the bride.

Rukhsat

After all the rituals and ceremonies are over, the bride's family bids their daughter a tearful farewell as she starts for her husband's house. A brother or a maternal uncle carries the bride to the palanquin accompanied by sad songs sung by the women.

Other Tribes of Kashmir

Hanji

Hanji, the masters of water boats are a significant ethnic group of the valley of Kashmir. This sect of people, though Muslims, are confined to the rivers and lakes of the valley. Hanjis believe that they are the descendants of Prophet Noah. They row their boats with a long pole to start with and after that they switch over to a heart shaped oar.

Hanjis are a hard-working race. According to E. F. Knight,[16] "the Hanjis, or boatmen, form a separate class in Kashmir. They are fine-looking men, athletic, hardworking, and extremely courteous." He further says, "Their women, when young, are often beautiful and the children, of whom they appear to be very fond, are the prettiest little creatures imaginable."

Hanjis are divided into various sub-castes:

- Demb Hanz — These boatmen work on floating gardens and their occupation is to grow vegetables.
- Gari Hanz — These boatmen gather water-nuts and also collect lotus stems.
- Mata Hanz — These deal in ferrying wood.
- Dunga Hanz — Earlier all the Dunga boatmen would ferry passengers from one place to another. However, some of them have shifted to houseboat business. The owner, along with his family, lives in the Dunga and sublets to any tourist one or two rooms of the Dunga.
- Gad Hanz — The boatman is essentially a fisherman who catches fish with a net or fishing rod or a harpoon. It is interesting to see them catch a fish with the harpoon.
- Haakh Hanz — These boatmen are collectors of wood from water bodies.
- Bahatchi Hanz — These boatmen live in their boats and ferry various goods such as rice, wheat, or building material.
- Shikara Hanz — The boatmen's livelihood is mainly dependent on tourists. He takes the tourists on pleasure trips in the lakes or the river. Dal Lake has many such boats which are beautifully decorated to attract tourists.
- Houseboat Hanz — These boatmen are treated as an elite class of the Hanjis clan.

Their houseboats are very expensive and can match any room of a five star hotel. These boatmen even speak many foreign languages. They are imaginative and use many methods to lure the tourists. According to Sir Walter R Lawrence,[17] "Half the tales about Kashmir and the Kashmiris can be traced to the imagination of the Hanjis, who, after the manner of the Irish car-drivers, tell travellers quaint stories of the valley and its rulers."

Bhands

Bhands or Bhagats are the performers of Bhand Pather, an archetypal and traditional folk-form of Kashmiri culture. This tradition has travelled through generations from father to son. Earlier these performers would perform for marriages, fairs and festivals and earn their living by accepting anything from the audience—money or material goods. These people also travel from one place to another to put up performances. Most of Bhands /Bhagats are Muslim. According to Sir Walter R Lawrence,[18] "With the curious exception of the Akengam Company, which is formed of Pandits, the Bhagats are all Musalmans." This has been endorsed by veteran actor/ director, M K Raina, who says that a village called Muhurpur next to Akengam used to have Kashmiri Pandit Bhand performers.

These performers are mainly from Akengam in the Anantnag district of Kashmir. However, they did spread to a few other villages of Kashmir. These performers dress differently. They have long hair and mostly wear while clothes. They are imaginative and show their ingenuity by improvising according to the situation and props available when they put up a show.

Gujjars

Gujjars/ Bakarwaals are two beautiful ethnic tribes of Kashmir. Though they are the original inhabitants of Kashmir, and very close to each other, yet there is some difference in their way of life. The Gujjar clan has a long history. It is difficult to find their origin but there are some references in Ramayana as they joined King Dashratha of Ayodhya, in his fight against demons. In Mahabharata, Gujjars fought with the forces of Lord Krishna when he migrated from Mathura to Dwarka. There are different views about the origin of Gujjars. In India, it is said that Gujjars appeared in Northern India during the invasion of the Huns. They are also believed to be the descendants of ancient Yuchis or Kushans. Originally, they were Hindus (Kshatriya and Brahmins) but later on they converted to Islam.

However, there are some Gujjars who have clung to the Hindu religion. Irrespective of their accepting Islamic faith, Gujjars have retained their gotra such as Bhati, Chandel, Baniya, Lodha etc. Marriage in the same gotras is strictly prohibited. According to Sir Walter R. Lawrence,[19] "Their language, known as Parimu or Hindki, is wholly different from the Kashmiri language, and they really intermix with the Kashmiris, though, like them, they are Musalman by religion."

There are different explanations of the name Gujjar. In Sanskrit language 'Gur' means enemy and 'Ujar' means destroyer hence 'destroyer of enemy'. Some say that since the tribes migrated from Gujjar (Gujarat), therefore, they are named Gujjar, others believe that they migrated from Rajasthan. Gujjars in Jammu and Kashmir are found in hilly terrains such as Udhampur, Pir Pantsal, and Drass area of Ladakh. Traditionally the Gujjars had a patriarchal family set-up.

The main occupations of Gujjars are livestock rearing and milk production. Some have cultivable land and they produce maize, wheat, and also rear buffaloes and cows. They are also aware of traditional herbs which protect them from various illnesses. Gujjar tribes were initially migratory grazers. However, this nomadic life is now declining at a very rapid rate. They are now trying to settle and join the mainstream of life in the country. Gujjars do not have any written language. Nonetheless, they speak their own dialect and enjoy their own traditional tribal songs and dances.

Bakarwaals

Bakarwaals is a nomadic tribe that roams in the Pir Pantsal area of the Himalayan mountain range. 'Bakra' means goat and 'Waal' means to take care. The Bakarwaals of Kashmir have accepted Islam as their religion but their dress, language, manners and customs have no commonality with that of the people of Kashmir—urban or rural. They have different social, political and cultural ethos. They adhere to the tenets of Islam. According to Michael J Casimir and Aparna Rao,[20] "The valley Gujjar and Bakarwaals adhere to many of the principle observances enjoined by Islam—circumcision, fasting in the month of Ramadan, and when they can afford it, the pilgrimage to Mecca. They are considered by the rural Muslims of the Kashmir valley to be good and pious Sunni Muslims."

In addition to Jammu and Kashmir, Bakarwaals are found in other states such as Uttarakhand, Himachal Pradesh and Punjab. They are mainly found in hilly terrains, on the slopes and on mountain tops. In Kashmir, they roam in the hilly areas of Banihal and Qasigund. They are also seen in the districts of Jammu, Kathua, Udhampur, Poonch, Rajouri etc.

It is a typical sight to see the stout and handsome men with beards, wearing turbans, shirts, coat and pyjamas. The women wear pherans. They also wear a kind of headgear underneath which their intricately, stylishly knitted hairstyles with multiple plaits, makes them extremely fascinating and beautiful. These women carry their food on their heads. This consists of a nutritious diet of maize, bread, whey, jungle roots and fruits. These men, women and children walk with their herd of goats, lambs, sheep, buffaloes and even cows. The group also has ponies with them which carry their bag and baggage. They move in search of greener pastures from one place to another in the high mountains.

The group is incomplete without their dogs known as Bhotia. The dogs walk silently with the herd and keep a watchful eye on the erring animals. They are noted for their ability to protect the livestock. They provide protection not only to the livestock but the tribals too. The dogs subsist only on bread, milk products and avoid eating meat.

Communication, The language of Kashmiris

Though there is no agreement on the origin of language but it is estimated that man used language, about two million years ago when evolution travelled to the Homo Habilis Age—the end of ice age and beginning of Stone Age. Since then man has developed his concepts, ideas and notions through speech and writings. In India, it is believed that formal language started with Panini, the grammarian, during 5th century. Kashmiri language also developed gradually and has a history of about 2,000 years. Common folks name it as Koshur or Kashir Zaban (Kashmiri Language). This language also shares its sentence-structure with Indo-Aryan languages which are dominant in two-thirds of India as well as most of Pakistan and Bangladesh. George Abraham Grierson, the eminent linguist, considered Dardic languages a sub-family of the Aryan languages and Kashmiri language is one of the Dardic languages. Kashmiri language, though spoken by majority of people in the valley, has not been the official language. Initially it was written in Sharda script, now more or less extinct. The Sharda script is only used to write horoscopes or religious scriptures. Sanskrit was very widely read and spoken in whole of India. In 1833 AD, Sir Macaulay became the first Law Minister of British India. In order to introduce English language he destroyed lakhs of schools which were teaching Sanskrit. In modern times Muslims write Kashmiri language in Urdu and Hindus write it in Devanagri.

According to Rev James Hinton Knowles, a famous linguist missionary and physician of 1893 AD,[21] "Proverbs taught 'the real people's speech,' discovered 'the genius, wit and spirit of a nation', and embodied its 'current practical philosophy'." In the preface of his book *Folktales of Kashmir* he says,[22] "My primary object to collecting these tales was to obtain some knowledge of Kashmiri, which is purely colloquial language, my secondary object was to ascertain something of the thoughts and way of the people."

There have been many versions about the origin of Kashmiri language. Writes Heinz Kloss,[23] "Kashmiri is broadly grouped under the Indo-Iranian branch of Indio-European and is included under the Dardic group of languages." There is little doubt that the Kashmiri language is essentially of Indo-Aryan base and owes its roots to Vedic Sanskrit. Dr Shashi Shekher Toshkhani, an eminent linguist of Kashmir, says,[24] "There exists very strong evidence to support the claim that Kashmiri has descended from the Vedic speech." Some of the scholars have stated that Kashmiri language has close affinity with Shina. Shina is a Dardic language which is spoken in Gilgit and Baltistan areas of Pakistan. It is also known as Tshina language. But according to Shashi Toshkhani, "Morphologically too Kashmiri does not share any of the characteristics attributed to Pishachi." According to Aziz Kashmiri,[25] "However, this is a hard fact that Kashmiri language has sprung from Hebrew language and not from Sanskrit."

Kashmiri speaking people are divided into various communities such as Marazi, belonging to southern and south-eastern region and Kamrazi belonging to northern and north-western region. Another dialect is Kishtwari. Grierson says, Kishtwari is the only one true dialect. The language is spoken in the valley of Kishtwar. Poguli is a dialect spoken in the west of Kishtwar and to the south of Pir Pantsal range. Rambani is spoken in the Ramban area, which is between Jammu and Kashmir. Siraji is spoken in Doda area on the Chenab River.

The orthography of Kashmiri language is in four scripts—Sharda, Devanagri, Perso-Arabic and Roman. Kashmiri Pandits used Sharda script since Third Century BC. Rev Thomas Russell Wade wrote Kashmiri grammar in 1884. He says,[26] "Kashmiri is written in the Devanagri, Sharda and Persian characters." Nevertheless, gradually Sharda script became extinct and its place was taken by Devanagri and later on Roman-Urdu. Kashmiri language has its own vowels. He states,[27] "Words having Zh must be of Persian origin; those having Ts must be Kashmiri; those with Gh, Kh, Z, may be Arabic or Persian; those with P, Ch, G may be Persian or Indian; and words having any of the letters T, D, R, in them are of Indian origin."

Kashmir language poetry was first found in the thirteenth century, written by Acharya Srikantha. His famous treatise is *Mahanaya Prakasha*. This treatise is on Tantric cult. Though there was some poetry written before Srikantha, it is in the form of 'Chummapada'.

Kashmiri language has never been the official language, yet its richness and flavour is so great that it has been accepted by the poets, writers, dramatists, publishers, mass media etc. It is the only language amongst the Dardic group, which had the written tradition. According to Anand Kaul,[28] "Its grammar is perfect, the etymology and syntax are regulated by fast rules with rare exceptions." The language has developed through folk literature, folk tales, comic narratives, folk songs, proverbs and riddles. Kashmiri literature also has themes related to romance, adventure, miracles through anecdotes, fables, fairy tales, ghost tales and tales of wit and wisdom.

J Hinton Knowles has given a detailed description of Kashmiri sayings and proverbs. These are used in their day to day language.

During the fourteenth century there was a great thrust in the development of Kashmiri language. The poet Lall Ded spoke mystic verses known as Vaakh in Kashmiri language. She used metaphors, riddles and other mediums for expression. She amazingly translated terse and subtle philosophy into simple Kashmiri language. This was followed by Nund Rishi's verses in Kashmir language, which were a blend of Lalla's

Shaiva philosophy and Islamic Sufism. These two Sufi saints emerged to reshape the spiritual discipline and sacredness in the society. However, their sayings also gave a fillip of intellectualism to the Kashmiri language. These two became the source of inspiration of many writers and poets. Then came Roopa Bhawani. Roopa Bhawani added a divinenes to the language. Arnimaal and Habba Khatoon, brought romanticism in Kashmiri language. These poets wrote about love and passion blended with hope and joy.

Subsequent poets such as Mahmud Gami, Rasul Mir, Shamas Fakir, Samad Mir, Ahad Zargar, and Master Zinda Kaul also helped the Kashmiri language to grow. The poets and writers of the 20th century such as Rahman Rahi, Muzaffar Aazim, Ghulam Nabi Firaq, Amin Kamil, Shambu Nath Bhatt Haleem, Ali Mohammad Lone, Akhtar Mohiudin and Sarvanand Kaul 'Premi', Hari Krishan Kaul, Rattanlal Shant, Hirdhey Kaul Bharti, Nazir Jahangir, Moti Lal Kemu, also contributed in the development of the Kashmiri language.

The unfortunate political turmoil in the valley has impacted the language too. The Pandit community who have migrated to other parts of India have to depend on other languages for their daily routine. Their offspring are totally ignorant of this language. In the valley also people have to depend more on Urdu, it being the official language. English is the language in which all subjects are taught in educational institutes. Kashmiri language is not even an optional subject. Writes the celebrated linguist Brij B Kachru,[29] "In this interplay of language, politics, and power, the Kashmiri language never received patronage from the powerful or the court, except for a short duration during the reign of Sultan Zain-ul-Abidin (1420 – 1470 AD)." However, the media such as Doordarshan and All India Radio are contributing a bit to save the language.

Food habits of Kashmiri Hindus

Though the names of the dishes match those of the Wazwan yet Kashmiri Hindus do not use garlic or onion in their dishes. Their main dishes are Rogan Josh (meat preparation with Kashmiri chillies), Mach (minced meat rolls), Kalya (meat preparation with turmeric but no chillies), Yakhni (meat preparation with yogurt). The vegetarian dishes are Chaman (cheese). Chaman can be cooked in many ways. Dum aloo (potato), Chuk Vangun (egg plant/ brinjal, sour in taste), Sochal (a kind of leafy vegetable), Haak (Kashmiri spinach), Munja (Knoll Kohl), Nadur Yakhni (lotus stem cooked in yogurt) and Nadur Churma (lotus stem fried) are popular dishes Raw apples are also cooked. The spices used are cinnamon, cloves, and cardamom, fennel powder and dry ginger.

Yogurt is often used. Fennel powder and dry ginger powder are essential ingredients for the dishes. Earlier the use of onion, tomato and garlic was not permitted. However, now these are also used .

Pickles and Ketchups of various fruits such as cherry, apricot, plum and walnut are used both by Hindus and Muslims. However, it is surprising that neither Hindus nor Muslims eat a sweetdish after the meals, which is very common elsewhere in India.

Kahva/ Mogil Chai/ Kehvi (Green Tea)

It is interesting that sweets do not play any part in Kashmiri food. Yet at the end of the day when the meal is over, a cup of rich and flavoured green tea, known as Mogil Chai/Kehvi or Kahva is refreshing. The tea leaves are known as Bombay Chai. Perhaps the tea leaves of China were brought to Kashmir via Bombay (Mumbai), hence its name 'Bombay Chai'. The tradition goes that Kanishka ruled Kashmir in the second century and a royal prince was kept hostage in Kashmir. The prince's entourage brought green tea and pears along with them.

The tea is prepared in a Samovar, which is very common in a Kashmiri family. Crushed almonds, cinnamon, cardamom, saffron and sugar are put in the tea. Mogil Chai is relished without milk.

Nun Chai/Sheer Chai/Pink Salted Tea

This is a different kind of tea in which the leaves are semi-fermented. It is brewed with bicarbonate of soda. First tea with a little water is boiled for quite some time so that the leaves are drained of its colour. Then a little bicarbonate of soda, milk, salt is added. Once boiled and poured in cups, cream can be added. The colour of the tea is pink and quite fascinating.

Wazwan, the Muslim tastes

Wazwan is the most fascinating and delicious part of Kashmiri cuisine. It is difficult to trace the exact origin of the Wazwan though tradition says that in 15th century when Timur invaded India many migrants reached Kashmir. These people were skilled in various trades. Among them there were master cooks from Samarkand. The royalty employed them in their kitchens and since then Wazwan started. The master chefs could prepare 36 course meals. Wazwan literally means 'Cook's shop' wherein Kashmiri cuisine is prepared for a marriage ceremony. However, it has now found place in every festive function in Kashmir. Wazwan is now enjoyed even outside Kashmir.

Main items of Wazwan

The main dishes of Wazwan are: Seekh Kababs, Methi Korma, Tabakh Maaz, Safed Murg, Zafrani Murg, Rista, Rogan Josh, Daniwal Korma, Aab Gosht, Yakhni, Marchwangan Korma and Gushtaba. It also includes vegetarian items such as Chaman (Cheese), vegetables such as Nadru and Haakh. Then there is rice pulao, both salted and sweet. Wazwan is enjoyed by Muslims though people from other communities also relish it. Spices used are Saffron, Cinnamon, Cloves, Cardamom, Kashmiri Chilli, Curds, Garlic, Ginger, and Onion.

Festivals of Kashmir

In addition to the religious festivals, the people of Kashmir celebrate social festivals also.

Badam Phuly

Badam Phuly (Almond flower blossom) means the dawn of spring. It is a strange phenomenon that during winter the trees are absolutely barren and when spring comes the first thing to appear are the flowers. Almonds, cherry, apple trees are full of white and pink blossoms.

Jhiri Mela of Jammu

Jhiri Mela means the festival of Jhiri. This festival is celebrated during the months of October-November to commemorate the sacrifice of a great farmer Baba Jattoo. People go to the place where he is buried and pay their respects.

Sindhu Darshan festival of Ladakh

Sindhu Darshan was introduced recently by the Government of India. The festival is celebrated by the Ministry of Culture, Government of India and Government of Jammu and Kashmir.

Fifteen
Pilgrimage in Kashmir

Since time immemorial, Kashmir has been called the land of saints. Scholars from all over India would come to learn various philosophies and sciences. Having places of pilgrimage in abundance, Hindus throughout the length and breadth of India came for pilgrimage. Sir Alexander Cunningham and F G Growse say that these places exhibit traces of the influence of Grecian art, and are distinguished by the graceful elegance of their outlines.

Sarada Shrine

Sarada Shrine/ Survana-Pitha has been one of the most pious and revered pilgrimage spots not only of Hindus of Kashmir but of the rest of India also. Kalhana has mentioned it as 'Saradasthana'. Kashmir was once known as Sarada Desh. Sarada Peeth was the famous temple of the Hindu deity Sarada (Saraswati, the goddess of learning). It was once a celebrated centre of learning of Kashmiri Brahmins. As per Anand Kaul,[1] "Throughout India, Kashi and Kashmir were from ancient times famous as the seats of learning, but Kashmir excelled even Kashi. The learned men had to come to Kashmir to complete their education." It is believed that King Kanishka built the Sharda University on the confluence of Kishenganga and Vitasta (now called Neelam and Jhelum rivers).

As per P N K Bamzai,[2] "The place of pride which the valley acquired in Sanskrit language and literature as well as in humanities like medicine, astronomy, astrology, philosophy, religion, law and jurisprudence, music, art and architecture is attributed to the grace and benediction of the goddess who revealed herself in all her divine grandeur to Muni Sandalya at Sarada-Vana in the Upper Kishenganga valley in the north of Kashmir."

The sanctum-sanctorum is situated on a hillock, in a remote village called Sarada. Saradi and Nardi are two mountain peaks overlooking Sarada in the valley. Raised on a base of 24 feet square and 5 feet 3 inches high, this is a typical Kashmiri architectural marvel. Kashmir, at the confluence of the Kisanganga-Madhumati rivers commands a panoramic view of the alpine forests. According to Dr V N Drabu,[3]"Sarada enables her worshippers to be both creative and communicative, whereby they make a significant contribution to society and culture." While translating Kalhana's *Rajatarangini*, M A Stein visited this place and states,[4] "The temple of Sarada rises in a prominent and commanding position above the right bank of the Madhumati and the Kisanganga mingle."

Shankaracharya, while on his visit to Kashmir also visited Sharada Peeth. The famous Persian scholar who accompanied Mohammad Gaznavi, Alberuni visited Sharada Peeth temple in 11th century. He has ranked it second only to the grand Surya Temple at Multan. The pilgrimage was very popular during the period of Jonaraja. The famous Muslim king Zain-ul-Abidin also visited the sanctum- sanctorum. Afterwards, the image of the goddess was desecrated and people stopped visiting the place. According to M A Stein,[5] "The Mohamadian Rajas of Karnav ruled as practically independent chiefs in Kisanganga valley. Under one of them the shrine is said to have been used for the storage of gunpowder, the explosion of which blew off the original roof."

The legends: Tradition goes that Lord Shiva was angry with Ravana. Sensing the danger Ravana turned to Goddess Durga. She told him to perform Yajna. Meanwhile, she told Rama that in case she stayed there Ravana could never be defeated. She told him that he should make arrangements so that she was taken away from the place of war. Hanuman was summoned and asked to take Durga away from there. Hanuman refused to do so. Durga told him that she would go in the form of water. He had to drop only one drop of water from the Kamandal which

Hanuman did at Kasheer Bhawani (Kheer Bhawani). Then Hanuman kept the remaining water along with the Kamandal at Sharada and that is how the sanctums anctorum of Sharada shrine came into being. The other legend is that after the *Amrit Manthan*, the *Amrit* got into the hands of demons. The Goddess transformed herself into a dancer and somehow took the *Amrit* from the demons. She then threw the *Amrit* at that place, which is known as Sharada.

Martanda, the Sun Temple

Martanda in Sanskrit means Sun. It is also known as Pandav Larr (House of Pandavas). Tradition goes that the kingdom of Pandavas included the Kashmir valley also and that is why the temple is till today known as Pandav Larr. Situated on the left bank of Lidar River, the temple of Martanda is dedicated to the Sun God. It is on top of a plateau, near the town of Anantnag. It is a medieval temple dedicated to Bhaskara, the Sun God. King Lalitaditya, a Kshatriya of Surya dynasty, got the Martanda temple constructed to commemorate Surya in 7th – 8th Century. This beautiful temple has a courtyard with the shrine in its centre. Built with 84 columns, it offers a magnificent view of the Kashmir valley. Martanda temple of Kashmir is amongst the best and most memorable works of King Lalitaditya. *Imperial Gazetteer of India* states,[6] "Among the numerous temples, two may be noticed—Martanda and Payech (a temple in Pulawama has been named as Payech); the first for its grandeur, and the second for its excellent preservation."

Writes Bansi Lal Malla,[7] "Ancient Martanda, which overlooks the modern village of Matan (also called Bhavan) is situated on the lofty plateau in Anantnag district. The city of Martanda derived its name from the presiding deity of the place, Martanda, the Sun God. Next to Konark, Martanda was probably the most monumental temple complex dedicated to the Sun God."

As per Cunningham,[8] "Erection of the Sun-temple was suggested by the magnificent sunny prospect which its situation commands. It has the finest view of Kashmir. Beneath it lies the Paradise of the East, with its sacred streams and cedar glens, its brown orchards and green fields, surrounded on all sides by vast snowy mountains whose lofty peaks seem to smile upon the beautiful valley below." He further says, "The vast extent of the scene makes it sublime, for this magnificent view of

Kashmir is no petty pier on a half-mile glen, but the full display of a valley 30 miles in breadth and 84 miles in length, the whole of which lies beneath the ken of the wonderful Martanda." According to Sir Walter R Lawrence,[9] "Occupying, undoubtedly the finest position in Kashmir, this noble ruin is the most striking in size and situation of all the existing remains of Kashmir grandeur."

While visiting Matan one finds a spring and large interesting caverns. Commenting on these caverns, Hugel Baron reminds us about when King Nara went to the serpent sisters, Iravati and Chandralekha and asked one of them to satisfy his lust. When their father came to know about this he fought with the King. Hugel Baron has mentioned in his book,[10] "A storm was accordingly called up and the earth opened and swallowed up the king and his whole court. The sister of the serpent-god assisted him, and hurled on the city huge stones from the Baman Mountain. The caverns of Matan are said to be on the spot where these rocks were thrown."

According to John Keay,[11] "In Kashmir, where Muslim immigration and conversion had resulted in the installation of a Muslim dynasty in 1339, the normally cordial pattern of Hindu-Muslim relations were interrupted in the early fifteenth century. The great Sun temple of Martanda was destroyed and heavy penalties imposed on the mainly Brahman Hindus." In addition to Kashmir, there are Sun temples in other places in India and abroad too.

- Dakshinaarka Temple at Gaya, Bihar (13th century)
- Bhramanya Dev Temple at Unao, Madhya Pradesh
- Sun Temple at Surya Phar, Assam
- Suryanaar Temple, Tamil Nadu (13th century)
- Suryanarayanaswamy Temple, Andhra Pradesh (7th century)
- Sun Temple at Modhera, Gujarat (11th century)
- Sun Temple at Konark, Orissa (13th century).

We also find Sun temples in Multan (Pakistan), Karnak (Egypt), Mayan (Columbia), Abu Simbel (Egypt) Mesa Verde (USA), Abu Ghurab (Egypt), Nuissere, and Mesoamerican (Mexico). According to Younghusband,[12] "But it is at Martanda that there is the finest—not only typical of Kashmir architecture at its best, but built on the most sublime site occupied by any building in the world, be it the Parthenon (in Greece), the Taj, St Peters, or the Estuarial."

Amarnath Cave

Situated in a narrow gorge at the farther end of Lidar valley, Amarnath stands at about 3,888 meters above the sea level and is 44.8 km from Pahalgam and 141 km from Srinagar. Amarnath cave is one of the holiest places of Hindu pilgrimage. Every year during the month of Shravana, on the full moon in August, a pillar of ice is believed to be an ice lingam, the phallic symbol of Lord Shiva. Two smaller ice stalagmites represent Parvati, his wife, and Ganesh, his son.

The discovery: According to the tradition, once a sadhu gave a Muslim Gujjar named Buta Malik a sack of coal to use. When the Muslim reached home, he opened the bag and found it full of gold coins. Deliriously happy, Buta Malik rushed back to the place to find the sadhu so that he could thank him. But he found a cave instead. Eventually, the place became a pilgrimage for all believers. It is surprising that to date a percentage of the donations, which the people offer, go to the Malik family.

The legend: A legend says that once Parvati asked Shiva to tell her the secret of immortality. Lord Shiva tried to find a secluded place where nobody except Parvati could know the secret. He went to the Amarnath cave. He left Nandi, the bull he used to ride, at Pahalgam. At Chandanwari, he released the Moon from his hair (Jatta). At the banks of Lake Sheshnag he released the snakes. He decided to leave his son Ganesh at Mahaguna. At Panjtarni, Shiva left the Five Elements behind (Earth, Water, Air, Fire and Sky) which make up a living being. It is believed that as a symbol of sacrificing the earthly world, Shiva and Parvati did the Tandava dance. Then, Lord Shiva entered the holy Amarnath cave along with Parvati. He took his *samadhi* on a deer skin and concentrated. To ensure that no living being could hear the tale, he created Rudra and ordered him to spread fire to eliminate every living thing in and around the holy cave. Then he started narrating the secret of immortality to Parvati. However, one egg, which was lying beneath the deerskin, remained protected. The pair of pigeons born out of this egg became immortal having listened to the secret of immortality from God Shiva himself.

Shankaracharya temple

Situated on a hill, a thousand feet in height, stands the ancient stone temple of Shankaracharya, earlier known as Jyeshtia Rudra. This splendid temple is in the heart of Srinagar. *Rajatarangini* states that it was first built by Jalauka, the son of Emperor Asoka, about 200 BC. It was later rebuilt and dedicated to Jyesthesvara by king Gopaditya. Initially, the hill was known as Jyesthesvara, then 'Jetha Larak' and later it was renamed 'Gopadri.' The village at its foot is still called 'Gopkar'. Kalhana writes, "After consecrating a shrine of Jyesthesvara on the Gopa hill (Gopadri), this wise king bestowed the Gopa-Agrahara on Brahmans born in Aryadesa." Also according to M A Stein,[13] "We have in Gopadri the ancient designation of the conspicuous hill now popularly known as Takht-e-Suleiman, immediately to the east of Srinagar."He further clarifies that, "Shiva, under the name of Jyesthesvara, has been worshipped from early times to the present day at Jyesthyer in the immediate vicinity of Takht hill."

The Temple was repaired by Zain-ul-Abidin who ruled from 697-734 AD. It is surprising that Sikandar Butshikan did not destroy it.

It is also said that during the ninth century, Adi Shankaracharya, a famous Hindu saint, came to Kashmir from South India to revive Hinduism. He stayed on top of the hill for some time and the hill thus came to be known as Shankaracharya hill.

As per Baron Hugel, the temple of Takht-e-Suleiman is stated to be the earliest of all the temples in Kashmir. He records that its erection is ascribed to Gopaditya or the Gonerdya dynasty, 370 BC. He says,[14] "Having with great difficulty clambered up the mountain pompously styled the Throne of Solomon, the first object which presented itself was an ancient Buddhist temple (Deval), composed of masses of rock, with a curious doorway, evidently of very high antiquity. The temple was, in later times, converted into a mosque; a Persian inscription of more modern date, gives no information as to the original temple, but to Solomon is ascribed the honour of being the founder. It is said moreover that a very ancient Sanskrit inscription is now buried underground. At present, Hindus call the temple Shankaracharya."

According to C E Tyndale Biscoe,[15] "On the top of this hill is a very ancient Hindu temple; it was built by Raja Sandiman, who ruled Kashmir during the period 2629 -2564 B C. It was repaired by Gopaditya (426 – 365 BC). Sikandar did not destroy it because Sultan Mahmud of Gazni had offered prayers in it." The statement seems doubtful as

Sultan Mahmud Ghazni did not enter Srinagar. He fought a war with the Shahi kings, Anandpala and Trilochanapala and Tunga the commander of Queen Didda helped Trilochanapala. Trilochanapala and Tunga were defeated by Mahmud Gaznavi. The Shankaracharya hill was named as Takht-e-Suleiman by Abul Fazal.

Kheer Bhawani

There is hardly any Kashmiri in the world who has not visited Kasheer Bhawani or Kheer Bhawani. This sanctum sanctorum is situated about 24 kms from Srinagar, north of Kashmir in the village of Tulamulla. It has a spring. The devotees offer milk and *Kheer* in the spring and that is why it is known as Kheer Bhawani.

The legend: A legend goes that Goddess Kheer Bhawani/ Syama/Kali was living in Ceylon and during the Ramayana period she was removed from Ceylon to Kashmir. Once, Ravana wanted to perform a human sacrifice before the goddess. He had invited lord Rama also. According to Madhu Bazaz Wangu,[16] "When Rama and Sita appeared in the middle of the worshipping area, Ravana, with a terrible look, announced to Rama that if he wanted to stay alive he should leave Sita and go home, otherwise he would be sacrificed to the goddess. Rama refused to leave and said, 'I will destroy you and then take Sita and Syama home'. Ravana became very angry. He took out his sword and ran to attack Rama. A terrible war was fought. By now the angry goddess Syama, her voice thundering like clashing clouds, said to Ravana, 'Shame on you! I am going to the valley of Kashmir in the Himalayas and I vow to follow vegetarianism'. Hearing her, Rama asked Hanuman, the foremost of his devotees, the epitome of sexual renunciation, to take the great goddess to Kashmir. Syama rode on the back of Hanuman and reached the village of Tulmul (Tulamulla)."

The discovery of Kheer Bhawani has yet another legend. It is said that the goddess once came in the dream of Pandit Govind Joo Gadroo of Bohri Kadal, Srinagar, and told him to visit the place. He arranged a boat and went to Tulamulla. He poured milk in the spring. The place has become a pilgrimage for every Kashmiri pandit.

On every Durga Ashtami, people in thousands visit the sanctum sanctorum. As per S N Pandita,[17] "A curious phenomena observed here is that the water of the spring changes colours occasionally like purple, green and so on." Tradition also says that when the water of the spring changes to blackish it is a warning that something disastrous is going to happen. According to *Rajatarangini*, the jageers of the priests of Tulamulla were once confiscated by King Jayapida (753 to 784 AD). Ninety-nine Brahmins jumped in the river Chandrabhaga. One of the priests named Ittila cursed the king for his impious deeds and a golden pole of the canopy suddenly tumbled down upon the king from which he sustained serious injury resulting in his death."

Hari Parbat

There is hardly any place like Hari Parbat anywhere. It reflects how the people of Kashmir lived together respecting each other's religion. The place symbolises the real unity in diversity of religions. There is a Hindu temple, Muslim mosque and Gurudwara at the same place.

Hari Parbat, the hill of Sharika, is abode of Mahashakti, the divine mother Jagadamba, and Sharika Bhagwati. It is a very famous pilgrimage for Kashmiri Hindus. It is situated within the Srinagar city. The Hindus in Kashmir go to Hari Parbat in the wee hours at Chakreshawri temple for prayers.

Tradition goes that once two demons lived there. These demons would always harass the rishis. The rishis prayed to Goddess Parvati. The goddess transformed herself into a Mynah bird (Har in Kashmiri language, therefore Hari Parbat), took a pebble and dropped it on the demons. The pebble grew into a hillock and the demons were crushed and the rishis got rid of them. There is another legend that says that while draining the lake Satisar, the gods struck the bed of the gorge at Khadnyar, below Baramulla. Jalodbhava continued to offer resistance until Goddess Durga appeared in the form of a bird and dropped a pebble on the errant demon. The pebble assumed the form of the hillock Hari Parbat.

The Mughal Emperor Akbar constructed a fort on the peak of the hill and named it Nagar Nagar/Nager Nagor. He wanted to segregate his army who had accompanied him from the civilians and therefore ordered his army to stay in the fort. According to Abdul Majid Mattoo,[18] "Akbar directed Yusuf Khan Rizwi to construct houses for the soldiers. They were forbidden to occupy private houses." He also ordered that people be employed for the construction of the fort. It was for the first time that the labourers were paid their wages in cash. Two huge gates Sangeen Darwaza and Kathi Darwaza are on the rampart, of the fort. Kathi

Darwaza, highlights influence of Persian architecture during Mughal rule. It contains Persian inscriptions on it.

Just below the Nagar-Nagar Mughal fort is Sheikh Hamza Makhdoom Sahib's shrine. It also cradles the shrine of Sufi saint Akhun Mullah Shah, the teacher of Prince Dara Shikoh. Hari Parbat has been renamed as 'Koh-i-Maran'.

Jyesthteshwara

It is a temple near the famous Parimahal between Shankaracharya temple and Cheshma Shahi. The pilgrims throng the place on Zeth Ashtami (during May - June) and observe their auspicious day.

Jawala Mukhi temple

Jawala Mukhi is the goddess of fire known as Ishtdevi of Pandit community. This temple is situated near the village of Khrew in Pulawama district. Its position is on the east of Zabarwan hills about 20 km from Srinagar. According to Tarikh Hassan, King Driptadav constructed a temple dedicated to Jawala Mukhi.

Shrine of Shah-i-Hamadan

The Shrine of Shah-i-Hamadan was built by Sultan Sikandar in 1395. It is situated between the third bridge (Fateh Kadal) and fourth bridge (Zaina Kadal). According to *Baharistan-i-Shahi*[19], "Sultan Qutbu'd-Din ruled for sixteen years. During his time, his holiness arrived in Kashmir. Sayyid Ali Hamadani, God sanctify his soul, consecrated the land of Kashmir by planting on its soil his most august footsteps."

According to Baron Hugel,[20] "The Shah Hamedan Musjid (Shah-i-Hamdan Mosque) is a modern-looking building, the prototype of every mosque in Kashmir, and if not exactly resembling a Chinese temple, is certainly unlike Indian architecture in general, though some of the same form may be occasionally seen in the British Himalaya." Writes DN Saraf,[21] "Shah Hamadan Mosque, one of the oldest mosques in Srinagar, has fine Papier Mache work on the walls and ceilings, as well as exquisite wood-work." The sanctum sanctorum of Khanqah-i-Maula is situated on the banks of the river Jhelum. It is the first mosque ever built in Srinagar in the year 1395 AD, and it was at this place where Shah-i-Hamadan used to offer prayers. He was the first Muslim to spread Islam in Kashmir. The Khanqah of Shah Hamadan is a wooden structure whose chief aesthetic feature is its beautifully carved eaves and hanging bells. The interiors are richly carved and painted, and the antique chandeliers give it an air of opulence.

According to R C Kak,[22] "It is difficult to determine the date of the present structure, but it is practically certain that it does not belong to the time traditionally ascribed to the migration of Sayyid Ali Hamadani to Kashmir. Baron Von Hugel, who visited Kashmir in 1835, speaks of it as a modern-looking building. But there is no doubt that a mosque or some such religious edifice stood here at least as early as the reign of Akbar; for Abul Fazal in his *Ain-i-Akbari* says that Mir Sayyid Ali Hamadani resided for some time in this city (Srinagar) and monastery founded by him still preserves his name."

The mosque was twice destroyed by fire. In 1732 Abdul Barkat Khan rebuilt the mosque.

Jama Masjid

Jama Masjid, the famous mosque was built by Sikandar Butshikan in 1407 AD. It is said that there existed a Buddhist temple which was destroyed by Sikandar and transformed into a Masjid. Situated at Nowhatta, in the middle of the old city, it is considered an important mosque in Srinagar. Later, the son of Sultan Sikandar, Zain-ul-Abidin got the mosque extended. The attractions of the Jama Masjid of Srinagar, Kashmir include beautiful Indo-Saracenic architecture, a magnificent courtyard and 370 wooden pillars. Another feature of the mosque is the peace and tranquillity inside it which stands out amidst the hustle and bustle of the old bazaars around it. Thousands of Muslims assemble at the mosque every Friday to offer their prayers. According to Abdul Majid Mattoo,[23]"It was devastated by fire a number of times. In 1622 AD while Jahangir was in Kashmir, the mosque was completely destroyed. He directed Malik Haider to rebuild the mosque. It was again destroyed during the reign of Aurangzeb, but was again restored."

Hazratbal Shrine

The Hazratbal Mosque is situated in Srinagar district, on the western banks of the picturesque Dal Lake. Facing the beautiful Nishat Bagh, the mosque offers a spectacular view of the lake and the mountains. Some of the other names of the Hazratbal mosque are Asser-e-Sharif, Madinat-us-Sani and Dargah Sharif. One of the most revered Muslim shrines, Hazratbal is an epitome of the love and respect of Muslims for the Prophet. It is located in a place of the same name on the banks of the Dal. Its pristine white marble elegance is reflected in the waters of the lake.

Hazratbal's special significance is derived from the fact that it houses a hair of the Prophet Muhammad. This is put on view to the public on religious occasions, usually accompanied by fairs. Apart from these occasions, Friday prayers are offered at Hazratbal and attended by throngs of people. Hazratbal is remarkable for being the only domed mosque in Srinagar; the others having distinct pagoda like roofs.

Chrar-e-Sharif

Chrar-e-Sharif has a 600-year-old wooden shrine, dedicated to the memory of the Sufi saint Sheikh Noor-ud-Din Noorani. This is not only sacred to Muslims but non-Muslims also. It is located on the way to Yusmarg, about 30 km from Srinagar. The shrine has been a symbol of religious harmony and Kashmiriyat. It is also a symbol of composite culture in the valley as both Hindus and Muslims go to the shrine to offer prayers.

According to Jagmohan,[24] "the Chrar-e-Sharif Dargah of Sheikh Nuruddin is one of the most sacred dargahs of the country. It was built in 1808-1810 AD by the Afghan Governor, Atta Mohammad Khan, in honour of the Sheikh who founded the famous Sufi-Rishi order of Kashmir at the end of the 14 century."

During recent times, an Afghan militant by the name of Mast Gul along with his men occupied the shrine from March to May 1995. The Indian army then laid siege to the sanctum sanctorum. However, sensing trouble, Mast Gul torched the Shrine on May 11, 1995 and escaped.

Pather Masjid

Standing close to the Shah Hamadan is Pather Masjid that was once a state granary. It is said that the mosque was never consecrated as its builder, Empress Nur Jahan, apparently hurt the sentiments of the religious leaders of the time. According to R C Kak,[25]"the mosque is said to have been built in AD 1623 by the Empress. There is a story that, being questioned regarding the cost of its construction, she pointed to her jewelled slippers and replied 'as much as that'. The jest was reported to the mullahs who unanimously decreed that by this sacrilegious allusion the mosque had been desecrated, and was unfit for religious use. For this reason, the Pather Masjid has never been used as a place of prayer."

"The style is quite simple and lacking in any kind of ornamentation. The interior is divided into three passages by two rows of massive stone arches,"[26] says Abdul Majid Mattoo.

Rishi Peer

Rishi Peer, is situated at Ali Kadal (5th Bridge), Mahrajgunj, Srinagar. It is known popularly as Peer Pandit Padshah Har Dujahan Mushkil Aasan". According to Mohan Lal Ogra,[27]"this shrine is believed to be the birthplace of Rishi peer, one of the Kashmir's greatest saints of his times. The title suggests a great kindly learned Brahmin saint capable of giving solace and relief to the people in distress."

Tradition goes that the mother of Rishi Peer was going in a boat to Srinagar when the child was born. He would speak to the people irrespective of their religion, caste and creed that God is one and all religions are, in their ultimate essence, one. What is needed is a life of piety and purity, no matter what faith one follows.

The legends: Tradition says that Rishi Peer had great love and reverence for his mother. However, when he attained the age of 12 years, the mother wanted to baptise him to Hindu faith. It is said that he went to the riverbank and jumped into the river. When he came out his head was clean shaven and there was a holy thread around his neck.

During Saif Khan's tenure as governor, Emperor Aurangzeb directed him to bring to his court two important persons of Kashmir, namely Rishi Pir Pandit Padshah and Mulla Tahir Ghani. Mulla Tahir Ghani was the greatest Persian poet of his time. According to Sir Walter R Lawrence,[28] "A legend is told of his persecution of the famous Rishi Pir Pandit Padshah, a Hindu ascetic. A messenger was sent citing the Rishi to appear before the emperor at his court in India. The Rishi travelled in one night through the air to India, and appeared in a terrible form, mounted on a lion, as the emperor lay asleep. Aurangzeb, in his fear, agreed to the Rishi's retaining his title of Padshah but the legend does not say whether the emperor relaxed from that time his persecution of the Hindus."

Chatti Padshahi

The sixth Guru of Sikhs, Guru Har Gobind Singh, visited Kashmir and preached Sikhism to the people at the place where the Gurudwara is constructed. Chatti Padshahi Gurudwara is located close to the Kathi Darwaza which is the main access for Hari Parbat Fort.

Vaishno Devi temple

The Hindus of the world consider a pilgrimage to Mata Vaishno Devi Temple at Trikuta Mountain the holiest. Millions of pilgrims visit the holy shrine every year. Situated at an altitude of 5,200 feet above sea level, it is about fourteen km trekking from Katra. There is a mention of Trikuta mountain in the *rig veda*. Geological studies say that the cave is a million years old. During Mahabharata war, Arjun invoked the blessing of Goddess Vaishno Devi.

The Legend: According to a Hindu epic, Vaishnava Devi was born in the house of Ratnakara Sagar in South India. The childless parents had undergone lot of penance and prayed before god for a child. A female child was born. They were amazed to see a beautiful baby having a halo of light around her. Perhaps it was their intuition that made them realise that the redeemer of their ills, miseries, misfortunes —a goddess in the form of a girl was born. Her parents named her Trikuta.

People would flock to have *darshan* of this child. At age nine she sought permission from her parents to go for meditation to the seashore. She prayed to Lord Vishnu who then had taken birth as Rama and was searching for Sita. Lord Rama suddenly found her. Trikuta told lord Rama that she had accepted him as her husband. Lord Rama advised her that she should go to Trikuta Mountain and meditate in the cave and he assured her that he would meet her in Kalayuga.

Bahu temple

Bahu Temple is situated inside the Bahu Fort. Raja Bahu Lochan built the fort. The original structure is believed to be as old as 3,000 years. It is also known as Mahakali Temple. On Tuesdays many pilgrims visit the temple and offer prayers.

Sixteen
Literary Development in Modern Era

Kashmiri literature came into existence in the twelfth century. It started with some works written on Shaivism. Shiti Kanth's *Mahayana Prakash*, Lall Ded and Sheikh Nur-ud-Din introduced Kashmiri language into the literary field. Though they spoke philosophy, they translated the philosophy into the language of common folk.

Sheikh Muhammad Mohsin Fani, 1615-1671 AD

Mohsin Fani was born in Kashmir. He was a learned scholar and a poet of Persian language. He flourished in the seventeenth century during the period of Mughal Emperor Shah Jahan. He composed *Masdur ul Asas* (the source of Science). His other famous work is *Debistan-l Mazahib* (School of Religions). These works were translated by David Shea and Anthony Troyer. Mohsin Fani also enjoyed the honourable office of the Chief Judge of Allahabad in the court of Shah Jahan.

Abdalkurreem Kashmiri Ibn, 1785 AD

Abdalkurreem was born in Kashmir. He was the son of Khojeh Akebut Mahmood. He is considered to be a man of distinction. His famous works are *Bayan-i Vaqi-The Memoirs of Khojeh Abdalkurreem*. It is the history of Nadir Shah after his return from Hindustan to Persia. Khojeh Abdalkurreem visited Bagdad, Damascus and Aleppo. He also visited

Medina and Mecca. From Jeddah he came back to India and sailed to Hooghly in Bengal. His works include *History of India from 1739 to 1749 AD*. The works later were translated by Francis Gladwin. Abdalkurreem died in the year AD 1785.

Pandit Ishwar Kaul, 1833-1893 AD

Pandit Ishwar Kaul is known as the Panini of Kashmir. In fact, Aurel Stein called him the 'Kashmiri Panini'. He was born on 4 July, 1833. His father Pandit Ganesh Kaul died when he was still a child. He learnt Sanskrit from the renowned Sanskrit Scholar Pandit Tikka Ram. In the year 1871 he was appointed as Head Teacher of Sanskrit Pathshala. His work *Kashmir Shabdamrit* was acclaimed by the scholars. It gives perfect knowledge of the linguistic structure of Kashmiri language. He also headed the Translation Department of Jammu and Kashmir State.

Pandit Ishwar Kaul was a pioneer Lexicographer of Kashmiri language. He was the first person to use Devanagri script for translating Kashmiri words, both in his grammar and his dictionary. He was well versed with Persian and Arabic and could translate any work into Sanskrit or vice-versa. He died on 28 August 1893.

Shamas Faqir, 1839-1916 AD

Shamas Faqir was a famous Sufi poet of Kashmir. He was born in 1839 AD in Chinkral Mohalla Srinagar. His real name was Muhammad Sidiq Bhat. His mystic poetry tells of his love for the holy Quran. He emphasised oneness of God and love for humanity. He was revered by Muslims as well as Hindus. After his death in 1916 AD, he was buried at Karim Shora Badgam. People from other religions also visit his shrine.

Govind Kaul, 1846-1899 AD

Pandit Govind Kaul was born in Kashmir in the year 1846 AD. He was the eldest son of Pandit Balbhadra Kaul, an eminent scholar of his times. Pandit Govind Kaul was related to the famous Pandit Birbal Dhar, who went to Maharaja Ranjit Singh for help. He kept up his family traditions and attained mastery over Sanskrit, and, interestingly, English language also. Maharaja Ranbir Singh appointed him incharge of the Translation Department for translating Sanskrit literature into Hindi.

Without his help, Aurel Stein would not have been able to translate Kalhana's *Rajatarangini* and the compilation of Kashmiri Folk Tales. Aurel

Stein mentioned this when he was awarded the Knighthood that he took help from Pandit Govind Kaul at every step.

Nityanand Shastri, 1874 AD

When George Grierson and Sir Aural Stein started their monumental work *Dictionary of Kashmiri Language*, and translation of other works, they could find no one better than Pandit Nityanand Shastri to help them in their stupendous task. Pandit Madan Mohan Malaviya, an admirer of Pandit Nityanand Shastri, invited him to head the Sanskrit faculty of Banaras Hindu University. When Vivekananda visited Kashmir, Pandit Nityanand Shastri was one of the important Kashmiri Pandits who met him.

Nityanand Shastri was a great devotee of Lord Rama. He started teaching Sanskrit at the age of sixteen. After graduating in Sanskrit he became Professor of Sanskrit in Sri Pratap College at Srinagar. His famous work is *Sriramacaritabdhiratna*, the life story of Lord Rama. Another prominent work by him is *Ramakathakalpalata* in Hindi.

Sir Aurel Stein, Professor Maurice Winternitz, J Ph Vogel and George Grierson had great respect and reverence for him. The letter written by them to Pandit Nityanand Shastri is still available.

Abdul Wahab Pare, 1845-1913 AD

Abdul Wahab Pare, born in the year 1845, was called the Firdaus of Kashmir. He belonged to Hajin. He transalated Firdausi's *Shahnama*, (23,491 verses), and *Khilafatnama* into Kashmiri language. He also translated *Akbarnama*. He was a noted Persian poet. Wahab Pare was like a saint. He was always worried about the wellbeing of the people and would comment on the apathy of the government departments.

Krishan Joo Razdan, 1850 AD

Pandit Krishan Joo Razdan, son of Ganesh Raina, was born in the year 1850 AD, in the district of Anantnag in village Vanpoh during the reign of Maharaja Pratap Singh. He was a Sanskrit scholar of repute; at the same time he was well versed in Persian language.

Krishan Joo was influenced by Lall Ded and Nund Rishi. His famous works are *Shiv Parinav*, *Shiv Mahima* and *Harihar Kalyan*. He was also a great musician of his times. He used to play the sitar with great ease.

Sahaz Bhatt, 1862-1935 AD

Pandit Sahaz Bhatt, a profound scholar, was born in Kashmir in 1862 AD. He was just a child when he lost his father. His elder brother Pandit Sat Kak, Royal Physician in the court of Maharaja Ranbir Singh brought him up. In school he learnt English, Sanskrit, Arabic and Persian. He mastered Arabic and Sanskrit. He then learnt the Unani system of medical science. Pandit Sahaz Bhatt became the legendry Unani Hakim in Kashmir. In view of his multifaceted personality, Maharaja Ranbir Singh appointed him in the department of translation in 1890 AD. He supervised the publication of Sanskrit texts on philosophy, medicine and other subjects. He also guided Sir Aurel Stein and Pandit Govind Kaul in compiling various manuscripts.

In the year 1935 AD, this great scholar and legendry physician left for his heavenly abode.

Poets of Kashmir

Samad Mir, 1894-1959 AD

Samad Mir was born at Narwara, Srinagar. His parents belonged to district Badgam of Kashmir and later shifted to Narwara. He was a Sufi-mystic poet. His famous work is *Akanandun*. In this work he has tried to synthesise Tassawuf (Sufism) and Trika (Shaivism).

Rasul Mir, 1870 AD

Rasul Mir was born in Mirmadan Duru, District Anantnag. His father was a Namberdar. In his youth he fell in love with a Hindu girl of his village, known as Kongmal. Unfortunately, fate had something else in store for him. The parents of Kongmal married her to someone else. The parting was very painful and the love turned into madness .

Rasul Mir wrote the famous poem

'*Rind poshmal gindanay drai lo lo*'

(The flower-faced debutant is out for love play).

In this poem, Rasul Mir has used the swan bird which has a majestic neck. There is an ancient belief that the swan is silent during his lifetime until the moment just before it dies. While dying, it sings a beautiful song. It may be a legend, but one can feel the muteness of Kongmal, who in spite her love and devotion for Rasul Mir, could not express it.

Rasul Mir wrote hundreds of Ghazals, Vatsun (short lyrics) and 'Naats'. *Zeba-Nigar* was his famous work but is now lost. He drew his inspiration from Persian literature.

According to tradition, Rasul Mir was tall, handsome and had a graceful personality.

Master Zinda Kaul, 1884 -1965 AD

Pandit Zinda Kaul is a famous Kashmiri poet. The magnificent landscape of Kashmir deeply affected him and his imagination. He could be termed as a mystic yet humanistic poet. Born in Kashmir in 1884 AD, he was a versatile poet and wrote in many languages. He wrote poetry in Hindi, Urdu, Persian and Kashmiri.

Masterji's magnum opus is *Sumran*. He was honoured with the State Cultural Academy award in 1960. He was awarded Sahitya Akademi Award in 1956. He had mastery over English language too. He translated Parmananda's poetry into English. Master Zinda Kaul wrote terse poetry. He was a voracious reader and had read many authors like Arnold, Vivekananda, Ram Tirtha, and Galib and of course Bhagawat Gita. He had thoroughly studied Shaivism of Kashmir. He died in the winter of 1965. One is reminded of an Urdu couplet by Masterji, which says:

"*Yeh mehfil bhi kisi se kam na hoogi husun-o-seerat mein,*
Abhi aaney to dey is par shabab aahista aahista."

(This mehfil will be no less in beauty and virtues
Let it mature and bloom slowly and gradually)

Mahjoor, 1887-1952 AD

Mahjoor is the immortal poet of Kashmir. He was born on 11 August 1887, at Metragam in Pulawama. His father was a Persian and Arabic scholar. His mother died when he was only two years old. His passion for poetry was enormous and he spoke of nature, flowers, romance and love. His famous poem is *Poshe-mati-jaanaano.*

His famous song goes:

'Bage nishat ke gulo naaz karaan karaan valoo'

(You the glory of Nishat garden come with a feeling of pride).

He gave life to inanimate objects which earned praise from Rabindranath Tagore.

Mahjoor's real name was Gulam Ahmed. He also worked as a Patwari. Rabindranath Tagore called him the William Wordsworth of Kashmir. He was a freedom fighter too. His poem, *Valo ha Baaghvaano* inspired people to rise to attain freedom. Mahjoor died in 1952 AD, and with him ended the romantic literature. But he lives through his poems.

Mahjoor zara bas kar – pari kus ashqun daftar
Thav lol dilas ander lolas chaay kharidari
(Oh Mahjoor! Just leave it now–who learns love from books
Let the love dwell in hearts for love is not for deal)

He was candid in his expression and was even arrested for his blunt talking. However, the National Conference Government, which had arrested him, made him the National Poet after his release. In 1947, Mahjoor wrote:

Zuv te jan vandaha Hindustans
Dil chum Pakistans seit
(I sacrifice my body, my life for Hindustan,
Yet my heart goes to Pakistan)

Abdul Ahad Azad, 1903-1948 AD

Abdul Ahad Azad is one of the great poets Kashmir has produced. He revolutionised Kashmiri poetry and brought modernism in it. He brought realism of life in his compositions. Azad was the son of Sultan Dar. His brother, Ali Dar, was a doctor by profession. Ali Dar educated the village boys and he made his younger brother join the group. Abdul gradually learnt the Holy *Quran*. He acquired a workable knowledge of Arabic, Persian and Urdu Languages, Muslim Jurisprudence and History. He was only in his teens when he got a job as a teacher in the same school where he had studied.

In 1931 AD, when there was revolt against the Maharaja, Azad also joined the uprising. As a punishment he was transferred to Traal and had to face a lot of problems. However, his problems became a boon for his literary works. His poems caught the attention of the intellectual class. He befriended intellectuals like Prem Nath Bazaz, and learnt from him the philosophy of M N Roy.

On April 4, 1948, he passed away and was buried in his own village Ranger near Chrar-i-Sharif.

Aariz Kashmiri, 1916-1965 AD

Aariz Kashmiri's name was Gulam Nabi. He completed his primary education in 1928 AD, and went to Srinagar to study further. After attaining training from the Forest Training School, he was appointed a forest officer. Aariz's style of poetry is impressive and unusual. His language is lucid and simple.

Dinanath Nadim, 1916-1988 AD

Dinanath Nadim is one of most famous poets of Kashmir. He was born in 1916 AD in Srinagar. His father Pandit Shankar Kaul died when he was only eight years old. His first teacher was his mother who would sing Vaakh and Wanvun to him.

After his graduation, he worked as a teacher in the Hindu High School. After independence he joined Government service as Assistant Director in Social Education Department. His poetic excellence and craftsmanship made him experiment with various styles in poetry. He introduced a new phase in Kashmiri literature. He was the first poet who wrote blank verse. He depicted the beauty of nature in his works. He also wrote the dance-dramas *Vitasta, Heemal- Maegrai, Bombur Yemberzal* (Bumble bee and the Narcissus) which were widely appreciated. His book of poetry *Shuhul Kul* earned him the Sahitya Akademi Award in 1986. He was also awarded the Soviet Land Nehru Award in 1971 AD.

Amin Kamil, 1924-2014 AD

Amin Kamil, a versatile poet of Kashmir was born in Kaprin in Kulgam District of Kashmir. He became a lawyer but instead of practicing in the court he joined as Editor in the Academy of Art and Culture and Languages. His memorable works are *Saqi Namah*, *Lavah Te Praveh*, *Bey Suy Paan*, *Padis Pod Tsaay*, *Yim Mayany Sokhan*. He was awarded Sahitya Akademi Award in 1967 for the book *Lavah Te Pravah*. He was also awarded the Padma Shri in the year 2005.

Daya Shankar Kaul Nasim, 1877-1845 AD

Daya Shankar Kaul Nasim was an Urdu poet of the 19th century who won fame for his epic *Gul Bakawali*.

Amar Nath Kak, 1889-1963 AD

Amar Nath Kak was a prominent Kashmiri lawyer. He was the brother of the famous archaeologist and politician Ram Chandra Kak. Amar Nath

Kak was an important Hindi writer and has many books to his credit. The most famous books he wrote are *Hamara Vrittanta* and *Gayatri* which depicts the life of Kashmiri Pandits.

Moti Lal Saqi, 1936 -1999 AD

Moti Lal Saqi emerged as a great literary writer and a progressive poet of Kashmir. He was born in Bijbihara in the year 1936 AD. His contribution as literary critic is very much appreciated. He dedicated his whole life for promotion and development of Kashmiri traditions. He was an authority on the Rishi cult. His work on Nund Rishi and the Sufi poet Samad Mir, is considered a masterpiece. He also compiled Kashmiri folk songs. He was awarded the Sahitya Akademi Award and then Padma Shri for his literary work in Urdu also. He edited Urdu-Kashmiri dictionaries by Jammu and Kashmir Cultural Academy. His other works are *Modury Khawab* (sweet dreams), *Niri Nagma* (Songs of the green meadows), and *Mansar*. Moti Lal Saqi enriched Kashmiri language and literature in several ways. He will be remembered for all times to come.

Jagan Nath Shivpori

Pandit Jagan Nath Shivpori, popularly and affectionately known as Master ji was a class apart. He devoted all his life to teach music to young boys and girls irrespective of their religion. He opened a school in Kraala Khud, Srinagar. Hundreds and thousands of students attended the school to study Indian Classical Music.

Mohan Lal Aima

Mohan Lal Aima was a legendry musician of Kashmir. His lilting melodies are still echoing in the ears of the people of Kashmir. According to Moti Lal Kemu, "Nadim wrote Bombro Bombro chorus with simple, forceful words and when set to tune by Aima Saheb every actor and musician congratulated the director." He was among the moving spirits of the post 1947 revival of Kashmiri music. He lifted the Kashmiri 'Chakri' from its plebeian moorings and gave it popularity and respectability among the high-born Kashmiris."

Mohan Lal Aima introduced his own style of rhythm on Naut and Tumbaknari. His style of singing and playing mesmerised people into listening to him.

Some famous Artists/Performers

Subhan Bhagat, 1927-1993 AD

Mohammad Subhan Bhagat was born in 1927 in Akengam (Kukarnag) of Kashmir. He was a versatile folk actor-director. He popularised the famous folk form 'Bhand Pather'. Though he belonged to the family of Bhand performers, yet he got his excellence in the Bhand tradition from his teacher Ustad Kamal Bhagat. With many awards to his credit, he will be remembered as a great performer of Kashmir folk theatre. He died in 1993.

Pushkar Bhan, 1926-2008 AD

Pushkar Bhan was a great and dynamic man. He was born in Babapura, Habba Kadal in 1926. After graduating he went to Bombay to try his luck in films. He came back and started working for an Urdu daily *Inquilab*. He left the job and joined Radio Kashmir and then there was no looking back. His radio plays *Zoon-e-Dab* and *Machama*, created history in the broadcasting field. *Zoon-e-Dab* was on air everyday for nineteen years. Pushkar Bhan's plays brought laughter to the people through satire. They were message oriented and included criticism of the Government's working. His works had aesthetic significance and originality. He was also acclaimed for his acting talent. He has acted in films such as *Mainziraat, Shayer-e-Azam Mahjoor*. For his outstanding contribution in the field of art he was awarded Padma Shree in 1974.

Tibet Baqal, 1914-1982 AD

Mohammed Abdullah Tibetbaqal was born in the year 1914. His father's name was Khwaja Abdul Ghani. Tibetbaqal, as a singer, demonstrated uncanny artistic talent in his early years. Born in an orthodox family, his art became a source of frustration for his family which was in the Pashmina trade. But his passion drove him to pursue singing. He learnt Sufiana Kalaam from Ghani Joo and Ramzan Joo. He also learnt Persian and Arabic. He then joined Radio Kashmir as a singer and became very popular.

One of his famous compositions in Sufiana Kalaam style is

"*Bell tey madal ven gulab pamposh dastay*
Puza-e-lagav param shivas shavnathas tey"

The song was in praise of God Shiva. In spite of being a Muslim, it was with complete devotion he sang this song and enthralled the Hindu community of Kashmir.

Gupa-Bacha alias Gopi Nath, 1920-2001 AD

Gopi Nath was born in the year 1920 in Achabal, in Anantnag District of Kashmir. He was the first Kashmiri Pandit who learnt the art of dancing. He was given the sobriquet of 'Gupa-Bacha'. Gopi Nath's dancing was the Bach Nagma style of Kashmir, where male dancers wear the costumes of women. Gopi Nath was not only a good dancer, he was an equally good singer. He sang *Leela* (religious songs of Hindus), *Naats* (religious songs of Muslims), *Chakri* and *Roaf*. He could play most of the instruments such as Harmonium, Nout (pitcher), Tabla, Banjo, etc. He drove a tonga to earn his livelihood.

Gulam Hassan Sofi, 1932-2009 AD

Gulam Hassan Sofi is a legendry singer of Kashmir. He is the undisputed melody king of Kashmir. Usually he would compose his songs himself. He played the Rabab, Sarangi, Nout, flute and Tumbaknari. He worked many years for the Song and Drama Division of the Ministry of Information and Broadcasting.

Painters

Maheshwar Nath Dhar, 1888-1971 AD

Pandit Maheshwar Nath Dhar was born in 1888 AD at Bana Mohalla of Srinagar, Kashmir. This self-taught artist impressed everyone including Maharaja Pratap Singh who took him to Jammu to design a painting studio. His paintings reflected mysticism. After Maharaja Pratap Singh died, Maharaja Hari Singh closed his studio. Sir Gopalaswami Ayyengar utilised his services for renovating the sun temple Martanda.

Manohar Kaul, 1925-1999 AD

Manohar Kaul was born in 1925 in Srinagar. He has been termed as one of the best painters of 20th century. He took training in Art at Amar Singh Technical Institute, Srinagar, and from City Institute, London University. A famous poet Keshav Malik says about Manohar Kaul's paintings, "His work is only of joy, but perhaps, joy is the supreme quality in art."

After putting up many exhibitions, he took over as Chairman, All India Fine Arts and Crafts Society. Manohar Kaul has many books to his credit such as *Kashmir Hindu, Buddhist and Muslim Architecture, Trends in Indian Painting—Ancient, Medieval, and Modern.*

Gulam Rasool Santosh, 1927-1997 AD

He was born in a poor Muslim family of Kashmir at Chinkral Mohalla. His father died when he was in school. He had to take up various jobs to support the family. He had talent for sketching, painting in water colours or oil paints. He studied under a celebrated painter, professor N S Bandre at University of Baroda.

He married a Hindu girl known as Santosh. This gave a jolt to Hindus as well as Muslim society of Kashmir. He assumed her name also and came to be known as Gulam Rasool Santosh.

He started his carrier as a Cezanne and Cubist artist. In 1965 there was a complete metamorphosis in his works, behaviour and personality. He switched over to mysticism of religious philosophies such as Islamic Sufism, Tantra of Buddhism and Trika system of Kashmir Shaiva Philosophy. His paintings *Shiva Shakti*, *Zalla* and *Tantra Painting*, exhibit his keen insight. His paintings, full of vibrancy of colours, neat lines and spiritual energy earned him a name in the field of art. He held as many as 30 painting exhibitions in various countries such as United State of America, Japan, Hong Kong and Singapore.

Awards

He was a class playwright and poet and was bestowed with Padma Shri in 1977. He was also awarded Sahitya Akademi Award in 1979 for his poems *Besoakh Ruh*.

Suraj Tikku, 1929-1997 AD

Suraj Tikku was born on 14th June, 1929. His father, Pandit Govind Ram belonged to a middle class family. When he was just a child, he lost his father. Although his early years were marked by personal tragedy and financial hardship, yet his drawings and paintings are fascinating. According to Dr R K Tamiri, "His outstanding talent and great personal qualities made him a legend in his lifetime. Tiku did not have godfathers. Had an opportunity come his way, he would have emerged as an artist of national fame in all genres he pursued."

Suraj's greatest creative triumphs are his watercolour landscapes. His paintings have harmony of colours and aesthetic perfection.

He worked in many stage plays, radio plays and films.

As a designer of the settings he had no rival in the valley. He designed sets for hundreds of productions.

In 1966, Suraj Tikku was selected as 'Scenic Designer' in the Srinagar Centre of Song and Drama Division of the Ministry of Information and Broadcasting, Government of India.

It consisted of actors, actresses, instrumentalists, singers, folk performers etc. The great performers of that time were Omkar Khazanchi, Omkar Nath Raina, Krishan Langoo, Makhan Lal Bhatt, Inder K Chaku, Gulam Mohammad Rah, Ali Mohammad Nishtar, Rashid Hassan, Rajinder Raina, Krishna Wali, Ali Mohammad Bamboo, Gulam Mohammad Dar, Asha Kaul, Khemlata Dhar, Veena Gaind, Kantiyani Ganjoo and Santosh Kaul. Suraj designed sets for each and every prducion these artists performed. The set design for the producion of *Nefa Ki Ek Shaam* was memorable. A man of deep compassion for other human beings, an admirer of art and artists, he had deep quest for learning. His paintings depicted life in its authentic form but in a subtle way. Suraj Tikku passed away on January 26, 1997.

Bansi Nirdosh, 1930-2001 AD

Bansi Nirdosh was born in Badyar, Srinagar. His father Shyam Lal was a journalist. Bansi Nirdosh started his career as a journalist in an Urdu Daily *Naya Zamana* published in Amritsar. When he returned to the valley, he joined All India Radio. He wrote short stories in Kashmiri language. His novel *Akh Daur*, became very famous. People also appreciated his play *Bas Akh Tamah*. His other works include novels *Mukjaar*, *Girdab* and *Bal Marayo*.

Film Makers

Arun Kaul, 1933-2007 AD

Arun Kaul, a famous film maker of Kashmir, was born in 1933. He worked as Screenplay Assistant to veteran filmmaker Gulzar in his films *Lekin* and *Ijaazat*. He won the Filmfare Critics Award for Best Movie for the year 1992. Arun Kaul also produced a film *Ek Adhrui Kahani* which was directed by Mrinal Sen.

From Films Arun Kaul switched over to Television. He died in 2007.

✦ ✦ ✦

REFERENCES

Chapter 1

1. *Ranjit Singh*: Lepel Henry Griffin, p 36
2. *History of Sikhs*: Joseph Davey Cunningham, p 106
3. *Press and Freedom Struggle In Jammu and Kashmir*: (Article) by Zahid G Muhammad
4. *Ranjit Singh*: Sir Lepel Henry Griffin, p 39
5. *Maharaja Ranjit Singh—the Last to Lay Arms*: Kartar Singh Duggal, p 107
6. Ibid, p 112
7. *A History of Kashmiri Pandits*: Jia Lal Kilam, p 252
8. Ibid, p 252–253
9. *Ranjit Singh*: Lepel Griffin, p196
10. *Valley Of Kashmir*: Walter Roper Lawrence, p 199
11. *A History of Kashmiri Pandits*: Jia Lal Kilam, p 255–256
12. *Ranjit Singh*: Lepel Griffin, p 196
13. *Kashmir*: Francis Younghusband, p 160
14. *Travels in Kashmir, Ladakh, Iskardo*: Godfrey Thomas Vigne, p74
15. *Ranjit Singh*: Sir Lepel Henry Griffin, p 195

16. *Travel Adventures of Rev Joseph Wolff*: Joseph Wolff And Alfred Gatty, p 115
17. *Travels in Kashmir and the Punjab*: Baron Charles Hugel, p 109
18. *History of Sikhs*: Joseph Davey Cunninghamm, p 234
19. *Thirty five Years in the East. Adventures, Discoveries:* John Martin Honigberger, p 107
20. *Travels in Kashmir, Ladakh, Iskardo*: Godfrey Thomas Vigne, p 73
21. *Cultural and Political History of Kashmir*: P N K Bamzai, p 633

Chapter 2

1. *Ranjit Singh*: Lepel Henry Griffin, p 14
2. *A Short History of Jammu Raj*: Sukhdev Singh Charak, p 288
3. *The History of Struggle for Freedom in Kashmir*: Prem Nath Bazaz, p 120
4. *Travel to Kashmir and Ladakh*: William Moorcroft, p 293
5. *Kalhana's Rajatarangini*: Introduction Comments M A Stein

Chapter 3

1. *Duggar Ka Itihas*: Shiv Nimohi (Hindi), p 64
2. *History of the Sikhs*: Joseph Davey Cunningham, p 182
3. *A Short History of Jammu Raj*: Sukhdev Singh Charak, p 141
4. *Duggar Ka Itihas*: Shiv Nimohi (Hindi), p 67
5. *History of Punjab*: D N Kundra, p 309
6. *Letters from India*: Victor Jacquemont, Vol II p 2
7. *Soldier and Traveller*: *Memoirs:* Alexander Gardner, p 234-235
8. *Duggar Ka Itihas*: Shiv Nimohi (Hindi), p 70
9. *Culture and Political History of Kashmir*: P N K Bamzai, Vol III p 738
10. *A Short History of Jammu Raj*: Sukhdev Singh Charak, p 293
11. *Adventures of a Lady in Tartary, Thibet, China & Kashmir*: Mrs Hervey, p 250-251
12. *A Short History of Jammu Raj*: Sukhdev Singh Charak, p 179
13. Ibid, p 184

14. *Ladakh, Physical, Statistical, and Historical*: Sir Alexander Cunningham, p 353
15. *Duggar Ka Itihas*: Shiv Nimohi (Hindi), p 77
16. *Texts in Context: Traditional Hermeneutics*: Edited Richard Timm, p 152-153
17. *Rajatarangini Comments*: M A Stein, Vol II-p 383-384
18. *Duggar Ka Itihas*: Shiv Nimohi (Hindi), p 77
19. *Kashmir*: Francis Younghusband, p 174
20. *The Valley of Kashmir*: Walter Roper Lawrence, p 202
21. *Memorial of Mistakes Converted Kashmir*: Narendra Sahagala, p 197
22. *A History of Kashmiri Pandits*: Jia Lal Kilam, p 284
23. *The Valley of Kashmir*: Walter Roper Lawrence, p 202
24. *Memorial of Mistakes Converted Kashmir*: Narendra Sahagala, p 198
25. *The Valley of Kashmir*: Walter Roper Lawrence, p 202
26. Ibid, p 214-215
27. Ibid, p 375
28. *Culture and Political History of Kashmir*: P N K Bamzai, Vol III P 686
29. *A History of Kashmiri Pandits*: Jia Lal Kilam, p 281-282
30. Ibid p 282
31. *Culture and Political History of Kashmir*: P N K Bamzai, p 695
32. *The Valley of Kashmir*: Walter Roper Lawrence, p 2
33. *A History of Kashmiri Pandits*: Jia Lal Kilam, p 285
34. *Hindu Rulers Muslim Subjects*: Madhu Rao, p 136
35. *Memorial of Mistakes Converted Kashmir*: Narendra Sahagala, p 188
36. *Where Three Empires Meet*: E F Knight, p 28-29
37. *Political Awakening in Kashmir*: Ravinderjit Kaur, p 11
38. *Kashmir in Conflict*: Victoria Schofield, p 10
39. *Duggar Ka Itihas*: Shiv Nimohi (Hindi), p 105
40. *Urdu in Jammu and Kashmir:* (Article) Nishat Ansari
41. V*ivekananda*: (Article) Swami Bodhasarananda

42. *A History of Kashmiri Pandits*: Jia Lal Kilam, p 290
43. *Duggar Ka Itihas*: Shiv Nimohi, p 112
44. *Our Summer in the Vale of Kashmir*: F Ward Deny, p 127
45. *The Princes of India in the Endgame of Empire 1917-47*: Ian Copland, p 51
46. *The Indian Princes and Their States*: Barbara N Ramusack, p 17
47. *The Princes of India in the Endgame of Empire*: Ian Copland, p 131
48. *Political Awakening in Kashmir*: Ravinderjit Kaur, p 174-175
49. *The History of Struggle for Freedom in Kashmir*: Prem Nath Bazaz, p 160
50. *Kashmir Past and Present*: M L Kaul
51. *Memorial of Mistakes Converted Kashmir*: Narendra Sahagala, p 188
52. *The History of Struggle for Freedom in Kashmir*: Prem Nath Bazaz, p 151
53. Ibid, p 152
54. *Culture and Political History of Kashmir*: P N K Bamzai, p 731
55. *The History of Struggle for Freedom in Kashmir*: Prem Nath Bazaz, p 153-154

Chapter 4

1. *The Clash of Fundamentalisms: Crusades, Jihads and Modernity*: Tariq Ali, p 226
2. *The History of Struggle for Freedom in Kashmir*: Prem Nath Bazaz, p 176
3. *The Clash of Fundamentalisms: Crusades, Jihads and Modernity*: Tariq Ali, p 229
4. *Islam and Political Mobilization in Kashmir*: Article, *Pacific Affairs* Ian Copland
5. *Culture and Political History of Kashmir*: P N K Bamzai, p 739
6. *The History of Struggle for Freedom in Kashmir*: Prem Nath Bazaz, p 164
7. *The New Cambridge History of India*: Garaldine Forbes, p 239
8. *The History of Struggle for Freedom in Kashmir*: Prem Nath Bazaz, p 220 -222

9. *Kashmir in Conflict: India, Pakistan and Unending War*: Victoria Schofield, p 24
10. *Low Intensity Conflicts in India*: Vivek Chadha, p 96-97
11. *Remembering Partition, Nationalism and History in India*: Gyanendra Pandey, p 29
12. *Crafting Peace in Kashmir through a Realist Lens*: Varghese Koithara, p 28

Chapter 5

1. *Kashmir in Comparative Perspective*: Sten Widmalm, p 38
2. *Kashmir's Constitutional Status*: Santosh Kaul, p 21-22
3. *Frozen Turbulence in Kashmir*: Jagmohan, p 84
4. *The Constitution of Jammu and Kashmir*: Justice A S Anand, p 63
5. *My Life and Times*: Syed Mir Qasim, p 31
6. *The History of Struggle for Freedom in Kashmir*: Prem Nath Bazaz, p 318
7, *Kashmir 1947*: Prem Shankar Jha, p 4
8. Ibid, p 46
9. *The New Cambridge History of India*: Geraldine Forbaes, p 246
10. *Jinnah, Pakistan and Islamic Identity*: Akbar S Ahmed, p 119
11. Ibid, p/136
12. *Drawing the Indo Pakistani Boundary*: (Article) Lucy Chester
13. *The Sole Spokesman Jinnah, the Muslim League and the Demand for Pakistan*: Ayesha Jalal, p 246
14. *India Wins Freedom*: Maulana Abdul Kalam Azad, p 198
15. *The Partition of India and Mountbatten*: LA Sherwani, p 49
16. *Shameful Flight: the Last Years of British Empire in India*: Stanley Wolpert, p 10
17. *Freedom at Midnight*: Larry Collins and Dominiue Lapierre, p 179
18. *Rajatarangini Translation*: MA Stein, Vol I – p 30
19. *Drawing the Indo Pakistani Boundary*: (Article) Lucy Chester
20. Ibid
21. *Freedom at Midnight*: Larry Collins and Dominique Lapierre, p 186

22. *Drawing the Indo Pakistani Boundary*: (Article) Lucy Chester
23. *The Aftermath of Partition in South Asia*: Gyanesh Kudeshia, p 96
24. *Jinnah, Pakistan and Islamic Identity*: Akbar S Ahmed, p 117
25. *The Other Side of Silence*: *Voices From the Partition of India*: Urvashi Butalia, p 3
26. *India Wins Freedom*: Maulana Azad, p 203
27. Ibid p 207
28. *The Other Side of Silence*: *Voices From the Partition of India*: Urvashi Butalia, p 3
29. *India Wins Freedom*: Maulana Abdul Kalam Azad, p 196

Chapter 6

1. *The Sole Spokesman Jinnah, the Muslim League and the Demand for Pakistan*: Ayesha Jalal, p 285
2. *The Great Disclosures*: Hilal Ahmed, p 108
3. *Kashmir in Conflict*: *India Pakistan and the Unending War*: Victoria Schofield, p 25
4. Ibid p 47
5. *Gandhi through Western Eyes*: Horace Gundry Alexander, p 169
6. *Crafting Peace in Kashmir through a Realist Lens*: Verghese Koithara, p 34
7. *My Life and Times*: Syed Mir Qasim, p 37
8. *Slender Was the Thread*: *Kashmir Confrontation 1947–48*: Lionel Protip. Sen, p 38
9. *Kashmir*: *a Wailing Valley*: M L Gupta, p 106
10. *Slender Was the Thread*: *Kashmir Confrontation 1947–48*: Lionel Protip Sen, p 38
11. *My Life and Times*: Sayyid Mir Qasim, p 37
12. *Kashmir 1947*: Prem Shankar Jha p 135
13. *Culture and Political History of Kashmir*: P N K Bamzai, p 718
14. *Between Two Fires*: Iqbal Singh, p 74
15. *Kashmir 1947*: Prem Shankar Jha, p 4
16. *Slender Was the Thread*: *Kashmir Confrontation 1947–48*: Lionel Protip Sen, p 36
17. *A History of Struggle for Freedom*: Prem Nath Bazaz, p 326

18. *Kashmir 1947*: Prem Shankar Jha, p 7
19. Ibid, p 92
20. *The Aftermath of Partition in South Asia*: Tai Hong Tan, Gyanesh Kudeshia, p 8
21. *Kashmir 1947*: Prem Shankar Jha, p 11
22. The *History of Struggle for Freedom in Kashmir*: Prem Nath Bazaz, p 327-328
23. *Culture and Political History of Kashmir*: P N K Bamzai, p 761
24. *Conflicts in India: An Analysis*: Vivek Chadha, p 41
25. *Slender Was the Thread: Kashmir Confrontation*: Lionel Protip Sen 1947-1948, p 103
26. *Jammu and Kashmir War, 1947- 48*: Kuldip Singh Bajwa, p 117
27. *Slender Was the Thread: Kashmir Confrontation 1947-1948*: Lionel Protip Sen, p 102
28. *Culture and Political History of Kashmir*: P N K Bamzai, p 763
29. *Slender Was the Thread: Kashmir Confrontation 1947-48*: Lionel Protip Sen, p 104
30. *Freedom at Midnight*: Larry Collins and Dominique Lapierre, p 357
31. *Low Intensity Conflicts in India*: Lt Col Vivek Chadha, p 74
32. *Pakistan's Endgame in Kashmir*: (Article) Husain Haqqani
33. *Kashmir 1947*: Prem Shankar Jha, p 47

Chapter 7

1. *Culture and Political History of Kashmir*: P N K Bamzai, p 802
2. *Jammu, Kashmir, Ladakh: Ringside Views*: Shyam Kaul, Onkar Kachru, p 59
3. *Between Two Fires*: Iqbal Singh, p 88
4. *Kashmir 1947*: Prem Shankar Jha, p 92
5. Ibid p 92
6. *Times of India (15th April 2008)*: Article
7. *Hindu Rulers, Muslim Subjects*: Madhu Rao, p 260
8. Ibid p 285
9. *Who Shaped India*: (Article) Pran Chopra *India Today*
10. *The History of Struggle for Freedom in Kashmir*: Prem Nath Bazaz, p 254

11. *My Frozen Turbulence of Kashmir*: Jagmohan, p 79
12. Ibid.
13. *Low Intensity Conflicts in India*: Lt Col Vivek Chadha, p 83
14. *Who Shaped India*: (Article) Pran Chopra *India Today*
15. *The History of Struggle for Freedom in Kashmir*: Prem Nath Bazaz, p 666
16. Ibid p 210
17. *Kashmir: A Wailing Valley* M L Gupta, p 120
18. Ibid p 121
19. *War and No Peace over Kashmir*: Maroof Raza, p 19
20. *My Frozen Turbulence of Kashmir*: Jagmohan, p 78-79
21. *The History of Struggle for Freedom in Kashmir*: Prem Nath Bazaz, p 549
22. *Kashmir in Crucible*: Prem Nath Bazaz, p 180
23. *The History of Struggle for Freedom in Kashmir*: Prem Nath Bazaz, p 180
24. Ibid p 176
25. *Hindustan Times (October 16, 1948)* Article
26. *A Betrayal of Nehru*: B Krishna (Article) *Kashmir Sentinel*
27. Ibid
28. *The History of Struggle for Freedom in Kashmir*: Prem Nath Bazaz
29. *Kashmir: A Wailing Valley*: M L Gupta, p 121
30. *Low Intensity Conflicts in India*: Vivek Chadha, p 83
31. *Kashmir, Myth of Autonomy*: Mohan Kishen Teng, p 31
32. *Kashmir in Conflict: India, Pakistan and the Unending War*: Victoria Schofield, p 77-78
33. *Culture and Political History of Kashmir*: P N K Bamzai, p 809
34. *The History of Struggle for Freedom in Kashmir*: Prem Nath Bazaz, p 681-682
35. Ibid p 686
36. *My Frozen Turbulence in Kashmir*: Jagmohan, p 98
37. Ibid p 99
38. *My Life and My Time*: Syed Mir Qasim, p 81
39. *The History of Struggle for Freedom in Kashmir*: Prem Nath Bazaz, p 685

40. *My Frozen Turbulence in Kashmir*: Jagmohan, p 100
41. *My Life and My Time*: Sayyid Mir Qasim, p 96
42. Ibid p 93
43. *Hijacking and Terror in the Sky*: Giriraj Shah, p 20
44. *My Life and My Time*: Syed Mir Qasim, p 94
45. Ibid p 86-87
46. *A Region in Turmoil: South Asian Conflicts Since 1947:* Rob Johnson, p 11
47. *Kashmir, a Wailing Valley*: M L Gupta, p 130
48. *A Region in Turmoil: South Asian Conflicts Since 1947*: Rob Johnson, p 117
49. *Crisis in Kashmir*: Sumit Ganguly, p 45
50. *My Life and My Time*: Syed Mir Qasim, p 102
51. *Crisis in Kashmir*: Sumit Ganguly, p 52
52. *Kashmir in Conflict: India, Pakistan and Unending War:* Victoria Schofield, p 106
53. *The History of Struggle for Freedom in Kashmir*: Prem Nath Bazaz, p 511

Chapter 8

1. *Pakistan Its Ideology and Foreign Policy*: Arif Hussein, p 131
2. *Indian Muslims, Where Have They Gone Wrong*: Rafiq Zakaria
3. *Kashmir in Conflict: India, Pakistan and the Unending War*: Victoria Schofield, p 106
4. Wikipedia *Operation Gibraltar*: Internet
5. *Pakistan's Drift in Extremism*: Hassan Abbas, p 44
6. *Kashmir in Conflict: India, Pakistan and the Unending War*: Victoria Schofield, p 107
7. Ibid p 108
8. *Culture and Political History of Kashmir*: P N K Bamzai, p 883
9. Wikipedia '*Operation Gibraltar*: Internet
10. *Pakistan's Drift in Extremism*: Hassan Abbas, p 45
11. *Who Shaped India*: (Article) Pran Chopra *India Today*
12. *Indian Airports: Shocking Ground Realities*: Kishin R Wadhwaney, p 122-123

13. *Terrorism, History and Facts in the World and India*: N S Saksena, p 25
14. *Crafting Peace in Kashmir*: Verghese Koithara, p 40
15. *Can Pakistan Survive? The Death of a State*: Tariq Ali, p 95
16. *My Life and My Times*: Syed Mir Qasim, p 1
17. Ibid p 10
18. *My Frozen Turbulence in Kashmir*: Jagmohan, p 105
19. Ibid p 108
20. *Kashmir and the Freedom Movement*: Parmanand Parashar, p 60
21. *Jammu Kashmir, Ladakh*: *Ringside Views*: Shyam Kaul, Onkar Kachru, p13
22. *Global Terrorism*: Ramesh Chandra, Vol 6, p 99

Chapter 9

1. *Pakistan and the Emergence of Islamic Militancy in Afghanistan*: Rizwan Hussain, p 202
2. *The Virulent Wahabi Virus*: (Article) Murad Ali Baig, *Hindustan Times* April 11, 2009
3. *Kashmir 1947*: Prem Shankar Jha, p 5
4. *My Frozen Turbulence in Kashmir*: Jagmohan, p 373
5. *The Virulent Wahabi Virus*: (Article) Murad Ali Baig *Hindustan Times* April 11, 2009
6. *My Frozen Turbulence in Kashmir*: Jagmohan, p 2
7. *My Kashmir*: Habibullah, p 99
8. *Pakistan: Its Ideology and Its Foreign Policy*: Arif Hussain, p 131
9. *Culture and Political History Of Kashmir*: P N K.Bamzai, p 729
10. *The Wild Wild North West*: (Article) Amit Baruah
11. *Times of India*: Ram Chandra Guha (Article) September 19, 2008
12. *With Malice Towards One And All*: Khuswant Singh
13. *My Frozen Turbulence in Kashmir*: Jagmohan, p 393
14. Ibid p 342
15. *Terrorism in Kashmir*: Rakshit Puri, p 16-17
16. Ibid p 19
17. *My Frozen Turbulence in Kashmir*: Jagmohan, p 355
18. Ibid p 440-441

19. *Pakistan and the Emergence of Islamic Militancy in Afghanistan*: Rizwan Hussain, p 202
20. *War and No Peace over Kashmir*: Maroof Raza, p 126
21. *India-Pakistan in War and Peace*: J N Dixit, p 20
22. Ibid, p 16
23. Ibid, p 13
24. *Peace Parks Conservation and Conflict Resolution*: Saleem H Ali, p 280

Chapter 10

1. *Ancient Monuments of Kashmir*: R C Kak, p 164
2. Ibid p 160
3. *Nilamatapurana*: Translation Ved Kumari Ghai SL,p 252-259
4. Ibid SL 260-261
5. Kalhana's *Rajatarangini*: Translation M A Stein, p 32
6. *Valley of Kashmir* Walter Roper Lawrence, p 294
7. Ibid p 299
8. *Kashmir under the Mughals*: Abdul Majid Mattoo, p 201
9. *Culture and Political History of Kashmir*: P N K Bamzai, p 406-407
10. *Ain-e-Akbari*: Abu-al-Fazal Translation H S Harrett, p 365
11. *Ancient Monuments of Kashmir*: R C Kak, p 95
12. *Kashmir under the Mughals*: Abdul Majid Mattoo, p 201
13. *Ancient Monuments of Kashmir*: R C Kak, p 102
14. *Kalhana's Rajatarangini*: Translation M A Stein, p 456
15. *Ancient Monuments of Kashmir*: R C Kak, p 103
16. *Jammu Kashmir and Ladakh*: Desh Bandu, p 29
17. *Kashmir under Mughals*: Abdul Majid Matoo, p 201
18. *Travel in the Mogul Empire AD 1556-1668*: Bernier Francois, p 415
19. *Kashmir under Mughals*: Abdul Majid Matoo, p 198
20. *Jammu Kashmir and Ladakh*: Desh Bandu, p 25
21. Ibid
22. *Ancient Monuments of Kashmir*: R C Kak, p 97

Chapter 11

1. *Valley of Kashmir*: Walter Roper Lawrence, p 332
2. *On Yuan Chwang's Travel in India*: Translation, Thomas Watters, p 262
3. *Gathering Kashmir's Saffron*: (Article) Daniel Lac, Journalist BBC
4. *Tuzuk-e-Jahangiri*: *Jahangir* Translation Alexander Rogers and Henry Beveridge, p 137
5. *Valley of Kashmir*: Walter Roper Lawrence, p 348
6. *Silk and Empire*: Brenda M King, p 76
7. *Travels in the Mogul Empire AD 1656 – 1668*: Francois Bernier, p 399
8. *Akbarnama*: Abul Fazal Translation H Beveridge Chapter XCIX, p 266
9. Ibid, p 329
10. *Glimpses of History of Jammu and Kashmir*: Pathik Jyoteesh, p 8
11. *Travel in Kashmir, Ladakh, I*skardo: Thomas Vigne Vol II, p 15
12. Ibid, p 95

Chapter 12

1. *Aesthetics*: Yuri Borev, p 55
2. *Travels in the Himalayan Province of Hindustan*: Moorcroft William and George Trebek, p 169
3. *Journey from Bengal to England*: George Forster, p 19
4. *Travels in Kashmir and the Punjab*: Baron Charles Hugel, p 8
5. *Ladak:* Alexander Cunningham, p 200
6. *Art and Crafts of Jammu and Kashmir*: D N Saraf, p 10
7. *Travels in the Himalayan Province of Hindustan*: Moorcroft and George Trebek, p 165
8 *Travels in Kashmir and the Punjab*: Baron Charles Hugel, p 403
9. *Encyclopaedia of Kashmir*: Suresh K. Sharma and Shiri Ram Bakshi, p 31
10. *Jammu Kashmir and Ladakh*: Bandhu Desh, p 43
11. *Diary of a Pedestrian in Cashmere and Thibet*: William Henry Knight, p 50

12. *The Valley of Kashmir*: Walter Roper Lawrence, p 375
13. *Art and Crafts in India and Ceylon*: Ananda K Coomaraswamy
14. *Art and Crafts of Jammu and Kashmir*: D N Saraf, p 89
15. *Kashmir in Conflict Pakistan and the Unending War*: Victoria Schofield, p 6
16. *Art and Crafts of Jammu and Kashmir*: D N Saraf, p 109
17. Ibid p 95-96
18. *The Valley Of Kashmir*: Sir Walter R Lawrence, p 250
19. *Kalhana's Rajatarangini Translation*: M A Stein Book –V/462
20. *Travel in Kashmir, Ladak, Iskardo*: G T Vigne, Vol II p/29

Chapter 13

1. *Aesthetics*: Yuri Borev, p 261
2. *Ain-i-Akbari*: Abu-al-Fazal Translation H Blochmann and Colonel H S Jarrett, p 373
3. *Nilamatapurana*: Translation Ved Kumari Ghai Vol. 1, p 99
4. *Zaina Rajatarangini*: Srivara Translation Kashi Nath Dhar 1/1/33
5. *Bhand Pather*: Article Javed Iqbal Bhat
6. Ibid.
7. *The Bhand Pather of Kashmir*: Article, M K Raina
8. *Architecture and Drama in Kashmir and North-West*: Article, *Koshur Samachar* R K Braroo
9. *The Valley of Kashmir*: Walter Roper Lawrence, p 256
10. *Vitasta Annual Number*: *XXXIV Various Forms in Kashmiri Lit.* Article, Mohiud-Din Hajini
11. *The Garland Encyclopaedia of World Music*: James Porter p 682
12. *The Traditional Music of Kashmir*: Sunita Dhar, p 50
13. Ibid, p 63
14. Ibid, p 12
15. Ibid, p 27

Chapter 14

1. *Modern India and the Indians*: Sir Monier Williams, p 151
2. *The Kashmiri Pandits*: Anand Kaul, p 37
3. *Valley of Kashmir*: Aparna Rao, Michael Witzal, p 41

4. *The Brahmins of Kashmir* Article: Michael Witzal September 1991
5. *Travels in the Mogul Empire AD 1656 – 1668*: Francois Bernier, p 409
6. *The History of Kashmiri Pandits*: Jia Lal Kilam, p 38
7. Ibid p 40
8. *The History of Struggle for Freedom in Kashmir*: Prem Nath Bazaz, p 53
9. *Where Three Empires Meet*: E F Knight, p 18
10. *Kashmir:* Francis Younghusband, p 126
11. *The Traditional Music of Kashmir*: Sunita Dhar (Preface)
12. Ibid
13. *The Valley of Kashmir*: Walter Roper Lawrence, p 302
14. *Kashmir under Mughals*: Abdul Majid Mattoo, p 133
15. Ibid p 155
16. *Where Three Empires Meet*: E F Knight, p 21
17. *The Valley of Kashmir*: Walter Roper Lawrence, p 314
18. Ibid, p 312
19. Ibid, p 316
20. *A Black Dog's Gaze*: Michael J Casimir, Aparna Rao,
21. *Kashmir Proverbs*: James Hinton Knowles (Preface)
22. *Folktales of Kashmir*: James Hinton Knowles (Preface)
23. *The Written Languages of the World* Heinz Kloss, *Vol 2* p/269
24. *Kashmiri Language*: *Roots, Evolution and Affinity*: Article, Shashi Shekher Toshkhani
25. *Crisis in Kashmir*: Aziz Kashmiri, p 55
26. *A Grammar of the Kashmir Language*: Rev Thomas Russel Wade, p 5
27. Ibid, p 7
28. *The Kashmiri Pandits*: Anand Kaul, p 32
29. *The Valley of Kashmir*: Aparna Rao, Article Brij B Kachru, p 310

Chapter 15

1. *The Kashmiri Pandits*: Anand Kaul, p 29
2. *Sarada Temple in Kashmir*: Article, *Koshur Samachar* P N K Bamzai

3. *Sarada-Mai: A Forgotten Cultural Link*: Article Dr V N Drabu
4. *Kalhana's Rajatarangini*: Translation M A Stein, Vol. II p 282
5. Ibid p 284
6. *Imperial Gazetteer of India*: *Provincial Series Jammu and Kashmir*, p 29
7. *Vaisnava Art and Iconography of Kashmir*: Bansi Lal Malla, p 18
8. *An Essay on the Arian Order of Architecture*: Alexander Cunningham, p 28-29
9. *The Valley of Kashmir*: Walter Roper Lawrence, p 171
10. *Travels in Kashmir and the Punjab*: Hugel Baron, p 135
11. *India: A History*: John Keay, p 288
12. *Kashmir*: Francis Younghusband, p 135
13. *Kalhana's Rajatarangini* Translation M A Stein Vol 1, p341
14. *The Foreign Quarterly Review*: Volumes-*36-37,* p 112
15. *Encyclopaedia of Kashmir*: C E Tyndale Biscoe, p 10
16. *Images of Indian Goddesses*: Madhu Bazaz Wangu, p 144-145
17. *The Temple Legacy of Kashmir*: S N Pandita
18. *Kashmir under Mughals*: Abdul Majid Mattoo, p 185
19. *Baharistan-i-Shahi*: Translation Kashi Nath Pandita
20. *The Foreign Quarterly Review*: Volumes 36-37, p 118
21. *Art and Craft Jammu and Kashmir*: D N Saraf, p 28
22. *Ancient Monuments of Kashmir*: R C Kak, p 78
23. *Kashmir under Mughals*: Abdul Majid Mattoo, p 187
24. *My Frozen Turbulence in Kashmir*: Jagmohan, p 720
25. *Ancient Monuments of Kashmir*: R C Kak, p 81
26. *Kashmir under Mughals*: Abdul Majid Mattoo, p 186
27. *Reminiscence*: Article Mohan Lal Ogra
28. *The Valley of Kashmir*: Walter Roper Lawrence, p 194

Bibliography

Kalhana's Rajatarangini, Kalhana
The Saga of the Kings of Kashmir, Kalhana
Dvitiya Rajatarangini, Jonaraja
Zaina Rajatarangini, Srivara
Vikramankadevacharita, Bilhana
History of Kashmir, Haydar Malik
Tarikh-i-Rashidi, Mirza Mohammad Haydar Duglat
A in-i-Akbari, Abu-Al-Fazl Allami Mubarak
Akbarnama, Abu-L-Afazl Allami Mubarak
Tuzuk-I-Jahangiri, Jahangir
Diwan-I Mahfi, Zib-al-Nisa
Halat-I Asad Big, Asad Big
Ancient Monuments of Kashmir, Ram Chand Kak
The Kashmiri Pandit, Pandit Anand Kaul
Desopadesa and Narmamala of Kshemendra, Kshemendra
Isvara-Pratyabhijna-Karika of Utpaladeva, Utpaladeva
Kashmiri under Mughals, Abdul Majid Matoo
India as seen in the Kuttanimatam of Damodaragupta, Ajay Mitra Shastri

Cultural and Political History of Kashmir, P N K Bamzai
The Philosophy of Sadhana, Deb Brata Sen Sharma
The History of Struggle for Freedom in Kashmir, Prem Nath Bazaz
Daughters of Vitasta, Prem Nath Bazaz
Kashmir in Crucible, Prem Nath Bazaz
Kashmir Myth of Autonomy, Mohan Kishen Teng
Essential documents and notes of Kashmir dispute, Pl Lakhenpal
Between Two Fires, Iqbal Singh
Kashmir under Sultans, Mohibbul Hassan
A History of Muslim Rule in Kashmir, R K Parmu
A Short History of Jammu Raj, Sukhdev Singh Charak
Nilamatapurana, (Author unknown)
Swacchanda-Tantra, Ksemaraja
Duggar Ka Itihas [Hindi], Shiv Dutt Nimohi
Ishvara Pratyabhijna Karika, Utpaladeva
A History of Kashmiri Pandits, Jia Lal Kilam
India Wins Freedom, Abul Kalam Azad
Memorial of Mistakes, Narendra Sahagala
Glimpses of History of Jammu and Kashmir, Jyoteeshwar Pathik
Hijacking and Terror in Sky, Giriraj Shah
Kashmir's Transition to Islam, Mohammad Ishaq Khan
History of Kashmir Saivism, Baljinnath Pandita
Vaishnava Art and Iconography of Kashmir, Bansi Lal Malla
History of Punjab, D N Kundra
Ancient India, R C Majumdar
Low Intensity Conflicts in India, Vivek Chadha
The Roads, Bhumesh Sharma
Hindu Rulers, Muslim Subjects, Mridhu Rai
Clash of Fundamentalisms, Tariq Ali
Kashmir 1947, Prem Shankar Jha
Slender Was the Thread, Lionel Protip Sen
Advance History of Ancient India, Shiri Ram Bakshi
Advance History of Medieval India, Shiri Ram Bakshi

A Text Book of Historiography, E Sreedharan
Crisis in Kashmir, Sumit Ganguly
The Aftermath of Partition, Tia Yong Tan
Remembering Partition, Gyanendra Pandey
India-Pakistan in War and Peace, J N Dixit
Bilhana, Prabhakar Narayan Kawthekar
Maharaja Ranjit Singh, Kartar Singh Duggal
History of Indian Theatre, M L Varadpande
Medieval Indian Literature, K Ayyappapanicker
Ancient Indian History and Civilization, Sailendra Nath Sen
The Splendor of Himalayan Art and Culture, Ashok Jerath
Dogra Legends of Art & Culture, Ashok Jerath
Kashmiri Scholars Contribution, S Bhat
The Evolution of The Artillery, R C Butalia
Kashmir: A Wailing Valley, M L Gupta
The Traditional Music of Kashmir, Sunita Dhar
Kashmir Shaivism under Siege, M G Chitkara
The Pratyabhijna Philosophy, Ganesh Vasudeo Tagare
Krama Trantricism of Kashmir, Navjivan Rastogi
The Other Side of Silence, Urvashi Butalia
Kashmir and United Nations Encyclopaedia of Kashmir Series, Suresh K Sharma/Shiri Ram Bakshi
An Introduction to Buddhist Esoterism, Benoytosh Bhattacharyya
Indian Literary Criticism, G N Davey
Crafting Peace in Kashmir, Verghese Koithara
Kashmir Roots of Conflict, Paths to Peace, Sumatra Bose
The Constitution of Jammu And Kashmir, Adarsh Sein Anand
Images of Indian Goddesses, Madhu Bazaz Wangu
Kashmir's Constitutional Status, Santosh Kaul
Vaishnava Art and Iconography of Kashmir, Bansilal Malla
Companion to Tantra, S C Banerji
Kashmir Myth of Autonomy, Mohan Kishen Teng
Indian Epigraphy, Dinesh Chandra Sircar

Ancient India, Dilip Kumar Ganguly
Remembering Partition, Gyanendra Pandey
Indian Muslims, Rafiq Zakaria
My Frozen Turbulence In Kashmir, Jagmohan
Rupa Bhavani, Shyam Lal Sadhu
Tales from Rajatarangini, Shyam Lal Sadhu
Indian Airports, Kishin R Wadhwaney
War and No Peace over Kashmir, Maroof Raza
Terrorism, History and Facets, NS Saksena
Saints and Saviors' of Islam, Hamid Naseem Rafiabadi
Language of Belonging, Chitralekha Zutshi
India wins freedom, Maulana Abul Kalam Azad
History of Ancient India, Ram Shankar Tripathi
Saints and Sages of Kashmir, Triloki Nath Dhar
A Concise History of Classical Sanskrit Literature, G S Bhattacharyya
The Encyclopaedia of Indian Literature, Amaresh Datta
Indian Poetics, T Nanjundaiya Sreekantaiya
Three Satires, Somadeva Vasudeva
Jammu Kashmir and Ladakh, Desh Bandu
Jammu and Kashmir War, 1947-1948, Kuldip Singh Bajwa
My Life and Times, Sayyid Mir Qasim
Low Intensity Conflicts in India, Vivek Chadha
On Yuan Chwang's travels in India, Yuan Chwang
Alberuni's India, Alberuni
The Happy Valley, W Wakefield
Travels In Kashmir and the Punjab, Baron Charles Hugel
A Journey from Bengal to England, George Forster
Tree and Serpent Worship, J Fergusson
Soldier and Traveller, Alexander Haughton Gardner
Thirty-Five Years in the East, J M Honigberger
Travels In Kashmir, Ladak, Iskardo, Godfery Thomas Vigne
Travel In the Mogul Empire, Bernier Francois
The Vishnu Purana, Horace Hayman Wilson

Ladakh, Alexander Cunningham
Al-Hind, Andre Wink
Folktales of Kashmir, J Hinton Knowles
Hinduism and Buddhism, Charles Eliot
Lallavakyani, George Abraham Grierson
Where Three Empires Meet, E F Knight
The History of India as told by its own Historians, Henry Meir Elliot
Kashmir, Francis Younghusband
Rulers of India, Stanley Lane-Poole
The Valley of Kashmir, Walter Roper Lawrence
History of Indian Literature, Moriz Winternitz
Our summer in the Vale of Kashmir, F Ward Denys
Tarikh-i-Firishta, Mohammed Qasim Firishta
A History of Sikhs, Joseph Davey Cunningham
Halat-i-Asad, Assad Big Kazvin
A Hindu Critique of Buddhist Epistemology, Kumarila Bhatta
Encyclopedia of Indian Philosophies, Harold G Coward
Encyclopedia of Erotic Literature, Gaetan Brulotte
A Historical Atlas of Islam, William Charles Brice
Kashmir in Conflict—India, Victoria Schofield
The New Cambridge History of India, Barbara N Ramusack
The Princes of India, Ian Copland
Kashmir in Comparative Perspective, Sten Widmalm
Jinnah, Pakistan and Islamic Identity, Akbar S Ahmed
The Sole Spokesman, Ayesha Jalal
Freedom at Midnight, Larry Collins/ Dominique Lapierre
The Aftermath of Partition, Tai Yong Tan
A Region in Turmoil, Rob Johnson
Pakistan, Arif Hussain
Pakistan and the Emergence of Islamic Militancy in Afghanistan, Rizwan Hussain
Peace Parks, Saleem Hassan Ali
Encyclopedia of Religion and Ethics, James Hasting

Silk and Empire, Brenda N King
India: A History, John Keay
A Dictionary of Kashmiri Proverbs and Sayings, James Hinton Knowles
The Written Languages of the World, Heinz Kloss
A grammar of the Kashmiri Language, Thomas Russel Wade
Modern India and the Indians, Monier Williams
Women, Religion and Social Change, Yvonne Yazbeck Haddad

INDEX

A

B

C

D